Client/Server
Architecture

Other Related Titles

0-07-060362-6	McDysan/Spohn	*ATM: Theory and Applications*
0-07-042591-4	Minoli/Vitella	*ATM & Cell Relay Service for Corporate Environments*
0-07-044362-9	Muller	*Network Planning, Procurement, and Management*
0-07-912256-6	Naugle	*Local Area Networking, 2/e*
0-07-046461-8	Naugle	*Network Protocol Handbook*
0-07-046380-8	Nemzow	*The Ethernet Management Guide, 3/e*
0-07-046321-2	Nemzow	*The Token-Ring Management Guide*
0-07-049663-3	Peterson	*TCP/IP Networking: A Guide to the IBM Environment*
0-07-051143-8	Ranade/Sackett	*Advanced SNA Networking: A Professional's Guide to VTAM/NCP*
0-07-051506-9	Ranade/Sackett	*Introduction to SNA Networking, 2/e*
0-07-053199-4	Robertson	*Accessing Transport Networks*
0-07-054991-5	Russell	*Signaling System #7*
0-07-054418-2	Sackett	*IBM's Token-Ring Networking Handbook*
0-07-057199-6	Saunders	*The McGraw-Hill High-Speed LANs Handbook*
0-07-057442-1	Simonds	*McGraw-Hill LAN Communications Handbook*
0-07-057639-4	Simonds	*Network Security: Data and Voice Communications*
0-07-060363-4	Spohn	*Data Network Design, 2/e*
0-07-069416-8	Summers	*ISDN Implementor's Guide*
0-07-063301-0	Taylor	*The McGraw-Hill Internetworking Command Reference*
0-07-063263-4	Taylor	*The McGraw-Hill Internetworking Handbook*
0-07-063295-2	Taylor	*Multiplatform Network Management*
0-07-063638-9	Terplan	*Benchmarking for Effective Network Management*
0-07-063639-7	Terplan	*Effective Management of Local Area Networks: Functions, Instruments and People, 2/e*
0-07-065766-1	Udupa	*Network Management Systems Essentials*
0-07-067375-6	Vaughn	*Client/Server System Design and Implementation*

Client/Server Architecture

Alex Berson

Second Edition

McGraw-Hill

New York   San Francisco   Washington, D.C.   Auckland   Bogotá
Caracas   Lisbon   London   Madrid   Mexico City   Milan
Montreal   New Delhi   San Juan   Singapore
Sydney   Tokyo   Toronto

To Irina, Vlad, and Michelle

Library of Congress Cataloging-in-Publication Data

Berson, Alex.
    Client/server architecture / Alex Berson. — 2nd ed.
       p. cm. — (J. Ranade series on computer communications)
    Includes bibliographical references and index.
    ISBN 0-07-005664-1 (hardcover)
    1. Client/server computing. 2. Computer architecture. I. Title.
II. Series.
QA76.9.C55B47 1996
004'.36—dc20   96-3254
                                                   CIP

McGraw-Hill

*A Division of The **McGraw·Hill** Companies*

1 2 3 4 5 6 7 8 9 0 DOC/DOC 9 0 1 0 9 8 7 6

ISBN 0-07-005664-1

*The sponsoring editor for this book was Jerry Papke, the editing
supervisor was Virginia Carroll, and the production supervisor was
Donald Schmidt. It was set in Century Schoolbook by North Market
Street Graphics.*

Printed and bound by R. R. Donnelley & Sons Company.

This book is printed on acid-free paper.

Contents

Preface

The last few years have seen the transformation of stand-alone personal computers into workgroup environments where workstations are interconnected via local and wide area networks and are integrated with the mainframe computers. This transformation has been combined with advances in microcomputer technology, graphical user interfaces, networking, and communications. As technology continues to evolve, users are capable of interconnecting various platforms efficiently and transparently, and distributing data and applications across heterogeneous systems and networks.

User's desires to reduce costs in hardware, software, application development, and operations; to improve software quality; and to reduce time-to-market for new products can now be realized by moving application development and operational systems from mainframes to more efficient, cost-effective, and powerful client/server environments. These are the main reasons for the rise of new types of computing and, at the same time, these factors have resulted in a new, often confusing vocabulary of terms and a number of new development methodologies. The picture has become even more complex with the advances in and acceptance of open systems, object-oriented technologies, and the Internet. Prominent among these new computing models is the client/server computing model and the underlying architecture of cooperative and distributed processing.

This client/server computing model is rapidly evolving from the one first introduced in the early 1990s to today's multitiered, widely distributed, data-rich cooperative distributed environment. No longer is it a matter of a client "simply" asking a server for data. The concepts of specialization introduced in the first edition of this book have matured and resulted in a second generation of client/server computing, one that deals with servers dedicated to applications, data, transaction management, systems management, and the like. Data structures supported by this enhanced computing model range from relational to multidimensional to unstructured to multimedia. Clients are now mobile, and remote access is universally accepted and planned for.

Almost every major business organization is considering a move toward a distributed environment, cooperative processing, object-oriented technologies, the Internet, and second-generation multitiered client/server architecture. These large reengineering and system integration projects require a significant investment in time, money, and resources. However, the lack of proper expertise and the confusion surrounding the issues of open systems, distributed cooperative processing, distributed objects, and client/server architecture often lead to (actual or perceived) project failures that affect business and computer vendors alike. Thus, the need to clarify the concepts, architecture, and evolution of the client/server computing model, coupled with the analysis of a popular and successful implementation of this model, become very pressing indeed. Understanding client/server architecture and relevant issues is central to the success of such open distributed cooperative processing initiatives as electronic commerce and data warehousing.

The purpose of this book is to introduce readers to the evolution, power, advantages, and pitfalls of client/server architecture and to discuss a number of complex issues surrounding the implementation and management of client/server systems. From that perspective, this book is intended to become the handbook and guide for client/server application developers, systems and database administrators, information technology managers, and users. Client/server architecture, its advantages, features, and usage, are discussed against the background of the evolution of the computing environment, standards and open systems, object-oriented technologies, client and server specialization, and the analysis of middleware. Using these topics as a foundation, the book proceeds to analyze multitiered second-generation client/server architecture and technologies such as data replication, distributed systems management, and data warehousing.

WHY THIS BOOK IS NEEDED

The amount of information related to the subject of client/server computing is tremendous. Conversely, as technologies continue to advance, new "hot" areas such as data replication, the World Wide Web, data warehousing, on-line analytical processing, data mining, and parallel database technologies are attracting the attention of developers, strategists, and users, while the amount of information about most of these technologies is still limited. Some of the material covered in this book can be found mostly in various vendor publications, trade literature, and international standards materials.

To sort through all the available client/server-related information and find a cohesive and complete description of second-generation client/server computing architecture and applications is extremely difficult. This is especially true because a significant portion of the available information is being changed on a regular basis. Various emerging standards and continuous product updates are examples of this dynamic nature. Various client/server implementations and related issues, described in this book, require detailed knowledge of different hardware and software platforms. Specifically, hardware platforms described in this book include mainframes, midrange systems, parallel processors, workstations, servers, and personal computers. Operating systems include MVS, UNIX, Windows/NT, NetWare, and OS/2. A description of open distributed environments includes Open Software Foundation's Distributed Computing Environment as well as Object Management Group's Common Object Request Broker Architecture. Database management system discussions are focused on key features of SYBASE, ORACLE, INFORMIX, MS SQL Server, and DB2/6000. Readers are also introduced to other extremely important client/server-related issues that deal with the presentation management (e.g., X Window System and MS Windows), distributed systems management, middleware, parallel database technologies, data warehousing, transaction management, data replication, and various industry standards.

Unfortunately, even if one decides to read all the available literature, it would be very difficult to obtain a clear picture of what client/server computing is all about. That is why the author's personal experience in developing client/server systems and extended involvement with high-performance commercial computing, distributed systems management, the Internet, and data warehousing proved to be invaluable in writing this book.

WHO THIS BOOK IS FOR

This book has been written as a result of the author's experiences of participating in several very large scale projects implementing client/server architecture in open systems environments.

In discussing the architecture, advantages, and benefits of the client/server computing model, the author met with many IT managers, system integrators, system administrators, database and data communications specialists, and system programmers, all of whom are potential readers of this book.

This book can be used as a guide for systems integrators, designers of distributed systems, database administrators considering the issues of open distributed databases, systems administrators, and network specialists looking for theoretical or practical knowledge of the distributed cooperative processing and second-generation client/server architecture.

Some specific client/server components described in this book can help IT managers, systems administrators, DBAs, network and communications specialists, and application developers to make informed decisions when selecting platforms and products to implement three-tiered client/server environments. The innovations that became available with the second generation of client/server computing are discussed in the book on such a level of detail that the book should be an invaluable tool for any professional developing distributed client/server applications, dealing with heterogeneous distributed databases, struggling with problems related to application and database interoperability, and, in general, solving a whole spectrum of issues and concerns related to downsizing or rightsizing. In fact, this book is a must for any information systems professional who deals with open systems and standards, client/server architecture, and distributed cooperative transaction processing.

Finally, those readers who are looking into such advanced topics as object-orientation and high-performance commercial computing, middleware and data replication, distributed systems management, and data warehousing will find this book extremely useful in covering the implications of client/server computing for their favorite technologies.

PREREQUISITE

Readers with any data-processing experience can understand this book. Those who deal with only COBOL batch programs will find this book useful. Those with CICS, SQL, DB2, or any other database expertise, including DBA experience, will benefit. UNIX, Windows and Windows/NT, OS/2 and NetWare application developers, systems and network administrators, and LAN specialists should not have any problems reading this book.

The author assumes that readers have little or no previous knowledge about client/server architecture. The book has been structured as a self-teaching guide, with the introduction to client/server architecture and generally related issues placed in the first parts, and the rest of the book dedicated to such important issues as the middleware, transaction management, distributed systems management, data warehousing, and client/server application development.

Part 1 begins with the evolution of computing environments and an introduction to the open systems phenomenon. Part 2 methodically analyzes the key aspect of client/server architecture—specialization of clients and servers—and demonstrates features and advantages of some client/server-related products over others. Important issues of client/server computing—communications and middleware—are discussed in Part 3 of the book. Part 4 deals with the issues of data management in distributed cooperative processing environments, including the analysis of the 12 rules of distributed DBMS first formulated by C. J. Date. Parts 5 and 6 look at the modern issues of transaction management, distributed systems management, and data warehousing. The book concludes with a brief look at client/server application development tools and organizational and management issues related to the implementation of the second-generation client/server systems.

STYLE USED

The book includes a fair amount of diagrams, figures, examples, and illustrations in an attempt to present a lot of rather complicated material in as simple a form as possible. Client/server architecture is a complex, involved, and often misunderstood subject, so that whenever possible, theoretical issues are explained through practical examples. Therefore, the author has made a serious effort to illustrate client/server architecture based on the theoretical foundation of the distributed cooperative processing model.

For those readers interested in theory, the book provides a sufficient theoretical overview of client/server architecture and today's client/server technology. In fact, this book is a comprehensive guide to client/server computing architecture as well as to many popular client/server products.

This book is about a very dynamic subject. All material included in the book was current at the time the book was written. A significant amount of material contained in the first edition of this book has been revised, and a number of new topics have been added. But the author realizes that, as the client/server computing model continues to evolve and as vendors continue to improve and expand on their product quality and functionality, changes would be necessary. The author intends to revise the book again if a significant development in the client/server arena makes it necessary to add, delete, or change parts of the text.

WHAT IS INCLUDED

Part 1 begins with an analysis of the evolution of computing environments and introduces the changes in the way computing is done today. The definition and advantages of open systems and the Open Software Foundation's Distributed Computing Environment are introduced and used as the reference model for the client/server architecture. Common

Object Request Broker Architecture is briefly described and used as an illustration of the wide acceptance of the client/server architecture. This part looks at the evolution of client/server computing itself and analyzes second-generation multitiered client/server architectures.

Part 2 continues the discussion by describing the specialization of clients and servers in distributed environments.

Part 3 deals with the critical issues of client and server interoperability: communications and middleware. Remote procedure calls, SQL interactions, messaging and queuing, and related data communications and networking issues in the client/server computing environment are described in sufficient level of detail.

Part 4 deals with distributed data management issues. It discusses ideal distributed DBMS requirements and proceeds to analyze data replication systems. This part also discusses several popular client/server database management systems such as ORACLE, SYBASE, INFORMIX, MS SQL Server, and DB2/6000.

Part 5 deals with transaction and distributed systems management issues in client/server environments. Several transaction management systems, including IBM CICS, Transarc's Encina, Novell's Tuxedo, and AT&T GIS TOP END are discussed here. This part also focuses the discussion on distributed systems management issues and approaches to systems management and software distribution. Microsoft Systems Management Server and Tivoli Management Environment are discussed here, among other tools.

Finally, Part 6 of the book looks at client/server as a mature architecture capable of supporting the enterprise. The discussion is focused around client/server-based data warehouse architecture and application development issues for client/server computing.

Acknowledgments

First and foremost, I must thank Jerry Papke for encouraging me to write this book. I would like to thank George Anderson for his energy, persistence, and dedication. Very special thanks to my many friends and colleagues at Merrill Lynch and Dun & Bradstreet for providing a creative and challenging atmosphere and for giving me an opportunity to learn and work in a very stimulating and challenging environment on the leading edge of computer technology. Specifically, I would like to thank Cynthia Wilson, George Lieberman, Peter Meekin, and Peter Bakalor.

I am very grateful to Dr. Ramon Barquin for his invaluable help and kindness by allowing me to include his insightful "10 Mistakes . . ." in this book. Special thanks to John Pezzullo of ICS for his friendship and continual support.

I would like to thank all those who have helped me with clarifications, criticism, and information during the writing of this book, especially Dawna Travis DeWire, who was patient enough to read the entire manuscript and made many useful suggestions. And of course, this book would have never been finished without the invaluable assistance and thoroughness of Ginny Carroll of North Market Street Graphics.

Finally, the key reason for this book's existence is my family. My very special thanks to Irina, Vlad, Michelle, and the rest of my family for giving me time to complete the book, understanding its importance, and for their never-ending optimism, support, and love. I am especially grateful to my son Vlad for his help in designing the illustration material (and my personal home page on the Web).

Alex Berson

Foundation

The client / server computing model is rapidly evolving from the one first introduced in the early 1990s to today's multitiered, widely distributed, data-rich cooperative distributed environment. No longer is it simply a client asking a server for data. The concepts of specialization introduced in the first edition of this book have matured and resulted in the second generation of client / server computing, the one that deals with servers dedicated to applications, data, transaction management, systems management, and the like. Data structures supported by this enhanced computing model range from relational to multidimensional to unstructured to multimedia. Clients are now mobile, and the remote access is universally accepted and planned for.

This evolving computing architecture has been recognized as powerful, flexible, and complex, and has been proven to provide the following benefits to its implementors:

- *The ability to achieve systems interoperability and data sharing*

- *The ability to speed up the implementation of new systems based on having many choices already defined*

- *Lower costs, due to the reduction of the support effort as the number of products and processes is reduced*

- *The general improvement in the system quality and the increased flexibility to make modifications more easily in the future*

- *The architected process, which is the communication of a common direction throughout the organization*

- *The ability to prevent the crisis of complexity that closely related to networked computing as the scope, size, and heterogeneity of the systems continue to grow, by reducing the total number of components and processes*

- *Improved maintenance and control through a more consistent approach to system management.*

This computing architecture, its components and their interrelationships, design and management issues, implementations, and emerging trends and applications are the subject of this book.

Introduction to Open Distributed Systems and the Client/Server Model

The term client/server originally applied to a software architecture that described processing between two programs: an application and a supporting service. At that time, the client program and the server program did not have to be physically separated—they could be calling and called programs running on the same machine. Thus, originally, the client/server discussions were limited to interactions between one client and one server. As computer science and the theory of programming evolved, however, the concepts of some programs capable of providing services or managing resources on behalf of a number of other programs became widely accepted. In fact, the client/server computing model represents a specific instance of distributed cooperative processing, where the relationship between clients and servers is the relationship of both hardware and software components.

The client/server computing model covers a wide range of functions, services, and other aspects of the distributed environment. Relevant issues include local and wide area networking, data distribution and replication, distributed processing, transaction management, software distribution and system management, data warehouse, middleware, standards, and open systems. Our discussion of the client/server architecture begins with a look at the evolution of distributed application environments and an introduction to open systems and standards.

1.1 EVOLUTION

How familiar is the statement "Client/server computing is the way of the '90s"? Claims have been made that client/server technology will eliminate application backlogs, reduce software maintenance costs, increase application portability, improve systems and networks performance, and even eliminate the need for minicomputers and mainframes. Instead of getting into a debate about which of these promises (if any) is realistic, let's first look at the evolution of computing environments and find a place for the client/server model.

1.1.1 Host-based processing

The client/server computing model implies a cooperative processing of requests submitted by a client, or requester, to the server, which processes the requests and returns the results to the client.

Client/server cooperative processing is really a special form of distributed processing, where resources (and tasks affecting the resources) are spread across two or more discreet computing systems. While distributed systems are a relatively new phenomenon, operating system–level distribution is well known and widely used. One example may be the distribution of arithmetical and input/output (I/O) functions between a central processing unit (CPU) and an I/O channel controller. Other examples include the distribution of network control functions between an IBM host running Virtual Telecommunications Access Method (VTAM) and a communication controller running Network Control Program (NCP), or distribution of operating system functions among multiple CPUs in a multiprocessor such as the IBM 3090/600 (six processors). However, for the purpose of this book, let's consider processing environments as they are viewed by a particular application.

Distributed systems evolved from the most primitive environment to support application processing. It is the host-based processing environment that does not have any distributed application processing capabilities (see Fig. 1.1).

Host-based application processing is performed on one computer system with attached unintelligent, "dumb," terminals. A single stand-alone personal computer (PC) or an IBM mainframe with attached character-based display terminals are examples of the host-based processing environment. From an application processing point of view, host-based processing is totally nondistributed.

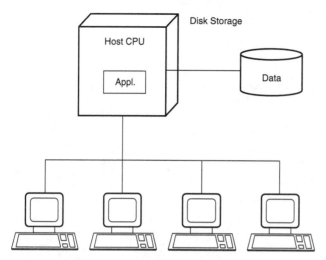

Figure 1.1 Host-based processing environment.

1.1.2 Master-slave processing

The next-higher level of distributed application processing is master-slave processing. As the name implies, in a master-slave system, slave computers are attached to the master computer and perform application processing–related functions only as directed by their master (see Fig. 1.2).

Application processing in a master-slave environment is somewhat distributed, even though the distribution of the processing tends to be unidirectional—from the master computer to its slaves. Typically, slave computers are capable of some limited local application processing, such as on-screen field validation, editing, or function-key processing. An example of a master-slave processing environment is a mainframe (host) computer, such as the IBM 30XX, used with cluster controllers and intelligent terminals.

1.1.3 First-generation client/server processing

The client/server processing model has emerged as a higher level of shared-device processing typically found in local area networks (LAN).

In a shared-device LAN processing environment, personal computers are attached to a system device that allows these PCs to share a common resource—a file on a hard disk and a printer are typical examples. In the LAN terminology, such shared devices are called *servers* (a file server and a printer server in our example). The name *server* is appropriate, since these shared devices are used to receive requests for

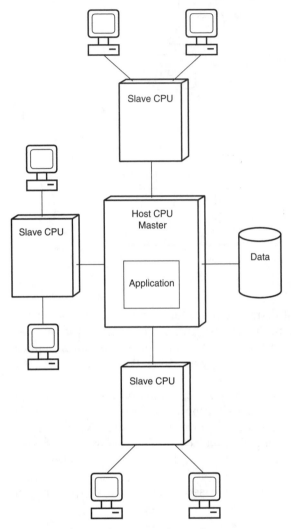

Figure 1.2 Master-slave processing environment.

service from the PCs for generic, low-level functions. (See Fig. 1.3.) In typical LAN-based, shared-device processing, these PC requests are usually limited to services related to shared-file or print processing (a common file can be read by several PCs, and some report pages can be sent by multiple PCs to the same printer). The obvious drawback of such an approach is that all application processing is performed on individual PCs, and only certain functions (print, file I/O) are distributed. Therefore, an entire file has to be sent to a PC that issued a

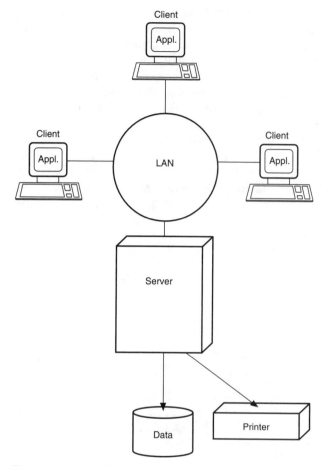

Figure 1.3 Shared-device processing environment.

READ request against this file. If a file has to be updated, the entire file is locked by the PC that issued the update request.

An example of shared-device processing can be Novell's NetWare, which allows a local area network to have a system dedicated exclusively to the file and/or print services.

The client/server processing model is a natural extension of shared-device processing. Evolutionary, as local area networks grew in size and number of supported workstations, the shared-device system, be it a file server or a print server, also grew in capacity and power. Gradually, these servers became capable of serving a large number of workstations. At the same time, the role of the workstations was also changing—the workstations were becoming *clients* of the servers. The main reason for the change was that, in a large LAN environment, sharing of file and print services among the workstations in a LAN group was representing only a fraction of a typical application. The significant part of the application functionality was also a good candidate for sharing among LAN users. Therefore, some of the application processing was distributed to a new server—the server that receives requests from applications running on workstations (clients) and processes them for each of its clients.

In this model, application processing is divided (not necessarily evenly) between the client and the server. The processing is actually initiated and partially controlled by the service requester—the client, but not in a master-slave fashion. Instead, both the client and the server cooperate to successfully execute an application. A database

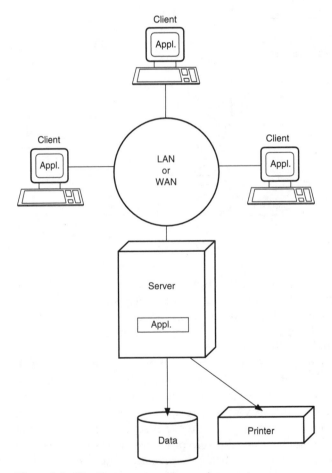

Figure 1.4 Client/server processing environment.

server such as SYBASE SQL Server is an example of the client/server processing environment. (See Fig. 1.4.)

An advantage of the client/server approach can be illustrated by a comparison between a file server and a database server. If a PC application needs particular records from a shared file, it sends a request to read the entire file to a file server, which makes this entire file available to the PC. The application running on this PC has to search the file to select requested records. The computing resources of the file server are used to process the entire file, while the PC's resources are used to run an application that reads every record of the file. If every file record is sent to the PC for processing, a significant portion of the available resources is used inefficiently, and communication lines are overburdened.

In the case of a database server, an application running on a PC sends a record READ request to its database server. The database server processes the database file locally and sends only the requested records to the PC application. Both the client and the server computing resources cooperate to perform the requested query.

To summarize, architecturally, client/server processing requires:

- Reliable, robust communications between clients and servers
- Client/server cooperative interactions that are initiated by a client
- Application processing distribution between a client and its server
- Server-enforced control over what services or data clients can request
- Server-based arbitration of conflicting client requests

1.1.4 Peer-to-peer processing

A client/server model distinguishes between clients that request services and servers that service these requests. All participant systems in peer-to-peer processing, however, are equals, and can request and provide services to and from each other.

This architecture is the ultimate in the distribution of application processing. The processing is performed wherever computing resources are available, including shared devices, CPU, and memory. A single system in peer-to-peer processing can act as a client for other servers and a server for other clients (including itself). In intelligent peer-to-peer processing, one server can distribute a workload among available servers and can even optimize such a distribution based on servers and network characteristics. (See Fig. 1.5.)

Ideally, such a peer-to-peer environment provides for transparent cooperative processing between applications possibly residing on a

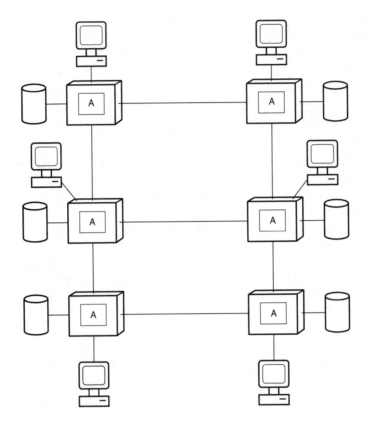

A—application

Figure 1.5 Peer-to-peer processing environment.

wide variety of hardware and software platforms. One goal of the peer-to-peer processing environment is the support of networked databases, where database management system (DBMS) users will be able to move seamlessly between multiple heterogeneous (i.e., different) databases.

1.1.5 Second-generation client/server processing

Since the first edition of this book was published in 1992, the client/server computing model has undergone rapid evolution from a simple, two-tiered client/database-server model to a multitiered, widely distributed, data-rich cooperative distributed environment. The client requests are no longer limited to just relational data. The second generation of client/server computing deals with servers dedicated to applications, data, transaction management, systems management, and the like. Data structures supported by this enhanced computing model range from relational to multidimensional to unstructured to multimedia. Clients are now mobile, and the remote access is universally accepted and planned for.

Indeed, the second generation of client/server computing is characterized by a multitiered architecture which promotes migration of the application logic from the client to the application server in a three-tiered environment (see Fig. 1.6).

At the same time, server-based application logic becomes less monolithic, and the advancements in the middleware and application development techniques allow for constructing applications from smaller reusable components. The increasing scaleability requirements for data size and performance, advancements in the middleware, and distributed systems enable application logic to be distributed across multiple servers. And finally, an integration of distributed architectures with the object models leads to evolution of procedural client/server systems to a distributed object computing model.

The actual development of distributed cooperative client/server and peer-to-peer environments is not a trivial task. To fulfill the requirements of cooperative processing between a client and a server and, by extension, between nodes in peer-to-peer processing, several questions have to be answered. Among these questions are:

- How do the clients and servers find each other across the network?

- Since clients and server often reside on separate systems (in separate address spaces), how do they (clients and server) share information?

- How can clients and servers that run on many heterogeneous platforms under many operating systems synchronize their processing across many network protocols?

These and other questions are addressed by the client/server architecture in general and the suite of emerging distributed computing standards in particular.

1.2 PARADIGM SHIFT

The emergence and wide acceptance of the client/server computing paradigm can be linked to several changes in today's computing.

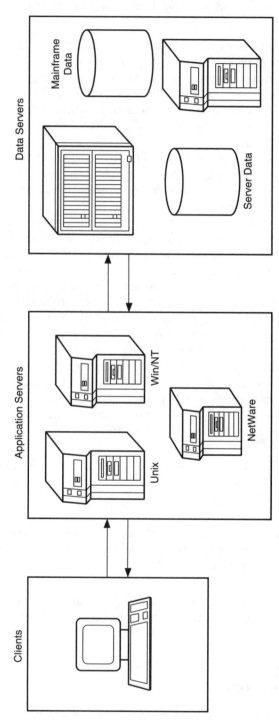

Figure 1.6 Three-tiered second-generation client/server model.

Clients

Application Servers

Win/NT

Unix

NetWare

Data Servers

Mainframe Data

Server Data

1.2.1 Computing paradigm

The first change can be characterized as a shift in a computing paradigm. A traditional view of computing might be that of a computer user who accesses a powerful tool—the computer—via a communication network. The emphasis here was on the need to access a known computer program that resided on a known, possibly remote, system, as was the case in host-based and master-slave computing.

A new way of computing is emerging now. Users use computers to solve problems and to request services. There is an implied understanding that the services the users require may not be found in a single system, but rather are distributed across a network. Users use their individual computers as entry points to get access to this distributed computing power. The global nature of today's business, the proliferation of workgroup computing and LAN/WAN environments, the strong focus on shared and reusable resources, the attention given to the promise of the Information Superhighway, and the wide use of global networking services like Internet and World Wide Web (WWW) are the evidence of this shift in computing paradigm. (See Fig. 1.7.)

This shift can also be observed in the way distributed client/server computing is being positioned in the enterprise. As more and more mission-critical applications are being placed (ported to or developed for) on this new environment, the early client/server solutions are proving to be inadequate to solve today's business problems. This inadequacy affects both the run time and the development aspects of client/server computing. The major changes affecting the way client/server computing is implemented do not invalidate the client/server architecture but rather introduce a set of additional, more demanding requirements on the environment. Among these trends the following three appear most prevailing:

- *Object-orientation*—The promise of development productivity of the object-oriented analysis, design, and programming cannot be ignored any longer. The implicit or explicit acceptance of object-orientation

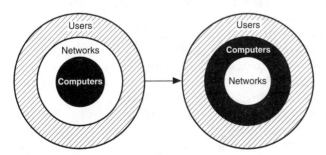

Figure 1.7 Computing paradigm shift. (*Gartner Group.*)

by information technology practitioners, coupled with the emergence of object-oriented standards and availability of related development and run-time tools, result in the need to adopt the client/server model to handle objects, mostly in the form of object request brokers (Common Object Request Broker Architecture is discussed later in this chapter).

- *Middleware*—The layer in the client/server architecture that transforms a simple two-tier client/server computing model to a more complex client-middleware-server model. Middleware is discussed in Chap. 5.

- *High-performance commercial parallel computing and very large database (VLDB) processing*—traditional servers are often incapable of handling large volumes of data, large numbers of users, and the high demands on performance and throughput required of the new breed of applications (data mining, multimedia, speech and character recognition, visualizations, etc.). Computer engineers and scientists turn their attention to different computer architectures and new ways of database processing to satisfy these demands. Massively parallel processors and parallel databases are examples of these efforts. Both are discussed later in the book.

1.2.2 Business paradigm

An impartial observer may notice that the advancements in computing technology manifest themselves in a change in the way we do business. Indeed, the proprietary systems and mainframe-based computing of the 1960s and 1970s moved a traditional business enterprise from the manual back and front office to an automated back office and the proliferation of on-line transaction processing (OLTP). Essentially, though, these automated systems were designed to duplicate traditional manual operations, and while these innovations improved processing speed and throughput, they did not change the way the businesses worked.

But rapidly changing market dynamics, competitive pressures, globalization of commercial markets, reduced profit margins, and other similar factors forced business to review its structures, approaches, and strategies. Users are demanding more value for the money and are well aware of the competitive offerings. The world map is changing as previously closed markets become available, and the speed of market penetration as well as the flexibility and adaptability of the products and services differentiate successful enterprises from previously inconceivable business failures.

Aggressive rightsizing, business process reengineering, changes resulting from the introduction of workgroup computing to the way the front office works, a prominent role given to decision support systems and their users (executives and information workers), the paperless office, just-in-time delivery of products and services that exceed customer expectations—are just a few examples of what a new business enterprise may need to stay competitive. And technologies like client/server computing, distributed computing, object-orientation, the Web, multimedia, extensive use of artificial intelligence and expert systems for data visualization and data mining, voice and image recognition, mobile computing, personal communication systems, and handheld computers may help businesses to achieve these goals. (See Fig. 1.8.)

1.2.3 Advantages of client/server computing

Very few products today even claim to support peer-to-peer processing. There is a spectrum of outstanding technical issues that make the implementation of peer-to-peer processing a rather difficult task. However, the client/server model, while not yet the peer-to-peer ideal, is a reasonable approach to the development of distributed systems. This model provides significant benefits and can be used in today's business solutions. Aside from strictly marketing considerations—

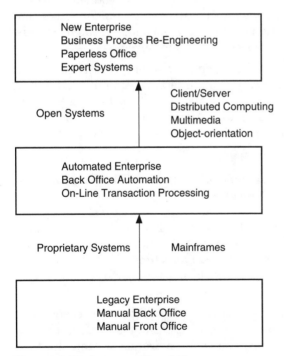

Figure 1.8 Business paradigm shift.

most of the development of application-enabling technology (including computer-assisted software engineering, or CASE, tools) is being focused on client/server tools—there are real benefits in adopting a client/server architecture. Specifically, it:

- Allows corporations to leverage emerging desktop computing technology better. Today's workstations deliver considerable computing power, previously available only from mainframes, at a fraction (sometimes more than an order of magnitude) of mainframe costs.

- Allows the processing to reside close to the source of data being processed (client/server architecture is a special form of distributed processing: cooperative processing); therefore, network traffic (and response time) can be greatly reduced, and effective throughput and carrying capacity on a heavily loaded network is increased. Conversely, the network bandwidth requirements and, therefore, cost can be reduced.

- Facilitates the use of graphical user interfaces (GUI) and multimedia applications. These new interfaces can be delivered to customers in a variety of visual presentation techniques, together with easy and intuitive navigation and standards-compliant consistency. Indeed, a picture is worth a thousand words. As a result, investment in training and education can be leveraged better, and new products that exceed customer expectations can be developed faster; end user resistance to accepting new products can be minimized.

- Allows for and encourages the acceptance of open systems; indeed, the fact that clients and servers can, in fact, be running on different hardware and software platforms allows end users to free themselves from particular proprietary architectures, thus taking economical, marketing, and competitive advantage of the open market of available products.

To be sure, the client/server model is not perfect. There are some disadvantages to using a client/server model:

- If a significant portion of application logic is moved to a server, the server may become a bottleneck in the same fashion as a mainframe in a master-slave architecture. The server's limited resources will be in ever-higher demand by the increasing number of resource consumers—end users.

- Distributed applications, especially those designed for cooperative processing, are more complex than nondistributed. This is true for the application development, run-time environment, and the tools used to manage this distributed environment.

However, some of this complexity can be offset by reducing a large problem into a set of smaller, possibly interdependent problems, similar to modular system design. There are certain claims made by various software vendors and industry experts relative to a client/server computing model. Some of them are probably true, while the others look like a marketing/sales push. For example, the claim that client/server will turn nontechnical users into professional software developers is highly questionable. The same can be said about a claim that client/server will force minicomputers and mainframes to disappear.

However, it is highly probable that a *properly implemented* client/server model will reduce software maintenance cost, increase software portability, boost the performance of existing networks, and even eliminate application backlog by increasing the developer's productivity and shortening the development life cycle.

The true client/server architecture encompasses much more than just data. It includes networks and data communications, distributed presentation and distributed transaction processing, standards, and open systems. This book attempts to look at all these issues in order to give the reader as complete a picture as possible of the client/server architecture.

1.3   STANDARDS AND OPEN SYSTEMS

Before discussing various aspects of the client/server architecture, it is useful to look at the difference between an architecture and a product. An architecture is a set of definitions, rules, and terms that are used as guidelines for building a product. A product is a specific implementation of an architecture. The architecture alone, without a product implementing it, is not very usable. A product that implements the architecture is what makes that architecture usable.

Well-designed architecture should be implemented in one or more products, and should have a lifetime well beyond that of a specific product. To achieve these goals, such an architecture should be based on industry standards and, conversely, may initiate the introduction of new standards. Products that implement such an architecture will promote and support standardization. The client/server computing model is a maturing architecture. The wide variety of products that implement this architecture today differ significantly in functionality, interfaces, and even level of compliance to the standards that should regulate the architecture. What's more, not all standards relevant to the client/server architecture are finalized to date or even fully developed. Therefore, the discussion of the client/server will start with a look at relevant industry standards, especially those related to open systems.

1.3.1 Open systems

From an information technology point of view, a typical business enterprise is a collection of different systems residing on a wide variety of different, quite often multivendor, mutually incompatible hardware and software platforms, running myriad business, scientific, and engineering applications. Today, customers want to link their entire enterprise into a coherent whole, tying together all their systems, irrespective of the vendor platform these systems are running on. Moreover, customers want to extend their businesses by linking enterprise-wide systems with business's suppliers, distributors, and customers. To be able to interconnect all these systems and to move applications from one system to another, these existing proprietary systems should open their architectures by adopting standards-based interfaces. Interoperability means that existing multivendor systems should be able to talk to each other. Open interoperability means that new applications should be built in such a way that neither the design nor the implementation of the system would lock the application into a particular vendor hardware or software platform. In other words, open systems applications should be portable across all customer-specified platforms to avoid lock-in onto a particular system. In addition, as business applications grow in scope, customers should be able to move these applications to a larger, more powerful system without the need to modify applications—an open system should facilitate application scaleability for performance and throughput. Of course, for open systems to fulfill interoperability and application portability requirements, such systems must be built according to industry-accepted standards. Only when a system conforms to industry standards, can it seamlessly interoperate with another standards-compliant system, and only then can applications be ported from one such system to another.

It is very important to notice that an open system does not automatically mean a UNIX operating system. Openness is not a function of the operating system. Open systems should have the following features:

- Compliance with industry standards for programming, communications, networking, system management, presentation, system services, and interfaces between applications and system services
- Portability of applications across systems
- Scaleability of applications performance and throughput
- Interoperability across systems

In fact, the Institute of Electrical and Electronics Engineers (IEEE) Technical Committee on Open Systems (TCOS) offers the following definition of open systems:

... A comprehensive and consistent set of international information tech-nology standards and functional standards profiles that specify interfaces, services, and supporting formats to accomplish interoperability and porta-bility of applications, data and people.

Of course, some customers might be interested only in application portability, systems scaleability, and interoperability. Such a position is usually justified by saying that these features bring the highest return on investment. However, without standards compliance, the full poten-tial of open systems cannot be achieved. There are many important ramifications of the wide proliferation of proprietary standards:

- Customers that are locked in to one vendor's systems and are looking to change the vendor/system/architecture face a very high cost of switching from one vendor to another.

- As a rule, users of proprietary systems have already written a lot of business-related software and supporting documentation, and trained their employees in system-specific skills. Not all these in-vestments can be saved when migrating to another environment.

- Independent software vendors tend to develop software for vendors with large installed customer bases, thus giving the largest system vendors additional competitive advantage.

Thus, many users are forced into proprietary systems. The real prob-lem arises when, for various reasons, a proprietary system's vendor no longer meets customers' needs or when a business built on proprietary systems decides to extend its reach to another business (e.g., a merger, an acquisition, or a joint venture) and that other business relies on a different proprietary system.

Client/server architecture is no exception: standards will allow differ-ent vendors' clients and servers to communicate, to port applications from one platform to another without abandoning the client/server architecture, and to move applications to systems of different sizes to achieve scaleable performance and throughput.

Among standards organizations that play key roles in the open sys-tems arena are:

- *POSIX,* the Portable Operating System Interface for the computer environment, which has been defined by the IEEE TCOS to provide greater consistency across unlike operating environments.

- *X/Open,* a nonprofit organization founded in 1984 to solve problems caused by software and systems incompatibility. X/Open plays an important role in defining a Common Application Environment (CAE), specifications, which are contained in the X/Open Portability Guide (XPG4 in the fourth release of this guide).

- *International Organization for Standardization* (ISO), whose goal is to develop, accelerate, and promote various standards and products that implement them. Among them is the Open Systems Interconnection (OSI) reference model.

- *Corporation for Open Systems* (COS), which concentrates its efforts in the area of OSI, ISDN, standards conformance testing, and certification.

- *Object Management Group* (OMG), an international organization involved in system and software development in the framework of object-oriented technology.

- *Open Software Foundation* (OSF), a major technology provider for open system environments.

The current mission of the OSF is to end the existence of factions in the open systems industry and present users with a far more comprehensive framework for standards development than currently exists. With the acquisition of the UNIX Software Laboratories by Novell, the OSF will attempt to attract Novell's UNIX Systems Group and SunSoft—the software arm of the Sun Microsystems—into its fold. OSF may even become host to another open systems vendors alliance—the Common Open Software Environment (COSE)—and will focus on developing common and unifying public-domain specifications for the various aspects of the open systems standards. These actions should help converge existing open systems standards and technologies into a common open systems continuum.

1.3.2 Beneficiaries of open systems

The ultimate goal of an ideal open computing environment is to make possible truly distributed networks where:

- Computing can occur transparently across the network.

- applications, resources, functionality, and power can be shared seamlessly throughout the environment.

- Users will be provided with the greatest possible portability, interoperability, and scaleability of applications.

Creation of such an open computing environment does not mean the elimination of proprietary operating systems. Nor—and this is very important—does it imply that open systems must be purely UNIX-based. Open systems are more than UNIX. Open systems environments accomplish interoperability and portability of applications and data by supporting a comprehensive and complete set of internationally accepted technology and functionality standards. And truly open systems will coexist with proprietary operating systems, including various flavors of UNIX. This coexistence will be accomplished by providing interfaces and connection points, so that vendor lock-in is avoided and users' investments in existing technology, applications, and training are better leveraged. A truly open computing environment will benefit system vendors, independent software vendors, and end users as follows:

- Hardware and software system vendors will benefit from open systems by lowering the costs of operating systems development, thus shortening time to market for new products. Instead of spending time and effort on creation of proprietary systems, vendors will be able to improve the architecture, features, and functionality of new products.

- Open systems do not eliminate competition; conversely, vendors will compete and add value to their products to achieve specialization of products and hardware platforms, quality, service, and proprietary optimization solutions.

- Independent software vendors will benefit from an open computing environment by developing products based on international standards.

- Compliance with standard interfaces will practically guarantee new wider markets for their products.

- End users will be the biggest beneficiaries of the open computing environment. Their hardware purchasing strategies will allow end users to purchase systems without fear of buying the "wrong box." In open systems, end users will be assured of having the same operating environment with any system they purchase—mainframe, minicomputer, workstation, or supercomputer. Mixed-vendor interoperability and networking connectivity will be simplified. Software development, training, and maintenance costs will be lowered, and more off-the-shelf products will be available at more competitive prices. Entire corporations and individual business units will have more flexibility in choosing products and systems that best suit their business requirements.

While a truly open computing environment is still the future goal of many vendors, standards bodies, and end users, there are many encouraging developments today that bring us closer to the open systems environment. Among these developments is a promising version of the open computing environment from the OSF: the Distributed Computing Environment (DCE). A similar specification was developed by the former UNIX International: Open Network Computing (ONC).

A detailed discussion of the various open system solutions is beyond the scope of this book. But, from the perspective of client/server architecture, it is useful to look closely at the foundation and key of client/server architecture: distributed cooperative processing. And since distributed processing is one of the main goals and beneficiaries of truly open systems, the picture will not be complete without discussing one of the best-known candidates to become a de facto standard for open and distributed computing environments: OSF's Distributed Computing Environment.

1.4   OSF DISTRIBUTED COMPUTING ENVIRONMENT

OSF's Distributed Computing Environment empowers both end users and software developers to take advantage of truly distributed open systems. The DCE provides the foundation that is needed to use and develop distributed applications in heterogeneous hardware and software environments.

Through its open Request For Technology (RFT) process, OSF has selected and integrated the best technologies available to date. The selected technologies were mostly derived from the DECorum proposal jointly submitted by Hewlett-Packard (HP) / Apollo, IBM, Digital, Microsoft, Locus, and Transarc.

The resulting architecture (DCE) provides solutions to several fundamental questions facing the developers of the distributed cooperative client/server environments. Among them are the client's and server's abilities to locate each other across the network, the mechanism to share information between clients and server across the network, and the ability to synchronize processing among many distributed systems to achieve true cooperation.

1.4.1   DCE architecture

In general terms, the Distributed Computing Environment is an integrated environment consisting of the following components:

- Distributed file system
- Directory service
- Remote procedure calls
- Threads services
- Time services

See Fig. 1.9.

1.4.2   Distributed file system (DFS)

Distributed file systems operate by allowing a user on one system that is connected to a network to access and modify data stored on files in another system. From the point of view of client/server architecture, the system on which the user is working is the *client,* while the system in which the data is stored is the *file server.*

When data is accessed from the file server, a copy of that data is stored, or *cached,* on the client system, so that the client can read and modify it. Modified data is then written back to the file server. An obvious problem arises when multiple clients attempt to access and modify the same data. One solution to this problem is to force the file server to keep track of clients and their cached data. DCE DFS uses a set of

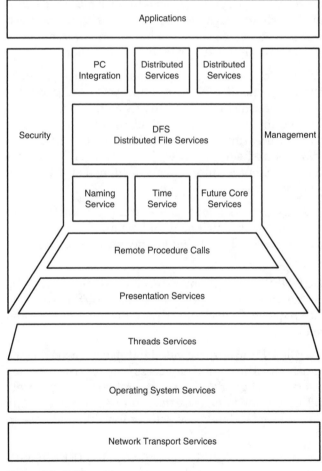

Figure 1.9 DCE architecture.

tokens to keep track of cached information. The tokens are allocated to a client by a server when the client caches the data, based on the type of access the client requested. For data modification, a client must request a *write token* from the server. Once the write token is allocated, the server can inform other clients that the write token is issued. If other clients had the same data allocated and cached to them for read purposes, they will be notified that their data is no longer current and the server can revoke their tokens.

DCE DFS provides the following advanced distributed file system features:

- *Access security and protection.*   While original UNIX systems were notorious for their weak security, DCE DFS implements enforced security by supporting both user *authentication* (Kerberos system allows clients to exchange encrypted information with the authentication server, so that clients carry Kerberos tickets that, in effect, prove that a client is who he/she claims to be) and an *access control list* mechanism for awarding file access to authorized clients.

- *Data reliability.*   While distributed systems theoretically allow elimination of the single point of failure, improperly designed distributed systems may force a single client to rely on a number of critical resources, loss of any one of which would result in the client's inability to continue processing. To prevent this problem, DCE DFS supports *replication* for all its network services—if one of the servers becomes unavailable, a client is automatically switched over to one of the replicated servers.

- *Data availability.*   DCE DFS allows the system administrator to perform routine maintenance (such as data backup, file movement, etc.) on network resources without bringing the network or any of its servers down.

- *Performance.*   DCE DFS is an efficient, extensible system. By caching file status information and data on a client system, DFS is reducing the number of data requests from clients, thus reducing a server's and network's workload.

- *Manageability.*   DCE DFS uses distributed databases to keep track of file location, authentication and the access control lists used by both clients and servers. These databases are broken into separately administered and maintained domains that can be accessed by any client. In addition, these databases are self-configuring and easy to operate.

- *Standards conformance.*   DCE DFS conforms with the IEEE POSIX 1003.1 file system semantics standard.

- *Interoperability with Network File System (NFS).* DCE DFS provides gateways that allow clients using NFS to interoperate with DCE DFS servers, thus providing a migration path from NFS to DCE DFS.

DCE DFS is based on the Andrew File System from Transarc Corporation. It differs from Sun's Network File System (NFS)—a current de facto standard—in these two main categories:

- DFS uses global file space (all network users see the same paths to accessible files). Global file names ensure uniform file access from any network node via a *uniform name space*. In NFS, each network node has a different view of the file space.

- DFS provides integrated support for both local and wide area networks. NFS was designed primarily to operate in a local area network environment.

1.4.3 Directory service

Computer networks, like people, require names and directories to describe, record, and find the characteristics of the various services and information they provide. Like a real mail system, an electronic mail system must be able to locate a user's mailbox in order to deliver the mail.

In a distributed computing environment, the mail delivery application will contact a directory or name services application to look up the user's name and location (address). In the DCE, anything that can be named and accessed individually (e.g., network services, electronic mailboxes, computers, etc.) is called an *object*. Each object has a corresponding listing (an *entry*) in the directory service. Each entry contains *attributes* that describe the object. Name entries are collected into lists called *directories*. In the DCE, directories can be organized into hierarchies, in which a directory can contain other directories. An example of such a hierarchy is an international telephone listing that contains directories of individual countries.

The name and directory services are central to the DCE. That is because all DCE objects are defined by their names, and applications and services gain access to objects by accessing an appropriate directory entry and retrieving its attributes. Thus, object characteristics are separated (decoupled) from the object itself, and, most importantly, the *location independence* of objects is assured. Such an organization allows applications and services to access objects even if the object moves or changes several of its attributes. The DCE Directory Service is integrated with the other DCE components, including DCE DFS, and possesses the same advanced characteristics (security, reliability, availability, manageability, performance) as the DCE DFS.

The DCE Directory Service is designed to participate in the CCITT's and ISO's (International Standards Organization) Open Systems Interconnection (OSI) X.500 worldwide directory service. Local DCE users can be tied into X.500 directory service and, conversely, users in other parts of the world are allowed to access local names via X.500. To implement this feature, DCE supplies naming gateways called *Global Directory Agents,* or GDAs.

In a client/server DCE environment, a local client in one part of the DCE network (in one domain) that needs to look up the name of a remote client sends its request to a local GDA residing on a name server. The GDA on that server forwards the request to the worldwide X.500 service, which looks up a name and returns the result to the GDA, which in turn passes it back to its client.

To ensure portability and interoperability and to isolate application programmers from the details of the underlying services, the OSF DCE uses a service-independent *application programming interface* (API). This API is based on the X/Open Directory Services (XDS) API specifications. Applications that use XDS can work with the DCE Directory Service and with X.500 without modifications.

1.4.4   Remote procedure calls

Remote procedure calls (RPCs) syntax, semantics, and presentation services represent the extension of high-level language subroutine calls. RPCs allow the actual code of the called procedure to reside and be executed on a physically remote processor in a manner transparent to the application. The RPC mechanism is the most critical aspect of the entire DCE architecture—it acts as the glue that holds all DCE components together. The basis of the OSF DCE RPC is the HP/Apollo Network Computing System (NCS) version 2.0 remote procedure call. DCE's RPCs are easy to use, are designed to be transparent to various network architectures, and support threads (described in Sec. 1.4.5).

1.4.5   Threads services

A typical network computing environment achieves its goals by linking all participating processors. Therefore, opportunities exist to implement a certain degree of parallel processing. Among many strategies in existence to implement the parallel processing code, the OSF selected the threads strategy for its Distributed Computing Environment. The threads strategy uses subprocesses (threads) that exist and operate within a single instance of the executing program and its address space. The program itself can use special synchronization tools, such as semaphores, to control access to a common, modifiable resource shared by several users (memory variable, for example). Of course, there are many other methods of implementing parallel processing (i.e., shared memory among multiple programs or use of explicit synchronization verbs to exchange messages among several programs). However, these methods usually involve resources external to the program. Digital's Concert Multithread Architecture (CMA) is the foundation of the DCE's threads services. It offers portability and supports the POSIX 1003 application and system services interface specification.

1.4.6   Time services

The function of the time services component is to synchronize the clocks of all network nodes with the clock that controls the network as a whole. Due to its completeness and simplicity, OSF selected Digital's distributed Time Synchronization Service.

1.4.7   The result—DCE client/server model

The OSF DCE is designed to fit into the client/server paradigm. Therefore, DCE components must be present on the service requester, DCE client, and the service provider, DCE server (see Fig. 1.10).

DCE is not simply a software package that can be installed on a server. In fact, DCE components are placed "between" applications and networking services on both the client and the server. Even though DCE is a multilayered architecture containing a number of basic services, the DCE client/server model hides the actual details of these services from end users.

Essentially, DCE components represent an integral part of the distributed computing model being developed by such standards bodies as the ISO.

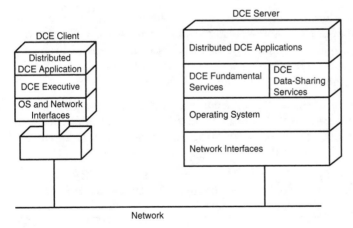

Figure 1.10 DCE client/server model.

1.5   CORBA

Some of the major obstacles in building a seamlessly distributed computing environment are related to the quality, cost, and lack of interoperability of the software. Indeed, while the hardware costs are on the downward trend, the costs of acquiring, developing, and managing distributed interoperable software are on the rise. The Object Management Group (OMG) was formed to help reduce the complexity and lower the costs of new software solutions.

To achieve these goals, the OMG defines Object Management Architecture (OMA). Its object-oriented computing paradigm focuses on the ability to encapsulate data and processes (methods) into reusable software components called *objects.*

Conceptually, OMA-compliant applications consist of a set of internetworking object classes and instances that follow that theory via interfaces defined in an object model and the Common Object Request Broker Architecture (CORBA). CORBA can act as the connection engine for all other forms of distributed computing as well as object-oriented computing. The intention of the OMA is to impose as few design constraints as possible and only at the highest level. The OMA identifies major separable components of a distributed object system, characterizes their functions, explains interrelationships and relationships with the external operating environment, and identifies required protocols and interfaces.

As defined by the OMG, the OMA will provide the following benefits to end users:

- Applications can share and reuse application and system objects; the result is reduced development time and cost, as well as the development of consistent user interfaces.

- An object-oriented (OO) user interface allows users to view and manipulate application objects as objects of the real world, thus providing a common and consistent look and feel that is easier to see and use than to remember and type. Examples of OO user interfaces are Microsoft Windows 95, NextSTEP, and OSF/Motif.

- Encapsulation of data and methods inside objects, as well as using object class hierarchy and inheritance, allow building applications in a truly modular fashion, preventing unintended interference and improving software quality.

- Using shared and reusable objects and standards describing their behavior provides for enhanced interoperability among applications.

OMA divides objects into three groups: Object Services, Common Facilities, and Application Objects (see Fig. 1.11). Object Services, the first component to be standardized, is defined in phases, the first being the Common Object Services Specification (includes Life Cycle services such as *object create, destroy, move, copy,* Event and Naming Services, and Persistence), and the second group including transaction, concurrency, relationship, externalization, internationalization, and time services. Common Facilities is expected to include a compound document interface and print services. It is possible that Application Objects will be standardized by vertical markets, rather than by the OMG.

One of the theories of distributed object computing is that objects of any type can request services of other objects, at any time, and with no concern for where the two objects are or how they accomplish their respective tasks, just as animate objects can do in the real world. An object that cannot perform the requested service will say so.

Therefore, the communication heart of the OMA standard is the architecture that describes the object request broker (ORB). This architecture provides an infrastructure that allows objects to communicate independently of the specific platforms and techniques used to implement these objects. Known as the Common Object Request Broker Architecture (CORBA), it is aimed at providing portability and interoperability of objects over a network of heterogeneous systems. CORBA defines an object-oriented switching mechanism for the messages passed between objects. This mechanism is the ORB, and it is designed by the Object Management Group to fit closely into the client/server architecture.

Within the semantics of the object model, a CORBA-compliant ORB should provide:

- *Name services*—maps requestors to methods through some type of object location service.

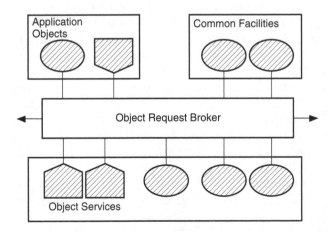

Figure 1.11 Object Management Architecture (OMA).

- *Request dispatch*—determines which method to invoke.
- *Parameter encoding*—maps the requestor's local parameter representation to the recipients.
- *Delivery*—delivers requests and results using transport protocols such as TCP/IP or ISO standards.
- *Synchronization*—provides a means (e.g., asynchronous, synchronous) for a recipient to reply to a requester in a meaningful and timely manner.
- *Activation*—actually invokes the method; provides means for objects that hold persistent information in non-object-storage facilities such as flat files or relational databases.
- *Exception handling*—provides restart/recovery resources.
- *Security*—provides authentication and protection.

A central CORBA premise is that there are definitions of object interfaces in an interface definition language. This language defines the types of objects according to the operations that may be performed on them and the parameters needed by those operations. Once a client makes a request, the ORB is responsible for all the mechanisms required to find the *object implementation* in the network, prepare it to receive the request, and transmit the request. The client object does not care where the implementation is located, what programming language it is implemented in, or what underlying protocols/operating system/chip technology it operates on. Specifically, CORBA defines an object as an identifiable, encapsulated entity that provides one or more services that can be requested by a client. A client's request may have parameters and causes the service to be performed by an object on the client's behalf. The outcome of the request (the result) is returned to the client according to the request definition. Objects can be created and destroyed as an outcome of issuing requests. Clients are aware of the object *interface*—a set of possible operations that a client may request of an object.

In this context, an object can be considered as a server process. What differentiates this from a simple client/server model is the fact that the client request is given to the referenced object by the object request broker. The ORB is responsible for all the mechanisms required to find the specific object implementation for this request, to prepare the object implementation to receive the request, and to communicate the request to the object. Thus, the object interfaces visible to the client are completely independent of the object location and implementation specifics (i.e., language, internal structure, etc.). The OMG defines the Interface Definition Language (IDL) that is used to specify interfaces between clients and servers. The CORBA IDL is flexible enough to support static (compiled) interfaces as well as the Dynamic Invocation Interface, which interprets and passes requests on the fly. (See Fig. 1.12.)

In essence, CORBA defines an object-oriented *middleware* software layer that could facilitate the emergence of the open peer-to-peer distributed network computing (the discussion on middleware can be found in Chap. 8). Many object-oriented systems, particularly those developed in-house using standard OO development environments, can use CORBA-compliant products for objects distribution and interactions. With the completion of the CORBA specifications, C language binding, and Object Service Specifications, the OMA and CORBA have a potential of rapidly becoming a viable development and execution environment.

However, as is the case with many emerging standards, CORBA is also not without problems. One is the complexity of this new and different distributed object-oriented application development environment. To cope with this complexity, an elaborate, expensive, and prolonged effort to acquire necessary professional-level skills is required of many programmers. Another and somewhat related problem is CORBA's timing—not too many off-the-shelf applications are CORBA-compliant today. The immaturity and incompleteness of version 1 of the CORBA specification results in the inability of ORBs from different vendors to interoperate even though it is claimed that they are built to the CORBA specification. Hopefully, the CORBA 2.0 specification, when published, will help eliminate the ORB interoperability problem.

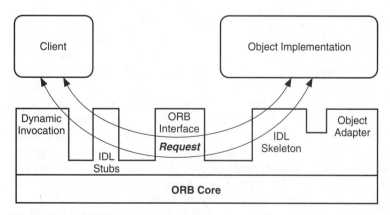

Figure 1.12 CORBA.

1.6   THE COMPLETE PICTURE—A NEW
GENERATION OF THE CLIENT/SERVER
COMPUTING MODEL

The Distributed Computing Environment represents a valuable contribution to the development of open distributed computing. This maturing of the client/server and distributed computing environment is also being strongly influenced by the advent and industrywide acceptance of object-orientation. Among the most popular standards that are emerging to respond to the fast-growing object-oriented computing model, software vendors and IS organizations alike pay special attention to Microsoft's Object Linking and Embedding (OLE), OpenDoc, and CORBA. Although promising, these standards are good examples of the lack of interoperability among several object-oriented approaches vying for marketplace dominance.

Among the three, Microsoft's OLE technology is probably the nearest to de facto status. OLE is a key technology for Microsoft and represents Microsoft's direction toward an object-oriented operating system that will follow Windows NT. This *objectware* is defined as an environment where applications are composed of object components that are combined at run time to provide a total application solution across networks and on multiple platforms. As described in Chap. 3, OLE uses a document-editing metaphor, where the contents of a document have embedded links to the relevant application or set of applications. OLE allows the embedded information to be manipulated and displayed seamlessly from the container document.

OpenDoc can best be described as an attempt by its sponsors to produce a competing, nonproprietary OLE superset aimed at reducing industry reliance on Microsoft technical direction. The OpenDoc sponsors—Apple, IBM, Borland, WordPerfect, Novell, Oracle, and Xerox—formed a consortium, Components Integration Laboratories (CIL), which has defined an architecture similar to OLE. Some experts say that OpenDoc architecture as defined is even superior to OLE in some areas. OpenDoc should have greater cross-platform interoperability than OLE by supporting UNIX, OS/2, Mac, and Windows. What's more, OpenDoc is defined to be CORBA-compliant by including some of the IBM's Systems Object Model (SOM) technology, which provides an interface to IBM's own CORBA-compliant object request broker.

CORBA, briefly described previously, is an object-oriented switching mechanism for the messages passed between objects and does not follow a document-centric metaphor. Although all three front-runners in the standards race are different, there appear to be a common theme among them, and that commonality is built around ORBs. Thus, CORBA could be the glue that ties together OpenDoc and OLE. Even though OLE today is not designed to be CORBA-compliant, Digital Equipment Corporation, in cooperation with Microsoft, works to add interoperability between its ORB, known as Digital ObjectBroker, and OLE, using technology licensed from Microsoft. This will allow the development of distributed and heterogeneous applications using custom and off-the-shelf components. Furthermore, this work will support OLE links to UNIX, because ObjectBroker runs on OSF/1, AIX, HP-UX, and SunOS.

To complete the discussion on the open computing environment architecture, two additional efforts need mentioning:

- To make applications easily available for a multitude of hardware and software platforms, vendors and organizations such as the OSF are working toward the development of the *Architecture-Neutral Software Distribution Format* (ANDF). If and when it is implemented, ANDF technology will increase the appeal and power of open systems by making available a rich set of applications for a broad range of computing platforms.

- As distributed computing becomes a reality, the need to define a consistent approach to managing networking systems, irrespective of the underlying hardware and software platforms, becomes more pressing; Several proposals are on the table today. Tivoli's proposed solution to a uniform framework for the efficient management of open systems is the *Tivoli Management Environment* (TME). It is a complicated issue, and TME has a way to go to become a widely accepted management solution for distributed heterogeneous environments.

Standards-based architectures like the DCE and CORBA should be used as a proper foundation for development of an open client/server architecture.

1.7 SUMMARY

This chapter has briefly covered a lot of material, including the evolution of computing environments from host-based–centric to a distributed cooperative model of client/server processing. We showed that the client/server model is not the end-all model, that it's dynamic and continues to evolve from one generation to the next. This chapter also discussed open systems and standards as key components of open distributed computing. What follows in the next chapter is a closer look at the distributed computing models.

Approach to Distribution

The evolution of computing environments, as described in the previous chapter, brought to life various forms of distributed processing. Distributed computing is the next evolutionary step beyond file sharing. A distributed computing environment such as Open Software Foundation's Distributed Computing Environment, or DCE, makes a collection of loosely connected systems appear to be a single system. Distributed computing makes it easier to develop and run applications that use resources throughout a computer network. Applications can be distributed to run on the computers best suited for the task. Various tasks can be run on parallel, providing higher performance and better resource utilization. Client/server architecture is built on and represents a special case of distributed computing: cooperative distributed processing. Today's client/server requirements include the freedom to store data and run applications on a wide variety of interconnected platforms. Client/server implementations should be available in an open, flexible, standardized, multivendor computing environment. The importance of standards and open systems has already been described in the previous chapter. The next critical building block of the client/server architecture deals with distributed environment models and is the subject of this chapter.

2.1 DISTRIBUTED MODELS

The development of a distributed computing architecture has been affected by two opposing forces that prevail in today's computing environment. The first force breaks up applications and pushes the resulting pieces (fragments) toward the end users. There are at least two reasons for this behavior:

- Development and execution of applications on workstations and PCs provide significant price/performance gains.

- End users' demands for local autonomy and additional functionality (such as flexible and consistent graphical user interfaces) increase users' productivity.

The second, opposing force, has its roots in the end user's need to access corporate data. This need affects systems integration requirements and results in the centralization of applications on large, powerful servers and mainframes. That second force increases the need for ever-higher levels of integrity, performance, and availability.

These requirements are rarely achievable on a single, small system. The answer lies in the development of a distributed model consisting of a large, centralized platform connected to a network of sufficiently powerful workstations operating in local area networks (LANs). The main architectural questions in such a model are:

- How and where in the model computing are resources distributed?

- How should intercommunication facilities be implemented among all participating computing resources?

To answer the first question, let's take a closer look at cooperative distributed processing of the client/server computing model.

2.1.1 Cooperative client/server processing

Cooperative processing is the foundation and driving force of the client/server architecture. The distinguishing characteristic of a cooperative processing application is the high degree of interaction among various application components (or application fragments). In a client/server architecture, these interactions are the interactions between the client's requests and the server's reactions to the requests. To understand these interactions, let's look at the general application components. A typical application consists of the following components (see Fig. 2.1):

- *Presentation processing logic.* It is a part of the application code that interacts with a device such as an end user's terminal or a

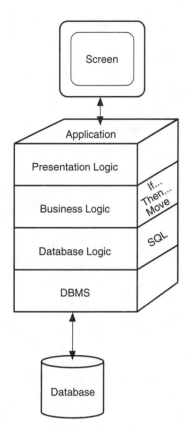

Figure 2.1   Typical application components.

workstation. Presentation logic performs such tasks as screen formatting, reading and writing of the screen information, window
management, and keyboard and mouse handling. Some of the facilities that provide character-based presentation processing logic are
IBM's CICS, IMS/DC, and TSO for a centralized mainframe environment. Graphical user interfaces (GUIs) are provided by facilities
such as Microsoft's Windows and Windows/NT, OS/2 Presentation
Manager, X-Windows, and OSF/Motif.

- *Business processing logic.*   It is a part of the application code that
  uses the input data (from a screen and/or database) to perform business tasks. Typically, this code is user-written in any of the supported
  programming (i.e., COBOL, C, C++, SmallTalk, MS VisualBasic).

- *Data manipulation logic.*   It is a part of the application code that
  manipulates data within the application. The data is managed by a
  database management system (DBMS). Data manipulation in rela-

tional DBMSs (RDBMS) is done using some dialect of the Structured Query Language (SQL). SQL's Data Manipulation Language (DML) is typically embedded into the 3GL or 4GL application code.

- *Database management system processing.* It is the actual processing of the database data that is performed by the DBMS. Ideally, the DBMS processing is transparent to the business logic of the application. However, from the architectural point of view, database processing is an essential part of the cooperative processing interactions and should be considered as a component of cooperative application processing.

In host-based processing, these application components reside on the same system and are combined into one executable program. No distribution is taking place, and, in general, the application is restricted by the limited resources of the platform it runs on. With the advent of distributed computing, new opportunities are being opened to system developers and end users. Portable scaleable applications capable of running on networks of open systems transparently to the end users can now be developed. By distributing computing resources across the network, significant cost-benefits can be achieved. To *distribute* means to take something, divide it into fragments, and spread these fragments out. In distributed computing, to distribute means to divide available computing resources into fragments and spread them across a network. (See Fig. 2.2.) The question is: what resources should be distributed, and what are the consequences of such a distribution?

When only data is distributed among several locations, a single application can conceivably access the data from any location, in a fashion totally transparent to the application. Certain benefits (such as placing data close to its source, data distribution for higher availability, etc.) can be derived from such a distribution. However, the singularity of an application can create a bottleneck, a limiting factor in achieving higher performance, portability, and the cost-benefits of application scaleability.

If, however, in addition to data, some application processing is also distributed across the network, various computing resources can be better utilized, especially considering the significant price/performance characteristics of PCs and modern workstations. Of course, once application components are distributed, they must cooperate in the processing of a business application. The client/server architecture employs distributed cooperative processing to:

- Distribute application processing components between clients (typically presentation and some part of the business logic) and servers (typically some parts of the business logic, database logic and DBMS).

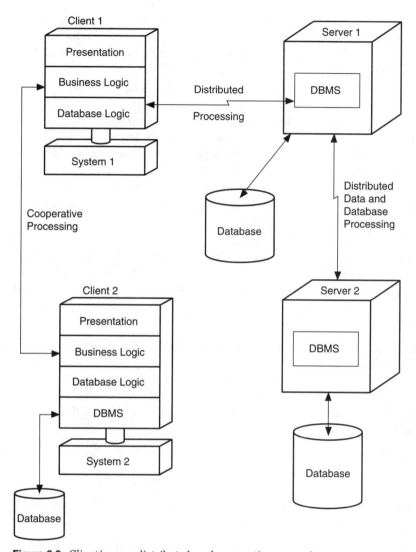

Figure 2.2 Client/server, distributed, and cooperative processing.

- Support cohesive interactions between clients and servers in a cooperative fashion.

One of the questions every client/server system designer must answer is how to distribute application components between clients and servers. In a multitiered architecture, this question is extended to the component's placement into various tiers. While there is no universal recipe for the "proper" distribution of application components, some general recommendations can be made:

- In general, a presentation logic component would have its screen input/output facilities placed on a client system. These clients are typically placed in the lowest tier of the multitiered environment (PC and workstations).
- Given the available power of the client workstations and the fact that the presentation logic resides on the client system, it makes sense to place some part of the business logic also on a client system. It should be true for at least the part of the application logic that deals with the screen-related editing, and maybe for those pieces of the code that are specific to a particular client.
- If the database processing logic is embedded into the business logic, and if clients maintain some low-interaction, quasi-static data, then the database processing logic (such as local data manipulation) can be placed on a client system.
- Given the fact that a typical LAN connects clients within a common-purpose workgroup, and assuming that the workgroup shares a database, all common, shared fragments of the business and database processing logic and DBMS itself should be placed on the server. (See Fig. 2.3.)

Similar principles can be used to decide the placement of a client/server application component in an environment consisting of client systems, departmental servers, and enterprise servers (i.e., mainframes). Such an environment is often referred to as a *platform-based three-tiered architecture,* and it is discussed in more detail later in this chapter.

To a large extent, the question of component placement should be decided by:

- The quantity of data relevant to any given application
- The number of active users running applications against this data
- The number of interactions between various application components
- The technical characteristics of the platforms selected for clients and servers

For example, if the application requires frequent read and write access to a large corporate database, that database and its processing logic are placed on the enterprise server or the top tier (see Fig. 2.4). If the access is infrequent, or is mostly read-only, it may be feasible to place relevant copies of the data onto a second-tier server. The server-based DBMS (often different from the host DBMS), database processing logic, and common shared components of the business logic should also be placed there. In this case, every tier contains its own database, and system designers face the problem of heterogeneous data access (this

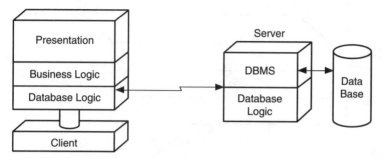

Client/Server Processing with Data on the Server Only

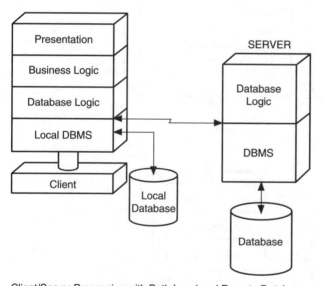

Client/Server Processing with Both Local and Remote Databases

Figure 2.3 Client/server processing.

problem is discussed in greater detail later in the book). Figure 2.4 illustrates such an architecture, where the top tier contains a mainframe IBM host that accesses MVS/DB2 database. The second tier is a database server running a relational DBMS such as SYBASE SQL Server, and the third tier contains Intel-based PCs running MS Windows and MS Access database.

2.1.2 Application components distribution points

The separation of application logic into the general categories previously described is not always straightforward, and the boundaries

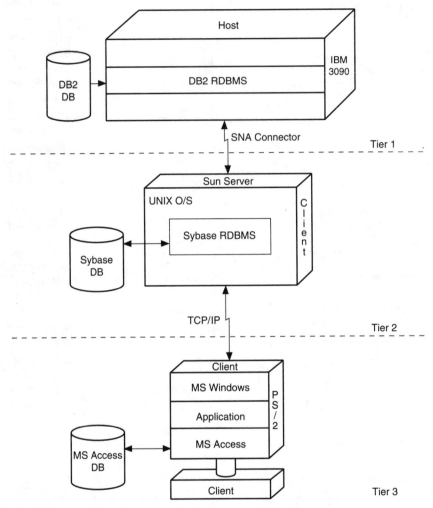

Figure 2.4 Three-tiered architecture with heterogeneous data access.

between the components are not always clearly defined. However, applications developed with structured programming techniques and proper software engineering guidelines can help separate these components. Moreover, proper application of object-oriented techniques, especially encapsulation and inheritance, can facilitate these often intuitive efforts.

In general, an application is limited by the limited resources of the platform it runs on. In a distributed environment, multiple systems are connected into a network of resources, all of which are conceivably available to the application. To make all these resources available and useful to the application, the application components should be distributed in such a way that cooperative processing between them becomes possible. The client/server architecture employs distributed cooperative processing to:

- Distribute application processing components between clients (typically presentation and some part of the business logic) and servers (typically some parts of the business logic, database logic, and DBMS).
- Support cohesive interactions between clients and servers in a cooperative fashion.

The high-level view of cooperative processing describes some general scenarios for the distribution of application components: distributed presentation, distributed business logic, and distributed data management. However, a closer look reveals that a finer granularity in application components distribution exists. This view leads to several possible styles of cooperative processing between various distributed applications (Fig. 2.5).

Depending on the distribution points (or lines) chosen for a particular application structure, the following *atomic* cooperative processing styles can be defined:

- Distributed presentation (DP)
- Remote presentation (RP)
- Distributed business logic (DBL)
- Distributed data management (DDM)
- Remote data management (RDM)

This classification deals with the atomic, elementary styles of cooperative processing. Of course, only certain combinations of cooperative processing styles are possible or even desirable. For example, distributed business logic can include distributed data management, or remote data management can be combined with the distributed business logic styles.

Note that the preceding classifications should be considered from the point of view of the application core—the business function. It is, in fact, the principal reason the application exists in the first place.

To summarize, a cooperative application can be split:

- To separate presentation logic, data management logic, and/or business logic from each other
- To combine and/or distribute parts of the application across multiple systems

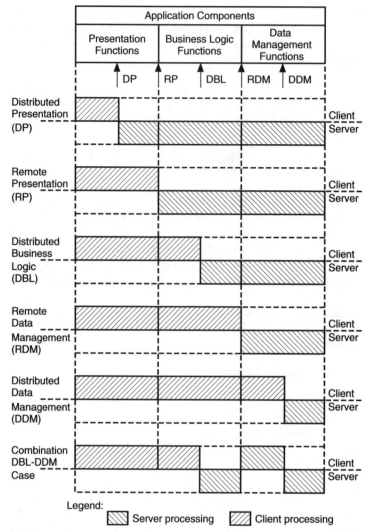

Figure 2.5 Application components distribution points.

In this context, business logic cannot be considered remote. Indeed, it cannot be remote to itself, but can only be distributed between two or more platforms.

Each of the cooperative processing styles described here is defined and accounted for in the client/server architecture.

2.2 MULTITIERED ENVIRONMENTS

The client/server computing model continues to evolve to meet the challenges of complexities and scope associated with growing beyond workgroup computing to the entire enterprise. This evolution has been reflected in the growing complexity and flexibility of the client/server architecture, from the earlier two-tiered model to scaleable, manageable multitiered environments.

2.2.1   Two-tiered model

The two-tiered client/server computing model is a direct result of applying the five styles of application component distribution previously described to the two platforms—a client and a server. Clearly, such a model fits well into a small-scale workgroup environment, and typically is implemented as one of these styles:

- *Remote data management*—In this model, the presentation logic and the business logic (application code) reside on the client, with the server supporting database (and file) services. This application-on-the-client, database-on-the-server model represents a common view of first-generation client/server computing and is often referred to as a "fat" client.

- *Distributed business logic*—A model where some of the business and data manipulation logic resides both on the client and on the server.

- *Remote presentation*—In this model, all application and database functionality is placed on the server, with a "thin" client performing presentation functions. The business logic in this model is often implemented as stored procedures in the database management system.

The two-tiered model works best in a homogeneous environment, where all database servers are of the same type and where the business logic is relatively simple. The two-tiered model has demonstrated some serious drawbacks as developers started to extend it to the enterprise level.

- *Connectivity to heterogeneous database environments*—The two-tiered model was typically implemented as a specialized client designed to interact with a specific server in the most efficient way. When a given client application had to connect to different server and DBMS systems, the client code frequently required modifications that had to be extended to all client systems in the enterprise.

- *Support for transaction processing*—Typically, two-tiered models rely on the DBMS to ensure data integrity and consistency in a transactional sense. The problem arises from the fact that in a heterogeneous DBMS environment a given server cannot guarantee the integrity of the transaction if a different DBMS server is involved

- *Synchronous processing*—Typically, a two-tiered model is implemented as a synchronous processing model where clients are connected to servers and wait for the server response to continue processing.

- *Portability of server code*—Using proprietary server code to implement stored procedures, triggers, and rules was often a necessity dictated by the lack of appropriate standards, limited platform size, and demanding performance and throughput requirements. At the same time, this approach resulted in locking two-tiered client/server systems to a specific DBMS.

- *Scaleability*—The two-tiered model offers limited scaleability as the number of clients and transaction volumes continues to grow. For example, in this model, each client has to establish its own database connection to the server, with a number of connections rapidly exceeding the server, DBMS, and/or network limits. Although it is always possible to upgrade server hardware or to add another server, it may require expensive changes in the infrastructure and, potentially, changes in the applications, especially if database partitioning is involved. Similarly, as additional applications have to be placed on the client (in the "fat" client model), the client systems may have to be upgraded, which could result in a very expensive and prolonged effort.

- *Maintainability*—An enterprise-level two-tiered client/server model can result in a large number of client systems widely distributed (possibly globally) throughout the enterprise. A change in client software becomes a challenge of distributing the change, reconfiguring client systems, and possibly upgrading client hardware.

2.2.2 Platform-based multitiered model

In the efforts directed toward *rightsizing,* and to better position themselves for the deployment of client/server applications, most large organizations have been moving toward what has become known as a platform-based, three-tiered architecture. The roots of this three-tiered architecture can be found in a familiar hierarchical, traditional master-slave computing paradigm. Examples of this paradigm are IBM's System/390 and the original implementations of the Systems Network Architecture (SNA).

The platform-based, three-tiered client/server architecture represents an extension of the two-tiered model and is a high point of the first generation of the client/server computing model. It has added distributed and cooperative processing capabilities to the hierarchical computing model. In the most trivial implementation of such an architecture, the computing resources are distributed vertically. Specifically, the top tier is usually occupied by the most powerful system and the source of the corporate data, the mainframe. The second tier contains powerful LAN servers, which have dual properties: they act as top-tier clients that send appropriate requests to the mainframe. At the same time, they function as servers for the workstations and PCs that reside in the third tier. An example of such a vertical three-tiered architecture would be an organization that extends its central single-host data center capabilities by building LANs in each of its headquarters departments and connecting corresponding LAN servers to the host.

It is interesting to note that this model is driven by a number of market forces: price-performance, functionality, and, local autonomy push the distribution downward, while the need for a high level of availability, data integrity, manageability, and security restrains the distribution trend (see Fig. 2.6).

Of course, such an architecture can be expanded horizontally by adding mainframes to the top tier and local area networks and servers to the second and third tiers. For example, an organization that desires to extend its East Coast operations by building a second data center on the West Coast can put LANs into each regional sales office. Office LAN servers can be physically located in remote (relative to a host) locations and can be connected to either host via a wide area network (WAN). (See Fig. 2.7.)

The network management, system performance, data integrity, and reliability in such an extended three-tiered model require a degree of an intratier communication (intercommunication between hosts in the first tier and between servers in the second tier). Therefore, the resulting architecture becomes more complex to build and manage. However, the resulting computing capacity has also increased, probably in orders of magnitude.

The platform-based, three-tiered model appears to eliminate some of the drawbacks of the two-tiered model. For example, this architecture is more scaleable. This means that as the number of workstations grows, additional local area networks, more powerful servers, and even additional tiers can be put into operation. If designed properly, the changes to the infrastructure (network, systems management, etc.) can be minimized. Frequently, the growth in the number of users (an important aspect of the scaleability) can be supported without changes to the applications. The main shortfall of this model is its tight dependency on the platforms used. For example, client systems in this model are designed to interact with server DBMSs of a given type and the server software, if finely tuned to interoperate with the enterprise server (mainframe) and its data stores. In short, the platform-based model is lacking the degree of abstraction and the architectural view of

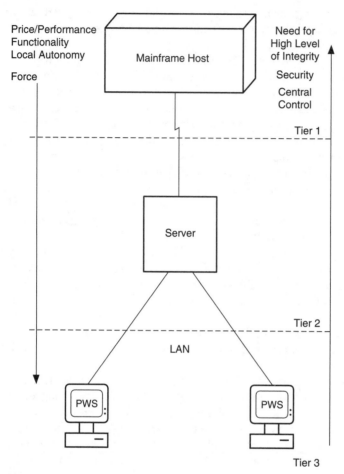

Figure 2.6 Three-tiered architecture and market forces.

the flexible and adaptable function-based multitiered model that has emerged as a second-generation client/server computing architecture.

2.2.3 Second-generation multitiered client/server models

Two-tiered and multitiered solutions came from different sources. While two-tiered implementations originated with database vendors offering client-database server systems, the multitiered approach has its roots in open systems, distributed, enterprise-wide computing, where the main goal is the distribution and cooperative interoperability of applications on the network. Merging of these two approaches results in the second generation of client/server computing that is characterized by:

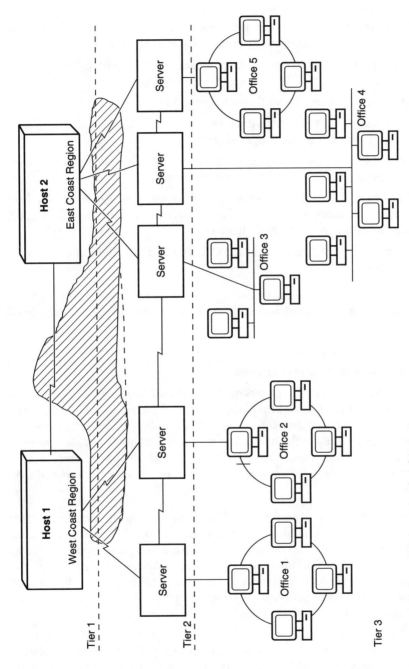

Figure 2.7 Extended three-tiered architecture.

- Multitiered architectures

- Asynchronous connectivity between clients and server that involves messaging and synchronous remote procedure calls

- Support of on-line transaction processing (OLTP) by using transaction managers (or TP monitors)

- Data distribution via replication technologies

- Data access that provides data location (and often structure) transparency for distributed applications

- Ability to integrate complex data types including documents, voice, images, multimedia, and full-motion video

- Advanced information processing techniques that are based on data warehouse concepts (i.e., on-line analytical processing, or OLAP, data mining, and data visualization)

- Support of very large databases (VLDB) and parallel database technologies.

These and similar requirements have resulted in the architectural changes that partition new applications across multiple specialized servers.

Function-based three-tiered model

This model extends the two-tiered model and improves the platform-based three-tiered model by defining an architectural middle tier (the one between a client and the server) that consists of one or more application servers on which the bulk of the business and data logic resides (see Fig. 2.8). The resulting three-tiered functions-based architecture divides application components across three different classes of systems:

- *Clients* perform presentation functions, including graphical user interfaces and local edits; run local application code that may access local (client-resident) databases; and execute communication front-end code that provides access to the network. Additionally, the realization that client/server interactions may involve distributed transaction management is reflected in the fact that a client may also be a client of a distributed transaction manager.

- *Application servers* are members of a new architectural layer (tier). They are designed to off-load common functionality from the clients to properly designed and positioned systems. Application servers perform workgroup application functions, support the network domain operating system, store and execute common business rules,

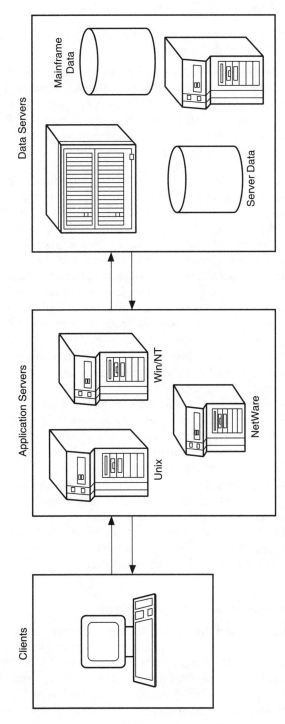

Figure 2.8 Three-tiered function-based model.

support a data directory, provide messaging and queuing services, and participate in global transactions.

- *Data servers* are focused on providing data-related services, including support for relational and object database management systems, data warehouse services, and systems management configuration databases. In addition, this class of servers provides backup and recovery services, represents transaction management control point, and supports legacy applications.

Notice that this model allows application placement on all three tiers. This is partly because often the lines between application logic, data logic, and presentation logic are blurred. The actual placement of application components depends on often-conflicting factors based on ease of development, testing and administration, server scaleability, system and network performance, and throughput.

This model addresses the main drawbacks of the two-tiered model by eliminating the "fat" client syndrome, improving scaleability, heterogeneity, and manageability. Indeed, concentrating most of the application code on the application servers (rather than clients) allows for more manageable maintenance and configuration. The client-based application code is now isolated from the DBMS-proprietary stored procedure languages and can be developed using standard languages (i.e., C, C++, SmallTalk, COBOL).

Middle-tier servers can participate in global transactions by supporting the X/Open transaction interface protocol (XA protocol) that is supported by the majority of database vendors. Application servers can also multiplex transactions, thus improving scaleability as it relates to the number of concurrent users.

In addition, this model eases the development and deployment of specialized applications such as on-line analytical processing, or OLAP, (discussed later in the book) using designated application servers. Thus, the three-tiered function-based model can support mixed processing environments where both OLTP and decision support systems (DSS) can coexist and interoperate.

Services-based multitiered model—middleware

The previous discussion illustrated that, as the complexity and size of client/server systems continue to grow, a relatively simplistic two-tiered approach to the application components distribution in a client/server computing model becomes ineffective and has to be replaced with a more sophisticated function-based distribution model—the model that addresses the distribution and placement of application components on clients and servers.

In a real business enterprise computing environment, with the multitude of applications, platforms, and networks participating in distributed cooperative client/server processing, an important additional functionality is required to make that distribution and cooperation work. This functionality can be placed on a separate architectural component, with a set of formal interfaces between it and the client and server. Since, architecturally, this layer sits between the client and the server, it can be considered as an enterprise middleware component that can perform services necessary to support enterprise client/server computing. (See Fig. 2.9.)

Among these services are security, message routing, directory services, integrity, and recovery. While the discussion on middleware is the subject of a separate chapter (Chap. 8), the important point is that, when considering enterprise-wide client/server architecture, two-tiered and three-tiered models should be extended to a multitiered client/server model that incorporates clients, application and data servers, and the middleware.

2.3 SINGLE SYSTEM IMAGE

A successful client/server architecture takes advantage of network computing and price/performance advances in microcomputer technology by off-loading traditional mainframe processing onto powerful servers and workstations. The fact that certain functions needed by an application are performed on a different system, potentially miles away from the client site, should not affect the way applications appear to behave. In other words, distributing application components between clients

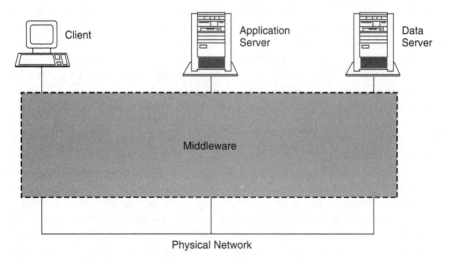

Figure 2.9 Multitiered client/server with middleware.

and servers should not change the look and feel of an application. Many different systems may participate in the execution of a single client's request. To the end users, however, the entire distributed multi-client/multiserver environment should appear as a single-user powerful system. To summarize, properly implemented, a client/server distributed environment should provide end users with a *single system image,* or SSI.

In practical terms, single system image means that all client/server interactions between distributed application components should be performed in a transparent, timely, and effective fashion. Obviously, SSI is a highly desirable feature of client/server architecture. However, its implementation requirements are quite different for the presentation, application processing logic, and data distribution.

The next sections of this chapter look closely at how the distribution of the application components affect single system image.

2.4 PRESENTATION DISTRIBUTION

The first application fragment that interacts with the end user is the presentation logic. The presentation logic is the application's window into the outside world. It is this logic that interfaces with the end user, and, at the same time, interacts with the business logic. In a stand-alone or host-based environment, presentation and business logic are bundled together. With the advances in workstation technology, new capabilities have been opened to presentation logic developers. Traditional character-based terminals are being replaced by high-resolution screens with a practically unlimited number of colors. Today, presentation functions perform such tasks as screen formatting, dialog management, reading and writing of the screen information, window management, and keyboard and mouse handling. Advanced presentation functions can handle general input editing, data type and data range validation, cross-field editing, context-sensitive help, session transcripts, message logging, and user access control. In addition, high-quality audio systems are now available to almost any workstation platform. As a result, *multimedia* workstations equipped with point-and-click devices, such as a mouse, rich graphics, computer scanning and imaging, audio-video input/output facilities including full-motion video, are now widely available. These innovations allow application developers to design applications with visual, intuitive graphical user interfaces that offer such features as windows, scrolling bars, pull-down and pop-up menus and push buttons. Use of these tools and intuitive input devices not only increases end-user productivity, its ease of use allows for shorter training, thus providing better leverage for the investment in application development and training.

To illustrate the power of a GUI interface, let's consider a real estate application. Imagine a contemporary real estate office. When a new customer walks into an office and asks to see all new-construction houses in a particular area, a real estate broker enters all of the parameters into a computer and receives a display of a color map of the desired area, with all potential houses clearly marked. The broker uses a mouse to point to one of the candidate houses, and a color picture of the house appears on the screen, together with the pertinent information. Point and click on the entrance, and the next window pops up with a view of the foyer. A guided tour of the house can be accomplished by audio comments. Another example is a home shopping application using a multimedia catalog. A user connects to the *home page* of the retailer via a World Wide Web browser like Mosaic or Netscape, and proceeds to browse the latest catalog for the available selection of desired products. The user can select, for example, a shirt from the catalog, zoom in to look at the buttons, rotate it for a better view from the back, chose a color and size, and even send a purchase order for the selected shirt via a built-in modem. These illustrations are not science fiction. Products that provide facilities and applications similar to the ones described here exist and are implemented using client/server architecture.

Technically, the presentation portion of such an application is distributed to a client site and runs on a powerful workstation equipped with appropriate input/output devices. The reasons for the presentation distribution are quite compelling:

- High-resolution graphics require significant processing power. Each individual picture dot on a screen (pixel) is controlled in its placement, intensity, and colors, and there may be over a million pixels in a high-resolution monitor. The entire screen is "painted," pixel by pixel, and a large number of floating-point calculations are associated with every new screen.

- All windowing environments are event-driven. Most of the processing is controlled by a mouse pointer moving from one window to another, by pressing a mouse button, or when a scrolling bar or a menu item are touched. This processing requires significant computing resources.

- Workstations are often designed to perform high-function graphics. Their on-board processors are enhanced to handle 2-D and 3-D graphics, as well as audio output.

The computing power requirements for most of the currently used graphical user interfaces and multimedia applications make it economically beneficial to off-load the presentation logic onto a platform that is designed specifically to handle such requirements. And just by the nature of presentation, such a platform is designed for human interactions and should be at a user site. To satisfy the single system image requirements, interactions between the presentation fragments and the rest of the application logic should be accomplished in a user-transparent fashion.

One of the best-known technologies that allows applications to transparently access displays on a networked workstation was developed at The Massachusetts Institute of Technology and was called *X Windows*. X Windows architecture is based on the client/server model. It provides a communication protocol between an application and its presentation logic, which may reside on a remote display workstation. X-Windows and other presentation standards are described in more detail later in the book.

From the cooperative processing point of view, the way the presentation functions are separated from the rest of the application determines the two styles of cooperative presentation: distributed presentation and remote presentation.

2.4.1 Distributed presentation

In the context of a cooperative application structure (see Fig. 2.5), distributed presentation corresponds to the DP split point of the application. Thus, presentation functions are distributed when the presentation part of the application code is split between two or more network nodes. Figure 2.10 illustrates distributed presentation, where a portion of the user interface logic is located on one node, while the rest of the presentation, together with the remainder of the application logic, is located on another node.

The typical distributed presentation model consists of front-end and back-end components. Front-end components handle the physical part of a user interface: screen displays, graphical user interfaces, window management, color, fonts, audio, mouse, and keyboard. Therefore, the distributed presentation front end is located on an end-user interface device: a terminal, a personal computer, or a workstation. In client/ server terminology, the front-end presentation component resides on a *client node*.

The back-end presentation components reside on a node different from the front end's node and perform some common, shared presentation functions. In the client/server architecture context, the back-end presentation components reside on a *server system*.

The important feature of distributed presentation is the fact that the cooperative processing is performed between the front end and the back end of the presentation components, and both the nodes' hardware and software are responsible for this cooperation.

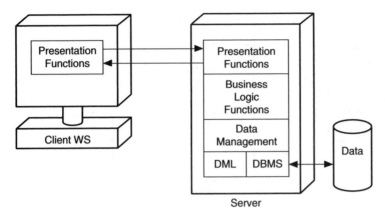

Figure 2.10 Distributed presentation.

The front-end/back-end processing of distributed presentation represents one of the techniques used to develop cooperative applications.

2.4.2 Remote presentation

In the context of the cooperative application structure (see Fig. 2.5),
remote presentation corresponds to the RP split point of the application. Therefore, presentation functions are said to be remote (from the
business logic component) when a presentation part of the application
code is placed in its entirety on one node, while the rest of the application is located on another node (see Fig. 2.11).

The remote presentation style of cooperative processing is best
suited for certain types of nonconversational applications where end-
user interactions are predetermined. Such predetermined interactions
can lead to fully specified, static user interfaces. The presentation
functions can thus be limited to a single message being sent from the
end-user node (where remote presentation functions are placed) to the
application code residing at another node, with a single reply coming
back.

Remote presentation processing is cooperative processing between
presentation functions and other application functions. This mode of
cooperative processing can be supported by remote procedure calls or
by some form of program-to-program communication (for example,
APPC). An example of remote presentation is Digital's transaction
processing system (Digitaltp), running on VAX. The presentation is
performed by the Digitalforms software (screen generation, input
validation). Once the input is received, the transaction request is sent
to the VAX server for processing.

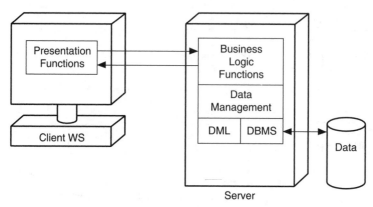

Figure 2.11 Remote presentation.

2.5 DISTRIBUTED PROCESSING

Application logic functions are designed to fulfill the business reasons for the application to be in existence. Within the client/server framework, there appear to be three possible architectural alternatives.

Alternative 1. Application processing logic is placed entirely on a client system. Some of the advantages of this approach are:

- It places the application processing logic as close to the source of the terminal I/O data as possible. The alternative is to send screen data to the server for processing and back to display results over the network.

- It reduces network traffic between presentation and application processing logic.

- There is no need for the synchronization between application processing logic fragments, which would be necessary if the fragments were distributed between clients and servers.

Some of the disadvantages of this approach are:

- The need to maintain multiple copies of the same business logic on every client workstation represents a serious systems management problem.

- The benefits of a common shared modular code cannot be realized.

- The power of a server machine is not fully leveraged. At the same time, client systems could be overloaded, which might necessitate a hardware upgrade and additional investment in multiple workstations.

Alternative 2. Application processing logic is placed entirely on a server. Some of the advantages of this approach are:

- It eliminates code redundancy, simplifies systems maintenance, and allows for better leveraging of the investment in the server hardware.

- It reduces network traffic between an application and a database.

- There is no need for the synchronization between application processing logic fragments, necessary if the fragments are distributed between clients and servers.

Some of the disadvantages of this approach are:

- It could result in overloading of the server resources, thus necessitating a server hardware upgrade. That is especially true when many different applications have to share the same server system.

- Interactions between the presentation and business logic can significantly increase network traffic and the response time for real-time applications.

- The power of client workstations could be underutilized, thus reducing the return on investment.

Alternative 3.   Application processing logic is fragmented, with the fragments distributed between the client and the server.

In general, the first two alternatives represent the most trivial case of a distributed environment, where application functions are contained in a single system—a single node in a network. This approach can be justified for certain low-activity, limited-access applications in relatively small networks.

However, such a design, while relatively simple, creates at least three significant problems:

- A single application location can result in a throughput bottleneck, especially in a high-volume transaction processing environment.

- A single application location makes the entire system less reliable by creating a single point of failure.

- Distributed computing resources are poorly utilized and the application-hosting node may need to be constantly upgraded to keep up with the ever-increasing transaction workload.

The natural way to alleviate these problems is to distribute application logic functions across several nodes.

2.5.1 Distributed functions

In the context of the cooperative application structure (see Fig. 2.5), distributed business logic corresponds to the DBL split point of the application. The business logic functions are split so that they can be placed on different systems (nodes). This way, the execution of the business transaction is performed as a cooperative effort between all business logic components with the cooperative participation of both presentation and data management functions.

A typical split of the business logic functions is done in already familiar front-end/back-end fashion (see Fig. 2.12). The front-end/back-end cooperation usually includes the front-end component's initiation of the interactions and the back-end component's reaction to the front end's requests. This mode of operation resembles client/server interactions and is reflected in a client/server architecture implementation of distributed business logic functions. In this scenario, the front-end components are logically placed at client nodes, while the back-end components reside on a server system.

Distributed business logic functions are particularly well suited for complex, highly interactive, and database I/O-intensive client/server applications. Indeed, the portion of the business logic related to the presentation functions typically resides on the end-user node (i.e., client workstation). The database-related business processing is ideally placed on the node containing the database management system (i.e., the DBMS server). As a result, the number of messages that the application fragments must exchange during a cooperative transaction can be seriously reduced, thereby improving response time and better utilizing available computing resources. The underlying technology to support distributed business logic applications includes various RPC implementations as well as conversational program-to-program communication mechanisms such as IBM's APPC. Distributed business logic functions are typically the most difficult cooperative processing applications to design and develop. Even in its simplest form, a distributed business logic application consists of two separately compiled

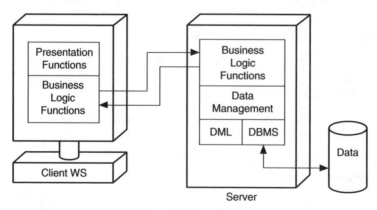

Figure 2.12 Distributed business logic functions.

programs, which must nevertheless be designed to be aware of each other and be capable of working together in cooperative fashion.

Obviously, as the number of cooperating programs and the nodes they reside on grows, the complexity of application design and management grows as well.

Another complication of distributed business logic applications arises from the power and flexibility of the client/server architecture. Consider, for example, the variation of the distributed functions that allows one node (client) to include some local database and self-contained functionality together with the distributed functions. It is not an uncommon situation considering the capabilities of modern workstations and the frequent desire of end users to store/process some data at a local site. Examples of such local data may be word processing private or sensitive documents and spreadsheets (e.g., a manager might want to keep employee evaluations and salary records at his/her workstation rather than at a shared facility). The design of such a distributed application must allow for different types of processing and, possibly, different DBMS access depending on the input received from the presentation component of the application.

2.5.2 Transactions and distributed transaction processing

Distributed business logic functionality is closely related to the notion of transactions and distributed transaction processing. A transaction can be defined as a sequence of predefined actions, performed on behalf of an application, that take a computing system and its resources from one consistent state to another in order to accomplish the desired business functionality. This predefined sequence of actions represents a logical unit of work (LUW) performed by a transaction. Both terms, *transaction* and *logical unit of work,* therefore, are used interchangeably throughout this chapter.

The information affected by transactions is stored in a computing system and can be accessed and/or changed in real time by executing these transactions. Such a computing environment is referred to as an on-line transaction processing system, or OLTP. Transaction processing (TP) systems are most commonly used in controlling access to such computing resources as databases by interacting with the corresponding resource managers (e.g., database management systems). Transactions and LUWs possess the following "ACID" properties:

- *Atomicity*—The entire LUW must be either completed or aborted; the sequence of actions cannot be partially successful.

- *Consistency*—A transaction takes a computing system and its resources from one consistent state to another.

- *Isolation*—A transaction's effect is not visible to other transactions until the transaction is committed.

- *Durability*—Changes made by the committed transaction are permanent and should tolerate system failures.

An additional property—*serialization*—means that as long as a transaction in progress depends on certain information, this information is locked to prevent any other transaction from changing it.

To support these properties, transactions as atomic units of work require some kind of recovery and concurrency mechanisms to be in place. Another requirement is that the execution of a transaction must be controlled by a transaction processing (TP) management system, sometimes called a *TP monitor* (TPM). TPM ensures consistency and data integrity in the event of a program or system failure. For example, IBM's Customer Information Control System (CICS) is the most widely used TP monitor for the mainframe OLTP environment.

In a nondistributed environment, TPM performs its functions by running on the same system as the application functions, presentation functions, and DBMSs. An example is a CICS running on an IBM mainframe together with such database management systems as IBM's IMS/VS and DB2, and Computer Associates's IDMS.

The picture becomes much more complicated when the business logic functions, and therefore the work they are designed to do, are distributed among several systems. Each distributed node performs its share of the work in its portion of the still atomic "local" transaction.

While all local transactions maintain their properties for their local systems, the cooperative processing in which distributed business functions participate requires a new concept of distributed atomicity, consistency, isolation, and durability. This new concept is that of *distributed transactions* and *distributed transaction processing* (DTP). TP monitors, recovery and consistency mechanisms, and all transaction management issues now have to deal with the realities and complexities of the distributed environment and cooperative processing. Support for data integrity, recovery, and consistency (including two-phase commit protocols) on a transaction basis are among the most complex in a distributed transaction processing environment.

2.6 DATA DISTRIBUTION

So far, the analysis of the distribution of application components has concentrated on the presentation, business, and database logic. Each of these components, however, deals with data. Database logic accesses the data from a DBMS, business logic processes the data, and presentation logic displays the data to end users. In fact, the processing of data is the main purpose of an application. Indeed, data in general, and corporate-wide critical data in particular, becomes a critical resource for the enterprise. Reliability and timely availability of this critical information may improve the overall corporate position, assist in critical tactical and strategic decision-making processes, reduce time to market for new products and services, and give a corporation a significant competitive advantage.

Several vital questions relate to the issues of the distributed data in a client/server environment. Some of these questions are:

- Is the data distributed or centralized?
- What role does a database server play?
- Where is the data located if distributed?
- How is the data fragmented if distributed?
- Is data replicated in multiple locations, and, if yes, how are all the copies kept current?
- How can data in multiple locations be accessed in an application-transparent fashion?
- How can data integrity and availability be guaranteed?
- What are the data administration issues in a distributed environment?

2.6.1 Distributed data and data management architecture

There is a distinction between data as an information resource and the data management functions that help store, maintain, and retrieve data. In computer systems, data can typically be stored in two classes of data storage:

- *Files,* which are low-level operating systems and, often, hardware-dependent entities. Files store data in records and blocks of records, are managed by the operating system's utilities, use the operating system's input/output subsystem, and usually are not transparent to the application. A typical file access is coded in the application's 3GL or 4GL code itself and is rather difficult to port from one file access type to another.
- *Databases,* which are designed to provide independence between applications and data. Databases can be viewed as operational, administrative entities, unified by a common business purpose and a common access method—database management systems (DBMSs). A DBMS implements a particular data model (hierarchical like IBM's

IMS, networked like CA's IDMS, relational like SYBASE SQL Server, etc.) and insulates applications from the intricacies of the actual data input/output. A DBMS provides applications with a consistent means of data access by supporting data definition and data manipulation languages throughout various implementations of a given DBMS on all supported platforms. A DBMS can provide data independence, consistency, integrity, security, and recovery. A DBMS can, therefore, help develop applications that can be used in distributed heterogeneous environments.

Their advantages over traditional files have resulted in wide acceptance of various DBMSs (especially relational database management systems) on practically every computing platform.

To sum up, the data management logic functions are designed to be able to:

- Store, retrieve, and update large volumes of data
- Maintain the integrity and security of data stored in the database
- Provide a consistent user and programming interface to the application
- Support multiple users and provide reasonable response time to user requests

In general, a cooperative distributed environment architecture is characterized by:

- The data being distributed among several computing systems (nodes)
- The processing being distributed among several nodes and managed by a distributed transaction manager (network control, processes coordination, synchronization, and scheduling)
- The distributed data access being provided by such multilayer functions as application and user language interfaces, data input/output controllers, data dictionary, directory, and catalog
- The data management systems (database and file management systems) being distributed alongside the data

A conceptual architecture that can satisfy these requirements can be implemented in many ways. Several database vendors have already implemented a distributed client/server environment fulfilling some of these requirements. These implementations typically contain components that support functions performed by transaction controllers (at least to a certain degree), data I/O controllers, data dictionary/directory, and query/report processing.

The components of such an architecture can be found in client/server environments where data can be distributed among several servers and "local" data may even reside at a client's workstation. Distributing data is an important step in designing distributed systems not only because it allows data to be placed closer to its source, but also because it provides for higher data availability. For example, by placing multiple copies of the critical data at different locations, a potential single point of failure can be eliminated.

When data is placed among several nodes (distributed data) or on a remote node (remote data), all or part of the data management logic must accompany it. Two different styles of data management in a cooperative distributed environment can be defined: remote data management and distributed data management. A particular style depends on whether the data is distributed among several nodes or is remote (relative to the application logic) and on how much of the data management logic is actually distributed (relative to the application business logic).

2.6.2 Remote data management

In the context of the cooperative application structure (see Fig. 2.5), remote data management logic corresponds to the RDM split point of the application. In the remote data management approach, an application is *directly* connected to the DBMS and requests a server-resident DBMS to access data (as opposed to an *indirect* connection, where a client application requests remote data through an intermediary—local DBMS). A single system image for remote data management can be implemented by supporting data location transparency for every client, irrespective of the server location and DBMS type. The design logic behind remote data management is derived from the following considerations.

- Data management logic typically consists of two components: data manipulation logic and database processing.

- The database processing functions must reside on the same system as the database itself, while the data manipulation logic (functions of the data manipulation language, or DML) may be placed close to the DBMS or close to (embedded within) the application business logic.

Therefore, when all data, data manipulation logic, and DBMSs for a given application reside on a single system separate from the application node, it is considered as remote data management (see Fig. 2.13). In this case, an application transaction deals with a single data location at a time.

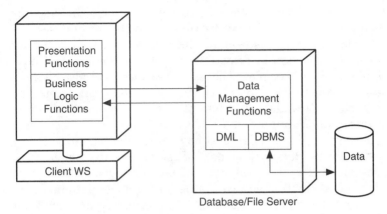

Figure 2.13 Remote data management.

Architecturally, remote data management is implemented via a front-end/back-end processing model, where the front-end system contains the business logic portion of the application, while the back end contains the database and runs the DBMS itself. Remote data management represents a classic file or database server approach, reflected in a relatively simple (many clients, single database server) client/server architecture. Essentially, since remote data management in a single-server/many-client environment assumes that data is *not* distributed, such an architecture represents a traditional, central database design that can be found in any nondistributed environment. Many commercial database management systems are capable of supporting remote data management (i.e., DB2, ORACLE, SYBASE SQL Server, INFORMIX ONLINE, CA/Ingres, to name just a few).

In the case of relational databases (RDBMS), remote data management is implemented by a special type of cooperative processing technique: SQL client/server interactions. These client/server interactions are based on the power of the relational data model and the Structured Query Language (SQL). The SQL client/server model is well suited for decision support applications, relatively simple queries, and dynamic (ad hoc) requests. The actual client/server interactions in a remote data management environment can be implemented by such mechanisms as synchronous and asynchronous remote procedure calls, program-to-program communications (i.e., APPC), messaging (i.e., MQI), or any communication protocols supporting reliable message exchanges between the front-end and the back-end nodes. The latter is especially true for nondatabase access to remote data (files). Remote data management can also be implemented in what traditionally was never considered to be a client/server environment. For example, IBM's CICS allows for data access functions to be shipped (the facility is called *func-*

tion shipping) from one mainframe CICS application to another. That other CICS application may reside in a different address space of the same system, or even on a different system. CICS function shipping allows data access to remote files, queues, and IMS databases.

The remote data management style of cooperative processing is relatively easy to implement. Application transactions deal with a single source of data; therefore, the issues of distributed data consistency and integrity do not have to be dealt with. In many cases, remote data management provides end users with a single system image of complete data location transparency, which makes it ideal for application and database portability. However, remote data management has its drawbacks, as follows.

- The remote data management architecture (as defined here) places databases on a single system (i.e., database server), thus creating a performance bottleneck.

- Remote data management requires all data requests and responses to be transmitted by the network between a server and the application, thus creating potentially significant communication overhead.

- The database server is limited in its functionality to the processing of the DML requests sent from the front end.

- A single source of data and single DBMS location create a single point of failure.

- While, by design, considerable computing resources are available in a cooperative distributed computing environment, the singularity of a database server prevents it from taking advantage of all available resources.

To eliminate potential communication overhead in the network, remote data management is best suited for applications characterized by low-volume, infrequent user-directed ad hoc query processing (decision-support applications) that produce simple, small data volume results.

The drawbacks of remote data management are dealt with in the section on distributed data management.

2.6.3 Distributed data management

The distributed data management style of cooperative processing is intended to eliminate problems introduced by remote data management. In the context of the cooperative application structure (see Fig. 2.5), distributed data management logic corresponds to the DDM split point of the application.

Distributed data management deals with data (databases) distributed among multiple nodes. Such distribution allows us to place data closer to its source, provides for higher data availability by placing multiple copies of the critical data at different locations, and eliminates a potential single point of failure.

When data is distributed among several nodes, all or part of the data management logic must also be distributed to accompany the data. Thus, at least some portion of the database processing logic (DBMS) must reside on the same system as the database itself. In general, data integrity and administration issues related to distribution of data would have to be resolved. For example, if the application data is spread across multiple servers (horizontally within a server tier or vertically between a LAN server and a host), distributed database management or distributed request processing with the two-phase commit is required to guarantee *data integrity across DBMS nodes*. By definition, an *indirect* connection between a client application and a server DBMS, where an application requests remote data through an intermediary—a local DBMS—falls into the category of distributed data management.

The distributed data management environment is characterized by two-way distribution:

- The data and DBMS are distributed among multiple nodes, including the node with the application logic.
- Data management functions are distributed between a front-end system (data processing logic, or DML) and the back-end server performing database functions (see Fig. 2.14).

Such an architecture can reduce network traffic due to the fact that data access requests (DML requests) are sent from an application business logic to the data processing logic on the same node. Data processing logic performs initial syntax checking, parsing, compiling, and determination on the required data location. If the local data is required, the DML request is satisfied without it being sent to the remote database server. Similarly, invalid DML requests are rejected before being sent into the network.

Distributed DBMS (DDBMS) employs such cooperative processing techniques as remote procedure calls, program-to-program communications (i.e., APPC), front-end/back-end synchronous distributed transaction processing, and such special mechanisms as stored procedures and triggers. Distributed data management is ideally suited to be implemented in a client/server architecture. There are several products available today that implement a distributed DBMS in a client/server architecture (SYBASE SQL Server and ORACLE 7.x are just a few

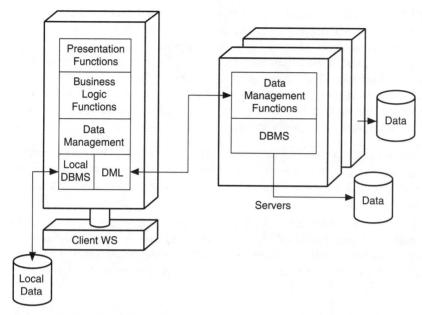

Figure 2.14 Distributed data management.

examples). Properly designed, a DDBMS provides end users with data location transparency, data integrity, consistency, and reliability.

However, the distributed data management style of cooperative distributed processing introduces many serious issues associated with the distribution of data and data management. These issues deal with the ways the data should be distributed, the issues of heterogeneous database access, data synchronization, consistency, locking, integrity, transparency, reliability, and administration. To illustrate the potential problems with data distribution in a three-tiered distributed client/server environment, consider the following scenario. A life insurance company structures its individual policy unit as a three-tiered organization:

1. The central office, which maintains all corporate books and financial records

2. Regional service centers (RSCs), which handle all customer service transactions for a particular region

3. Insurance agents, who service a number of their customers

To improve customer service, the company decides to equip agents with portable personal computers. Periodically, agents should connect to the servers in the RSCs to off-load transactions (new clients, changes in policies, etc.) and to acquire current rate and policy data from the central office and RSC computers. The business requirement for the company is that no change is valid until the corporate books are updated.

Architecturally, this scenario calls for a true client/server environment, with agent laptop computers in the third tier, RSC servers as a second tier, and the central office's mainframe as the first tier. However, for successful implementation, all client/server–related issues mentioned in previous sections need to be resolved:

- Agents take their laptop PCs to their customers and run appropriate applications. Thus, at least some of the customer data must reside on the agent's laptop PC. Laptop PCs are running MS Windows and MS Access database.

- RSC servers must handle all data related to the agents assigned to that RSC, plus some additional data necessary for an RSC management decision support system. In order to achieve maximum price/performance, RSC servers are running a UNIX operating system and SYBASE SQL Server.

- The central office maintains corporate books and all relevant customer records. The central office mainframe is running IBM's MVS/ESA and DB2 and IMS database management systems.

- The updates performed by agents to the MS access data must be propagated to the RSC server and central office DB2 and IMS databases. For some transactions, data integrity is mandatory—if the propagation fails on any tier, all changes must be backed out from databases on other tiers.

- To achieve application portability, an agent's applications must be designed in such a way that the required data can be accessed transparent of its location or the underlying DBMS. Each DBMS involved in this environment uses its own data manipulation language, and one of the DBMSs (IMS) is not even SQL-based (i.e., it is not relational).

This example demonstrates a degree of complexity that designers of the client/server environment have to solve. In respect to distributed data issues, some of the problems and corresponding requirements had been formulated by C. J. Date, one of the first designers of relational databases. These distributed database requirements (C. J. Date's 12 Rules) are listed in App. B and discussed in more detail in Chap. 10.

2

Client and Server Specialization in the Distributed Environment

The client / server computing paradigm is becoming the dominant force that will influence computing in the 1990s. Demand for new systems capabilities follows and is often ahead of the advances in computing technology. At the same time, computing environments are undergoing an evolution from general-purpose, centralized systems towards architectures characterized by the collective power of many specialized systems interconnected via advanced networks. Indeed, even nature has successfully demonstrated similar trends. Consider single-cell organisms that evolved into more complex specialized multicelled creatures because more complex systems offer greater capabilities. Cells became specialized, because relatively small specialized parts can evolve to achieve the desired functionality more successfully than large general-purpose parts. In a computing environment, cells are individual systems. Combining the specialized systems into a collective computing entity can be accomplished by making all system nodes interconnected in a network and allowing the nodes to enter into desired internode relationships.

In the client / server paradigm, the application components (presentation logic, business logic, database logic, DBMS) and data are distributed across the network. Network nodes can be classified as clients (those who request services) and servers (those who perform requested services). Clients and servers cooperate through a two-party relationship established for each client / server pair, even though there can be a many-to-one relationship between a collection of clients and their server.

3

Client Specialization in the Client/Server Environment

In a client/server architecture, an individual system is designated as a client or as a server, depending on which activity (requesting a service or performing a service) the system performs in a given node-to-node relationship.

If the client/server designation is not permanent, then, theoretically, clients and servers should be designed as general-purpose systems with equal capabilities. This is true for a peer-to-peer computing environment. However, cooperative client/server processing does not entail interactions between equals. For example, it is a client who initiates the application and, as a result, an interaction with its server. It is also true that client systems, not servers, interface directly with end users. Generally speaking, there are certain functions that clients perform best in a client/server environment. Similarly, there are other functions best performed by servers. For instance, database management systems (DBMSs) usually run on servers, not on clients. The optimum design should call for node specialization aimed at achieving the highest benefits from the cooperative processing between clients and servers.

Therefore, specialization requirements put clients and servers on different sides of the internodal relationship. However, another requirement for developing a complex client/server distributed networking system puts clients and servers close to each other. It is the requirement of high-performance interoperability. As discussed earlier, the best way to achieve the desired levels of interoperability are standardization and open systems. Open systems are inspired by and help achieve application portability, scaleability, and interoperability, which are also the goals and benefits of a client/server architecture.

In addition to the evolution of open systems, the client/server architecture is also influenced by node specialization in a complex client/server distributed environment. These two characteristics are reflected in the functionality of clients and servers, and the distributed environment in which they operate.

The focus of this chapter is the functional and architectural specialization of clients. This specialization is illustrated through examples of a client's presentation functionality.

3.1 CLIENT'S ROLE AND FUNCTIONS

Since client nodes are typically designed to interact with end users, their functionality and implementation can be specialized for these interactions. Similar to developing specialized sensory cells in humans and animals, client nodes must be designed to deliver such functions as high-resolution graphics and sound at acceptable performance levels. However, complete application requirements often exceed those of client node interactions and can be satisfied only as a result of the collective performance of all system nodes.

The major functions performed by a client system in a client/server environment are presentation functions and some business logic (anywhere from none to all). End-user interactions with an application are performed through the presentation logic. The presentation logic is the layer of the architecture that, on one hand, interacts with the business logic of the application and, on the other hand, interacts with end users. The latter includes all interactions with the physical device (terminal) and handling of actual end-user-performed input/output (screen I/O, keyboard I/O, mouse, etc.).

Traditional presentation functions dealt with character-based displays, where the processor displayed characters received from an application sequentially in a fixed font on a screen. Continuous evolution of presentation functions has been closely linked with high-performance workstations offering graphical display capabilities.

These displays allow the processor to control individual picture elements (pixels) on a screen. Modern client workstations can combine these display capabilities with images, full-motion video, sound, optical character recognition, pen-based input, and interactive multimedia.

These capabilities allow software designers to create uniquely effective, intuitive application interfaces that can actually blur boundaries between applications. For example, using Microsoft's Object Linking and Embedding (OLE) allows users to work on complex documents without realizing what particular application is invoked at any given time. The text portion of a document is handled by the MS Word word processor, spreadsheet by Excel, sound by multimedia extensions, etc. To achieve acceptable performance, throughput, and robustness, at the very minimum, a client system that has these capabilities has to specialize in graphical presentation management.

3.2 PRESENTATION MANAGEMENT AND GUI

The specialization of client systems for presentation management must conform to the common goals of the client/server architecture in an open distributed environment. Presentation management should be based on standards to allow systems to interact with users in a consistent fashion. It should be portable across a wide variety of hardware platforms, be able to interoperate with other open systems applications, and, most importantly, should improve system usability.

The design of usable systems requires that usability engineering be made an integral part of the development cycle. There are many methods that can be used at different phases of the usability engineering process. The usability engineering process can be implemented at different stages of development.

For a system to be usable, it is important to understand the users and their work. This understanding includes individual user characteristics, the user's current and desired task, functional analysis, and, particularly important for reengineering, the evolution of the user and the job.

Usability engineers should perform a competitive analysis that includes user and task observation. This observation includes current versions of products, competitive products, prototypes, and alpha and beta versions.

Some steps in usability engineering may include:

- Setting usability goals.

- Parallel design, which includes having several designers working on preliminary designs.

- Scenario development and the use of paper prototypes. Lotus Development Corp., for example, uses paper prototyping early in development to get feedback on conceptual designs before they commit to writing code. The goal here is to explore design alternatives before selecting a single approach.

- Participatory design, which includes getting customers and users involved in design efforts, from requirements gathering to detailed design.

- Development and use of GUI standards and guidelines.

- Prototyping.

- Empirical testing and formal user interface inspections. The latter is similar to code inspections and is used to check for consistency with standards and usability bugs.

- Iterative design.

- Usability feedback collection from field use.

Many of these stages are already in the development methodologies employed by various companies.

Consistent usable interfaces between users and applications represent a key requirement for open systems. This requirement is extremely important since user interfaces affect both developers and end users alike. Indeed, while some program or database interfaces are hidden from the users, application presentation is visible to every developer and even to a casual system user. The presentation interfaces between users and applications are called *graphical user interfaces* (GUI) and are designed to present information to users in graphic form. Graphics do not necessarily mean pictures. Word processor or desktop publishing software with multiple text faces, sizes, and styles also require graphic presentation.

The wide variety of currently available interfaces (including character-based) may confuse users and developers. Each new interface requires users and developers to be retrained and applications to be modified. A new graphical user interface may cause the entire set of applications to be rewritten for a new platform which supports the desired GUI. Typically, applications written for one GUI are not portable to other GUI environments. Often, developers must make difficult and costly decisions, limiting their product development to particular interfaces.

Examples include incompatible native interfaces developed for the Macintosh, Microsoft Windows, and OS/2 Presentation Manager. Thus, a standard GUI with a single common application programming interface (API) and a standard look and feel will have a significant beneficial impact on developer and user productivity.

3.2.1 General requirements for standard GUI

Industry acceptance, support by hardware and software vendors, as well as end-user organizations' preferences for a particular GUI make that GUI a potential candidate for the GUI standard. However, a standard graphical user interface for open systems should also satisfy the following requirements:

- *Portability.*   Applications and user skills should be portable across various open system platforms. A standard GUI should maintain a stable API for every platform, thus allowing for quick and easy port from one platform to another. A standard GUI should maintain a consistent look and feel on all platforms, thus reducing the need to retrain and easing the transfer of required user skills.

- *Standards compliance.*   This requirement is the key open system requirement. It is also a necessary condition for a GUI to attract large corporate and government customers. A best known de facto standard for an open system's GUI is the MIT X Windows System. The X Window System serves as a model for NIST (National Institute of Science and Technology), ANSI and IEEE standards, and X/Open specifications. The MIT X Consortium has published a set of specifications that allow client applications to communicate and work together. These specifications are listed in the *Interclient Communications Conventions Manual* (ICCCM), and are important for enabling a high degree of applications interoperability.

- *Development tools.*   Any GUI that is considered to be a standard must be accompanied by a comprehensive set of development tools. These tools can speed up application development, allow for developer-defined extensions, and are capable of building GUI applications for a wide variety of platforms.

- *Flexibility.*   A standard GUI must be flexible and extensible enough to accommodate new types of displays and other input/output devices that will become available in the future.

- *Internationalization.*   In today's global markets, internationalization is another way to achieve application portability. It includes other country's languages, numbers, monetary units, date and time formats, and special symbols and messages unique to that country's culture.

- *Platform independence.*   To be truly open and standard, a GUI must be designed to operate independently of the operating system or hardware platform it runs on. Similarly, in a networking environment, a standard GUI should operate independently of the underlying networking protocols.

3.2.2 GUI features

In general, GUIs present information on a screen in rectangular areas called *windows*. Windows can overlap each other. Users are allowed to perform several manipulations on windows, such as changing their size and position. Windows can contain *objects* that can be selected by users by clicking a mouse pointer on small object pictures called *icons*. An entire window can be minimized in size to become an icon, and a user can restore an icon to its normal size (before minimization).

Advanced GUIs almost completely eliminate the need to type commands by allowing users to select commands from menus using a mouse or function keys. Windows can also contain other graphical entities (such as scroll bars, sliders, and buttons) that allow users to control the content of the window and that provide additional input to the application.

When compared to conventional programming, the most significant difference in the presentation logic that controls a GUI is the notion that the user must always be in control of the logic. Thus, the traditional structured programming with its housekeeping section, processing section, and an output section has to be modified. GUI programming should be able to accept and process asynchronous events initiated by a user or a system at any time.

The set of supported user-generated input and system-generated events differs from one GUI implementation to another. Among the common types of events are:

- *Mouse events,* which occur when a user has moved the mouse pointer into or out of the entity, clicked on a mouse button within or without an entity, or released the mouse button

- *Keyboard events,* which occur when a user has pressed or released a keyboard key

- *Menu events,* which occur when a user selects a command from the menu

- *Window update events,* which occur when a portion of the picture of an application window has been damaged (possibly because it was overlapped by another window) and has to be redrawn

- *Resizing events,* which occur when a user has changed the size of the window

- *Activation* and *deactivation events,* which are generated by the GUI to allow a user to change the current, active, window

- *Initialize* and *terminate* events, which occur when a GUI entity has been created or destroyed so that the application can perform necessary setup or cleanup logic

These and other events should be processed by the presentation logic in cooperation with the application logic. The necessary processing is distributed among the GUI itself, the application logic, and the API of a particular GUI. Typically, an API is a set of GUI-specific library routines that perform such functions as creating windows and displaying various graphics. There are several models for event distribution processing:

- The *event loop* model specifies that an application must contain an event loop. The event loop calls a particular library routine to see if there are any pending events. Each pending event causes the application to dispatch an event-handling routine before control is returned to the event loop. To preserve the user's impression of always being in control, the application must return to the event loop very quickly, even if event processing has not yet been completed. (See Fig. 3.1.)

- The *event callback* model requires the application to register an event-handling function for each GUI entity that it creates, thus freeing the application from significant event loop overhead. When a GUI detects an event (such as a menu command or a keystroke) for the entity, it calls the appropriate application event routine. The application gets control only at entity initialization time and when one of its event-handling routines is called. (See Fig. 3.2.)

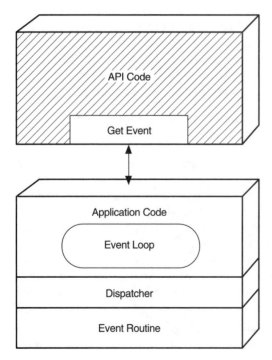

Figure 3.1 The event loop model. Note: The event loop, dispatcher, and event routines reside in the application code.

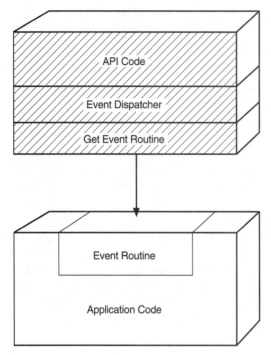

Figure 3.2 The event callback model. Note: The event dispatcher is in the API code. The event routine is called once for each event.

- The *hybrid* model, which combines an event loop model and an event callback model. Microsoft Windows employs a model where an application must contain an event loop which calls a routine to get the next event. At that point, an application can call another API routine, which can, in turn, call the application's event handler.

Similarly, there are many features of GUI output that distinguish one GUI from another:

- *Coordinate spaces* describe the two-dimensional coordinate system that allows the GUI to address individual pixels on a screen by defining a starting point and the resolution of the drawing space. Most of the GUIs place the starting point at the upper left corner of the display, with the coordinate increasing down and to the right. Other interfaces (for example, OS/2 Presentation Manager) differ in direction by placing the starting point in the lower left corner, with coordinates increasing up and to the right. Applications must be aware of the coordinate spaces and resolution of a given GUI in order to paint the correct picture on a screen.

- *Drawing algorithms* describe the way a particular GUI draws, centers, and connects lines. The difference often appears to be negligible. A three-pixel-wide line between two points, for example, can be centered on the end points or below or above the end points. On certain low-resolution platforms, the lines will look the same, but on a higher-resolution display, lines may appear to be disconnected or overlapping.

- *Color* affects the look and feel of the presentations drawn by a GUI. Unfortunately, colors differ widely from one display device to another. Also, GUIs themselves can treat colors differently and use different numbers of bits to represent colors, which in turn determines the precision with which colors can be selected.

- *Text* presentation in a graphical environment is different from that of a character-based presentation. Text under GUI is treated like graphics and can be displayed with a wide variety of options. These options include colors, character size, fonts, and style. GUIs used for desktop publishing software, for example, can allow users to create documents with fonts and styles varying from a small script (for footnotes) to a 48-point Times Roman bold italic for a document title.

3.3 X WINDOWS SYSTEM

The variety of available graphical user interfaces and the richness of their features justify the client's specialization in presentation management. However, some of the best-known GUIs do not need nor use the advantages of the client/server architecture.

In the network of the specialized nodes participating in collective application processing, the need arises to allow clients to perform presentation services for the applications running elsewhere in the network. In the client/server distributed environment, presentation management requires the technology that will support the following critical issues:

- Applications running on servers must be able to transparently access presentation logic that resides on client systems.

- Presentation logic on a client system performs services requested by the application running on a server. In effect, the client acts as a presentation server, while the server runs a client for that presentation server.

One of the best-known technologies for allowing applications to access displays on a networked workstation transparently is the *X Windows System,* also known as X. X was developed jointly by the Massachusetts Institute of Technology, IBM, and Digital in an effort known as Project Athena. X architecture is based on the client/server model. It provides:

- A network-transparent communication protocol between an application and its presentation logic which may reside on a remote display workstation
- High-performance device-independent graphics
- A hierarchy of resizable, overlapping windows

In the X Windows System, multiple applications can display simultaneously using one or many windows. (See Fig. 3.3.)

X popularity starts with the fact that it is in the public domain and is therefore available for all vendors to use and develop in their own ways. By exploiting a client/server computing model, X accomplished a breakthrough in distributed presentation. X is particularly useful in distributed heterogeneous environments where PCs, workstations, and minicomputers from different vendors need to run the same application. The X Windows System allows developers to write programs that can display information and accept input on one node, while running on a different node on a network.

The *X model* is the architectural framework of the X Windows System (see Fig. 3.4). It consists of a display, a server, and client programs. The X display is the hardware that includes a bit-mapped screen, keyboard, and mouse interfaces. An *X server* program controls

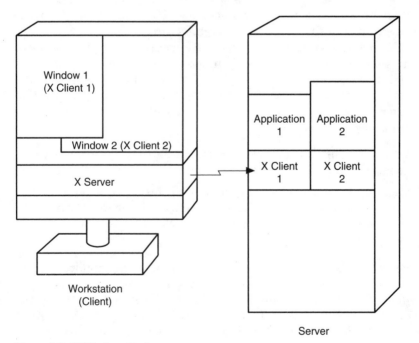

Figure 3.3 X Windows System.

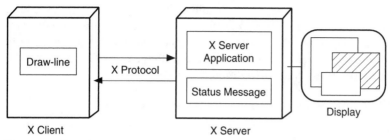

Figure 3.4 X model.

the display and provides an interface between itself and *X clients,* which are usually application programs. The X clients and X server may be running on the same or different network nodes and communicate with each other by exchanging specific messages. Different types of messages are collectively called the *X protocol.*

X is an *event-driven* system. After initialization, X clients are generally suspended until an event occurs on the X server. X clients are restarted when the X server sends them special X protocol messages (i.e., window size has changed, a key has been pressed, etc.).

The X Windows System supports a *window manager,* which is a separate program that enables window movement, resizing, and iconizing. An X window manager is treated as an X client in the X model. It interacts with client applications through the X server, controls the positioning and size of client's windows, and determines the way input is directed to client applications. An X client communicates with an X server via requests sent using the X protocol known as X11 protocol. There exists a library of C routines designed to facilitate these interactions. This library is called *Xlib* and is usually the lowest-level interface available with the X Windows System; Xlib is limited in its scope and capabilities. To alleviate the Xlib limitations, X Windows System applications are usually written using another program layer built on top of Xlib: the *toolkit,* which provides high-level graphics functionality, including menus and special window objects called *widgets.*

A fundamental concept of the X Windows System is that it intends to provide functionality rather than policy. In other words, an X server allows windows and graphics to be displayed without making any rules about the appearance of the windows or the GUI itself. The window manager determines the look and feel of the GUI, while X clients should be written to function with any window manager (or none).

In client/server architecture terminology, the node that displays and accepts information and interacts with the user is the client node. However, in X terminology, the presentation logic that resides on a client is called an X server. Conversely, X clients contain the functional application logic written by a developer and typically reside on a "server" system in the client/server network. Although the designations of X clients and X servers seem to contradict the definitions of clients and servers in a client/server topology, it in fact follows the proper client/server computing model. Indeed:

- X clients initiate interactions with their server, the X server.
- X clients request an X server to perform display or screen I/O functions.
- One X server can service multiple X clients.
- X client and X server can reside on the same machine.

In essence, the X Windows System provides for the interoperability between applications and their components operating within the X Windows client/server computing model.

3.4   OSF/MOTIF

The X Windows System is not a complete GUI. It is a package of windowing, graphics, and event-handling routines that form the basis for several popular GUIs—OSF/Motif, SUN Open Look, and DECwindows. Even though the X Windows environment may be sufficient for many applications, it is usually complemented by a window manager, a separate program whose exclusive purpose is to manage windows (move, resize, iconify windows) and provide a GUI with a particular behavior and appearance. For example, the two GUIs, *OSF/Motif* and *Open Look,* while based on the X Windows System, demonstrate different behavior and appearance because they employ different window managers and different programming interfaces.

The OSF/Motif graphical user interface is the result of the Open Software Foundation's Request For Technology process. The OSF/Motif GUI, released in July of 1989, is based on the X Windows System and incorporates the best features from DECwindows, HP's toolkit and window manager, and Microsoft's Presentation Manager.

The OSF/Motif GUI is implemented using a single API for all supported platforms. The API is based on DECwindows technology, extended to support Presentation Manager-style behavior, and has a unique three-dimensional appearance. OSF/Motif runs on over one hundred platforms, including IBM's RS/6000, Digital's VAX and ALPHA, SUN SPARC, MIPS, HP PA-RISC, Intel x86, i860, Motorola 680x0 and 88000, and PowerPC architectures.

Due to its X Windows foundation, OSF/Motif-compliant applications are isolated from underlying system dependencies and require only a small portion of a code to be modified when an application is ported from one platform to another. In addition, OSF/Motif complies with the *Interclient Communications Conventions Manual,* which enables OSF/Motif applications to share data and network resources with other ICCCM-compliant applications. It also allows the OSF/Motif window manager to run all X-based ICCCM-compliant applications even if they are not developed with an OSF/Motif GUI. Conversely, OSF/Motif applications can run under any ICCCM-compliant window manager.

OSF/Motif is supplied as an enabling technology to hardware and software vendors and end-user organizations. Application developers are supported by the *User Interface X Toolkit;* the *User Interface Language* (UIL), which is the specification language for describing the visual aspects of a GUI in a OSF/Motif application; *OSF / Motif Window Manager,* which is a separate program designed to allow users to manage the windowing environment; and a growing number of third-party development tools that support OSF/Motif. These tools include, but are not limited to, file managers, workspace managers, and interactive graphical interface design tools. OSF/Motif complies with X/Open's Portability Guide standards for Native Language Support. In addition to 8-byte character sets, OSF/Motif supports 16-bit and compound strings for use in European and Asian languages.

Because of strict conformance with the X standard, OSF/Motif contains very few operating system and network protocol dependencies. It is supported by approximately 72 percent of worldwide computer hardware and software suppliers, including Data General, Digital, Dell, HP/Apollo, Groupe Bull, Hitachi, IBM, NEC, NCR, Siemens/Nixdorf, SCO, Sony, Unisys, Wang, and others. OSF/Motif is specified as the GUI of choice by major end-user organization such as American Airlines, Boeing, the European Economic Community, Lockheed, NASA, and Shell Oil. Over 70 percent of U.S. government Requests For Proposals specify the OSF/Motif as the preferred GUI.

The list of operating systems that support OSF/Motif includes, but is not limited to, such popular environments as AIX, 4.3 BSD, Data General UX, Dell UNIX System V, MS-DOS 3.0 or later, HP-UX, Macintosh, MIPS RISC/OS, SCO UNIX, OS/2, SunOS 3.5/4.0 and Solaris 2, Ultrix, UNIX System V R3.2/4.0 or later, and VMS.

For comparison, let's discuss the *Open Look* graphical user interface that was developed by Sun Microsystems and AT&T. Although it was very popular, especially among users of SUN and AT&T systems, it is being steadily replaced by the OSF/Motif as a standard GUI. Similar to OSF/Motif, the Open Look specifications are independent of any particular implementation. Open Look portability is ensured by three APIs that can be used to develop Open Look-compliant applications. Sun's NeWS Development Environment (NDE) API for the NDE toolkit is supported on Sun platforms. Sun XView provides an API to the Xlib level of the X Windows System and is supported on Sun SPARC and Digital VAX systems, Intel x386, and Motorola 680x0 architectures.

Xt+ API from AT&T is supported on various AT&T platforms. The Open Look GUI provides users with a consistent and easy-to-use presentation, although the behavior and appearance of the Open Look GUI differs significantly from those of MS Windows, OSF/Motif, and OS/2 Presentation Manager. Similar to OSF/Motif, Open Look is based on the industry standard X Windows System. Open Look's XView and Xt+ APIs are based on X11 protocols. Therefore, these APIs are isolated from underlying system dependencies, requiring only a small portion of code to be modified when an application is ported from one platform to another. However, Open Look does not comply with the ICCCM for interclient communications. Therefore, the Open Look Window Manager is required to ensure the proper operation of Open Look applications.

There are several toolkits that have been developed to facilitate the development of Open Look-compliant applications. Among them are:

- *NeWS Development Environment* (NDE), developed by SUN Microsystems and representing an emulated PostScript interpreter modified to support a windowing system

- *XView* that was developed by Sun Microsystems and implements an Open Look API on top of the Xlib level of the X Windows System (in comparison, OSF/Motif implements this API in the X toolkit built on the higher level of the X11 Intrinsics)

- *Xt+* toolkit from AT&T, which contains graphical objects (widgets and gadgets) built on the X Windows System X11 Intrinsics

- A separate development tool that provides Open Look-compliant powerful graphical file and desktop management facilities

- *Open Look User Interface Development Tool* (Developer's Guide), available from Sun Microsystems, to be used within the Sun Open Windows environment

Open Look implementations are currently limited to 8-byte character sets and are English-based, but can be expanded for European and Asian language support. As with OSF/Motif, strict conformance with the X standard allows Open Look to contain very few operating system and network protocol dependencies.

3.5 MS WINDOWS

OSF/Motif is the GUI of choice for UNIX-based client systems. However, the vast majority of desktop systems today run Microsoft

Windows, Windows NT, or Windows 95 (a follow-on to Windows 3.x). Microsoft is an indisputable leader in desktop computing. Microsoft Windows is more than just a GUI—it is a comprehensive and mature GUI-based desktop operating environment. Its Windows 3.x has expanded MS-DOS capabilities and practically eliminated most of the DOS drawbacks of memory limitations and single-task processing.

3.5.1   Windows Open Services Architecture (WOSA)

Microsoft Windows has become much more than just a presentation services application component. In fact, it has become its own operating environment, which aims to be as open and as widely accepted as possible. The Windows environment today includes DOS-based Windows 3.x, multitasking Windows/NT and Windows 95, and object-oriented Cairo (a next Windows/NT). At the heart of the Windows family of products lies the Windows Open Services Architecture (WOSA). It is an open architecture that enables Windows workstations to connect to heterogeneous system environments across a wide range of services. WOSA is designed to achieve the following objectives:

- Make application development easier with a consistent set of interfaces for all services.

- Provide an open architecture and consistent standardized set of APIs for developers and independent software vendors to work together.

- Provide a model of interoperability.

- Work with the industry to establish this architecture.

- Provide the ability to plug in service provider implementation independently.

- Allow multiple providers simultaneous access for any one service.

- Establish Windows as the universal client.

To accomplish these objectives, WOSA encapsulates the Windows environment with vendor-independent APIs for a wide variety of services. These APIs are organized into a layered architecture that is placed between Windows applications and service providers (see Fig. 3.5).

The services that are provided by WOSA APIs are divided into three groups: common application services, communication services, and vertical market services.

Common application services include:

- *Data access.*   WOSA data access for relational databases is provided by Open Database Connectivity (ODBC) API. ODBC is based on the

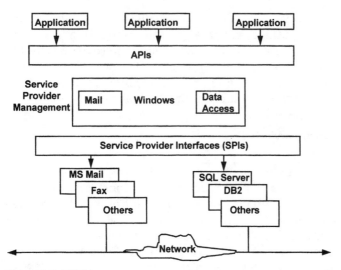

Figure 3.5 WOSA.

Structured Query Language (SQL) Call Level Interface (CLI) defined by the SQL Access Group (SAG). ODBC enjoys broad industry support. There are many ODBC drivers available today, including those for the SYBASE SQL Server, ORACLE, and INFORMIX. Vendors such as Apple, Digital, Gupta, Hewlett-Packard, Information Builders, Informix, Lotus, NCR, Novell, Oracle, PowerSoft, CA, Progress, Sybase, Tandem, and Unify all support ODBC.

- *Messaging.*   This service is provided by the Mail API (MAPI). MAPI is designed to allow mix and match mail front-end applications and service providers, easy development of MAPI-aware applications, and availability of mail and scheduling functionality to all applications. Such vendors as AT&T, Banyan, British Telecom, CompuServe, Digital, HP, and Novell support the MAPI standard. (See Fig. 3.6.)

- *Licensing.*   The License Service API (LSAPI) aims to provide license system independence and isolate the application from the licensing policy. LSAPI is supported by a number of vendors, including Apple, Banyan, Digital, HP, Lotus, Novell, Oracle, OSF, SPA, and Word-Perfect Corporation.

- *Telephones.*   In business, a typical desk has a PC and a telephone. However, today the desktop PC and telephone are not integrated. The Windows Telephony API (TAPI) aims to define and establish a telephony interface standard to support visual call control, personal productivity improvements, integrated messaging with e-mail, voice mail, fax, and voice/PC integration for annotation and playback, to name just a few.

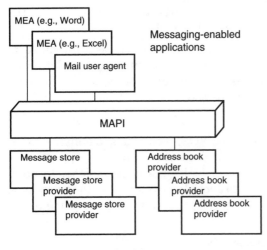

Figure 3.6 MAPI.

Communication services include:

- *Windows Sockets API.* This API is designed for easier integration of Windows and UNIX applications across the network. The Sockets API provides a single interface for Windows applications to communicate with sockets-based applications. Corporations such as 3COM, Digital, FTP Software, HP, IBM, NetManage, Novell, Sun Microsystems, Ungermann-Bass, and Wollongong Group represent a short list of companies supporting the Windows Sockets API.

- *Windows SNA API.* This API is designed to create a standard SNA interface for Windows and Windows/NT environments. The SNA API goal is to support all major SNA protocols—HLLAPI, APPC, CPI-C, and LU0. Corporations such as Attachmate, DCA, IBM, Multisoft, NCR, Novell, Olivetti, Siemens-Nixdorf, Systems Strategy, and Wall Data represent a short list of companies supporting Windows SNA API.

- *Windows RPC.* The Remote Procedure Call API is designed to establish the RPC as a strategic interprocess communication mechanism for Microsoft. The Windows RPC supports the OSF DCE RPC protocol.

Vertical market services include the following.

- WOSA extensions for financial services, which include interfaces for branch banking applications. Well-known vertical financial application providers such as Andersen Consulting, EDS, ICL-Futjitsu,

NCR, and Unisys, to name just a few, are participating in the Windows Banking Systems Vendor Council.

■ WOSA extensions for real-time market data. These are defined to allow any Windows application to access real-time market data from any provider. Providers such as ILX, Knight-Rider, Quotron, Reuters, and Telerate are participating in the Windows Open Market Data Council.

WOSA is a dynamic architecture. WOSA continues to enhance existing services, with the emphasis on data access, messaging, software licensing, communications, and vertical market extensions. In addition, WOSA is being extended to include new services for telephony, directory services, distributed security, and systems management.

3.5.2   Windows Clipboard, DDE, and OLE

The Windows operating environment supports features like Clipboard, dynamic data exchange (DDE), and OLE (Object Linking and Embedding), which represent significant steps toward improvement of application interoperability under Windows as well as a strong affinity toward object-orientation in GUI implementations.

Clipboard

The Windows Clipboard is an operating environment facility built within Windows. Therefore, every implementation of Microsoft Windows has Clipboard support. Applications need only take advantage of the Clipboard APIs to implement basic data sharing between Windows applications and, therefore, a degree of applications interoperability into their solutions.

As an inherent part of every implementation of Microsoft Windows, the Windows Clipboard is a very mature and easily implemented feature for experienced Windows programmers. Indeed, many Windows users take advantage of the Clipboard features by employing cut-and-paste techniques. Additionally, many high-level solution development tools provide built-in functions for Clipboard-enabling applications.

DDE

In addition to the Clipboard, the Windows operating environment supports a higher level of application interoperability, which deals with data interactions between application processes. The mechanism for Windows application interprocess communication is the Windows *dynamic data exchange* (DDE) facility. DDE is a message-based method of interprocess communication. It uses shared memory to exchange data between applications and synchronizes the passing of data through the DDE protocol. There are three types of DDE applications:

- Message-based
- Dynamic data exchange management library (DDEML)
- Network DDE

DDE applications follow the client/server computing model and can be categorized as a client and a server (also included are a monitor for debugging purposes and client/server categories). An example of DDE usage is the inclusion of Excel spreadsheet data into a Microsoft Word word-processing document.

DDEML is a higher-level implementation of DDE which utilizes a *dynamic link library,* or *DLL.* The use of DDL ensures a consistent means of implementing the DDE protocol in applications. DDEML functions make sending, posting, and receiving DDE messages simpler. Among the functions provided by DDEML are such services as string handling and data exchange. With both DDE and DDEML, data exchange follows a client/server interactions model and can occur in one of three ways:

1. A client can request data on a one-time basis from a server.
2. A client can send data to a server application.
3. A server advises the client that an item has changed value.

In addition, the interactions that originate on the server can be communicated to the client in one of two ways:

1. A server sends the client a change notice, but not the new data.
2. A server sends the client a change notice and the new data.

These DDE client/server data exchanges are characterized as DDE *data links.* There are three types of data links:

- *Cold link*—the client requests data, and the server immediately sends it.
- *Warm link*—The server sends the client notice of new data, but not new data.
- *Hot link*—The server sends new data whenever data changes, which ensures automatic updates.

The power of the hot links can be illustrated by the previous example of a spreadsheet incorporated into a Word document. Assume that the document contains a pie chart of sales data by region. Hot links will allow the pie chart within the document to change automatically every time the underlying spreadsheet data is changed.

While DDE and DDEML are not network-capable today, network DDE solves this problem. Network DDE hides the communication issues of data links from the local program. As a result, the local program behaves as if the interapplication communication is happening on the local machine. Network DDE is provided in Windows for Workgroups and Windows/NT products.

Network DDE processes all application DDE requests and carries out the network operations necessary to start and maintain the network DDE conversation. DDE in its various forms provides for data interoperability, saves time, combines or changes data presentation, and allows flexibility and speed in combining data manually or automatically.

The Windows dynamic data exchange facility is an inherent part of every implementation of Microsoft Windows. Therefore, it is a very mature feature that can be successfully utilized in applications by experienced Windows programmers. Additionally, many high-level solution development tools provide built-in functions for DDE-enabling applications.

OLE

Object Linking and Embedding is built upon and adds functionality to both the Windows Clipboard and the Windows dynamic data exchange facility. OLE is a set of Microsoft Windows services (APIs) for implementing object-oriented *compound document* features to business solutions. A compound document is created in one application, referred to as the *container,* and consists of information from different applications and from different sources to present a business solution. The pieces of information used to create a compound document are called *objects.* An object can be almost any type of information, including text, bitmap images, vector graphics, and even voice annotations and video clips. In an ideal implementation of a compound document, the user is unaware that different source applications are being invoked. The process of browsing, selecting, and editing information is seamless—users can manipulate various types of information within the body of a single document without the inconvenience of switching from one application to another. Users can create a single document that either links (references) or embeds different objects (packets of information)—thus the term *object linking and embedding.* OLE was developed by Microsoft because there are situations that are not adequately served by either Clipboard or DDE linking: specifically, the features of compound documents. OLE does not replace either DDE or the Clipboard, but rather extends the capabilities of them by providing this additional functionality.

OLE processes are design within a client/server computing framework, and, as such, they require a dialog between client and server. Any OLE application can be a client, a server, or both. In this context, an OLE client is a container application that produces the container document. For example, if a Microsoft Excel chart is embedded within a Word document, then Word is a client application and the document is the container document. The OLE server is the source application that produces the linked or embedded object. Indeed, an OLE client (MS Word) requests a service (Excel chart) from a "remote" application—Excel, which remotely creates, updates, and displays its chart in the container.

OLE-enabled solutions can be thought of as document-centric versus application-centric. OLE allows the user to focus on the task versus the details of the application and information exchange methodology. OLE provides easy sharing of data and functionality among different applications, even from different vendors. OLE provides embedding in the sense that the document's native data and its presentation format is stored in the document and is forwarded with it. The data for a linked document, by contrast, is stored in another file, not within the document. The linked object that is put into a document has the presentation for its data and a pointer to the file which contains the data. The data, in turn, has a pointer to the application and knows how to deal with the object data.

OLE also has powerful facilities for accessing programmable objects in applications in order to allow one application to "drive" another application. These facilities are called OLE Automation and Visual Basic for Applications (VBA). OLE Automation defines a standard mechanism for an application to expose subsets of functionality that can be queried and utilized by another OLE-enabled application. Additionally, VBA provides a common macro language that can be utilized in conjunction with many of the Microsoft productivity tools and integrated with solutions built with Microsoft's Visual Basic. These facilities are intended by Microsoft to be utilized as the glue to tie together reusable components and objects and incorporate them into a broad range of business solutions created by any number of vendors. Third-party vendors are attempting to provide embeddable common scripting products for providing OLE Automation capabilities to non-Microsoft products.

The powerful capabilities of OLE become very important as corporations increasingly focus their application development resources on providing decision-support business solutions. OLE services will become an inherent part of every Microsoft Windows implementation.

Although OLE-enabled applications are easy to use, they are not easy to develop. Developers using the Windows GUI should focus on learning and understanding OLE capabilities as an effective approach to object-orientation under Windows. More details about the OLE role, trend, and directions can be found in Chap. 8, which discusses middleware.

3.5.3   Windows 95

Windows 95 has dramatically expanded the capabilities and features of Windows 3.x. It is an operating system as well, and neither relies on nor requires MS-DOS. Starting from its installation, Windows 95 demonstrates a wealth of new capabilities. Among them are:

- Preemptive multitasking

- 32-bit support

- Plug-and-play—technology that automatically discovers and configures all desktop devices

- Easy navigation, from the start button, that allows access to all programs and files, to the *taskbar* that allows for easy switching between programs, to shortcuts that allow users to navigate from one program to another with a single click of a mouse button

- Long filenames—Windows 95 supports file names up to 250 characters long

- Built-in access to the Microsoft Network (fee-based access to e-mail, the Internet, electronic bulletin boards, etc.)

- Built-in access to the Microsoft Exchange in-box to send and receive e-mail and faxes

- Powerful multimedia with improved video and sound

Windows 95 is an example of the evolution in client specialization—it is designed to make client/server computing easy by leveraging the available computing power of client platforms, providing the client system with speed and 32-bit multitasking for local autonomy, and with transparent connectivity to local and remote (e.g., the Internet) servers.

3.6   GUI PORTABILITY

A client/server architecture does not limit any particular implementation to high-resolution terminals. Therefore, it would be beneficial for developers and users alike to be able to develop and run applications on any and all of these platforms using the same presentation's look and feel. Another benefit would be the ability to port an application from one platform to another without changing the look and feel of the GUI. One way to achieve this goal is to use tools that make the differences among different GUIs transparent to the applications.

One way to make GUI development easily portable from one GUI to another is to provide a common denominator to all GUIs via a special-purpose *compatibility* tool. With such a tool, application developers will be able to learn and use one tool to generate a desired graphical user interface on a given platform rather than mastering several different interfaces. It means that, depending on the particular GUI an application decided to use, the application code would have to perform a set of the GUI's API-specific functions. This set varies from one GUI to another. (See Fig. 3.7.)

For example, when an application that uses the OSF/Motif GUI needs to be ported to an MS-DOS platform with MS Windows GUI support, the application would not have to be changed. All GUI interactions in this case will be handled through a common tool API. The tools that bridge differences in various GUI implementations should take into account differences in application programming interfaces, event-handling logic, coordinate spaces, drawing algorithms, colors, text, and fonts used by various GUIs. At the same time, these tools should retain as much of the native GUI look and feel as possible. Another requirement for such tools is not to provide the least common denominator, which simply eliminates all advantages of a particular GUI; rather, such tools should provide a set of functions at least as rich as the most advanced of the supported GUIs and, preferably, exceed it.

Creating an API for such a tool is not a trivial task, since there are widely different levels of native GUI interface support. Given the need for and advantages of such a tool, it is no surprise that several vendors have embarked on the development of compatibility products. Among them are ORACLE Toolkit and XVT-Power++ from XVT, Inc. The latter, for example, both runs under and creates portable GUI applica-

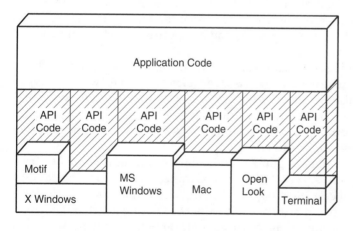

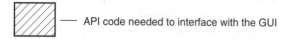
— API code needed to interface with the GUI

Figure 3.7 Various GUI APIs.

tions for Windows, Windows/NT, OSF/Motif, Open Look, MacOS, and OS/2. XVT-Power++ expands the portability of the GUI to include not only windows, but also all native GUI controls. A single resource file can be used by XVT-Power++ to create applications that run on multiple platforms, each with the appropriate native look and feel.

Another approach used by several vendors is to select a standard GUI and "port" it to other GUI environments. Given the popularity and widespread acceptance of Microsoft Windows, it is not surprising that vendors attempt to implement the Windows environment on non-Windows (UNIX) platforms. Two different approaches emerged as clear winners: develop Windows APIs to run Windows applications natively under UNIX (Windows Applications Binary Interface, or WABI) or emulate Windows APIs under UNIX by running an emulator program (e.g., SoftWindows from SoftBench).

Tools like these will allow developers to keep pace with advances in GUI technology and to facilitate applications portability and consistency of presentations while the GUI standards are being finalized.

3.7 APPLICATION DEVELOPMENT

The advent and popularity of GUI client platforms have affected the way client/server application development is done. Application development organizations have many classes of vendors from which to choose in building client/server applications, including single-vendor life-cycle solutions, vendors of modeling tools (CASE) for requirements analysis, 4GL vendors, vendors of 3GL toolkits or 3GL generators, and 3GL application development environments. And to make life more complicated, many subcategories and competitors exist within each of these categories.

Those organizations that use a 3GL development approach have realized that the productivity of 3GL development, even with the availability of a full-function GUI library, is not as high as that of a visual environment. As a result, these development organizations typically employ either an application generator or a GUI toolkit to be effective for client/server application development.

Alternatively, some organizations adopt a 4GL development strategy. Today, client/server 4GLs vary significantly in their suitability across a wide spectrum of application and environmental complexity.

The ease of use and intuitive nature of the GUI resulted in the transformation of programming environments for client/server. With the advent of powerful GUIs and client/server computing, application development has rapidly been transformed to more visual programming metaphors. Everything from user interfaces to database joins to application logic can be developed graphically on a workstation in a standard windowing environment. The trend in application development is to move strongly toward more graphical, visual means of application development. But the visual paradigm does not entirely replace the power and functional capabilities of a high-level programming syntax for professional developers coding highly complex applications.

Client/server 4GL tools represent a wide range of portability across platforms, presentation services, and database management systems, with different levels of support for each. The visual, highly intuitive nature of the tools should not mislead development organizations into concluding that all complex tasks related to a heterogeneous distributed client/server environment can be solved by dragging and dropping icons on a GUI screen. For example, a tool's support of multiple heterogeneous databases does not necessarily mean it will support complex joins across those databases or the porting of applications across those databases without substantial rewriting of code. The problem scope increases as the planning for today's environments and requirements has to be supplemented by positioning the development organizations to leverage the tools they are selecting for use against potential future key requirements.

Another factor that adds to the complexity of the application development is the emergence and acceptance of the object-oriented paradigm. There is a significant pool of solutions that incorporate the productivity benefits of a 4GL with the reuse benefits of object-orientation. However, often the tool that is the most object-oriented is not always the best for a given application.

While the object-oriented paradigm may affect the way the GUI is constructed (some may argue that Microsoft Windows, for example, does not follow an object-oriented metaphor), it is questionable whether object-orientation represents a separate class of development technologies. As an approach, object-oriented development principles should be applied to all types of development tools and approaches. In short, object-orientation should be considered as a powerful means of achieving the benefits of application component reuse and complex domain modeling.

This leads the discussion to another interesting issue. When object-orientation becomes pervasive throughout all new client/server implementations, it may affect the role and functionality assigned to a client platform today. Specifically, the following questions can be asked. Will the object-oriented paradigm change the role of the client platform from a mostly presentation management platform to an objects "playground"? Will the X Windows Systems architecture be changed? And, if that is the case, how will it affect client specialization? Whatever the answer, one fact appears certain: the client platform should be specialized to satisfy the functional requirements assigned to it in the most efficient and effective fashion.

Chapter

4

Server Specialization in the Client/Server Environment

As was stated in Chap. 1, one of the key principles behind the client/ server computing model is the physical separation of the user's presentation management from other application services. In the complex client/server distributed environment, this idea is helping the evolution of client and server systems toward the specialization that is aimed at particular functional tasks in a unique way. This specialization has already been shown (in the previous chapter) to facilitate such client functions as client-user interactions, with the emphasis on presentation functionality.

Server nodes can also be specialized to perform server functions more efficiently. This chapter will examine typical server functions, certain specialized design features used to facilitate these functions, and several examples of specialized server implementations.

Server specialization is best reflected in the functionality and design of database servers. Basically, database servers should be able to provide large amounts of fast disk storage, significant processing power, and the ability to run many applications (clients) simultaneously. However, as technology continues to evolve, specialization is extending to such functions as communications, terminal emulation, fax, library management, and electronic mail (e-mail). The focus of this chapter is the functional and architectural specialization of servers. This specialization is illustrated through examples of the server's hardware architecture and operating system implementations.

4.1 SERVER FUNCTIONS

Architecturally, a server is a logical process that provides services to requesting processes. In client/server computing, a client initiates the client/server interaction by sending a request to its server. The functions that a server should perform are determined in large part by the types of requests that clients can send to the servers. Conversely, if a server is unable to perform a function requested by a client, then this server cannot participate in cooperative client/server interactions. Ideally, a client should not be sending an unsupported request to such a server. In general, however, once clients and servers are interconnected in a network, the following functions may be required of servers by users:

- *File sharing.* In a workgroup environment, clients may need to share the same data file—for example, an insurance rates file in an insurance office. The rates file is placed in a shared file processor—a *file server*—and clients send their file I/O requests to the file server. Usually, the file server provides the client with access to the entire file, so that when one client updates a shared file, all other clients are unable to access this file. Another typical use of file servers is a file transfer between clients.

- *Printer sharing.* In a workgroup environment, one high-capacity printer may replace all individual client printers. Then all clients may send file print requests to a *print server*. A print server maintains a queue of all files to be printed, sending each print file, in turn, to a shared printer (usually, a high-output, high-quality printer). Typically, all individual print files are printed with a special separator page that indicates the client name and file name.

- *Database access.* In a client/server environment, application processing is divided between client and server systems. Servers may execute some portion of the business logic and database logic. Similar to file servers, *database servers* provide clients with access to data that resides on a server. However, database management systems (DBMSs) are more sophisticated than basic file I/O access methods. DBMSs provide concurrent data access with various levels of locking granularity and data integrity. DBMSs eliminate data redundancy, allow for user-transparent data distribution, and even allow parts of application-specific data access logic to be incorporated into the DBMS itself. Clients request access to desired data (contrary to a file server's access to the entire file), and all necessary manipulation on the required data is performed at the database server. Thus, multiple clients can access a database concurrently.

- *Communication services.* In a workgroup environment that is connected to a remote host processor, all communications software and hardware can be concentrated on a special *communication server,* to which clients may forward their communication requests for processing.

- *Facsimile services,* which usually require special equipment and software, are now more frequently trusted to dedicated *fax servers.* Clients send and receive fax documents by requesting appropriate services from a fax server.

Other client-requested functions, such as electronic mail, library, network, resource, and configuration management, are being handled in today's client/server environment by appropriate servers. (See Fig. 4.1.)

A server node in a client/server model can be specialized to perform its particular function in the most efficient way. However, besides indi-

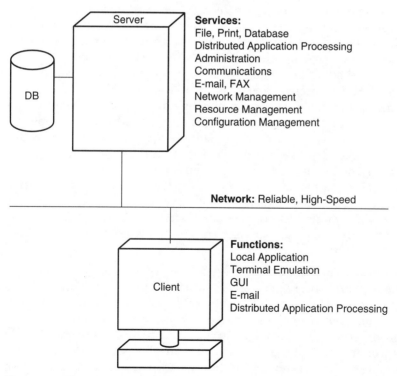

Server

Services:
File, Print, Database
Distributed Application Processing
Administration
Communications
E-mail, FAX
Network Management
Resource Management
Configuration Management

DB

Network: Reliable, High-Speed

Client

Functions:
Local Application
Terminal Emulation
GUI
E-mail
Distributed Application Processing

Figure 4.1 Client and server functions.

vidual, function-specific specialization, servers as a class of systems can be specialized to satisfy the following general-purpose requirements:

- *Multiuser support.* Even in a small workgroup environment, a server should be able to service multiple concurrent clients. Clients running different tasks would expect a server to support multitask processing. Note that multitasking can be implemented in a single-user system (like OS/2), and is a necessary but not sufficient requirement for multiuser support (a multitasking system is not equivalent to a multiuser system).

- *Scaleability.* Scaleability is the property of a system which permits an incremental increase in capacity, performance, throughput, the number of supported users, etc., by adding required computing resources as needed and without changing the applications. As the number of applications, their resource requirements, and the number of users grow, a server should be able to satisfy these increasing demands on its resources; i.e., it should provide scaleable performance. Scaleability does not mean that users should buy an overcapacity server system at an extra cost. On the contrary, the system should satisfy current requirements and, at the same time, should be easy to expand. This expansion can be achieved by a *vertical* scaling of a server (perhaps by adding or upgrading a CPU or a hard disk unit) or by a *horizontal* scaling where multiple servers cooperate transparently to share the workload. Since vertical scaleability does not require additional administrative support as a system scales up, it is often the preferred method of developing scaleable systems. Horizontal scaleability can be implemented in loosely coupled systems and distributed environments (e.g., databases and applications), as these are becoming more mature and provide better support. One drawback of horizontal scaleability in loosely coupled systems is the requirement for additional system administration support, which can affect the degree of scaleability an organization can afford. A less attractive and more expensive alternative to scaleability would be to replace the system every time it reaches the limits of its capacity, especially given the rapid change of today's business requirements.

- *Performance and throughput.* A server system should provide performance and throughput levels satisfactory to the business needs and user requirements in a multiuser client/server environment. For example, even if business requirements do not call for subsecond response time for every business transaction, users would hardly appreciate a system that takes more than a few seconds to respond to every user action. Similarly, if a workload on a server increases with the addition of new users, neither the performance nor the throughput should suffer. Since, like any other business requirements, application and user demands on a server can grow quite rapidly, a server system should be able to provide scaleable and easily tunable performance and throughput.

- *Storage capacity.* As the number of users and applications running on a server increases, and as advances in storage technology drive the costs of physical storage down, the demand for extra storage and faster access times becomes one of the critical requirements for a server system. The storage demands come from operating systems that need additional storage to implement new advanced features, from users that desire to store various data files on a server, and from applications such as DBMS and CASE tools that are some of the major storage consumers. For example, if a workstation that is running a CASE tool requires at least 16 MB of RAM (random access memory) and 300 MB of hard disk space, a server may need 64 to 256 MB of RAM and 1 to 3 GB of disk to support several of these workstations.

- *Availability.* As more and more mission-critical applications are migrated or deployed into a client/server environment, the availability of the server system becomes an essential business requirement. Similar to the mainframe data center environment, today's servers are expected to be up and running most of the time, and the 24-x-7 (24 hours, seven days a week) uptime for a server is not at all unusual. The key factors affecting availability are the server *robustness* and *on-line administration*. Robustness implies that the server system reduces the importance of any particular failure and recovers from it transparently and automatically. Hardware and software fault tolerance, including features like hot and warm standby servers, disk duplexing, and mirroring, and the use of RAID disk subsystems are all designed to improve server robustness. On-line administration is aimed at providing continuous operations, where both planned and unplanned outages are reduced or even eliminated. Operations such as database reorganization, backup and recovery, starting and stopping of server processes, system monitoring and configuration, user administration, and application/system upgrades should ideally be performed on-line, without taking the server down.

- *Complex data types.* As new applications and technologies become available, the demand for multimedia storage support is increasing. Image, video, and sound applications are becoming more and more popular. So, the requirements for a server system may include the ability to store not only digitized images on disk, but also hypertext on an optical storage device—WORM (write-once-read-many)—and video/sound data on video cassettes, compact disks, and video disks.

- *Networking and communications.* Client/server communications happen over a communication network. Both client and server systems should have built-in networking capabilities. Without networking there is no client/server interaction, therefore, no clients and servers. If a system is designed with the networking requirements in mind, the system hardware and software architectures can be optimally integrated with the networking interfaces and protocols.

One conclusion that can be drawn from the analysis of these requirements is that mainframe systems appear to be the best candidates for the server platform. As far as capabilities and functionality are concerned, mainframes are certainly well suited to be servers in client/server computing. In fact, it is the stated direction of computer vendors like IBM that mainframe hosts are to play a server role in a client/server environment that supports multiple clients. Mainframe-supported clients may require and obtain access to large amounts of corporate-wide data stored in various host DBMSs (DB2, IMS, IDMS, etc.). Indeed, mainframe-based transaction processing systems, such as IBM's Customer Information Control System (CICS), can today support thousand of users running on-line applications that can simultaneously access data stored in DB2, IMS, IDMS, and VSAM files. If mainframe applications can be distributed in such a way that application processing is performed cooperatively by host- and client-based application fragments, the result would be a two-tier workstation-mainframe implementation of a client/server architecture. Such implementations exist today and, for example, can utilize a CICS-based application running on a CICS/MVS host, with front-end presentation logic performed by such tools as Easel running on graphical workstations. (See Fig. 4.2.)
   Another example is a client/server architecture built on an OS/2 operating system that uses CICS for OS/2. Applications written for CICS OS/2 run on client workstations (IBM's PS/2) and are engaged in cooperative processing with CICS/MVS applications running on a host. However, using hosts as servers can be disadvantageous from the economy-of-scale point of view. New, high-powered workstations and servers allow end users to take advantage of the significant price/performance benefits of microcomputer technology. A typical mainframe costs orders of magnitude more than a server that is rated at the same processing speed. Processing power is often measured in MIPS (millions of instructions per second), MFLOPS (millions of floating-point operations per second), or, more useful for end users, how many transactions per second (TPS) a given application can process on a given platform. If the transaction volume and throughput requirements are known, the TPS cost can help to determine how much has to be spent to support a particular business application.

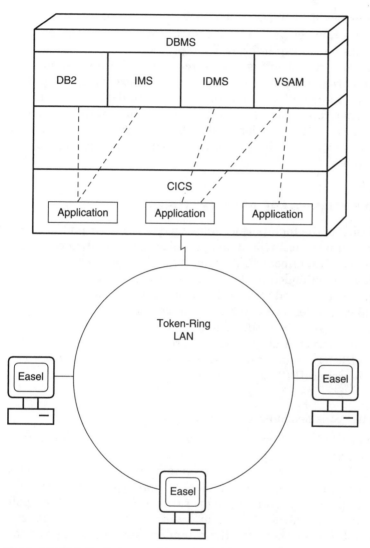

Figure 4.2 Mainframe as a server.

The economy of scale becomes very important when users compare typical price/performance characteristics on large-scale systems
(approximately $100,000 to $200,000 per TPS on an IBM MVS DB2
non-CMOS-based system) to the cost of a similar capacity system built
on the SUN SparcServer 1000 system (approximately $1500 per TPS).
The same ratio can be observed on the cost-per-MIPS comparison
between a mainframe and an average 25-MIPS server.

The price/performance advantage of microcomputer-based servers is
one of the reasons client/server architecture is being accepted by a

growing number of businesses. The power and capabilities of mainframes assure their critical role as central corporate servers and the best platforms for central information repositories.

However, not all business needs require mainframe computing power and storage capacity. Nor can every business or most applications justify a multimillion-dollar mainframe and data center–related expenses. Therefore, this chapter will look into several aspects of server platform specialization that allow hardware engineers to achieve the scaleable high-performance characteristics of today's microcomputers.

4.2   SERVER HARDWARE ARCHITECTURE

The discussion of the high-performance aspects of server platform specialization will be concentrated on specialization and advances in the server hardware architecture. This analysis of server hardware architecture trends is intended to clarify often misused and misunderstood technological jargon used by some hardware vendors, at the same time giving readers a reference point that can be used when a server purchasing decision is to be made. The focus of the discussion will be on three popular server architecture features: *Reduced Instruction Set Computer* (RISC), *symmetric multiprocessing* (SMP), and *massively parallel processor* (MPP) architectures.

4.2.1   System considerations

The basic principles of computer design describe, among other things, the factors that affect computer performance. In general, these factors include CPU architecture, the size and implementation methods of the instruction set, the ability of compilers to optimize for performance, computer chip technology, and the operating system. From the application's point of view, the CPU architecture, technology, and instruction set are the resources that the compilers and operating systems should be capable of exploiting to achieve the highest possible performance. Ideally, a system's hardware architecture, operating systems, and enabling software (i.e., compilers) are all balanced and tuned according to the nature of the application in order to achieve the highest possible performance and throughput. For example, applications that tend to be easily vectorized can benefit from running on a computer equipped with a vector facility (e.g., a supercomputer like the Cray Y-MP). Many applications, on the other hand, are not vectorizable and can best operate on systems with scalar performance. These applications may take advantage of a superscalar CPU design (i.e., the IBM POWER and POWER 2 RISC chips). Other architectures include distributed-memory massively parallel systems and clustered systems. In either case, in order to fully utilize often expensive hardware solutions, operating systems should be aware of the hardware configurations, and the compilers should be able to produce machine code optimized for these platforms.

Thus, the underlying instruction set becomes one of the critical performance factors. Indeed, computer performance can be described by the following symbolic formula:

$$\text{Performance} = \frac{1}{\text{cycle time} \times \text{path length} \times \text{cycles/instruction}}$$

The *cycle time* is the opposite of the system clock rate and is mostly limited by the underlying chip technology. Most of today's personal computers and workstations can operate at speeds from 60 to 130 MHz, although some high-end workstations offer commercial CPUs with higher speed. In general, faster clock speed may require new, higher-density chip technologies. The shorter the cycle time, the higher the performance.

Path length describes the number of machine instructions necessary to execute one command. The shorter the path length, the higher the resulting performance. The CPU architecture, underlying instruction set, and optimizing compilers are the factors that can reduce the path length.

The *cycles-per-instruction* factor describes how many computer cycles are necessary to execute one instruction. This number can vary from less than 1 (in RISC architectures) to greater than 1 in traditional CISC architectures. If the number is less than 1, then more than one instruction can be executed in one CPU cycle. Thus, performance is better. Computer designers continuously introduce innovative solutions to improve the cycles-per-instruction ratio. Superscalar and superpipelining are the two best-known approaches to this problem.

Other factors affecting computer performance include memory access times, external storage characteristics and I/O data transfer rates, and, in a networking environment, communications and networks.

Some systems can be optimized best for commercial environments, which are generally characterized by integer processing, transaction processing, file and disk subsystems manipulation, and a significant number of attached low- to medium-function terminals and workstations. Other systems may be best suited to scientific environments, which are generally characterized by very high floating-point performance requirements, and few high-function graphical workstations attached to the central server via very high speed interconnections. Still other systems may be designed to achieve a careful balance between integer and floating-point performance, thus extending the system's applicability to both commercial and scientific worlds. In any event, when system designers wish to address the performance issue, they may concentrate their efforts on one of the following:

- Shortening the instruction path length
- Improving the cycles-per-instruction ratio
- Speeding up the system clock

The designers may attempt to achieve the desired performance for the mix of integer and floating-point instructions, thus creating a universal high-performance architecture.

4.2.2 RISC versus CISC

In the early 1980s, some system designers argued that the then-current chip architectures could yield higher performance if new architectures would adopt the same principles as some of the best optimizing compilers. That is, optimizing compilers could produce almost as good code as the best programmers could write in assembler language. Analyzing the compiled code, David Patterson of the University of California at Berkeley found that compilers used the simplest instructions of an available instruction set. These simple instructions could be used more efficiently than the complex instructions if the system hardware was optimized for this task. Unfortunately, the opposite was true. Traditional computer architectures were optimized for more complex instructions. The instructions in these architectures were decoded by the microcode which was placed in the microprocessor hardware. Patterson proposed the *Reduced Instruction Set Computer* (RISC), as opposed to the traditional *Complex Instruction Set Computer* (CISC). In RISC architectures, instructions are decoded directly by the hardware, thus increasing the speed of the processing.

Originally, a RISC processor contained only the simplest instructions extracted from a CISC architecture, and the hardware was optimized for these instructions. Not only did the RISC design contain the simplest instructions, but the number of available instructions was significantly lower than with a comparable CISC design. Beginning in 1980, Patterson's group undertook the task of implementing RISC prototype processors, called RISC I and RISC II. RISC I contained 44,000 transistors, was completed in 19 months, and outperformed a Digital VAX 11/780 by a ratio of 2 to 1.

An interesting historical fact is that the first RISC machine (though not identified by that name) was the IBM 801 System—the result of a research project conducted by IBM from 1975 to 1979. Note that besides the performance, the apparent simplicity of RISC architecture provides another advantage: a designer can realize the RISC design in silicon chips faster. Therefore, time to market can be reduced and the latest in technology can be used in a current design more quickly than in a comparable CISC design.

The simplicity of RISC architecture is relative. Second-generation RISC designs introduced more complex instructions and increased the speed and the number of instructions. The real performance leverage in the second-generation RISC design is achieved by a carefully balanced tradeoff between complexity and simplicity via an optimized definition of the instruction set, machine organization, and processor logic design.

An important RISC feature is that each instruction is simple enough to be executed in one CPU cycle. In a "simple" RISC architecture, this may be true for a simple integer addition, but a floating-point addition may be simulated by several single-cycle instructions. To alleviate this and other similar problems, second-generation RISC architecture may be improved by a *superscalar* implementation (IBM's RS/6000, PowerPC, and Digital APLHA are examples of the superscalar RISC implementation). Superscalar design splits the processor into separate units so that the processor can sustain execution of two or more instructions per clock cycle. For example, the branch processor decodes instructions and assigns them to the other two units: the integer processor and the floating-point processor. Figure 4.3 illustrates the logical view of the IBM RS/6000 superscalar POWER RISC implementation.

Each of the three units can perform several instructions simultaneously. Integer and floating-point units contain multiple buffers to handle new operations before old ones are completed; the branch can initiate multiple instructions. The resulting instruction *pipeline* in effect breaks instruction processing into a series of stages connected like stations in an assembly line. In the RS/6000 example, the five-stage pipelining and superscalar design allows up to four instructions (one fixed-point, one floating-point, one branch, and one condition) or five simultaneous operations per cycle (three integer operations— fixed-point, branch, and condition, and two floating-point operations that constitute one floating-point instruction—multiply and add). That's why a superscalar RISC machine performs well in commercial, high-performance integer processing environments and in scientific, floating-point-intensive applications. Multiple vendors continuously work on the innovations in superscalar design, which results in frequent leap-frogging in performance among the vendors. For example, the next generation of the POWER architecture—POWER2—practically doubles the number of simultaneous instructions by integrating additional integer and floating-point units into the design. And the new PowerPC chips (the result of a joint IBM–Motorola–Apple ven-

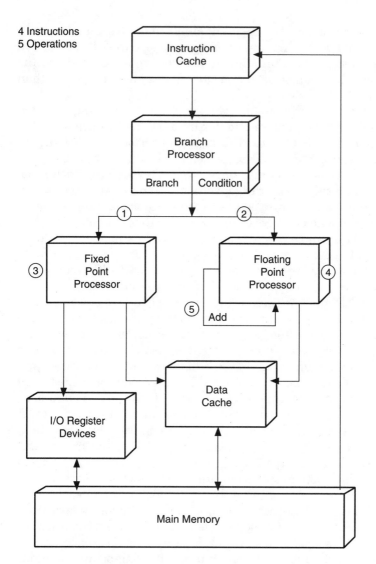

Numbers Indicate Order of Operations

Figure 4.3 Superscalar RS/6000 RISC architecture. (Numbers indicate the order of operations.)

ture) offer new levels of price and performance with relatively low cost and power consumption.

Another fundamental implementation technique used in RISC architectures is *pipelining*. As was previously described, pipelining is a technique that allows more than one instruction to be processed at the same time. A typical pipelined CPU uses several execution steps, or stages, to execute one-cycle-long instructions. Pipelining achieves high performance through the parallelism of processing several instructions at once, each in a different pipeline stage. To optimize the performance and increase the throughput of the pipeline, designers increase clock rates and introduce higher granularity of stages—superpipelining. For example, MIPS R4000 uses eight-stage pipelining, and Digital ALPHA uses parallel pipelines with different numbers of stages—10 for floating-point and 7 for integer and load/store instructions.

In a well-designed pipeline, all stages contain logic with approximately the same execution times. A careful balance between the number of instructions, clock speed, and the number of pipeline stages in superscalar RISC implementations will result in even higher performance levels of microcomputers, and workstations capable of hundreds of SPECint92 and SPECfp92 (Standard Performance Evaluation Corporation, or SPEC, benchmarks for the integer and floating-point performance) will be available in the near future at the cost of a regular PC. The performance advantage of the RISC architecture has to be leveraged by optimizing compilers and operating systems. To date, many UNIX-based operating systems and Microsoft's Windows/NT are capable of supporting RISC architecture.

4.3 MULTIPROCESSOR SYSTEMS

Multiprocessing is becoming an indispensable tool for improving the performance of computer systems struggling to support ever more complex and demanding applications. In fact, multiprocessing systems and parallel database technology (described in Chap. 12) promise to elevate client/server computing to new levels in performance, throughput, scaleability, and availability.

Generally, adding processors creates the possibility of performing several computing tasks in parallel, thus speeding up the overall execution of the program. As CPU costs decrease, users find that adding processors to their existing multiprocessor hardware is significantly more economical than either adding computer systems or replacing existing systems with more powerful uniprocessor systems. Conversely, adding entire computers to increase throughput has its drawbacks:

- Adding processors usually results in the addition of expensive peripheral devices. Stand-alone uniprocessors cannot share memory, unless they are networked at an additional expense. To speed up applications, an operating environment, including appropriate load-balancing software, must be in place to distribute and synchronize applications, usually at additional cost and complexity.

- Adding faster uniprocessors is more expensive than obtaining the same performance by increasing the number of processors.

Therefore, designers are focusing on computing architectures where the processing units are physically close and are often integrated by a single operating system. In such a system, the processing units (PUs) speed up a single computational task by executing it jointly (in parallel). These *parallel* systems have high-performance computing as their objective, but they also add such objectives as synchronicity, reliability, resource sharing, and extensibility. An additional and important goal is to achieve *linear* speed-up and scale-up; for example, doubling the number of processors cuts the response time in half (linear speed-up) or provides the same performance on twice as much data (linear scale-up).

In addition to these general objectives, multiprocessing systems and specialized parallel database management systems address a number of key business requirements:

- The need for fast response time on complex queries, a requirement for decision support systems (DSSs) and data warehousing.

- The need to support large (and growing) data sets. This is especially true for very large database (VLDB) support that goes beyond parallel query execution—parallel execution of database utilities that load, back up, and create an index is the only way to effectively manage large databases that exceed hundreds of gigabytes and even terabytes.

- The need to support a large number of concurrent users.

- The need for ever higher transaction rates for on-line transaction processing (OLTP) applications.

- The need to effectively support new, large-size data types such as multimedia, image, text, voice, full-motion video, and new application classes such as data warehouse, multimedia Internet access, home shopping, and video-on-demand.

As client/server computing matures into its second generation, multiprocessor systems are becoming the mainstream computing platform for high-end servers and demonstrate the clear need and advantages of server specialization. This chapter takes a closer look at the hardware configurations of multiprocessing systems. Multiprocessor systems can be classified by the following:

- The degree of coupling that measures how strongly the PUs are connected by evaluating the ratio of the amount of data exchanged among PUs to the amount of local processing performed by PUs in executing a task

- The interconnection structure that determines the network topology—bus, star, ring, tree, etc.

- Component interdependence that determines the level of dependence between PUs.

The principle distinction between different classes of multiprocessor systems is the degree of coupling between the processors and the memory. Specifically, multiple-processor parallel systems have either *shared* or *distributed memory*. Additionally, these systems can be implemented with either a *shared-* or *distributed-disk* subsystem, although the impact of shared versus distributed memory is much more severe from the general architecture and programming model viewpoints. In fact, a shared-memory system is typically one with a shared-disk design, while distributed-memory systems may have either shared- or distributed-disk implementations.

While in general the topology of a distributed system can change due to communication link failure, interprocess communications in distributed-memory parallel systems, for instance, are reliable and predictable.

4.3.1 SMP design

A *shared-memory* multiprocessor (typically, a symmetric multiprocessor, or SMP) incorporates a number of processors, called *processing units* (PUs) that share a common memory, common I/O, and various other common system resources. In other words, this is a *tightly coupled* design, where an SMP machine coordinates *interprocess communications* (IPC) through a global memory that all PUs share. A typical shared-memory multiprocessor consists of a relatively small number (4 to 30 on average) of processors. Processors select tasks to be executed from a common task pool and are interconnected via a high-speed common system bus, thereby providing extremely efficient interprocessor communications.

Shared-memory multiprocessing ensures that any processor completing one task is immediately put to work on another, the next available task. All PUs share a single copy of an operating system, and each PU executes a task selected from a common task pool.

Note. Not every operating system can support SMP. An SMP system requires an operating system that can take advantage of the shared-memory multiple processor configuration. The operating system requirements for the SMP are discussed later in this chapter.

Typically, in order to reduce the volume of shared-memory traffic, each PU has one or more memory caches. One or more memory controllers may be included in this architecture to support the high memory access requirements of multiple PUs.

A system where all PUs in a shared-memory multiprocessor have equal capabilities and can perform the same functions is called a *symmetric multiprocessor,* or SMP (see Fig. 4.4). Each PU in an SMP system can run user applications as well as any portion of the operating system, including such operations as I/O interrupt, operating system kernel functions, and I/O drivers. In addition, any task can be executed on any PU and can migrate from PU to PU as system load characteristics change.

The SMP implementation has a significant positive effect on scaleability. Indeed, if a system designates one PU to perform a particular task (e.g., service I/O interrupts), this PU will become overloaded as the number of I/O requests increases, and overall system performance will degrade.

SMP architecture provides two high-level features:

- *Seamless execution* is the ability of an SMP system to seamlessly, transparently to the user, support existing applications. In truly seamless implementations, all applications originally written for a uniprocessor will be able to run on an SMP system unmodified. By

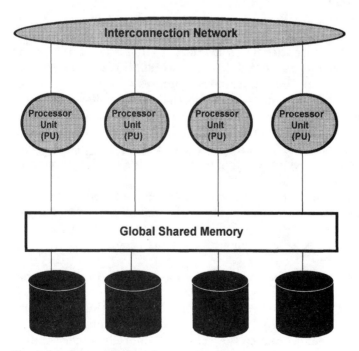

Figure 4.4 Symmetric shared-memory multiprocessor.

taking full advantage of multiprocessing, applications can achieve significant performance gains. This is especially important for servers running DBMSs and supporting transaction processing.

- *Limited scaleable performance* encompasses two components: computational growth and I/O growth. Computational growth can be achieved by adding processing elements, while I/O growth can be the result of adding peripherals and/or I/O buses. It is important to note that the addition of a PU increases the overall system performance up to a limit. The per-PU increase is not equal to the performance of the individual PU, but rather corresponds to a fraction of this PU performance. As the number of PUs grows, various factors (such as system bus and memory subsystem design, cache sizes, and the need to keep certain memory regions protected as they keep data specific to a given PU) all affect the resultant performance. Another obstacle to SMP scaleability is a feature called *cache coherency*—a frequency at which a cache has to be repeatedly emptied and filled as tasks continue to get scheduled and preempted (interrupted) for the execution on a given PU.

4.3.2 SMP features

If asked to name only the two most important SMP characteristics, it could be the following:

- The most significant benefit would be the use of a familiar traditional programming paradigm. Since the memory is shared, every program assumes that all memory is available for storage and retrieval. It is, in fact, the responsibility of the operating system (sometimes assisted by the hardware microcode) to ensure that multiple programs or threads of execution do not "step on" each other and corrupt each other's memory content. Today's SMP machines support standards-based operating systems and application enablers (compilers, tools, database management systems, etc.)

- The most significant drawback is related to the limited scaleability— the throughput of an SMP system does not demonstrate a linear growth in direct proportion to the number of PUs. Depending on the PU and system bus speed, the SMP throughput does not increase (and can even decrease, due to the local cache coherency problem) when the number of PUs exceeds some (machine-specific) number, typically less than 30.

Nevertheless, within its scaleability limitations, SMP-based systems provide the ability to increase performance incrementally. Therefore, SMP systems have become the mainstream of today's server platforms.

They allow for future upgradeability, and represent a cost-effective solution for such applications as DBMS, gateways, and transaction processing. Typically, these applications are composed of smaller, relatively independent tasks, that can be assigned to numerous processors. Applications like these are ideally suited to run on servers in a client/server environment.

Providing symmetry in shared-memory systems has an impact on both hardware and software architectures. Specifically, an operating system design becomes more complex on an SMP system. In fact, without an SMP-capable operating system it is very difficult to realize the potential scaleability benefits of a symmetric multiprocessor. Software features supporting scaleable SMP performance include the capabilities to execute the operating system kernel, I/O interrupts, and I/O drivers on all PUs.

SMP operating systems

Let's take a closer look at an SMP-capable operating system. Such an operating system is designed to assign work to available PUs based on a particular load-balancing algorithm. This work is represented by processes and lighter, finer-granularity *threads*. A thread, which is defined by POSIX as a single sequential flow of control within a process, allows developers to write cooperative routines, all sharing access to the same data in memory. Therefore, an operating system that does not support threads can take advantage of the SMP hardware only on the large-grain process level, while a threads-capable operating system can be much more efficient when running multiple applications as well as single multithreaded applications.

Shared-memory protection

The SMP operating system complexity is related to the locking strategy that is designed to prevent simultaneous updates to data structures and codes in SMP common shared memory. The locking strategy is designed to address the shared-memory nature of SMP systems, where an SMP-aware operating system has to be able to prevent processes from modifying each other's memory and system resources. In other words, the SMP OS must make sure that processor 1 does not let process A modify the memory that process B, running on processor 2, is using. Since, typically, there is no master PU in an SMP, the processors must let each other know about the processes they run and the memory area they use.

Dynamic load balancing

This feature is another critical requirement of an SMP software architecture. Indeed, if a PU has been added to an SMP system, the operating system and application software should be able to take advantage of the additional PU by dynamically redistributing the load among all available PUs.

Various SMP operating systems handle memory protection, multi-threading support, and load balancing differently, with various effects on scaleability and performance. For example, Windows/NT is multi-threaded and SMP-capable, with the multithreaded NT kernel managing resource allocation by acting as a non-preemptable master scheduler of processes and threads. Windows/NT memory protection is based on its non-preemptable microkernel architecture and protected subsystems, which copy data structures for a thread to a different memory area when this thread is passed to a new subsystem. While this approach limits the possibility for a conflict, copying data structures is time consuming.

UNIX operating systems vary in the way they support multithreading and SMP. The Open Software Foundation's OSF/1 operating system supports SMP by defining IEEE POSIX 1003.4 *P-Threads* standard-compliant threads. HP-UX and Sun Solaris are both multi-threaded and SMP-capable, while UNIX System V Release 4 (SVR4) is not multithreaded but supports SMP by using child processes that the operating system spawns on different PUs. Solaris is using a complex system of reader and writer locks to ensure memory protection.

Scaleable software architectures are not only designed to take advantage of the SMP hardware architecture transparently and seamlessly. They also provide for easy entry into parallel computing, where multiple applications can run simultaneously. There are several techniques for developing parallel applications capable of achieving maximum performance in a multiprocessing system. Among them are problem partitioning (dividing a problem into several smaller independent parts) and data decomposition for load balancing.

4.3.3 SMP implementations

High-performance SMP systems offer comparable or higher performance than traditional uniprocessors, while promising an impressive incremental performance scaleability within the design limits. Properly designed SMP systems allow for seamless execution and the ability of existing applications to execute transparently without modifications. That is why several SMP systems available today are used as DBMS servers, communication gateways, and transaction processing platforms.

Some popular shared-memory systems include products like Pyramid Technology's high-end machines, which combine SMP implementation with RISC technology; Sequent Computers Symmetry series; Sun SparcCenter 1000 and 2000; and HP's Enterprise Server, the T-500.

Even such a well-known supercomputer maker as Cray Research is serious about SMP architecture, as demonstrated by its CRAY SUPER-SERVER 6400 (Sun SuperSPARC–based, 4 to 64 PUs SMP system running Solaris 2).

Today's SMP servers are quite powerful and often exceed performance ratings traditionally attributed to high-end mainframes and supercomputers. Consider the SMP offering from a well-known and reliable UNIX server vendor: the T-500. The system combines HP's advanced PA-RISC processor architecture with symmetric multiprocessing software and a balanced high-end memory and I/O bus. The HP Corporate Business Server T-500 uses up to 12 state-of-the-art RISC-based processors, each equipped with a large, high-speed cache memory (1 MB per CPU for instructions and data each).

It is designed to be independent of the semiconductor and implementation technologies. Therefore, the T-500 can take advantage of leading-edge technologies as they develop. For example, the use of CMOS VLSI technology enables the entire CPU to be integrated into a single circuit-board module. The resulting reduction in complexity reduces system cost while increasing performance and reliability.

It is designed for growth by incorporating a 64-bit virtual address capability with the total addressing range of 256 TB.

The T-500 offers a high-speed processor memory bus capable of accessing main memory at the bandwidth of 1 GB/s. This bus is designed to minimize bus contention. Special hardware features ensure processor cache coherency, a well-known problem in SMP designs. Not only is such a system designed for high-performance computing; to satisfy commercial customers running large databases, the T-500 supports eight I/O channels with an aggregate I/O throughput of 256 MB/s. Its HP-UX operating system support is standards-based and compliant with POSIX 1003.1 and 1003.2, FIPS 151-1, and the X/Open Portability Guide Issue 4 (XPG4).

4.4 MASSIVELY PARALLEL PROCESSORS AND CLUSTER SYSTEMS

As previously described, SMP machines have an inherent architectural limitation on scaleability. One solution that avoids this limitation is a nontrivial approach employed by distributed-memory *massively parallel processors* (MPPs) and clusters of uniprocessors and SMP systems. These systems are often called *shared-nothing* systems, since neither the PUs nor the local memory are shared, thus eliminating the main reason for the limited scaleability of the SMP.

A common attribute of a distributed-memory machine, be it an MPP or a cluster, is a high-performance interconnection network that interconnects PUs and their local memory units. An interconnection network can be a high-speed *external* LAN (for typical SMP clusters), a high-speed *internal* switch, a connection tree, a hypercube, a star, a mesh, etc. Many of these solutions are proprietary innovative designs, but the standardization efforts move into this area as well; for example, there is a new interconnection system called the *Scaleable Coherent Interconnect* (SCI), which is an IEEE standard.

4.4.1 Distributed-memory architecture

In a distributed-memory machine, all PUs are connected to each other via an intercommunication mechanism and communicate by passing messages (see Fig. 4.5). In other words, distributed-memory systems are considered *loosely coupled* multiprocessor systems. Although both MPP and cluster systems adhere to the same distributed-memory computing model, they can be differentiated from one another by a number of attributes. For example, in the MPP design, a *proprietary* interconnect provides very high bandwidth and low latency communication between nodes. An MPP operating system that is designed to take advantage of this proprietary scaleable interconnection network is responsible for the inter-PU communications. These systems were originally designed to solve numeric-intensive processor-bound Grand Challenge problems and were once limited to specialized communities focused around a handful of centralized and extremely expensive computing facilities. MPP operating systems are optimized for programs that are often easily partitionable for parallel execution. As the number of PUs increases, these systems demonstrate excellent scaleability due to the nature of the applications they are designed to handle. Often, such an MPP system can contain and effectively use hundreds and even thousands of PUs.

One obvious drawback of the distributed-memory architecture is its requirement for a "new" distributed programming paradigm. Indeed, a traditional programming paradigm assumes that all memory is available to the CPU for storing and retrieving the data. In a distributed-memory system, a program that executes an instruction like $a = a + 1$ has to first locate the variable a in its local or remote memory (in the latter case, the processor needs to issue special instructions to retrieve the value of a from the remote location and to send it to this processor's memory). The result is a need for a *new operating system* design, *new compilers, new programming languages,* etc.

Distributed-memory systems can be classified by their interconnect architectures or by the way the messages are passed and synchronized. Parallel architectures can be divided into contemporary *multiple instruction multiple data* (MIMD) and older *single instruction multiple*

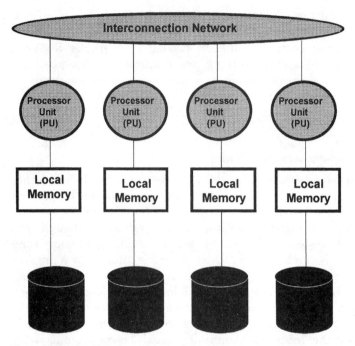

Figure 4.5 Distributed-memory architecture.

data (SIMD) machines. In MIMD systems (such as Intel Paragon's XP/S and IBM's SP-2), multiple processors can simultaneously execute different instructions on different data. Therefore, MIMD systems are inherently asynchronous computers that can synchronize processes by either accessing control data (semaphores, switches, etc.) in shared memory or passing synchronization messages in distributed-memory systems. MIMD systems are best suited to *large-grain* parallelism (on a subroutine and task level). An extension to the MIMD model is MPMD (*multiple program multiple data*), where multiple processors concurrently execute multiple programs accessing different data. The MPMD model supports parallel database processing for the commercial applications of the MPP technology as well as clusters of uniprocessors and SMPs.

SIMD machines (such as the Thinking Machine Corporation's CM-2, MasPar's MP-1, and MP-2) are by design synchronous parallel computers in which all PUs execute the same instruction at the same time (or remain idle). SIMD machines are typically controlled by a central control unit that broadcasts a single instruction to all PUs, at which time PUs execute that instruction in synchronous fashion on their local data. Fine-grained (instruction-level) parallelism is best suited for SIMD machines.

In general, distributed-memory MPP and cluster systems promise a tremendous increase in scaleable performance and throughput. Arguably, distributed-memory systems are the result of the shift in the computing paradigm, discussed in Chap. 1 and could become a dominant enterprise server architecture for mission-critical applications of today and tomorrow.

Distributed-memory shared-disk systems

A shared-nothing distributed-memory system can be very effective for those problems that lend themselves to easy partitioning. Sometimes called *embarrassingly parallel,* these problems can be solved by concurrently executing the same instruction against different data records read from individual disks. For example, consider a counting problem: count all records in a file that contains amounts greater than $100 in a *MONEY* field. Assuming a uniform distribution of the *MONEY* values throughout the file, to solve this problem on a shared-nothing machine could be as simple as:

- Partitioning the file into equal parts
- Running a program like *IF MONEY* > $100 *ADD* 1 *TO COUNT* on all processors
- Adding all *COUNT* values to get the final answer

If the file contains 1,000,000 records, partitioning it into 1000 parts can theoretically speed up the performance of the query by 1000 times, relative to a sequential (nonparallel) execution. However, if the problem becomes more complex (i.e., a multilevel selection criteria), or if the data are not uniformly distributed, the problem cannot be solved as effectively by blind partitioning—the elapsed time of the overall operation will be skewed toward the partition that has the most occurrences of the *MONEY* field that satisfy the selection criteria.

One way to reduce this data skew is a variation of distributed-memory shared-nothing architecture where the memory is distributed but the disk storage is shared (see Fig. 4.6). Such a system has many scaleability characteristics of the distributed-memory MPP system, but it also provides a single image of the disk subsystem that can be easily managed by a database management system.

In fact, this architecture assumes that all processors have direct access to all disks. To make this design effective for parallel database access, an extra software layer called a *distributed cache manager* is required to globally manage cache concurrency among processors. While the shared-disk design helps reduce DBMS dependency on data partitioning, it also introduces a potential limitation on the overall sys-

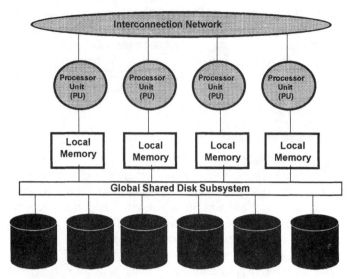

Figure 4.6 Distributed-memory shared-disk architecture.

tem scaleability for distributed-memory systems. A further discussion on the subject can be found in Chap. 16.

4.4.2 Research issues

Since distributed-memory architecture uses a different computing and programming paradigm, its emergence in the commercial marketplace is surrounded by a number of active theoretical and practical issues. The bulk of the issues is related to what is known as *paradigm integration* caused by the advent of high-power MPP machines and low-latency, high-bandwidth intercommunication networks. Paradigm integration means that a new MPP-compliant program should combine both task and data parallelism with a single application. The need for paradigm integration is driven by the code reuse requirement in a parallel architecture, heterogeneous models that combine multidisciplines of numeric-intensive tasks, data visualization, and commercial computing. The latter deserves special interest due to its often contradictory on-line transaction processing and decision support system requirements. Another important feature of commercial high-performance computing is the requirements and design complexity of parallel database management systems capable of very complex query and very large database processing. The discussion on parallel database management systems can be found in Chaps. 12 and 16.

Some of the current MPP research issues are listed as follows:

- Traditional performance measurements (MIPS, MFLOPS) have to be redefined for MPP/SMP systems, since they do not reflect real performance characteristics.

- Scaleability must be considered in terms of how MPP system performance is affected by problem size or by the number of PUs.

- Operating systems for distributed and parallel processing are in their infancy. Operating system design and construction is an open problem, especially given the state of accepted standards in the areas of microkernels, interprocess communications, object-oriented operating systems, load balancing, etc.

- Task scheduling is a rather complex issue that has lead so far to a number of heuristic solutions, each of which may or may not work under different circumstances.

- Innovative programming methods are needed since traditional sequential shared-memory programming methods may not work or may not be able to take advantage of the distributed-memory architecture. Issues like MIMD-based programming, data-parallel programming, functional programming, and tuple-space programming are just a few items that researchers are working on.

- Compiler and optimization work mostly focuses on two directions. The *implicit* approach modifies existing languages or introduces new ones that help conceal the underlying system from the programmer (the preferred way for commercial computing). Obviously, this approach shifts the burden of parallel complexity to the compiler developer. Currently, there is a shortage of good parallel compilers. The *explicit* approach extends existing languages or introduces new languages to express parallelism directly. This approach has a serious impact on the existing programmer's skill set.

- Database systems require special consideration. Many vendors and researchers in the scientific community are working diligently to develop truly parallel database management systems. Oracle, IBM, Informix, and Sybase already have *limited-functionality* versions of their products targeted for *specific* MPP environments (i.e., there is a production version of ORACLE 7—Parallel Query Option—for several MPP systems). Full-function parallel DBMS (PDBMS) development is facing the same issues of reliability, scaleability, performance, etc., that the rest of the MPP community is forced to deal with. Heterogeneous processing, reliability, and code portability are "traditional" distributed-systems issues that are becoming even more pressing with the advent of MPP and clusters, especially in the commercial arena.

The advent of the revolutionary distributed-memory architectures is a clear indication of the necessity and benefits of server specialization. Indeed, specialization would not go that far if the set of business problems facing the server did not require extraordinary measures.

4.4.3 Clustered systems

As previously mentioned, the distributed-memory MIMD/MPMD architecture maps well onto a collection of loosely coupled uniprocessors or SMPs connected by local area networks.

In a cluster environment, each PU executes a copy of a *standard* operating system, and inter-PU communications are performed over an open-systems-based interconnect (e.g., Ethernet, TCP/IP) by either special operating systems extensions or by add-on software components.

The relatively low bandwidth and high latency of the interconnection network limit the cluster's ability to efficiently communicate data between nodes. In fact, many clustered systems are more sensitive to communications, data sharing, and synchronization requirements than MPP systems, since the communication in clusters is frequently over a standard communication network and typically is based on standard communications protocols (e.g., TCP/IP), although systems using FDDI, ATM, HiPPI, and FCS (Fiber Channel Standard) are capable of supporting an extremely high bandwidth (e.g., up to an 800-Mbps link speed for HiPPI; 1065-Mbps for FCS). While the major cost element of the MPP system is the high-speed internal interconnection network, clusters of uniprocessors and SMPs shift the cost to the large number of software licenses that result from the need to install operating system software on each node in the cluster.

On the positive side, cluster systems are often designed for high availability by providing shared access to disks and better balancing between processor-bound and I/O-bound tasks. As such, cluster systems can be successfully deployed for both scientific and commercial applications. The promise of unlimited scaleability; the availability and price-performance of the SMP systems; continuous growth in server performance and throughput requirements; the emergence of new application classes; the need to support new data types, large amounts of data, and large user communities; and improvements in parallel database management system software all lead major server vendors to start the race to develop commercial distributed-memory SMP clusters.

The latest developments in machine hardware architectures result in significant improvements in all three approaches. SMP systems continue to improve the performance of the interconnect (system bus) and the operating system, thus increasing SMP scaleability beyond today's levels. Modern cluster systems demonstrate many characteristics of the MPP system, including a very high speed scaleable interconnection mechanism, compact *cluster-in-the-box* packaging, and support for hundreds of PUs. In turn, MPP systems are evolving to utilize SMP nodes, thus increasing per-PU power and taking advantage of intra-node shared-memory architecture (see Fig. 4.7). The net result of these developments is that the distinction between MPP and clusters will become blurred as architectures continue to converge.

An example of these developments in MPP and cluster systems can be found in existing and emerging products. Although IBM has a clear lead with its SP-2 and follow-on systems, many established vendors, including Hewlett-Packard, Sun, and Sequent, have plans to deliver competitive offerings within the next two to three years. These vendors plan to leverage their expertise in operating systems and SMP implementation by developing innovative interconnect technologies and using standards-based very high speed communications protocols.

Probably one of the best justifications for server specialization is the price-performance characteristics of the latest in server designs. Traditionally, system performance is measured in MIPS, SPECmarks, or the somewhat more meaningful transactions per second (TPS). The cost of each TPS rating is quite high for a high-end mainframe. The price-performance characteristics of specialized server systems compare very favorably with those of a mainframe-class machine. In fact, it is not unusual to achieve an order-of-magnitude improvement in price-performance when using a specialized high-end server. And as technology continues to advance, the price-performance of specialized servers is getting even better, thus justifying architectural specialization for a server platform.

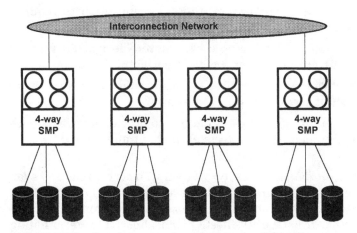

Figure 4.7 Distributed-memory cluster of four-way SMP nodes.

4.5 SERVER OPERATING SYSTEMS

Naturally, server specialization is not limited to its hardware architecture. The server operating system determines how quickly the server can fulfill client requests, how many clients it can support concurrently and reliably, and how efficiently the system resources such as memory, disk I/O, and communications components are utilized.

4.5.1 Requirements

In order to analyze the available server operating system, let's first consider some general requirements attributed to a server operating system in a client/server environment. By design, a server operating system has to support multiple users performing multiple, often conflicting, tasks concurrently. Therefore, a reasonable server operating system has to demonstrate at least the following:

- *Multiuser support*

- *Preemptive multitasking.* This feature allows a server to allocate time and resources among multiple tasks evenly or based on priorities. In preemptive multitasking, one (possibly a higher-priority) task can interrupt another task when necessary. Preemptive multitasking contrasts with cooperative multitasking (for example, implemented by Microsoft Windows), where one application has to be coded to give up control to another application.

- *Multithreaded design.* This allows a server operating system to employ lightweight processes to serve multiple requests and to distribute threads to multiple CPUs in a multiple-CPU server. Like multitasking within a single task, multiple threads can execute concurrently within a single process, thus reducing resource requirements and improving concurrency.

- *Memory protection.* This is a necessary feature designed to prevent multiple concurrent tasks from violating each other's memories.

- *Scaleability.* The server operating system should be able to scale up as the number of users and applications grows.

- *Security.* A server operating system has to provide its clients with a secure environment that protects each client and the corresponding resources.

- *Reliability/availability.* Clearly, a server that serves tens and even hundreds of users should not go down at will, especially if it runs mission-critical applications. A server operating system should protect the system from the ill effects of an abnormally terminating application (crash protection).

In addition to these requirements, servers (and clients) should be evaluated based on the operating system architecture, which is an important but often ignored characteristic of an operating system.

OS architecture—microkernel technology

In the traditional operating system, operating system services, such as process management, virtual memory management, network management, file system services, and device management, are all built into the kernel. The result is a large, complex, and often inflexible kernel that is difficult to enhance or port to different hardware platforms. These system kernels traditionally support uniprocessors and are inherently less secure. The new operating system architecture is based on *microkernel* technology, originally developed by Carnegie Mellon University. By design, the microkernel is relatively small and highly secure. It provides only the basic system services, such as task and thread management, interprocess communications, virtual memory services, input/output services, and interrupt services. These services are made available to user-level tasks through a set of microkernel interface functions. Unlike the traditional kernel-based operating system approach, services such as file system, network services, and device drivers operate outside the microkernel as user-level servers, thus reducing complexity, increasing portability, and requiring fewer interactions between user tasks and the microkernel to perform operating system services.

What is more, this architecture results in a highly modular operating system that can support multiple operating system "personalities" by configuring the outside services as needed. For example, the microkernel technology, which is based on Carnegie Mellon's Mach 3.0 microkernel, is used by IBM to allow DOS, OS/2, and AIX operating system personalities to coexist on a single machine.

In general, the benefits of the microkernel-based operating system can be summarized as follows:

- Simplified architecture
- Extensibility
- Portability
- Enhanced real-time support
- Multiprocessor support
- Robust system security

All of these benefits make a microkernel-based operating system a good candidate for the ideal server operating system.

4.5.2 UNIX

UNIX is a mature and established operating system. Developed in the late 1960s, UNIX has acquired a significant customer base and demonstrated its many strong features on real-life applications. Today, UNIX continues to increase its market share on an annual basis.

There are numerous UNIX versions developed by multiple vendors to run on practically any platform imaginable. Similarly, there are thousands of applications available to run on UNIX platforms.

Overall, UNIX is a true multiuser, multithreaded, fully preemptive multitasking operating system. It is portable to the majority of hardware platforms available today, including CISC (e.g., Intel) and RISC (e.g., RS/6000, PowerPC, Motorola, SPARC, MIPS, etc.). It is a scaleable operating system, designed to run on SMP and even MPP machines. UNIX advanced features include built-in networking, numerous operating system utilities, crash protection, administration, and diagnostics.

UNIX is a secure system. It is C1 and C2 secure, and is certifiable for B1 and B2 levels of security for distributed systems.

Applications developed for UNIX running on a particular platform are (generally speaking) source-code compatible with other hardware platforms that support UNIX, which enhances applications portability, especially for such applications like DBMS, Network File System, Source Code Library, etc. The portability and scaleability make UNIX an attractive server operating system.

The picture is a little different on the client system side. Multiple available UNIX versions cause confusion among ISVs and users alike. The lack of common UNIX kernel code and a common windowing API set continues to cause some hesitation on the part of users to adopt UNIX as the operating system of choice throughout the corporation. This lack of unity discourages some ISVs from developing shrink-wrapped software for UNIX, which may seriously affect vendors' efforts to position UNIX as a client operating system, but it probably has little if any effect on the adoption and growth of UNIX as a server operating system.

The UNIX operating system, tools, and applications have influenced the specification of many standards and, in fact, stimulated the emergence of open systems. The adherence to such standards as FIPS (Federal Information Processing Standard), SVID (System V Interface Guide), XPG4 (X/Open Portability Guide), and POSIX common operating system services, shell, tools, and real-time extensions further enhances portability. UNIX alliance vendors are working on bringing together various UNIX versions. The Common Open Software Environment (COSE) is a standard being developed by most major UNIX OS vendors, including Hewlett-Packard, IBM, Novell, SunSoft, and The Santa Cruz Operation. COSE specifies how each UNIX version should look, feel, and act.

4.5.3   Windows/NT

Microsoft's Windows/NT (New Technology) is an advanced operating system for Intel and RISC processors. By design, Windows/NT offers the best features of OS/2 and the UNIX operating system.

Windows/NT supports 16-bit DOS and Windows applications, OS/2 character-based applications, 32-bit native applications, preemptive multitasking, multithreading, and crash protection. Windows/NT uses an add-on product—LAN Manager—to provide the advanced LAN and multiuser capabilities required by a server OS.

Although not yet ported to as many hardware platforms as UNIX, Windows/NT is architected to be hardware independent. It supports several RISC processors (MIPS and Digital ALPHA), has C1- and C2-level security certification, and is POSIX-compliant (POSIX 1003.1— Base Functions). All these features are missing from OS/2.

Windows/NT offers software fault tolerance through a transaction-oriented recoverable file system (NTFS), disk mirroring, and memory-mapped files that simplify virtual memory operations. In addition, Windows/NT offers a Windows-like user interface, which makes it very easy to use by most current Windows and DOS users, of which there are millions.

The scope and promised functionality of NT has markedly affected the direction of the UNIX community during the past two years, causing UNIX vendors to seriously consider bringing different versions of UNIX together by developing standards for a common kernel, common APIs, and a common look and feel.

Many industry experts believe that NT will slow the progress of UNIX and erect impassable barriers on the advancement of nonportable operating systems. At the same time, an analysis of market trends leads to the conclusion that Windows/NT will not destroy UNIX's momentum.

4.5.4   OS/2

OS/2 was the first operating system specifically designed to provide preemptive multitasking for the Intel processor. Early versions of OS/2 (versions 1.x) were plagued with many problems and therefore were not adopted by the majority of the organizations as the operating system of choice. The shortcomings of OS/2 version 1 included heavy hardware requirements, poor performance, single processor support, and the lack of applications and ISV support.

With the release of OS/2 version 2, this operating system now is a stable platform that can provide advanced operating system features for workstations and servers alike. OS/2 version 2 can run 16-bit DOS and Windows applications as well as 32-bit applications specifically designed to take advantage of the 32-bit addressing and processing power of the operating system. OS/2 is a multitasking and multithreaded operating system and currently supports a total of 4096 threads and processes, with 64,000 semaphores per process. OS/2 uses Named Pipes as the preferred interprocess communication (IPC) mechanism and can use most popular network protocols to connect local and remote processes into a client/server system. OS/2 uses an add-on product—LAN Server—to provide the LAN and multiusers capabilities required by a server OS.

OS/2 can address up to 512 MB of virtual memory, with automatic paging to/from disk. One of the OS/2 strengths is its stability and crashproof memory protection. If a DOS, Windows, or native OS/2 application develops a serious problem, only this application can terminate—the rest of the system remains active, and an application such as a DBMS can continue to serve its clients.

OS/2 supports the High-Performance File System (HPFS), which is faster than the DOS FAT file system. HPFS uses an intelligent cache system and lays out files to minimize disk fragmentation. OS/2 can be tuned to optimize the use of I/O devices such as SCSI and SCSI-2 high-performance adapters.

One of the limiting factors in OS/2 acceptance is its inability to run on non-Intel processors. This diminishes OS/2 portability and scaleability as a server operating system.

4.5.5 NetWare

Novell's NetWare is another popular server operating system, especially for file and print services, although it is used today as a database server OS as well. NetWare offers many of the same facilities found in advanced operating systems such as OS/2, Windows/NT, and UNIX, but not without some severe limitations.

NetWare (version 3.11 and above) is a true 32-bit operating system with heavy emphasis on networking. In fact, it would be more accurate to call NetWare a network operating system (NOS). Its advanced file server features make NetWare one of the best in the networking world.

NetWare runs on Intel platforms only, which is a definite limitation. To achieve greatest performance, NetWare allows application developers to extend the system services associated with the file server by using NetWare loadable modules (NLMs). NLMs become a part of the NetWare kernel and run alongside the services already included in the NOS. Therefore, NLMs can demonstrate very strong performance, but not without a price. NLMs are not memory protected. Intel 386 and higher processors provide four levels of protection known as rings: Ring 0 has the highest number of privileges and is usually reserved for the operating system itself, while ring 3 has the lowest number of privileges. NLMs run at ring 0 and are able to get at and corrupt memory areas reserved for operating system processes and I/O device drivers, thus bringing an entire system down.

Unlike traditional virtual memory operations, NetWare does not page code to and from memory, which prevents additional NLMs from being loaded once the memory limitation has been reached—a severe impact on scaleability.

NetWare does not support preemptive multitasking, which means that NetWare cannot stop a running application to allow another application to continue execution. In addition, NetWare does not support threads, which limits server ability to support such services as RPCs.

Nevertheless, with the acquisition of UNIX Software Laboratories by Novell, NetWare could be a serious contender for a common operating system API, especially if it is ported to a new common kernel and later to a new microkernel on which it will likely coexist with UNIX.

4.5.6 OS summary

In the absence of other major portable operating systems, UNIX and Windows/NT should dominate the market for the server operating system, especially for new applications. The industry will probably choose between UNIX and Windows/NT mostly on vendor and marketing issues rather than on technical issues. Indeed, these two operating systems are quite similar in their technical capabilities, and one will be able to do almost anything that the other can.

UNIX is capable of handling most types of workloads today. Windows/NT is still relatively new, but could be ready to compete for most types of workloads in the near future. The application portability provided by these two environments and the freedom of choice of hardware platform available for these OS are the drivers that will foster their continued growth.

Today's trends in computing architecture emphasize the value of openness, portability, and interoperability. Therefore, the possibility of survival of nonportable operating systems is rather small, even though several established operating systems are now technically superior to UNIX and Windows/NT in many ways. An example of such a nonportable operating system is IBM's MVS. According to the Gartner Group, MVS is expected to decline at a rate of 9 percent annually through 1997, being roughly equal to Windows/NT in market size by 1997.

3

Networking,
Communications,
and Middleware

*Up to this point, the discussion of a client/server architecture
has concentrated on the characteristics of clients and servers
as specialized nodes in a distributed computing environment.
Client/server computing was defined as a specialized form
of distributed cooperative processing. In client/server
architecture, various application components are distributed
between client and server platforms which cooperate to
perform the desired application functions. Client/server
interactions were defined as those where a client initiates the
interaction and requests a particular service from a server.
The server reacts to the client's request by performing the
desired service and sending the response back to the client.
Such interactions do not make any assumptions on a topology
of the client/server architecture. In fact, there is nothing to
prevent a client and a server from existing on the same
physical machine. Nevertheless, these interactions require
reliable and robust communication facilities between clients
and servers. In very general terms, when clients and servers
are physically located on separate, potentially remote nodes,
client/server communications will have to be performed over
a suitable network. Such a network could be a local area
network (LAN) for a small workgroup or a wide area network
(WAN) for geographically dispersed nodes. Traditional IBM
Systems Network Architecture (SNA) networks, popular
Transmission Control Protocol/Internet Protocol (TCP/IP)*

networks, public networks utilizing packet-switching protocols, networks based on the standard Open Systems Interconnection (OSI) protocols could all be used for client / server communications. Understanding these networks and communication protocols is critical to an understanding of the client / server architecture.

Chapter

5

Communication Systems

In a distributed environment, various system resources (data, computing power, programs, etc.) are spread (distributed) across several locations. These resources utilize some kind of communication system to interact with each other. In this context, a communication system is a mechanism that allows the distributed resources to exchange control information and data. Communication systems, while essential for distribution, may be implemented in a way totally transparent to end users. Conversely, they may be visible enough for the end users to be aware of the network that provides actual resources interconnection. Whatever the implementation, communication between nodes is necessary, and this communication requires some kind of physical network that connects all interacting nodes.

5.1 COMMUNICATION AND DISTRIBUTION

Client/server architecture is a special case of cooperative processing. Cooperative processing, in turn, is a special case of distributed processing. A distributed processing environment, however, is not motivated by client/server computing model needs alone. Among factors that have contributed to the current interest in distributed systems are:

- Technological advances in microelectronics that have changed the price-performance ratio in favor of multiple low-cost, high-performance systems
- Interconnections and communication costs that have fallen dramatically in the past few years
- User demands for more economical, faster, more sophisticated and reliable facilities

One objective and benefit of distribution is resource sharing. A number of resources, such as computers, peripherals, special-purpose processors, programs, and data, are interconnected by a communication system in order to allow the sharing of resources. The interconnected systems form a *network* which is used by a communication system to switch messages or packets of information between different sites, systems, terminals, and programs.

Here are some definitions that will be useful when discussing networks and communications. A *communication system* is the collection of hardware and software which supports intersystem and interprocess communication between software components in distributed nodes. The *nodes* are interconnected by a network which provides a physical *path* between them (see Fig. 5.1). The direct connection between two or more systems is sometimes referred to as a *link*. A system that performs main application functions and controls the communication system is sometimes called a *host*. In a distributed system, the name of an object indicates a system, a process, or a node; an *address* indicates where the named object is, and a *route* tells how to get there.

One of the most common shared resources in distributed systems is data. Many applications require the sharing of data among diverse users with different computing facilities. By distributing data, reliability may be improved by replicating data into multiple copies. Access times may be improved by maintaining local copies of data by replication and partitioning. The data communication system may be used to transmit both data and data requests between different sites, systems, and programs. While interconnected systems may or may not form a distributed processing system by themselves, the data communication system used for message and data interchange can itself be considered a distributed system. Indeed, it is physically distributed, its components cooperate to provide common services, and it is controlled by a network management system.

5.2   COMMUNICATION SYSTEM FUNCTIONS

The following are some of the most important functions of a communication system:

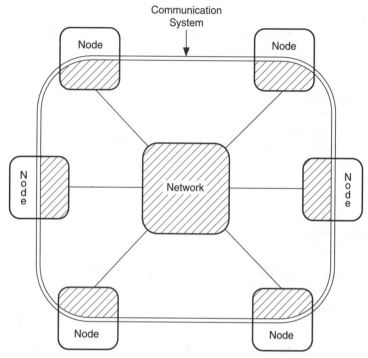

Figure 5.1 Network and communication system in a distributed environment.

Naming and addressing. A communication system has to manipulate names for objects such as processes, ports, mailboxes, systems, and sessions between users. Typically, users supply names in symbolic form (e.g., "system1"), and the communication system must translate (map) that symbolic name into a network address. Therefore, a communication system must maintain appropriate translation tables (directories). Routes are related to the address translation: a destination address is mapped onto a path or an intermediate object, such as a gateway.

Segmenting. If user messages or files to be transmitted are too long, the communication system might have to fragment a single message into multiple segments (see Fig. 5.2). Of course, once a message is segmented for transmission, the communication network has to be able to reassemble the message from its fragments before delivery to the end user.

There are several reasons for segmentation:

- Very long messages increase access delays for other users since they hold exclusive control over shared network resources for longer periods of time.

User Message

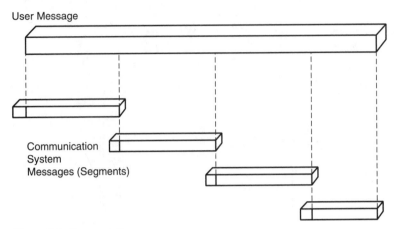

Figure 5.2 Segmentation.

- Shorter messages improve efficiency and reduce transmission error rates.
- Internal buffers, used by the communication system, can limit the transmitted message size.
- When various networks compose a particular transmission route, each of the component networks can have a different message size.
- Breaking long messages into small segments may allow the use of parallel data links (in some networks), thus supporting parallel transmission and reducing overall delays.

Blocking.   When a single message fragment is transmitted over the network, significant protocol overhead is incurred, especially when the message is short. Therefore, some communication systems use a blocking protocol to combine messages from different users into a single block for the transmission.

Flow control.   Many networks are designed to share limited resources among many users on the assumption that not all users will be active at the same time. In reality, however, communication networks may experience certain peak traffic scenarios where the resulting traffic exceeds the network throughput capacity (rush-hour traffic congestion is a good example). A network flow control function is designed to prevent transmission congestion and/or deadlock, and to optimize network performance, by regulating the flow of information between a pair of communicating entities. For instance, *pacing* protocols are used to prevent the sender node from sending more information than the receiver can handle.

Synchronization.   In order for a pair of entities to communicate with each other, their interactions must be synchronized. The receiver must be able to determine the start and the duration of each signal, byte, and block. Indeed, if a receiver is faster than the sender (transmitter), it may gain and misinterpret extra information. Conversely, it may lose some information if it is slower than the transmitter.

During communication, entities maintain their state information via a communication protocol. The communication states must be synchronized at initialization time and after a major failure.

Shared resources, such as shared data, require synchronization between processes to support resource integrity. An example of the multilevel synchronization protocol used in communication systems is IBM's Advanced Program-to-Program Communication protocol (APPC), which is discussed in Chap. 7.

Priority.   A communication system can assign a priority to messages to allow preference handling when competing for resources. High-priority messages (alarms, alerts, interrupts) should have shorter delays. A communication system should be able to assign priority statically or dynamically (according to message content, or based on a message source or destination).

Error control.   One of the prime objectives of communication system functionality is to provide reliable, error-free communication. Error control functions include error detection, correction, and recovery. Error detection can be performed by including redundant information, using control information that allows information corruption to be determined, or assigning sequence numbers to messages and detecting sequence errors. Redundant data can be compared in order to determine a possible error in the case of a mismatch. Control information can use various algorithms to calculate a check digit or a checksum of all information bits. Comparing calculated results with the one received, errors can be detected. Sequencing is used to determine lost, duplicated, or out-of-sequence messages. Error correction and recovery are often implemented by automatic retransmission, possibly via a different route, although sometimes error-correction codes can also be used.

Other functions, such as session management and control, are also very important. Some of the communication system functions, together with particular communication protocols, are described in greater detail in the next three chapters.

5.3 LAYERS, PROTOCOLS, AND INTERFACES

A communication system is responsible for supporting communication between nodes in a distributed system. It allows any network node to communicate with any other node connected to the communication network. Computer network architectures should facilitate interconnectivity among homogeneous and, especially in an open systems arena, heterogeneous systems. To better understand how a communication system is architected to support communications, let us consider a model of typical person-to-person communication. Three separate levels, or layers, can be defined:

- *The cognitive layer* includes concepts such as the understanding, knowledge, and existence of shared, mutually agreed-upon symbols; e.g., if one person communicates a description of a book to another, at the very least, both persons must understand what a "book" is.

- *The language layer* is used to put concepts and ideas into words. Obviously, if people do not have a common, mutually agreed-upon language, any communication will be impossible.

- *The physical transmission layer* provides the means for the actual communication, whether it is sound waves, paper for written communication, or any other medium.

All three layers are independent of each other in function, and the upper layers require the support of the lower ones. To communicate ideas, language and transmission are necessary, but the opposite may not be true.

The same principles can be applied to the building of distributed and communication system architectures. At the very least, all network architectures should share the same high-level objectives:

- *Connectivity* to permit various hardware and software to be interconnected into a uniform, single-system-image, networking system

- *Modularity* to allow building of diverse networking systems from a relatively small number of general-purpose components

- *Reliability* to support communications in an error-free fashion with error detection and correction availability

- *Ease of implementation,* use, and modification by providing general, widely acceptable solutions for network installation, modification, and management, and by supplying end users with network-transparent communication facilities

To achieve these high-level objectives, network architectures support highly modular design, where each module's functions are organized into functional, hierarchical, architected *layers.*

Layers are composed of *entities,* which can be hardware components and/or software processes. Entities of the same layer but in different network nodes are called *peer entities;* the same-level layers in different nodes are *peer layers.* Communication between layers is governed by a set of rules: *protocols.* Protocols include, but are not limited to, formats and the order of the information exchange, and any actions to be taken on the information transmission and receipt. The rules and formats for the information exchange across the boundary between two adjacent layers constitute an *interface* between layers. For example, a typical distributed system architecture may consist of the following functional layers:

- *The application layer* is the topmost layer of the architecture. Typically, it performs the management of application processes, distribution of data, interprocess communication, and decomposition of application functions into distributable processes. Application layer functionality is supported by lower-level layers.

- *The distributed operating system layer* provides systemwide distributed services required by the application layer. It supports naming and addressing, the sharing of local resources, protection and synchronization, intercommunication, and recovery. The distributed operating system unifies the distributed functions into a single logical entity and is responsible for creating the single system image (SSI).

- *The local management and kernel layer* supports the distributed operating system in the individual nodes. It also supports local interprocess communications, memory and I/O access, protection, and multitasking. This layer supports higher-level layers by providing the services requested by the distributed operating system layer and by communicating with its peer layer in other nodes.

- *The communication system layer* supports communication required by the application, the distributed operating system, and local management layers.

The layered architecture provides several important benefits:

- *Layer independence.* Each layer is aware only of the services provided by the layer immediately below it, but not of the implementation of the lower layers.

- *Flexibility.* An implementation change in one layer (for instance, new technology or different hardware) should not affect the layers above and below it.

- *Simplified implementation and maintenance.* This is due to the support of a modular layered design and architected decomposition of the overall system functionality into simpler, smaller sections.

- *Standardization.* Encapsulation of layer functionality, services, and interfaces into a precisely defined architected entity permits standards to be developed more easily.

5.4   ISO REFERENCE MODEL

Let's look at layered architectures in the example of data communication architecture. One of the most popular architectures, IBM Systems Network Architecture (SNA), was developed by IBM for data communication networks based mostly on the IBM and compatible hardware and software platforms. However, other vendors and organizations have also developed, or are in the process of developing, other architectures which can offer alternative methods of building data communication networks.

Thus, two important trends can be found in the marketplace:

- Almost every major vendor offers its own proprietary network architecture, and these architectures are not compatible.

- If a business customer uses multiple hardware platforms for its IS operations, the task of connecting different networks becomes more and more difficult.

Therefore, the need for a standard set of rules, or protocols, for the exchange of information between different, heterogeneous network architectures becomes urgent. Various standards organizations are working on developing standard architectures, protocols, and interfaces. The Consultative Committee on International Telegraphy and Telephony (CCITT) is an international standards organization that develops standards for various aspects of telephone and data transmissions (e.g., X.3, X.25, X.28, X.29). The Institute of Electrical and Electronics Engineers (IEEE) focuses on networking standards. In particular, the IEEE has developed a set of local area networking standards known as IEEE Project 802.

The realization that standards were needed to allow communication between different platforms, as well as the benefits and advantages of layered architectures, led the International Standards Organization (ISO) to develop a reference model with the express purpose of providing a common basis for communication system standards. This set of standards is called the *Open Systems Interconnection,* or OSI. The OSI model has adopted the best features of the existing architectures. It also provides additional features which make the heterogeneous communication networks interconnection easier and more efficient to develop.

Even though the OSI model is still being developed, the OSI architecture is often used as a reference model by vendors and standards organizations alike. Not surprisingly, it is a hierarchical, layered structure, which consists of seven architected layers. Each layer performs a specific OSI network function, services the next-higher layer, requests services from the next-lower layer, and communicates on a peer-to-peer basis with the corresponding layers in other nodes. (See Fig. 5.3.)

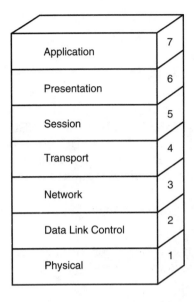

Figure 5.3 OSI layers.

To better understand the particular implementation of various communication systems, the next seven sections will briefly describe the basic functions of the seven OSI layers.

5.4.1 OSI physical layer

The OSI physical layer, or layer 1, is at the bottom of the OSI model. It deals with the physical implementation of a network. The OSI physical layer defines the electrical and signaling characteristics that are necessary to establish, maintain, and disconnect physical connections in the network. Currently, the physical layer of the OSI model includes these standards developed by the CCITT:

- V.35 and V.24 for analog transmissions
- X.21 for digital transmissions

The OSI physical layer describes how bits of information are to be sent and received but does not provide for data recognition.

5.4.2 OSI data link layer

The OSI data link layer, or layer 2 in the hierarchical structure, provides transmissions over a single data link. The OSI data link layer supports the following services:

- Data transport from one end of a link to another
- Data link activation and deactivation

- Data link error detection
- Data link sharing
- Transparent data flow
- Data link error recovery and notification

Among the protocols included in layer 2 of the OSI model at the present time are the American National Standards Institute (ANSI) Advanced Data Communications Control Procedures (ADCCP); the ISO High-Level Data Link Control, or HDLC; SNA Synchronous Data Link Control (SDLC); and a widely recognized standard called IEEE 802.2.

5.4.3 OSI network layer

The OSI network layer, or layer 3 in the hierarchy, provides control between two adjacent nodes. The following functions have been assigned to the OSI network layer:

- Network addressing (assignment, pairing, and matching)
- Blocking and segmenting of the message units
- Data units sequencing
- Switching and routing
- Local flow control
- Optional expedited data transfer control
- Error detection control
- Congestion control
- Error recovery and notification

All of these functions of the OSI network layer are included in the CCITT-recommended X.25, an international standard for packet-switched data networks.

5.4.4 OSI transport layer

The OSI transport layer, or layer 4 in the hierarchy, is defined to provide so-called end-to-end control between two user nodes. This layer takes packets of data from the OSI network layer and assembles them into messages. The OSI model defines the operation of the transport layer as a multiphased procedure:

- *Phase 1—establishment:* This phase establishes transport connections to lower layers.

- *Phase 2—data transfer:*   The data transfer phase transports data between OSI layers.

- *Phase 3—release:*   The release phase disconnects transport connections.

5.4.5   OSI session layer

The OSI session layer, or layer 5 in the hierarchy, provides network functions associated with the sessions. The following functions are defined in the OSI model for its session layer:

- Session initiation and activation
- Session termination and release
- Synchronization and resynchronization of the session connections
- Dialog control
- Normal and expedited data transfer

5.4.6   OSI presentation layer

The OSI presentation layer, or layer 6 in the hierarchy, provides the data stream presentation protocols. These protocols should allow a network to determine and maintain track of the information, such as message syntax, contained in the user data stream. The following functions have been defined for the OSI presentation layer so far:

- Transformation of data syntax, e.g., encryption of the data
- Selection of a presentation image syntax
- Virtual terminal
- Virtual file
- Job transfer and manipulation

5.4.7   OSI application layer

The OSI application layer is the topmost layer in the hierarchical model. At the present time, the application layer is defined to contain all the protocols between systems that are not included in any other OSI layer. The OSI application layer consists of the three parts:

- *Common application services.*   These are the services that can be used by all communicating parties. Common application services provide the protocols that can select the type of conversation to be held between users or the structure of this conversation, such as a file transfer structure. Common application services also provide such control protocols as commitment, concurrence, and recovery.

- *Specific application services.*   These services contain the protocols of all user information exchanges. These protocols may be private within a single communication or widely accepted even internationally recognized, communication standards. At this time, international communication standards for the OSI application layer include the X.400 Message protocol, the X.500 Directory protocol, and the File Transfer, Access, and Management protocol (FTAM).

- The *user element* in the OSI model represents the end points of the user information (e.g., final origination and destination points). If the user element is defined, there will be no need for a user interface above the application layer.

5.5   CLIENT/SERVER COMPONENTS CONNECTIVITY

In a client/server architecture, client and server systems are constructed from a number of interconnected components. Each component provides an interface through which it communicates with other components. Thus, communication between clients and servers can be viewed as the communication between relevant components. Two distinct classes of components can be defined:

- *Process components.*   Typically, these are software components that actively perform some functions.

- *Resource components.*   These provide the services requested by process components.

From the point of view of client/server interactions, an active resource component acts as a server, whereas the users of the resource component—process components, act as clients.

Process and resource components, as well as clients and servers, enter into an association with each other for the purpose of communication. This association is the *connection* between a sender of information (request, message, etc.) and a receiver of that information. The client/server connections can be static or dynamic. Static connections are set up at compile or load time, or at system initialization time, and cannot be changed. The dynamic connection can be changed in flight, at run time.

5.5.1   Communication and synchronization

In a cooperative client/server distributed environment, coordination and cooperation between components (clients and servers) is provided by the communication system's communication and synchronization functions.

Communication functions involve the exchange of information and are supported by flow control, error control, naming and addressing, blocking, and segmenting. Synchronization functions involve the coordination of actions between two or more components. Communication and synchronization are closely related. When communication is performed in shared-memory, closely coupled systems (such as the symmetric multiprocessing systems described in Chap. 4), software components such as semaphores or monitors are used for synchronization. In loosely coupled systems that are interconnected by communication networks, mechanisms such as message passing must be used for communication and synchronization. In either case, the communication service provided by a communication system can be *connectionless* or *connection-oriented*. Connectionless services are those in which each message transaction is independent of previous or subsequent ones. These are low-overhead services that are relatively simple to implement. An example is a *datagram* service, where the user is not provided with any form of response to a transaction. Typically, datagram services are used for broadcast or multidestination message transmission.

A connection-oriented service provides a relationship between the sequence of units of information transmitted by a particular communication layer. This is a more complex communication service. Most connection-oriented services have three phases of operation: establishment, data, and termination. An establishment phase can be used to negotiate connection or session options and, thus, a quality of service. A terminal session to a remote computer, or X.25 packet-switched network protocols, accepted by the OSI CCITT, are examples of connection-oriented services.

With respect to connections in general, the flow of information can be *unidirectional* (from a sender to a receiver) or the more complicated *bidirectional*. The latter involves a return message and synchronization in response to the initial request.

Bidirectional communications are an essential form of communication for client/server architecture. A client component requests some service to be performed by its (possibly remote) server, then waits until the results of its request (if any) are returned. Bidirectional client/server interactions can be provided by a message-oriented communication implemented in such request-reply protocols as IBM's Logical Unit 6.2 (LU6.2) or by a procedure-oriented communication such as remote procedure calls (RPCs).

5.5.2 Procedure-oriented communication—RPC

Procedure-oriented communication allows applications in a distributed computing environment, such as the Open Software Foundation's Distributed Computing Environment, to run over a heterogeneous network. The basic technology that enables this functionality is the *remote procedure call,* or RPC.

The RPC model is based on the need to run individual process components of an application on a system elsewhere in a network. RPCs use a traditional programming construct: the procedure call, the use of which is extended from a single system to a network of systems. In the context of a communication system's role in a client/server environment, an RPC requesting a particular service from a resource component (server) is issued by a process component (client). The location of the resource component is hidden from the user (client). RPCs are highly suitable for client/server applications, usually providing developers with a number of powerful tools that are necessary to build such applications. These tools include two major components:

- A language and a compiler that simplify the development of distributed client/server applications by producing portable source code

- A run-time facility that allows distributed applications to run over multiple heterogeneous nodes, thus making the system architectures and the underlying network protocols transparent to the application procedures

Among several RPC implementations and proposals competing for the role of standard RPC, DCE's RPC appears to be one of the strongest candidates, which deserves closer examination.

To develop a distributed, DCE-compliant client/server application, a developer creates an interface definition using the Interface Definition Language (IDL). IDL syntax is similar to the ANSI C language with the addition of several language constructs appropriate for a network environment. Once the definitions are created, the IDL compiler translates them into stubs that are bound with the client and the server (see Fig. 5.4).

The stub on a client system acts as a substitute for the required server procedure. Similarly, the server stub substitutes for a client. The stubs are needed to automate otherwise manual operations—copying arguments to and from RPC headers, converting data as necessary, and calling the RPC run time.

RPC run time should have the following features:

- Transparency and independence from the underlying networking protocols

- Support for reliable transmission, error detection, and recovery from network failures

- Support for a common method of network naming, addressing, and directory services, while at the same time being independent of network directory services

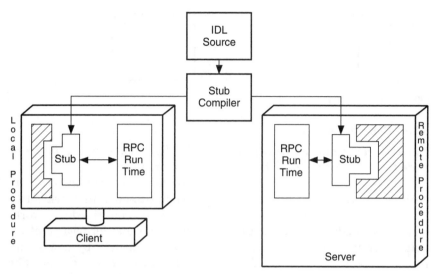

Figure 5.4 RPC implementation.

- Multithreading support for parallel and concurrent processing, and the ability to handle multiple requests simultaneously, thus reducing the time required to complete an application

- Portability and interoperability with various system environments

- Support for resources integrity and application security

The DCE implementation of remote procedure calls includes special semantics for both network transport independence and transparency. The DCE RPC includes a pipe facility to eliminate such resource limitations as inadequate main memory. ISO's X.500 standard is used to provide global directory services. The DCE RPC uses Kerberos authentication and authorization to support security service, and asynchronous threads to support concurrent and parallel processing.

More details about the RPC can be found in Chap. 8, which discusses middleware issues.

5.6 NETWORKS

A communication system was previously described as the collection of hardware and software which supports intersystem and interprocess communication between software components in distributed nodes. The actual links between nodes compose a *network,* which represents an ordered collection of physical *paths* between interconnected nodes. This chapter will introduce readers to the following aspects of networking: topology and basic network technologies.

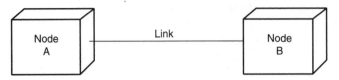

Figure 5.5 Point-to-point communication.

5.6.1 Classification

Network communications can be classified by the ability of a network node to communicate directly with one or more nodes.

Point-to-point communication allows one node to communicate only with an adjacent node. In its basic form, a point-to-point network is two directly connected nodes (see Fig. 5.5). Of course, a multinode network, where each node is connected to its adjacent node, also forms a point-to-point network. In this instance, adjacency is measured by how many logical steps it takes to get from one node to the adjacent node. For example, in Ethernet, all nodes are one logical step from each other.

A *multipoint* (multidrop) network is a network where all nodes share one line by sharing time on the line. Multidrop networks are similar to rural telephone party lines, where a user picks up a phone and checks to see if the line is occupied by someone else. If so, the user hangs up and tries again later. As the number of nodes grows, the possible delays become longer. Therefore, multidrop networks are useful where high-speed data transmission is not necessary but implementation costs are a factor. (See Fig. 5.6.)

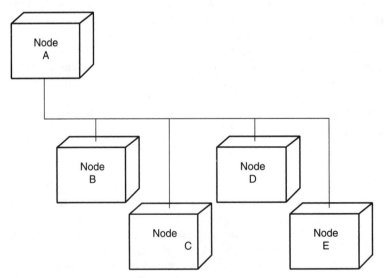

Figure 5.6 Multipoint network communication.

Network communications can also be classified by the way the messages are transmitted from node to node:

- *Broadcast networks* (mostly local area networks) are those where all nodes are connected to a common transmission medium, so that a single message can reach all nodes.

- *Store-and-forward networks* (mostly wide area networks) are those where a complete message is received into an intermediate buffer before being retransmitted toward its destination. The nodes in store-and-forward networks are interconnected by independent point-to-point transmission lines.

5.6.2 Topology

Network topology defines the basic interconnection structure of nodes and links. Topology can be viewed as the architectural drawing of the network components—the nodes (any system on a network) and the links between them. Links can be phone lines, private lines, satellite channels, etc. Basically, links can be divided into *physical* (actual, real) links and *virtual* links. Networks use virtual links to allow the sharing of the physical line by multiple network programs and data transfers. Virtual communications over physical lines are extremely valuable for providing cost-effective communications capabilities. Imagine, for example, the costs of providing a new physical line for every new network program if resource sharing via virtual links was not available. Let us review several network topologies.

A *fully connected network* is one in which each node is connected by a dedicated point-to-point link to every other node (see Fig. 5.7). Such a network is capable of high throughput, low delays, and high reliability. The main disadvantage of such a topology is its high cost. Indeed, n nodes require $n(n - 1)/2$ links, where each node must have $n - 1$ interfaces. Adding a node requires every other node to be modified.

A special case of a fully connected network is a mesh network. It has point-to-point links between some nodes. Store-and-forward transmission is required between those nodes not directly connected.

A *star* network consists of nodes that are connected to a single central switching node (see Fig. 5.8). This topology is often used when multiple terminals are connected to a central computer. The expansion costs of a star network are low, and delays should not exceed one intermediate node. The main disadvantage is poor reliability, since a central switch failure can stop all communications.

A *hierarchical* or *tree* network is a topology where one focal point is occupied by a host (central computer), which acts as a master in a master-slave relationship with the network nodes. A typical example is IBM's Systems Network Architecture (SNA) terminal network. Tree

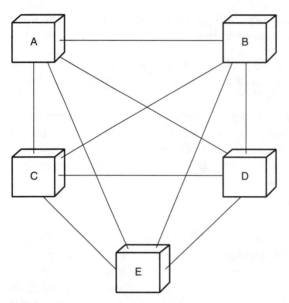

Figure 5.7 Complete interconnection.

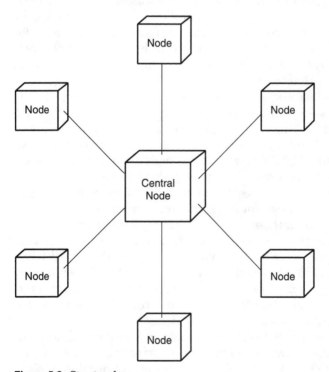

Figure 5.8 Star topology.

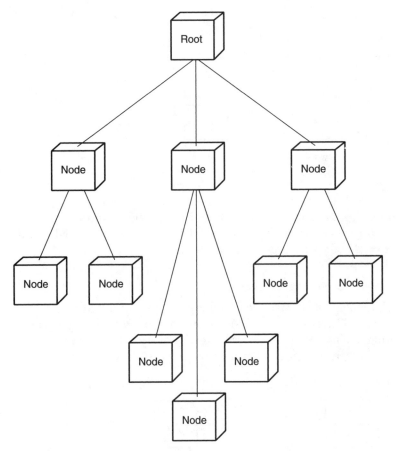

Figure 5.9 Hierarchical (tree) topology.

networks are useful for process control applications, since they reflect the hierarchical, master-slave nature of a control system. (See Fig. 5.9.)

A *bus* network is an example of a broadcast network implementation, where a shared transmission medium interconnects all nodes. Hence, the length of links and associated costs are minimized. A single interface is required to connect a new node to the network, which results in low expansion cost. Ethernet is an example of a bus network. (See Fig. 5.10.)

Note. IEEE 802 standards describe protocols that control logical links (IEEE 802.2) and media access protocols. Ethernet-like bus networks are described by the IEEE 802.3 standard.

A *ring* network consists of nodes linked to their neighbors by a unidirectional loop. Transmission can be broadcast or point-to-point. The signal is regenerated at each interface, which means that the ring

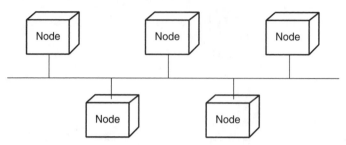

Figure 5.10 Bus topology.

length is not limited by line capacity (as in a bus network). Only one additional link is required for each additional node, and communication software does not require routing. IBM's token ring (IEEE 802.5) is an example of a ring topology. (See Fig. 5.11.)

5.6.2 Network switching techniques

Network topologies, as just discussed, illustrate that not all nodes have direct physical links between them. Therefore, a network must provide a function (relay function in ISO terminology) that switches data between links to provide a point-to-point path between some nodes.

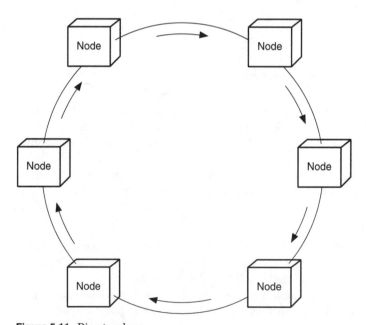

Figure 5.11 Ring topology.

There are two main switching techniques used in modern networks: circuit switching and packet switching.

A *circuit-switching* network operates by forming a dedicated connection (circuit) between two nodes (similar to a U.S. telephone system). While the circuit is in place, the sender is guaranteed that the message will be delivered to the destination. The capacity of this circuit is guaranteed; i.e., no other network activity should decrease the circuit capacity.

Packet-switched networks (usually used to connect computer systems) take a different approach. All traffic is divided into small segments (packets) that are mapped (multiplexed) into a high-capacity intersystem connection for transmission from one node to another. To implement packet-switching, packets must carry identification that allows network operating system (NOS) software to send packets to their destinations. The network hardware delivers packets to their destination, where the packets are reassembled by the network software.

The disadvantage of the packet-switching technique is that, as the activity increases, a given pair of communicating partners receives less resource capacity from the network. That is, contrary to circuit switching, the available capacity is not guaranteed. However, lower cost and high-speed networking hardware provide for high performance and wide acceptance of the packet-switching networking.

Sometimes, a message-switching technique is described as an alternative to both circuit and packet switching. It involves storing any size messages (including files) in the switching node's storage. Messages can be stored for hours or days until the destination node wishes to receive the message. This type of packet-switching technique is often implemented as an electronic mail application.

The networking functions, architecture, techniques, and characteristics discussed in this chapter will be used as a foundation for understanding local, metropolitan, and wide area networks, various standards, protocols, and particular implementations of client/server communications.

6

Local Area Networking

The proliferation of personal computers throughout organizations has resulted in the growth of PCs being used for a wide variety of business functions. It has also resulted in the ever-increasing need for personal computers to communicate. The communication needs include inter-communications among personal computers as well as communication with centralized data-processing facilities and the sources of corporate data. Several networking technologies have been developed to support this intercommunication. Among them are wide area networking, metropolitan area networking, and local area networking.

6.1 LOCAL AREA NETWORK CONCEPTS

Intelligent workstations, such as personal computers or UNIX-based technical workstations, can be used as stand-alone systems to support local applications. However, as workgroup environments become more and more popular, the reasons why these intelligent workstations should be interconnected in a network are getting more apparent. Among these reasons are:

- The need to access data stored in another, not local, system.
- The need for the members of a workgroup to share devices that are too expensive to be used by a single user only. A color PostScript laser printer is one example of such devices.

■ The need for workgroup members to exchange information electronically.

6.1.1 LAN, WAN, and MAN

The distance between network users is one of the factors that determines the required network type and, therefore, the underlying technology. One situation includes user requirements to access processing and data storage capabilities typically available from mainframes. Similarly, interconnectivity may be required by users widely separated geographically. In this case, the networking solutions may involve public telecommunication facilities for fast data interchange. The networks that tie all these users together are called *wide area networks* (WANs).

Sometimes it is useful to distinguish between wide area networks that can span remote locations at very large distances measured in hundreds and thousands of miles (e.g., users in New York, Los Angeles, and Tokyo) and networks that link users within a particular metropolitan area. Networks that operate within a city or those that can use physical telecommunications facilities typically associated with the city infrastructure (e.g., an underground cabling system), are sometimes called *metropolitan area networks* (MANs). A typical MAN provides voice, data, and video communications at speeds of 45 to 600 Mbps (million bits per second) at distances ranging from 1 to 50 miles.

Relatively short distance communication between intelligent workstations (such as personal computers) is supported by a networking technology known as *local area networks* (LAN). The Institute of Electrical and Electronics Engineers (IEEE) defines a LAN as a data communication system that allows a number of independent devices to communicate directly with each other, within a moderately sized geographic area, over a physical communication channel of moderate data rates.

Local area networks can be used for shared data, application and device access, electronic mail, process monitoring in a factory environment, and even for alarm and security systems. However, the most interesting feature of a local area network is its ability to support cooperative client/server applications, in which an application runs partly on LAN stations and partly on a LAN server or even a mainframe host, as was described in the previous chapters. Also, the range of LAN applications can be significantly extended by interconnecting several networks. LAN interconnection can be implemented over wide area networks, thus extending the communication capabilities of local area networks far beyond the traditional distance limitations of a typical LAN. At the same time, ease of use and direct interconnection typical of a LAN are still maintained.

6.1.2 LAN characteristics and components

The IEEE definition of a LAN provides LAN characteristics that distinguish local area networks from other networking technologies. Indeed:

- By allowing independent devices to communicate directly with each other, LAN supports peer communication between its nodes. This is in contrast with such centrally controlled hierarchical systems as, for example, IBM's Systems Network Architecture.

- By emphasizing a moderately sized geographic area, IEEE separates LAN from wide area networks. Typically, a LAN does not exceed a distance of about 6 miles and often is limited to a single building or a group of buildings placed close together (as in, for example, a college campus environment).

- By defining a physical communication channel with moderate data rates, IEEE contrasts LANs with wide area networks, which often use public switched communication facilities.

Moderate data rates used to imply that LAN data rates were to be slower than those of the direct mainframe links and channel-to-channel communication, measured in several million bits per second. However, with the advances in physical transmission technology, and especially the advent of the fiber-optics communications, local area networks can support data rates from 1 to 100 Mbps and higher.

A typical local area network that corresponds to the IEEE LAN definition consists of two general types of components: nodes and links between nodes. In LAN terminology, though, nodes, which can be any device attached to a network, are known as *stations*. All LAN stations are linked, or interconnected, via a *cabling system*, which includes physical communication channels (wire, cable) and any devices necessary to attach the stations to the network. For example, to avoid the loss of a signal over the length of the wire, signal regenerators, or repeaters, are sometimes installed in a LAN. (See Fig. 6.1.)

Each station must possess sufficient intelligence to handle the communication control functions. Thus, peripheral devices, such as printers and hard disk drives, are not LAN stations, but rather are attached to some of the intelligent stations.

As was illustrated in the previous chapter, networks, including local area networks, are characterized by the shape the cabling system takes—the network topology. In addition, different local area networks are characterized by:

- The *transmission medium*—the type of cable that is used in a given LAN

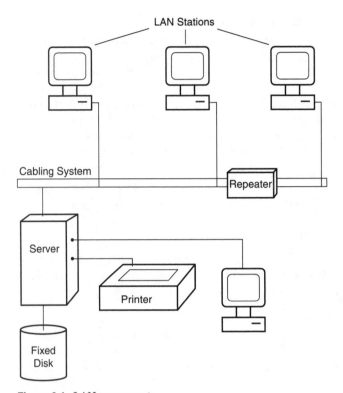

Figure 6.1 LAN components.

- The *transmission technique*—the technique that determines how the transmission medium is used for communication

- The *access control method*—the method by which LAN stations control their access to the transmission medium

These LAN characteristics are described in greater detail in the next section.

6.2   TRANSMISSION AND ACCESS CONTROL METHODS

The physical transmission of information over a local area network can be described by two main categories: the actual medium used for the transmission and the way this medium is used.

6.2.1   Transmission medium

A wide variety of physical communication links are used for the transmission of information. The telecommunication industry continues to expand the available transmission medium to achieve extremely high transmission rates while improving the costs and availability of the new physical connections.

Even though traditional media employed in conventional telecommunication applications can be used in local area networks, today's LANs are often implemented by using twisted-pair cable, coaxial cable, and fiber-optics links.

A twisted-pair cable consists of two insulated and braided strands of copper wire. Usually, such pairs form a cable by grouping pairs together and enclosing them in a common protective jacket. Typical intrabuilding telephone wiring is an example of such a cable. Relatively low cost and the high availability of such a cabling system have resulted in the popularity of the twisted-pair cable for LAN implementations. Twisted-pair cable can support transmission speeds of up to 10 Mbps.

To eliminate possible electrical interference, a twisted-pair cable can be enclosed in a special, high-quality protective sheath. Such cable is called a *shielded* twisted-pair cable and, even though slightly more expensive, it is used where higher reliability and higher transmission rates over longer distances are required. The IBM Cabling System Type 1 and 2 cables are examples of twisted-pair cables offered by a computer vendor.

Coaxial cable is familiar to television users, especially those with cable TV. Coaxial cable contains a central conducting core (usually copper) that is surrounded by the insulating material, another conductor (braided wire mesh or a solid sleeve), and yet another insulated protective and flexible jacket. Although more expensive, coaxial cable is better isolated from electrical interference than a twisted-wire pair. Coaxial cable can support transmission rates of up to 100 Mbps. DEC-connect Communication System's Thin and Standard Ethernet cables are examples of the coaxial cable used in LAN implementations.

Fiber-optic links are a relatively new transmission medium available for commercial LAN implementations. Optical fiber contains a core: an extremely thin glass cylinder, surrounded by a concentric layer of glass, called *cladding*. Optical signals take the form of modulated light beams that traverse the length of the fiber-optic link at the speed of light. The cladding is made of a material whose refractive index is lower than that of the core. Therefore, the light signals traveling along the core are reflected off the cladding back into the core. A number of such optical fibers are bound together into one fiber-optics cable, surrounded by a protective sheath. Fiber-optic cables are characterized by lighter-than-coaxial cable weights but significantly higher costs. However, the light signals transmitted over a fiber-optic cable are not subject to electrical interference. The optical transmission medium can support extremely high transmission rates—565 Mbps rates can be found in commercially available systems, and experiments have demonstrated data rates of up to 200,000 Mbps. IBM Cabling System's Type 5 cable is an example of fiber-optic cables used for a computer network.

Various implementations of these physical links can be found in a large number of commercially available cabling systems offered by general-purpose communication vendors as well as vendors of various computer networks. For example, IBM markets its own IBM Cabling System, and Digital Equipment Corporation offers the DECconnect Communication System.

6.2.2   Transmission techniques

Whatever the transmission medium employed in a given LAN environment, the LAN designer must select a technique the LAN will use to transmit signals over a physical communication link. In general, there are two available transmission techniques for the transmission over a physical communication channel: *baseband* and *broadband.*

Baseband transmission uses discrete signals (pulses of electricity or light that represent a binary 0 and 1) to carry information over a physical transmission medium. Such a signaling technique is called *digital signaling.* Baseband transmission uses the entire communication channel capacity to transmit a single data signal. Since multiple stations attached to a network have to share a common communication channel, a technique known as *time-division multiplexing* (TDM) is usually employed to allow attached stations to transmit signals one at a time.

One of the concerns with digital transmission is that as a signal travels along a channel it may get weaker, its form gets distorted, and the receiving station may have difficulty recognizing and interpreting the signal. In other words, the difference between a 0 and a 1 may become insufficient to distinguish between the two. Special devices—repeaters—are strategically placed along the route of a signal to overcome the signal deterioration problem. Repeaters totally regenerate the signal and retransmit it toward its destination.

Broadband transmission typically employs nondiscrete (analog) signals that are continuously transmitted over a transmission medium in the form of electromagnetic waves. Discrete information is encoded into analog waves by using amplitude, frequency, or phase modulation of the base (carrier) signal. In radio transmission, amplitude modulation is known as AM and frequency modulation as FM. In general, the higher the frequency of the carrier signal, the higher the volume of information that can be carried by this signal. The difference between the highest and the lowest frequencies that are carried over the channel reflects that channel's information-carrying capacity and is referred to as the channel *bandwidth.* The bandwidth is directly related to another measurement of channel capacity: the number of bits per second that can be carried over the channel, known as the *data rate.*

Similar to the time-division multiplexing of baseband transmission, analog broadband transmission employs *frequency-division multiplexing* (FDM), which divides available bandwidth into multiple communication channels. Some of these channels can be used for data transmission, while others can be employed for video, fax, or telephone transmissions simultaneously.

The majority of information transmitted in LAN environments is data—digital, discrete signals. When a broadband transmission is used, the digital signals must be converted into analog form by modulating the analog carrier signal. At the receiving station, these signals must be converted back (demodulated) into the original digital form. The modulation-demodulation process is performed by devices known as *modems* (modulator-demodulator). Various encoding schemes are employed by LANs to represent discrete 0s and 1s. Some of the better-known encoding schemes are the Electronic Industry Association's RS-232-C and zero-complemented differential encoding used in IBM's high-performance Synchronous Data Link Control (SDLC).

6.2.3 Transmission control

In general, various transmission control methods can be classified as:

- *Centralized control,* where one station controls the entire network and gives other stations permission to transmit.

- *Random control,* which allows any LAN station to transmit without being given specific permission.

- *Distributed control,* which gives the right to transmit to only one station at a time. The right to transmit is passed from one station to the next. All stations cooperate to control access to the network.

Each transmission control method offers its own advantages and disadvantages and has access control methods designed specifically to work best with that particular transmission control. For example, centralized transmission control provides for easier network coordination and management and requires simple station-to-network interfaces. At the same time, centralized transmission control, by definition, provides a single point of failure, and the central control point can prove to be a bottleneck. Access control methods are designed to facilitate and employ various transmission controls. Centralized control may employ the following access control methods:

- *Polling.* One station (master) sends a question-notification to all other (secondary) stations indicating that a given station is allowed to transmit. If the receiving (polled) station has a message to transmit, it sends the message to the master station. In turn, the master station forwards the message to its destination. While the polled station is being listened to, the secondary station is allowed to transmit more than one message, if there are other messages and enough time to transmit them.

- *Circuit switching* can be used successfully in a centralized control LAN implemented using a star topology. Here, a central station receives requests for a transmission from a secondary station and establishes a connection (circuit) between the sender and its intended receiver. Circuit switching is widely used in telephony, especially in private branch exchanges (PBXs).

- *Time-division multiple access (TDMA)* provides a specific time slot for each station on a network. The station is allowed to transmit only during this time slot. The time cycle is started and synchronized by a master station. TDMA can be successfully used on a bus LAN topology.

One of the best-known access control techniques for random transmission control is *carrier sense multiple access with collision detection* (CSMA/CD). It is one of the most commonly used LAN access methods, is employed by the Ethernet, and is also defined as one of the IEEE LAN standards. In CSMA/CD, before a station can transmit, it must listen to the network to determine whether or not another station is transmitting (sense the carrier). If the network is silent, the station can transmit its message, which arrives at every other station. Only those stations whose addresses are indicated in the message will actually receive the message.

It is conceivable, however, that two or more stations may transmit their messages simultaneously, resulting in message collision. If this happens, the receiving stations ignore the garbled messages, while the transmitting stations attempt to resend the messages. To avoid repeated collision, each transmitting station waits a period of time, determined by a random number generated by the station, before it transmits again. In light message traffic, CSMA/CD is very efficient and access to the transmission medium is fast. Heavy message traffic, however, leads to an increased number of collisions. As a result, access method efficiency and network performance deteriorate.

Distributed transmission control can be supported by such well-known access control methods as *token passing* and *carrier sense multiple access with collision avoidance* (CSMA/CA).

Token-ring passing is most widely used in ring topology networks (e.g., IBM's Token Ring). A token is a small message that is constantly circulating around the ring. Token passing can be used in bus or tree topology. Token bus methods are similar to those of a token ring, emulating the token-ring method on a logical topology level.

When a token that is marked "free" is received by a station, the station can transmit a message. Whenever a station transmits a message, it appends the message with a token marked "busy." Each station that should receive the message copies the message and updates the token's bits to indicate whether or not the station received the message. Finally, the message gets back to the sender. The sender station resets the token to "free" and removes the message. Token passing guarantees that each station has a chance to transmit at least one message during a predetermined period of time. The main disadvantage of the token-passing technique is its complexity and token processing overhead.

CSMA/CA is very similar to CSMA/CD access methods. Each station listens to the carrier while a transmission from one of the stations is in progress (if any). When the line is free, the stations begin to transmit their messages in the order of the station priorities assigned to them. In order to avoid potential message collisions, each station waits for a specific period of time before it begins the transmission.

When designing local area networks, many interdependent factors should be taken into consideration: the transmission medium, transmission control and access methods, network topology, bandwidth, and data rates. All these factors affect network performance and cost. Decisions regarding network topology, transmission control, and access control methods should be made based on the processing and cost requirements of a particular LAN.

6.3   IEEE 802 ARCHITECTURE

The IEEE plays a major role in defining LAN standards. Specifically, the IEEE has undertaken a special project, Project 802, that has as its goal the development of a flexible network architecture oriented specifically to local area networks.

6.3.1   LAN standards and IEEE Project 802

The IEEE has attempted to define LAN architecture in conformance with the ISO's Open System Interconnection architecture, described in the previous chapter. However, the scope of IEEE Project 802 is limited to only the two lowest OSI layers—the physical layer and the data link layer (see Fig. 6.2). The functions performed by the higher OSI layers are left up to individual LAN vendors and even users.

These functions are provided by a network operating system (NOS). The NOS is typically implemented as a software product that is capa-

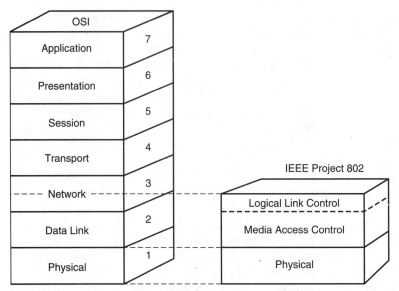

Figure 6.2   OSI and IEEE Project 802.

ble of performing print server, file server, and electronic mail support (functions of the highest-application OSI layer); internetworking connectivity; and network management support (functions of the OSI session, transport, and network layers).

Since a single standard capable of meeting all LAN requirements was very difficult to define, the approach taken by IEEE Project 802 was to develop sets, or families, of standards. These sets of standards are organized in a hierarchical, treelike set of layers that correspond to the architected LAN layers. (See Fig. 6.3.)

IEEE Project 802 defines a single standard for the logical link control layer: IEEE 802.2. Physical layer standards include twisted-pair cable, coaxial, and fiber-optic cables, together with transmission types, encoding methods, and data rates. The media access control and physical layers are described by multiple IEEE 802 standards. Some of them are listed as follows.

6.3.2   IEEE 802.2: logical link control layer

The LAN logical link control layer is described by the IEEE 802.2 standard. This standard is a common element in all IEEE 802 standards. As the root of the IEEE 802 hierarchy, IEEE 802.2 isolates the higher layers of a network architecture from the specifics of a particular LAN implementation. The IEEE 802.2 standard defines both service interface specifications and peer-to-peer protocols. It is responsible for the

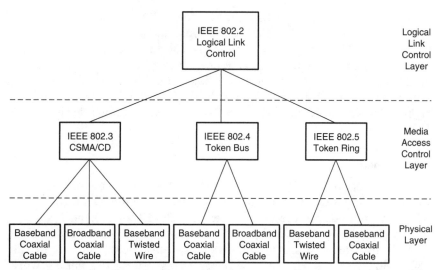

Figure 6.3 IEEE Project 802 Layers

exchange of protocol-specific control signals between LAN stations. Among the other functions defined by IEEE 802.2 are data flow organization, command interpretation, generation of responses, and error control and recovery.

6.3.3 Media access control layers and IEEE 802.3

The media access control (MAC) layers of the IEEE 802 standards are designed to support multiple devices that compete for access to a single physical transmission medium. The MAC layer defines the rules that stations must obey in order to share a common transmission medium. The media access control standard contains these functions:

- Media access management functions are used to control the sharing of transmission media among all stations in a network.

- A framing function identifies the beginning and end of a message by adding header and trailer information. Framing facilitates sender-receiver synchronization, routing, and error detection.

- An addressing function identifies devices participating in the sending and receiving of messages and determines the appropriate network addresses.

- An error detection function ensures that a message has been transmitted and received correctly.

IEEE Project 802 identified the carrier sense multiple access with collision detection (CSMA/CD), token-bus, and token-ring access control methods to support MAC standards. All three access control methods, described previously, interface with the same logical link control standard—IEEE 802.2. Project 802 has named its chosen access control methods as IEEE 802.3, IEEE 802.4, and IEEE 802.5, respectively. The first MAC method—CSMA/CD—is best known for its use in Ethernet networks.

6.3.4   Ethernet

Ethernet networks originated from the LAN development work performed by Xerox Corporation at its Palo Alto Research Center (PARC). The Ethernet design was very successful, and Ethernet specifications, jointly defined by Digital Equipment Corporation, Intel Corporation, and Xerox Corporation, provided a substantial contribution to the IEEE 802.3 standard. Many vendors today offer Ethernet network products that are compatible with various operating systems and the IEEE 802.3 standard. For instance, both Ethernet and IEEE 802.3 offer data encapsulation/decapsulation and data encoding/decoding. IEEE 802.3's media access management and physical medium attachment functions correspond to Ethernet link management and channel access management.

Ethernet is designed to provide network simplicity, low cost, flexibility and compatibility between different Ethernet implementations, high speed, low delay, stability, and maintainability of Ethernet-based LANs. Usually, Ethernet supports baseband transmission at a data rate of 10 Mbps, with a maximum cable length of 500 meters (approximately 1650 feet).

6.3.5   IEEE 802.4: token-bus standard

The IEEE 802.4 standard is one of the two IEEE 802 token-passing-based standards. IEEE 802.4 defines a token-passing standard for LANs implemented on a physical bus topology. In the IEEE 802.4 token-bus control method, each station knows the address of the station from which a token is received (predecessor) and the address of a station to which it must transmit a token (successor). An IEEE 802.4 token is passed (transmitted) from one station to the next. When the token is received, the station is allowed to transmit messages for a predefined amount of time. When the time limit has been reached, or a station has no messages to transmit, the transmitting station sends the token to the next station. Even though the physical topology of the IEEE 802.3 network takes the form of a bus, the logical operation is in the form of a logical ring (see Fig. 6.4).

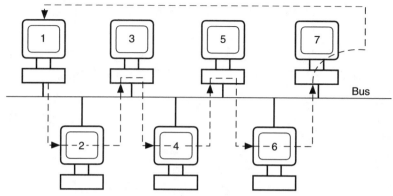

Figure 6.4 IEEE 802.4 token-passing bus. Note: The path of the token is shown as the dotted line. Station 1 initiates the token.

The IEEE 802.4 standard supports data rates from 1 Mbps up to 10 Mbps. General Motors' Manufacturing Automation Protocol (MAP) is an example of a networking architecture based on the IEEE 802.4 standard.

6.3.6 IEEE 802.5: token-ring standard

The IEEE 802.5 token-ring standard uses a logical model similar to the IEEE 802.4 token-bus architecture.

The IEEE 802.5 token-ring architecture consists of a logical ring implemented using a physical ring topology. Transmission of tokens and messages flows in a single direction (see Fig. 6.5). Information units are passed from one station to the next, and each station acts as a repeater.

Similar to the IEEE 802.4, in a token-ring network the right to transmit is controlled by a token. It is said that a *free* token is one that allows the station to transmit. When one of the stations that needs to send messages receives a free token, it changes the token to a *busy* state and is allowed to transmit messages for a predefined amount of time. The busy token is included by a transmitting station as part of a message. When the time limit is reached, the transmitting station transmits the token and a message to the next station. Each station receiving a message checks the message address to see if it has to process the message.

As the message travels around the ring, its originator finally receives it, changes the token to a free token, and removes the message. Besides station addresses, tokens can contain message priorities. The IEEE 802.5 standard specifies a baseband transmission technique over a twisted-pair cable with data rates of up to 4 Mbps, and over a coaxial

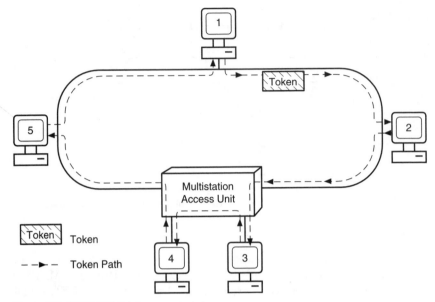

Figure 6.5   IEEE 802.5 token-passing ring.

cable with data rates of up to 40 Mbps. The IEEE 802.5 is the basis for IBM's widely used token-ring local area networks.

6.4   INTER-LAN CONNECTIVITY

Local area networks allow a group of computer users to communicate with one another and to share data, services, and devices. LANs are ideal for workgroup environments and client/server implementation on a geographically small scale. However, in reality, users of different local area networks need to communicate and share information with members of workgroups other than their own. Therefore, it is often necessary to interconnect existing LANs.

Local area networks can be interconnected directly or through higher-level networks—MANs and WANs. When interconnecting local area networks or LAN segments, several methods can be used.

6.4.1   Repeaters

Repeaters are the simplest method for network interconnection. A repeater's functionality is limited to interconnecting individual segments of similar smaller networks to form a larger network. Typically, repeaters are used in bus LAN topology.

6.4.2 Bridges

Bridges can interconnect networks that support different transmission protocols (i.e., CSMA/CD LAN and token-ring LAN). A bridge between two LANs receives messages from both networks, checks their destinations, and transmits the messages to the required LAN. Since messages are stored in the bridge system before retransmission, bridges are said to implement a store-and-forward technique. To properly handle messages, a bridge must know and understand the addressing scheme used on both networks. From the point of view of the OSI reference model, bridges operate at the physical and data link layers.

6.4.3 Routers

Routers perform the network layer functions of the OSI reference model. A router routes the message from the source node to the destination node through intermediate nodes. In this case, two addresses—the next node on the route and the final destination node—should accompany the message. The first address changes from one station to another along the route, while the second address remains constant. For a router to be able to work, the interconnected networks must be compatible at network and higher OSI layers (layers 3 and above), but may be different at the physical and data link layers. A key function of the router is determining the next node (station) to which a message is to be sent. (See Fig. 6.6.)

6.4.4 Gateways

Gateways are used to interconnect networks that may be built on entirely different architectures. Thus, gateways implement functions of all seven layers of the OSI model. Gateways handle any message, address, and protocol conversions necessary to deliver a message from one network to another. Gateways offer the greatest flexibility in internetworking communication. This flexibility comes at the cost of higher price and more complex design, implementation, maintenance, and operation of gateways. (See Fig. 6.7.)

6.4.5 Intelligent hubs

The intelligent hub can be described as a "LAN in a box." This device combines the features of a wiring hub, a multiprotocol router, and a network management station. Such a device can replace a backbone network and interconnect different media access control networks, including Ethernet, AppleTalk, and FDDI. As a result, the intelligent hub provides LAN-to-WAN routing and simplifies the management of a complex LAN environment. (See Fig. 6.8.)

TCP	Transport	Router			Transport	TCP
IP	Network	IP			Network	IP
Ethernet	Data link	Ethernet	LAP-B		Data link	LAP-B
	Physical		RS-232		Physical	RS-232
Ethernet cable			RS-232 cable			

(a)

TCP/IP						TCP/IP
IEEE 802.2	Data link				Data link	IEEE 802.2
IEEE 802.3		Bridge				IEEE 802.3
	Physical	IEEE 802.3			Physical	
Ethernet cable			10 BaseT wire			

(b)

Figure 6.6 Comparison between bridges and routers: (a) router; (b) bridge.

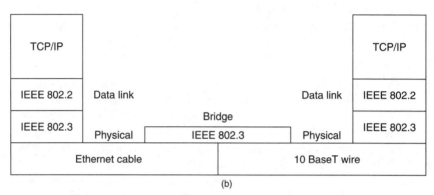

Gateway

		Routing, conversion and relaying			
X.411 MTP	Application	X.411 MTP	DIA DCA		DIA DCA
X.410 RTS	Presentation	X.410 RTS	Function management		Function management
X.225 BAS	Session	X.225 BAS			
X.224/C.O.	Transport	X.224/C.O.	Transmission control		Transmission control
X.25/PLP	Network	X.25/PLP	Path control		Path control
X.25 LAPB	Data link	X.25 LAPB	SDLC		SDLC
X.21	Physical	X.21	V.27		V.27
OSI media			SNA WAN media		

Figure 6.7 Gateway between OSI and SNA networks.

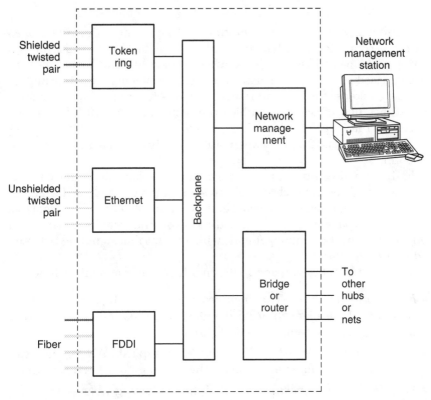

Figure 6.8 Intelligent hub.

6.5 HIGH-SPEED LAN

Conventional LAN technologies have been deployed practically every-
where to solve real local area network connectivity problems. However,
as is true with all technologies, eventually business requirements for
performance, throughput, scaleability, and connectivity outgrow the
conventional LAN technologies. Specifically, forces that make conventional LAN speeds obsolete include:

- Applications such as data warehouse, CAD/CAM, and multimedia
- The global, widely distributed nature of the businesses
- Topologies that span LAN and WAN

This section focuses on several LAN technologies designed for speeds
that are orders of magnitude higher than the conventional 10 or 16
Mbps.

6.5.1   FDDI

The *Fiber Distributed Data Interface* (FDDI) is already widely used in large computer installations that require LAN bandwidth of 100 +Mbps. The basic FDDI architecture is a token-passing structure that is composed of one or two rings—the latter implemented with counter-rotating tokens. Such an approach provides full redundancy for fault resistance and effectively doubles the bandwidth to 200 Mbps in the absence of failure. The dual ring can support up to 1000 stations over distances of about 2 km between stations, with overall fiber length of 200 km.

FDDI provides support for management functions, including connection management, which coordinates the physical and media access control components; entity coordination management, which controls an optical bypass switch to isolate the ring during troubleshooting; and physical connection management, which maintains signaling between adjacent stations.

The main benefits of using FDDI in a LAN environment include:

- *Fiber-optic capacity.*   This includes current 100 Mbps in each direction (for a dual-fiber cable), with a reasonable possibility of achieving much higher speeds in the near future.

- *Low signal loss per unit of fiber length.*   A typical LAN segment can extend several kilometers without the need for additional repeaters.

- *Very low noise transmission.*   A light-conducting fiber is virtually unaffected by the external electrical and magnetic interference.

- *Relatively high degree of security.*   It is very difficult to tap into the FDDI network without interrupting communications.

A major drawback of FDDI is its still relatively high (although continuously declining) cost.

A new FDDI standard is being defined to include additional capabilities. Called the fiber-optic follow-on LAN (FFOL), this standard will offer an improved link between LANs and the evolving technologies of SONET, ATM, SMDS, and B-ISDN (Broadband Integrated Services Digital Networks), improved performance, bidirectional data, and shortest-path routing.

6.5.2   100-Mbps Ethernet

Many Ethernet users complain about its relatively low effective speed. To address this requirement, the IEEE Ethernet standards committee is looking for a faster Ethernet that can produce FDDI-like transfer rates at a cost that is only fractionally higher than the standard 10Base-T Ethernet (based on twisted-pair cable).

From the wiring standpoint, the 100-Mbps Ethernet will be compatible with unshielded twisted-pair (UTP) installations. The issue of what particular type of UTP can support the new, higher transmission speed resulted in two approaches being considered for the 100-Mbps standard. Hewlett-Packard proposes a version called *100Base-VG* (voice grade) that is based on a demand priority access schema through a packet-switch hub. The counterproposal (from Grand Junction, Union City, California) specifies a more traditional CSMA/CD mode of Ethernet, but enhances that with the electrical attachment technique of FDDI.

6.5.3   Asynchronous transfer mode (ATM)

Asynchronous transfer mode is a packet-switching architecture designed to transfer data at very high speeds with a minimum of delays. ATM is the foundation of a number of WAN technologies (i.e., B-ISDN).

ATM uses small, fixed-length (53 bytes) packets called *cells.* Each cell consists of a 5-byte header and 48-byte information field. The primary role of the header is to specify the virtual path (similar to the virtual circuit) that allows fast hardware switching, reduces complexity, and adds capacity to a given virtual path by increasing the number of virtual channels allocated to it.

The fixed cell size is a compromise aimed to minimize the switch delay—variable-length packets like the ones used in X.25 and frame relay would be more effective for data transmission, but would also increase the complexity of the network switches, switching delays, and thus reduce the overall efficiency.

Like frame relay, ATM relies on the very high quality and low error rate performance of the transmission media to support speeds of up to 155 Mbps.

Network-grade ATM systems employ hardware technology to provide switched virtual circuits. Operating at gigabit-per-second (Gbps) speeds, the carrier-operated ATM switches should minimize latency within the nodes, while allowing any type of service to traverse the network in an efficient matter.

Using ATM for LAN connectivity provides a number of benefits, among which are the ability to interconnect LANs without the backbone network, protocol integration of various transmission protocols (ATM can support a wide variety of data and other services), and the potential for integrated network management services.

6.6   LAN-WAN INTERCONNECTION

From the connectivity standpoint, a general client/server system relies on public network services to interconnect LANs and WANs. The services used for the LAN-WAN interconnection can be grouped into the fixed-bandwidth services (i.e., T1 and SONET) and the bandwidth-on-demand services (frame relay and ATM). The list of services includes:

- Dial-up telephone service over a public switch telephone network
- Virtual private networks (VPN)
- Very small aperture terminals (VSATs)
- Packet-switched networks
- ISDN basic rate interface
- Fractional and full T1/E1
- Frame relay
- Switched multimegabit data service (SMDS)
- Asynchronous transfer mode (ATM)
- Broadband Integrated Services Digital Network (B-ISDN)

Some of these services are very briefly described here for completeness.

Fixed-bandwidth service. Fixed-bandwidth services provide point-to-point links at constant data rates. T1 provides data transmission rates of 1.544 Mbps and E1, 2.048 Mbps, with T1 consisting of twenty-four 64-Kbps channels, and E1 consisting of 32 channels. Even though the bandwidth is fixed, it is frequently subdivided (fractional T1/E1) to suit the particular needs of the users. T1 and E1 channels are leased from a telecommunication service provider or installed through a privately owned cable, microwave, or satellite link. An organization may purchase, install, and operate the appropriate multiplexers at multiple locations, typically where the variety of traffic can be aggregated. Even though the bandwidth on each link is fixed, the T1/E1 channels can be subdivided and rearranged to suit a variety of business needs. This can be done at any time by reconfiguring databases in each multiplexer.

The new standard for fixed-bandwidth transmission over fiber-optic cables was introduced by Bell Communications Research (BellCore) as the *Synchronous Optical Network* (SONET). It was adopted by ANSI in 1988 and further refined in 1990. Portions of the SONET standard have been adopted into the international Synchronous Digital Hierarchy (SDH) standard. SONET (and SDH) define an optical interface standard that allows internetworking of transmission products from different vendors on the same link. The standard defines a physical interface, optical line rates known as *optical carrier* (OC) signals, frame format, and a protocol for service management. The base rate (OC-1) is 51.84 Mbps, and higher rates are multiples of the base. For example, OC-3 is 155.520 Mbps, and the OC-48 (highest defined) is 2488.320 Mbps, or 2.48 Gbps.

Bandwidth-on-demand. The basic principle of bandwidth-on-demand is to allow the application to feed data to the network at the desired speed when it needs to. When the application network access is idle, other users can use the network switching and transmission infrastructure. Services that appear to have dedicated connectivity can actually be implemented through bandwidth-on-demand, provided there are idle periods or the information can be transmitted as periodic portions within a fixed time frame. The bandwidth-on-demand services originated with the U.S. government-sponsored ARPAnet, and became widely available from commercial service providers of packet-switched networks like Tymnet. The bandwidth of these earlier services was generally restricted to 56 Kbps or less, which is clearly inadequate for today's voice, video, and high-volume data transmission needs.

One of the first initiatives to provide greater bandwidth-on-demand is generally referred to as the *Integrated Services Digital Network* or ISDN. The most common implementations of ISDN in the United States provide two 64-Kbps circuit-switched channels and one 16-Kbps packet-switched channel, and are aimed at replacing traditional analog telephone. ISDN is also adopted and widely available in Europe and Japan. One of the most popular nontelephone applications of ISDN in France, for example, is PC-to-PC file transfer at the rate of 64 Kbps.

A version of ISDN called *Broadband ISDN* or B-ISDN is designed to address the higher bandwidth requirements of today's communications systems. The basic philosophy behind B-ISDN is to provide virtually any voice, data, and video services to the home or business over a public network. This, of course, requires a high-speed switching technology capable of transporting narrow band services (i.e., ISDN) like voice and low-speed data together with video conferencing and the full-motion-video requirements of cable TV. Such capabilities can be enabled through an underlying protocol stack like ATM.

Another example of bandwidth-on-demand services is *frame relay,* which is an interface standard defined under OSI and ISDN.

Frame relay is a relatively mature network standard with high bandwidth potential. The protocol functions at layer 2 of the OSI model, and provides a connection-oriented service called *permanent virtual circuit* (PVC). Access to the frame relay network is provided at multiples of 64 Kbps or T1/E1 speeds. This positions frame relay as a cost-effective, high-performance bandwidth-on-demand service, and as an interface option providing point-to-point PVCs on networks like ATM.

Frame relay technology is particularly valuable to diverse data communication needs because the protocols support statistical multiplexing inherent in fast packet switching—the protocol allocates logical channels to obtain additional bandwidth, up to the entire available spectrum, as needed. Therefore, several users can obtain needed variable-rate channels by sharing a fixed rate T1/E1 via frame relay. What's even more important, the bandwidth flexibility is well suited for client/server applications characterized by bursty traffic.

Switched Multimegabits Data Service (SMDS) is an outgrowth of the IEEE 802.6 standard. It provides high-speed cell switching using the same 53-byte cells selected for ATM. SMDS emphasizes the transmission of bursty traffic over a short period of time. Both SMDS and frame relay are targeted toward that LAN-to-LAN interconnectivity market. Some of the differences between the two include:

- *Speed.* Frame relay supports speed in the range of 64 Kbps to E1, while SMDS works in the range from T1/E1 to T3.

- *Coverage.* Even though both services can be national and/or global, it seems that frame relay is promoted by the long distance service providers, while SMDS is promoted by local telephone companies, thus narrowing the coverage from the metropolitan to national.

- *Connection type.* Frame relay is connection-oriented, compatible with X.25, and, as such, supports frame-based PVCs, while SMDS is connectionless, cell-based service similar to ATM.

6.7   WIRELESS LAN

LAN cables and their installation and maintenance are expensive. For each of the two predominant standards—IEEE 802.3 (Ethernet) and IEEE 802.5 (token ring)—many different wiring standards have been developed to meet various user requirements.

Wireless technology offers an alternative to expensive copper and fiber media, and is an attractive option for mobile computing. This alternative is often attractive for land-based local area networks since in most LAN environments the network bandwidth is rarely utilized to the full extent. Therefore, general wireless technology is a viable alternative where the LAN traffic is light to medium and where the number of users is small. This section will provide a brief look at some of the technology options for wireless LAN implementations.

6.7.1   Microwave

As their customer base continued to grow, the telephone companies began to make extensive use of microwave transmission technology, especially after the technology was successfully used in military applications.

Advances in microwave technology such as short-haul microwave allow antennas to be smaller. Short-haul microwave can transmit to 5 to 10 miles without repeaters, while long-haul microwave can transmit for distances in excess of 30 miles without repeaters. Of course, microwave transmissions are line-of-sight transmissions, and any obstacles to the direct line of sight will severely affect the transmission quality. The same is true for the weather conditions—extensive rain, sand storms, and heavy fog can interfere with the microwave signal.

Microwave technology represents the ability for an end user to own and operate its own end-to-end transmission facility, and thus bypass a local (and sometimes even the long-haul) communication carrier. Throughout the 1980s, microwave transmissions connected LANs on campuses and metropolitan areas. Today, microwave is used extensively for voice and data transmissions in cellular telephone systems. It is popular in large cities, where the transmitter can sit on top of a very tall building. In addition, the technology is often used as a backup link to the primary fiber-optics link.

6.7.2 Infrared

Infrared is a line-of-sight technology whereby one or more infrared devices relay their light beam back and forth to each other. Infrared technology can take advantage of the reflection of the light beam off the walls or other solid objects, similar to the remote control units of VCRs and TVs. Therefore, many vendors design their products to use reflection (i.e., a common spot on the wall or the ceiling) for LAN traffic. The infrared technology can operate at speeds of about 4 Mbps, and infrared LANs can support both MS Windows and Apple Macintosh worlds. Unlike microwave, infrared technology does not require FCC licensing.

6.7.3 Satellite

Satellite transmission, as it relates to telecommunications, is traditionally used to carry voice traffic. Like many other forms of wireless technology, satellite communications evolved from the extensive and successful use by the military for the weather forecasting, intelligence-gathering applications, and secure communications. Commercial businesses adopted satellite technology for a variety of applications, ranging from TV broadcasting to financial data transmissions to global paging and personal communications. In addition, businesses are always attracted to a technology that can save costs by bypassing local phone carriers (this is true for several wireless technologies, including microwave and infrared).

Satellite transmission brings a number of benefits to various applications. It is an excellent backup technology for designing backup and recovery strategy for a global network of primarily land-based components. Satellite can be used as a supplemental link for load balancing across WANs.

The two forms of satellite transmission are C-band and Ku-band. C-band is best suited for wide area coverage for multipoint communications. Ku-band is less susceptible to ground microwave communications, which makes it better suited for focused point-to-point coverage within metropolitan areas. The stronger signal of Ku-band allows for smaller, less expensive equipment to be located within metropolitan city limits. An example of a Ku-band application is a large retail store chain that relies on satellite transmission to link its point-of-sale terminals to remote data center systems.

6.7.4 Spread-Spectrum

Spread-spectrum radio transmission was used originally by the military in World War II for its antieavesdropping and antijamming capabilities. Spread-spectrum occupies three fixed radio frequency bands allocated by the FCC. The two primary forms of spread-spectrum are direct sequence and frequency hopping. *Direct sequence* is the ability to send a modulated (encoded) signal across several frequencies (spectrum) rather than just one. The ability to use multiple frequencies is good for security, since the receiver has to be configured to recognize the same frequency pattern as the sender. Since the spectrum is unique for a given system, two different spread-spectrum systems can broadcast across the same range of frequencies without interference.

Frequency hopping happens when the system forces the modulated signal to hop from one frequency to another. The receiving device must be in sync with the sender and must know the exact sequence of the frequency changes.

Currently, this technology is limited by its low power to distances of about 800 feet, supporting about 200 wireless nodes on the network. On the plus side, however, the technology can broadcast through walls, ceilings, and floors.

6.8 CONCLUSION

Both wired and wireless LANs have a critical role in enterprise networks, especially as relating to client/server computing. Wired LANs continue to improve their bandwidth and coverage. Wireless LANs are cost effective, flexible, and relatively easy to implement within their bandwidth limitations and the number of nodes that can be supported. Systems designers should be aware of and consider all available options in order to make appropriate business and technology decisions.

TCP/IP and SNA

Network architectures, such as the ISO's OSI, IBM's SNA, Digital's DNA, and TCP/IP, are designed to make the logical view of the communications network independent of its physical implementation. The OSI model, described in Chap. 5, deals primarily with the interconnection between systems and provides a generalized view of a layered network architecture. Various local area network architectures use the OSI model as a reference and conform with the OSI standards. In addition to the LAN standards and architectures critical for the client/server implementations in local area network environments, there are several network implementations so widely accepted that they have become de facto networking standards and are often used successfully in the client/server implementations based on these network architectures.

7.1 TRANSMISSION CONTROL PROTOCOL/INTERNET PROTOCOL (TCP/IP)

While IBM's SNA was developed primarily to satisfy the networking and communication requirements of IBM system users, significant research efforts have been made in developing technologies that allow disparate, heterogeneous physical networks to interconnect. The majority of this research was sponsored by various U.S. government agencies.

These organizations were first to realize and appreciate the importance and potential of network interconnection, sometimes called *internetworking,* or *Internet.* The leading Internet technology has resulted from the research funded by the Defense Advanced Research Projects Agency (DARPA). This technology, known as the Transmission Control Protocol/Internet Protocol (TCP/IP), includes a set of networking standards that specify the details of computer communications as well as conventions for network interconnection and network traffic routing.

7.1.1 TCP/IP internetworking

TCP/IP forms the base technology for a large Internet connecting major research establishments, universities, and government agencies. The result is the Internet, which connects, among others, such well-known entities as the National Science Foundation (NSF), the Department of Energy (DOE), the Department of Defense (DOD), the Health and Human Services Agency, and the National Aeronautics and Space Administration (NASA).

TCP/IP differs from other network protocols in the following features:

- *Network technology independence.* By design, TCP/IP is independent of any particular vendor's hardware. TCP/IP defines how information transmission units (datagrams) are to be transmitted on a particular network.

- *Any-to-any interconnection.* This allows any pair of computer systems to communicate with each other by assigning a unique address to each system that is recognizable throughout the Internet.

- *Source-destination acknowledgment.* TCP/IP supports end-to-end acknowledgment between the source and the ultimate destination of the message, even if the source and the destination reside in physically separate networks.

7.1.2 TCP/IP protocols

TCP/IP is a four-layer communication architecture that can be conceptually described as a hierarchy built on a physical network interface that provides communication interfaces to the network hardware (see Fig. 7.1).

The layer above the network services is referred to as the Internet protocol (IP) layer. It is a connectionless service that deals with the delivery of information packets. (It is connectionless because it treats each packet independently from all others.) The IP is essentially a datagram service designed to satisfy the following:

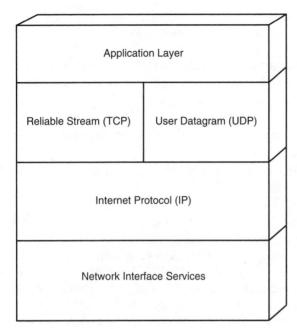

Figure 7.1 TCP/IP architecture.

- Definition of a basic unit of data transmission, used throughout the TCP/IP network

- Routing of data packets, including routing between dissimilar network architectures (for example, between IEEE 802.3 LAN and X.25 WAN)

- Best-effort (but not guaranteed) information delivery

IP includes the rules on how the packets should be processed, how and when error messages should be generated, and the conditions under which packets should be discarded, but IP, by design, does not guarantee delivery of data.

Guaranteed delivery, data concurrency, and sequencing are the responsibilities of the transmission control protocol (TCP) layer. In addition, TCP takes care of error checking, retransmission, and connection to applications on other systems.

TCP is a connection-oriented protocol, which uses connections between two points, and not individual end points, as its fundamental concept.

7.1.3 Addressing, sockets, and sequencing

TCP/IP was built primarily to allow a connection from a particular program on a particular node on a particular network to a remote program residing on a network node that may or may not be in the same network. The networks in question could be (and usually are) from different vendors.

To solve this interconnection problem, TCP/IP uses the following addressing mechanism that allows for delivery of information packets across dissimilar network architectures:

- Each program (known as a *process* in TCP) is assigned a unique address on each system—a local address.

- This unique local address is then combined with the particular node address to form a *port* address.

Processes by themselves are not TCP connection end points. TCP defines end points to be a pair (host, port), where the *host* is the IP address for the host and the port is a TCP port on that host.

Another important component of a TCP/IP network is a *socket*. Sockets are the basis for network I/O built in UNIX environments based on the Berkeley Software Distribution operating system. Sockets can be viewed as the result of a combination of the port address with the local network address.

A typical TCP/IP network may contain a large number of sockets, but each socket uniquely identifies one specific application on a specific node on a specific network. Through the socket mechanism, IP can get packets to the proper nodes where TCP will then deliver the packets to the proper program (process) on that node.

Two sockets that wish to connect to each other must use a particular mechanism to establish such a connection. TCP, being a connection-oriented protocol, provides several such mechanisms. One of the more common ways for TCP to establish a connection is by using an *active* or *passive* network *open*. When a socket that wishes to receive data declares itself open and available for incoming traffic, it is a *passive open*. A passive open may even be *fully specified*, which means that the socket that issued a passive open tells the network which socket may connect to it.

Unlike the passive open, the *active open* socket attempts to find a socket it wishes to connect with. An active open can be successful only if the requested socket cooperates by being a passive or an active open.

To establish a connection that supports correct synchronization between two end points, TCP uses a three-way *handshake*. The three-way handshake works as follows:

- The requestor of the connection sends a synchronization signal and an initial sequence number to the destination end point.

- A receiver receives the synchronization signal (segment) and sends back the acknowledgment, sequence number, and synchronization signals.

- On receiving both signals, the requestor sends the acknowledgment back to the receiver.

Since TCP is built on unreliable packet delivery services (IP), messages can be lost, delayed, duplicated, or delivered out of order. The three-way handshake is both necessary and sufficient for the proper synchronization. It guarantees that both sides are ready to transfer data (and know it), and both have agreed on initial sequence numbers. TCP uses packet sequencing to ensure proper order of packet delivery. TCP uses a checksum method for error detection, and further enhances the guaranteed delivery protocol by using retransmission of messages in the event of timeouts.

Once the connection is established, TCP provides for the transfer of data from one socket to another. The most popular methods for TCP data transfer are as follows.

- Segmented data transfer allows TCP to send data in segments across the network; segment sizes can be adjusted to provide for the best efficiency.

- The push mode forces TCP to send all data without network efficiency considerations being involved. It is used when an immediate data transfer is required.

7.1.4 Internet services

From the user point of view, TCP/IP internetworking appears to be a set of application programs, capable of communicating with each other over the network. Popular traditional applications of the TCP/IP Internet include:

- *Electronic mail (e-mail).*   This allows users to prepare memos and documents and to send them to other individual network users and user groups. TCP/IP supports the Simple Mail Transfer Protocol (SMTP), which provides for return receipts, message/mail forwarding, and other useful features.

- *File transfer.*   TCP/IP supports file transfer programs which allow users to send large files (e.g., images or entire libraries) across the network. File transfer facilities are provided by a mechanism known as the File Transfer Protocol (FTP), which allows for record transfer, block (a group of records) transfer, or image transfer (irrespective of the file content). FTP may support some character conversion (ASCII to EBCDIC, for example) before a transfer begins.

- *Remote access to a remote system—remote login.* It allows a user logged into one computer to connect to a remote computer and establish an interactive session with it. To a user it looks like the user's terminal (keyboard and display) is directly attached to the remote system. An example of the TCP/IP remote access application is TEL-NET, a virtual terminal facility that allows a user to connect to a remote system as if the user's terminal were physically attached to the remote system.

World Wide Web (WWW)

A new set of Internet applications has emerged recently. Commonly referred to as the Information Superhighway, this new phenomenon encompasses not only e-mail and FTP, but also numerous on-line services for private, educational, and commercial use.

The forces driving the Information Superhighway are all converging at the same time. First, the advanced networking technologies on which the Information Superhighway will be based are reaching a state of viability. Second, the U.S. government has encouraged the development of an Information Superhighway as a means of fostering economic growth, and judicial and regulatory decisions and pending legislation that will likely be passed soon will remove roadblocks for carriers to build new information delivery infrastructures. Finally, major companies are already investigating the role that interactive TV can play as a new means of marketing and selling products and services. A growing number of organizations recognize that marketing in the future will entail diverting billions of advertising dollars from certain print and broadcast media to the Information Superhighway. A number of countries, as well as state and local governments, all want to explore the Information Superhighway as a means of retaining as well as attracting business in their jurisdictions. Thus, more and more people and organizations now understand that the ultimate goal for the Information Superhighway is not simply to provide entertainment services, but to encourage the deployment of information technology to stimulate economic growth.

One of the better-known components of the Internet as Information Superhighway is the World Wide Web (WWW). Coupled with sophisticated, easy-to-use, and inexpensive navigation tools like Mosaic, the Web presents a unique opportunity for individuals to surf the net and for corporations to conduct business transactions over the Web.

The World Wide Web is a network of computers that presents information graphically through a hypertext-based system that lets users search for related "pages" globally by pointing and clicking with a mouse. Web pages can contain many types of data, from simple text to multimedia graphics and video.

Built on the concept of linking different types of information, the Web is the fastest-growing segment of the Internet and the most useful for commerce; it's the home of most of the business activity on the Net. To view Web billboards, you need a graphical Web browser such as Mosaic or Netscape, although a few Web browsers, such as Lynx, are text-based.

A few definitions

Hypertext Markup Language (HTML). This is the special language used to describe Web pages.

Hypertext Transfer Protocol (HTTP). The protocol used to send and receive HTML-encoded pages.

Mosaic. This is a client/server program that lets users navigate and view documents on the World Wide Web. Mosaic was invented at the National Center for Supercomputing Applications (NCSA) at the University of Illinois to facilitate easy, graphical browsing of the World Wide Web. It also supports Gopher, FTP, WAIS, and (with an additional program) TELNET. It is available for Windows, Macintosh, and UNIX platforms.

Common Gateway Interface (CGI). An interface and a scripting language that allows access to external data and applications from a Web server.

Secure Mosaic with transactions. Once Mosaic is able to handle transactions, mechanisms for securing messages will be needed. Several firms are addressing this requirement. CommerceNet's Secure Mosaic uses a high-level licensed technology—PKCS #7—from RSA Data Security to support digital signatures, digital envelopes, and cryptography. Secure Mosaic has an animated front end. For example, when an order with credit card information is sent, an envelope icon is sealed, with electronic sealing wax affixed, signifying that the message has been encrypted.

MIME (Multimedia Internet Mail Enhancements). This is a freely available standardized method of sending and receiving attachments. An attached file is specified, and the mail client encodes and sends it. The recipient's mail client decodes the attachment and displays it as part of the message. If the attached file has an extension, the mail client launches the associated application. MIME specification offers a way to interchange text in languages with different character sets and provide an ability to create, send, and receive e-mail with multimedia extensions over the Internet.

Firewalls. Companies looking to use the Internet for a variety of applications must protect their internal resources behind firewalls—hardware and software combinations that restrict access and filter data entering and leaving the organization. Diode routers, which are a configuration whereby an "inside" router initiates a message exchange with an "outside" router that connects to the Internet, with both routers implementing security rules, appear to be the most current firewall architecture.

WAIS (Wide Area Information Servers).   This is a program that allows relatively easy searching and retrieval from indexed text databases on remote computers. WAIS can be used to make your business documents and databases available to customers or other businesses. WAIS supports simple keyword searches.

7.2   SNA COMPONENTS, LAYERS, AND FUNCTIONS

Even though the material of this section may appear irrelevant to some readers involved in client/server application development, it is, in the author's opinion, extremely important. The importance of understanding SNA is due to the following:

- The very large installed base of SNA-based networks.
- An enormous number of existing legacy (i.e., mainframe-based) applications.
- The bulk of corporate data is still in "legacy" databases (i.e., IMS, IDMS, DB2, VSAM, flat files, etc.).
- As client/server systems grow from the departmental level into the enterprise, the need for application and data interoperability becomes even more critical.

IBM's Systems Network Architecture recently turned 20 years old. SNA has dramatically changed since it was first introduced. It supports a variety of applications and is widely used—IBM claims that it has issued over 40,000 SNA licenses. With the thousands of networks installed worldwide, SNA has emerged as one of the most accepted de facto networking standards. SNA provides a consistent set of communication rules, called *protocols,* and the communication access method, called ACF/VTAM.

SNA is designed to satisfy network user requirements efficiently and cost effectively:

- SNA provides resource sharing. It eliminates the need to install separate communication links for different types of workstations or applications since networking enables access to an application on any host processor and from any workstation.

- SNA enhances network dependability. SNA protocols recognize data loss during the transmission, use data flow control procedures to prevent data overrun, avoid overload and congestion, recognize failures, and correct many errors. Network availability is higher due to such SNA features as the extended recovery facility, alternate routing, backup host, and built-in control procedures in workstations, modems, and controllers.

- SNA helps users with network expansion and maintenance by providing open documented interfaces, which are implemented in all SNA products. That reduces the amount of programming involved in system integration.

- SNA simplifies problem determination by providing network management services in each network component and global management software, such as NetView.

- SNA maintains an open-ended architecture that helps to accommodate new facilities such as digital networks, digitized voice, distributed systems, electronic document distribution, fiber optics, graphics, satellites, and token-ring network.

- SNA provides a network interconnection facility which allows the users in one SNA network to access information and programs in other SNA networks by using SNA gateways. Therefore, SNA network boundaries are transparent to network users.

- SNA provides network security via its logon routines to prevent unauthorized users from accessing the network. For additional security, SNA provides encryption facilities.

7.2.1 Components

The following is a brief and incomplete discussion of the SNA components. An SNA network consists of many different hardware and software components connected via *links*. SNA defines a *node* as a portion of a hardware component and associated software components that implement a particular architecture-defined SNA function.

End users use the network to obtain network services, which are mainly the exchange of data between two points or nodes. In discussing SNA, the term *end user* is used to describe both the individuals interacting with the network through workstations and the application programs requesting the network services. Every end user gains access to an SNA network through a *logical unit* (LU). A logical unit provides a set of facilities which isolate the user from the physical characteristics of the network devices.

To summarize, SNA handles connections between users in a network in such a way that the underlying physical aspects of how the information unit is routed between users through the network are transparent to the user.

7.2.2 Seven SNA layers

IBM's SNA is a hierarchical, layered architecture. It consists of seven layers, each of which performs a specific function. The seven SNA layers are organized in a vertical, hierarchical architecture. In bottom-to-top order, the SNA layers are: physical control, data link control, path control, transmission control, data flow control, presentation services, and transaction services. Each SNA layer participates in the SNA hierarchy in the following fashion:

- It performs services for the next-higher layer.
- It requests services from the next-lower layer.
- It communicates with the corresponding layer in another SNA network.
- Changes to one layer do not affect the other layers.

Similar to the OSI reference model, the seven SNA layers are organized into a vertical hierarchy (see Fig. 7.2).

Transaction services layer. The transaction services layer is at the top of the SNA layered hierarchy. It is the layer in which SNA service transaction programs are implemented. The transaction services layer also provides certain services to control the network's operation. These include configuration services, session services, and management services.

Presentation services layer. Transaction programs communicate with each other in accordance with well-defined conversation protocols by using conversation commands (*verbs*). The presentation services layer defines these protocols for program-to-program communication. It also controls the use of the transaction program conversation level verbs.

Data flow control layer. Data flow on a session between two logical units (LU-LU session) needs to be controlled according to the session protocols used. The data flow control layer provides that control.

Transmission control layer., The transmission control layer is the lowest of the upper four SNA layers. It provides basic control of the network's transmission resources.

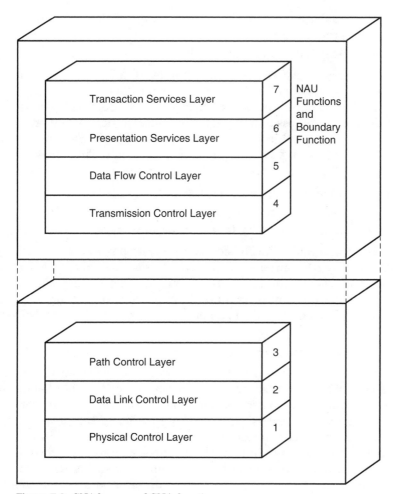

Figure 7.2 SNA layers and SNA functions.

Path control layer.   The path control layer is the highest SNA layer
of the three layers that provide the path control network functions.
The path control layer provides SNA protocols that route messages
through the network. The path control layer is used by all types of
sessions to:

- Perform path selection through the network.
- Route data through the network.
- Support segmenting and blocking protocols to combine and/or
  divide message units.

- Control virtual routes and virtual route rate of the throughput (i.e., virtual route pacing).
- Control explicit routes in the network.

Data link control layer.   As the name implies, the data link control layer provides functions for the data link elements of the path control network. The data link control layer provides protocols for message unit transfer across a link and for link level data flow and error recovery. The data link control layer supports SDLC, System/390 Data Channel, CCITT X.25, and token-ring protocols. The following functions are supported by the data link control layer:

- Transmission of message units across links
- Link level data flow management
- Error detection and recovery for transmission errors

Physical control layer.   The physical control layer provides a physical interface for any transmission medium used as a physical connection in the network. This layer defines the electrical and signaling characteristics needed to establish, maintain, and terminate the physical connections on which the links in a network are built.

Peer communications between SNA layers

Peer-to-peer communication enables the networks to be designed from the top down or from the bottom up, which was not possible before peer-to-peer communication became available. Furthermore, real peer-to-peer communication makes possible the creation of the networks that connect mainframes, minicomputers, and workstations into a cooperative computing environment. Distributed transaction processing and distributed databases can be implemented in such a network. Different hardware platforms can be used at different locations of the business enterprise, thus providing better leverage of the investment in information technology (IT).

Peer communication is the communication between equals. It differs from the hierarchical and master-slave types of communication where the communication is always initiated by a higher-level party (master), and the requests are sent from a master to a slave, but not in the opposite direction. Older network designs did not permit peer communication, often resulting in communication bottlenecks. The Systems Network Architecture allows peer communication between the SNA layers residing at the same levels within the hierarchy. In fact, the most advanced SNA logical unit, LU6.2, is defined to provide peer-to-peer communication capability between programs. As was mentioned before, each SNA layer performs services for the next-higher level, requests services from the next-lower level, and communicates as a peer with equivalent layers in another node. To support peer communication, each layer must be isolated from the internal procedures that another layer follows. (See Fig. 7.3.)

For example, the presentation services layer performs services for the transaction services layer, requests services from the data flow control layer (both in the same node), and communicates with other

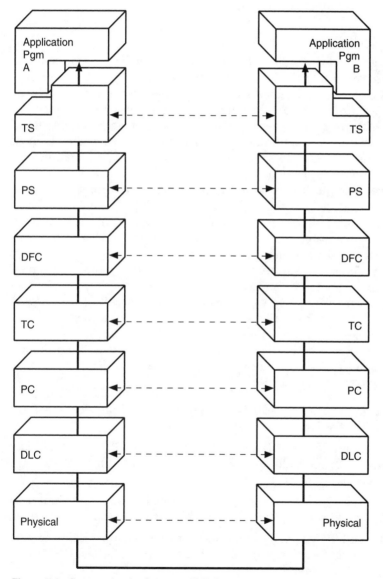

Figure 7.3 Communication between SNA layers.

presentation services layers in other nodes. The presentation services layer performs its functions independently of any other layer in the SNA architecture.

Since the SNA layers are defined to be functionally independent from each other, any layer may be modified or enhanced without disruption of the functions and operations of the other layers in the SNA network. That, in turn, allows SNA networks to grow, change, and, when necessary, migrate to new technologies.

7.2.3   SNA and OSI

The structures of the OSI model and the SNA model are very similar: both represent a hierarchical architecture consisting of the seven layers. The layers of both models have the same properties. Each layer performs a specific model function (SNA function or OSI function), the lower layers provide services for the higher layers, and layers of the same level can communicate with each other as peers. Indeed, both models are built to formally describe how communication networks should be implemented.

However, the purpose of the OSI model is different from that of the SNA model. The goal of the OSI model is to bring "law and order" into the diverse world of network communication architectures, to provide standard information exchange protocols for communication between autonomous, possibly different architectures.

IBM's Systems Network Architecture, on the other hand, is designed for the exchange of information between network nodes that belong to a single architecture. The existence of a single architecture allowed IBM to tailor both the hardware and software network components to achieve maximum efficiency and performance.

The functions of both SNA and OSI layers are similar, even though there is no one-to-one correlation between SNA layers and OSI layers. Specifically:

- Level 1—The SNA physical control layer and OSI physical layer are functionally equivalent.

- Level 2—The SNA data link control layer can use SDLC and the X.25 interface. SDLC is a subset of HDLC, which is used by the OSI data link layer.

- Level 3—The SNA path control layer provides functions similar to those defined for the OSI transport and session layers.

- Levels 4 and 5—The SNA data flow control and transmission control layers provide functions similar to those defined for the OSI transport and session layers.

- Levels 6 and 7—The SNA presentation services and transaction services layers provide functions similar to those defined for the OSI presentation layer and the common application services in OSI the application layer.

- Level 7—The OSI specific application services in the OSI application layer are considered to be end-user exchanges in SNA (see Fig. 7.4).

7.3 ADVANCED PROGRAM-TO-PROGRAM COMMUNICATIONS OVERVIEW

As stated previously, client/server computing is a special case of distributed processing. It is cooperative processing between clients and servers. Interestingly enough, Advanced Program-to-Program Communication (APPC) is a program-to-program communications protocol for IBM's cooperative processing strategy. APPC has been defined as a part of IBM's Systems Network Architecture and provides a rich set of interprogram communications services. APPC permits peer communications between distributed processing programs at SNA network nodes that support the APPC architecture.

APPC is based on the architecture of the SNA logical unit type 6.2 (LU6.2), and will be referred to as APPC/LU6.2 in this chapter. It is a set of protocols used by application programs in different processors to communicate with each other as peers in the execution of a distributed transaction. APPC/LU6.2 facilitates the development of distributed applications by providing an architectural foundation for program-to-program communications independent of the type of processor or operating system in which these applications exist. As such, APPC/LU6.2 is extremely important to the client/server architecture. It is widely used in various distributed and client/server implementations, especially those based on IBM products. Its architecture and features have been adopted into such standards as the OSI reference model and X/Open's XA architecture.

7.3.1 APPC design objectives

The structure and functions of APPC/LU6.2 are defined to satisfy the following requirements:

- *Simultaneous activation.* In a distributed transaction processing environment, APPC/LU6.2 allows the conversation partners to be active simultaneously so that the partners do not have to wait for each other for every action.

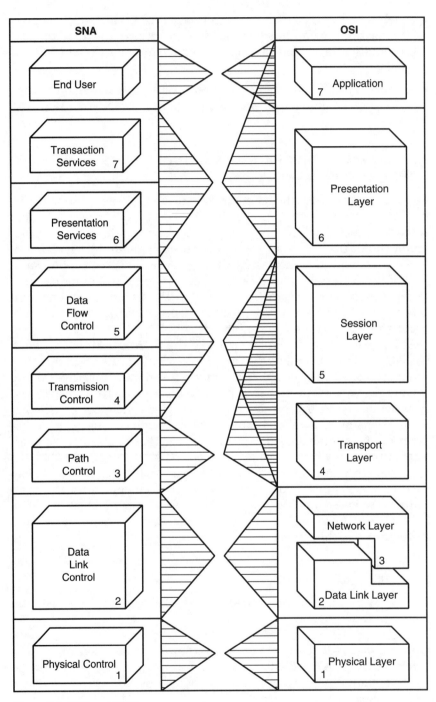

Figure 7.4 SNA and OSI layers.

- *Efficient allocation of resources.*   It includes not only local resources, but also sessions as communication resources. APPC/LU6.2 provides transaction programs with exclusive use of sessions in the form of conversations as part of their communication resources.

- *Minimum conversation overhead.*   APPC/LU6.2 achieves this by session scheduling and conversation allocation over a pool of available sessions.

- *Various conversation life.*   Conversations should last only for a period of time determined by the conversing programs. Thus, APPC/LU6.2 supports conversations varying from one short message to many-message, multiple-exchange conversations. If need be, APPC/LU6.2 allows conversations to continue indefinitely, terminating them only when failures occur.

- *Attention mechanism.*   APPC/LU6.2 provides an attention mechanism to handle asynchronous nonerror events.

- *Error detection and notification.*   APPC/LU6.2 provides the means to detect errors and notify conversation partners about them.

- *Commitment protocol.*   APPC/LU6.2 provides a synchronization protocol (syncpoint) to support error recovery and the distributed update capabilities of protected resources in a distributed transaction processing environment.

- *Mode of service.*   APPC/LU6.2 is designed to support a desired mode of transmission service (interactive or batch).

- *Flexibility via subset definitions.*   APPC/LU6.2 functions are grouped into subsets. These subsets allow APPC/LU6.2 to support a base function set common to all implementations of LU6.2, and optional sets, which may contain additional APPC/LU6.2 functionality.

7.3.2   Transaction programs and distributed transaction processing

APPC/LU6.2 is designed to provide application programs with support functions for program-to-program communication. Direct users of APPC/LU6.2 are application transaction programs. An *application transaction program* is a user-written program designed to perform communication requests and other functions of distributed applications. Utility and management services to application transaction programs (and SNA logical units) are provided by *service transaction programs.* Service transaction programs are different from application transaction programs. They are SNA-defined and are considered to be a part of APPC/LU6.2.

A typical transaction program (TP) is different from a program in general by the way it is invoked and the communication functions it initiates. A transaction program is invoked by another transaction program or by the LU6.2 via an *Attach* mechanism. The invoking TP (invoker) can initiate a conversation with another TP, which in turn is *connected* with its invoker via a *conversation*. For example, consider a CICS (Customer Information Control System) application transaction program that is designed to participate in CICS distributed transaction processing. In this case, the first application TP (TP-1) initiates a conversation with another TP (TP-2) by sending some data and control information. TP-1 uses special commands that are a part of the CICS implementation of APPC/LU6.2. The invoking program, TP-2, gets started by the TP-1 and receives the data sent to it by TP-1 (see Fig. 7.5).

A transaction program uses APPC/LU6.2 to communicate with other transaction programs by issuing transaction program *verbs*. Sometimes, an LU6.2 may issue transaction program verbs on behalf of a transaction program.

Distributed transaction processing, or DTP, is a process whereby two or more programs, usually residing in different systems, cooperate in

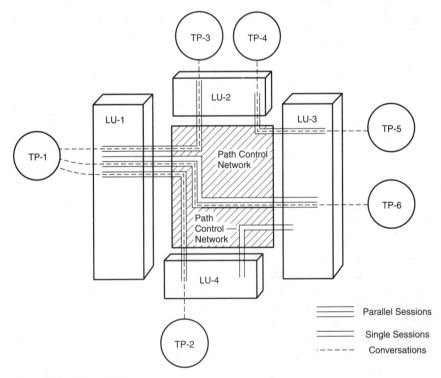

Figure 7.5 LU and SNA network.

order to perform certain required functions. That cooperation includes program intercommunication and local resource sharing. As a result, each program can use the other program's CPU cycles, databases, queues, and interfaces such as display and keyboard devices to perform its portion of the required functionality.

APPC/LU6.2 participates in the DTP by acting as an interface between programs and the network control layer (for example, SNA's Path Control Network layer). In essence, APPC/LU6.2 allows a transaction program to invoke remote programs and to communicate with them. It is important to realize that APPC provides only one type of communication: *program-to-program*. Workstation operators, for example, do not communicate with LU6.2 or use APPC directly. They use local workstation programming support which is designed to interact with the LU6.2 (e.g., keyboards and display terminals appear as microcode, or fixed programs, to the LU6.2).

To be able to communicate with each other, two transaction programs must establish a logical connection, or *conversation,* between them. APPC/LU6.2 assists one transaction program in initiating a conversation with another transaction program over a *session* held between two logical units (an LU-LU session). An active conversation has exclusive use of a session, even though transaction programs cannot explicitly request use of a particular session. Sessions are not "visible" to transaction programs, but conversations, on the other hand, are. Successive conversations are allowed to reuse the same session. While conversations, as logical connections between transaction programs, may be short-lived, sessions are long-lived and may be used by more than one conversation. Two SNA LU6.2s are capable of supporting multiple active APPC sessions between them. These sessions are called *parallel* sessions.

Another feature of APPC/LU6.2 is its ability to support many transaction programs concurrently, serially, or both. Each transaction program may have multiple conversations with one or more other transaction programs.

Each conversation connects a pair of transaction programs, and all active concurrent conversations constitute one *distributed transaction.* For example, consider that transaction programs TP-1 and TP-2 are connected by a conversation and TP-2 has an active conversation with TP-3 concurrently (see Fig. 7.5). At the same time, TP-3 is connected by a conversation to a TP-4. Then TP-1, TP-2, TP-3, and TP-4 are all participants in the same distributed transaction.

An extremely important feature of APPC/LU6.2 in a distributed transaction processing environment is that APPC provides synchronization services for *protected* transaction resources. These are local resources whose state changes are logged. Therefore, any changes performed by a transaction can be backed out and the resources can be restored to a consistent before-change state if a transaction fails. APPC/LU6.2 provides *syncpoint* and *rollback* functions for distributed transaction error recovery.

7.3.3 LU6.2 protocol boundaries and components

APPC/LU6.2 is designed as a universal method for peer-to-peer, program-to-program communications. As such, it can be implemented on a variety of hardware/software platforms and transaction programs written for different environments and in different languages. That is why the architectural definitions of APPC/LU6.2 are specified in generic terms, called the *transaction program protocol boundary,* and represent the APPC/LU6.2 interface to application transaction programs.

The interfaces between different implementations of APPC/LU6.2 and transaction programs are dependent on the particular environment. Each programming environment that provides an APPC/LU6.2 protocol boundary is called an *application programming interface,* or API.

Depending on the implementation environment, APPC/LU6.2 uses various subsets of the protocol boundary to interface with transaction programs. One set of transaction program verbs, for example, may consist of the subsets of verbs for mapped conversations, basic conversations, and SNA Distributed Services (SNADS).

In terms of the layered APPC/LU6.2 architecture, the subsets of the protocol boundary represent sublayers within APPC/LU6.2. Protocol boundaries exist between layers or sublayers of the node, as well as between peer components of the same layer (see Fig. 7.6).

A protocol boundary between two layers or sublayers of the same node defines data exchange rules called *layered protocols.* A protocol boundary between two peer components of the same layer is called a *peer protocol.* For example, the transaction program layered protocol boundary allows a transaction program to request LU6.2 services to communicate with other transaction programs. On the other hand, the transaction program protocol boundary can be viewed as a boundary between peers—two transaction programs. Actual exchanges between peers is accomplished by exchanges between layers (interlayer exchanges).

Figure 7.6 illustrates that concept by showing how peer exchanges between transaction programs occur. *Mapped* conversations between application transaction programs TP-1 and TP-2, and *basic* conversations between application transaction program TP-1 and service transaction program TP-3 are accomplished by actual information exchange between layers. Specifically, mapped conversation is reduced to a basic

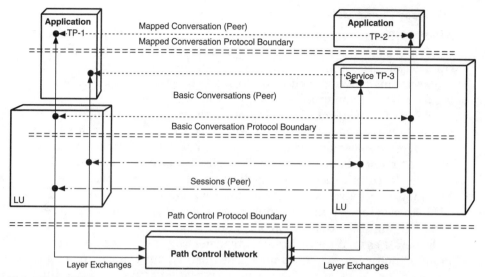

Figure 7.6 APPC protocol boundaries.

conversation. That, in turn, is accompanied by the information transformation within layers. For example, basic conversation itself is transformed into a session, the session is transformed into connections in the path control network, etc.

When compared to IBM's Systems Network Architecture, the APPC/LU6.2 architecture embraces the upper four layers of the SNA: transaction services, presentation services, data flow control, and transmission control.

To support APPC, logical unit type 6.2 contains two sets of components that implement the layered architecture. Similar to the SNA layered model, these sets of components are organized into two layers: upper and lower. One layer is designed for each LU6.2 protocol boundary. Each LU6.2 layer contains a group of processes that support a pair of corresponding SNA layers, and a management component that manages these processes.

7.3.4 APPC/LU6.2 conversations and states

Conversations are logical connections between logical units over which transaction programs and LUs can exchange data with one another. APPC/LU6.2 typically supports the data exchange over the conversation in one direction at a time. One TP has the right to send data, while another TP receives it until the sender gives up its right to send. This conversation protocol is called a *half-duplex flip-flop* protocol.

Send/receive protocols

APPC/LU6.2 acts as a traffic cop in enforcing the half-duplex send/receive conversation protocol. However, APPC allows the receiving transaction program to send an error indicator or a change-direction request, thus putting itself into the send state. Of course, a receiving transaction can abnormally terminate the conversation.

The exact implementation of the send/receive protocol depends on the application requirements. The degree of concurrency between sender and receiver can vary from high synchronous interactions, required by real-time, on-line inquiry applications, to asynchronous transfers, required by certain distributed applications. For example, real-time, on-line inquiry requires synchronous information transfer. Here, APPC/LU6.2 needs to keep the interprogram conversation (source and target TP) active until the completion of a transaction.

A special case of a synchronous transfer is the intermediate transmission no-response requirements of, for example, status-reporting applications. APPC uses a one-way conversation as a way of handling that special case of synchronous conversation. The source transaction program initiates a conversation with the target transaction program, sends data, and deallocates the conversation. A message reaches the target transaction program, which in turn is activated, receives a message, and deallocates the conversation. However, since the source TP does not expect any reply, it could have terminated itself while the message was in transit. Thus, the source and target transaction programs are allowed not to be active at the same time.

When a distributed application requirement is to allow both the sender and the receiver to exchange data at their convenience, as in the document distribution applications, APPC/LU6.2 provides support for *asynchronous* transfers via a *store-and-forward* protocol. Here, the sender sends data to the destination via a local service transaction program, which can store the message in a queue until such a time when the destination transaction program is ready to receive the message.

To alleviate the possible interpretation problems that may be encountered when different transaction programs use different internal data formats, APPC/LU6.2 provides common formats for data transmission, called *mapping*.

Conversation states

APPC conversations can exist in several architecturally defined states. These states are the result of actions taken by participating logical units and transaction programs. Conversation requests issued by a local or remote transaction program, as well as network errors, may all cause a conversation state to change. At the same time, the state of the conversation determines the actions that a particular transaction program is allowed to take (i.e., the commands that a TP is allowed to issue). If a communication request is issued for a conversation in the disallowed state, it causes state check ABEND conditions. For example, a SEND request issued for a conversation on which only receipt of data is allowed will generate such an error. The APPC/LU6.2 conversation protocol boundary defines the following conversation states:

- *Send state*—TP can send data, request confirmation or sync point.

- *Receive state*—TP can receive data from a remote TP.

- *Reset state*—TP can allocate the conversation.

- *Confirm state*—TP can reply to a confirmation request.

- *Defer state*—TP can request confirmation, sync point, or flush a send buffer, all in order to enter into Reset or Receive states.

- *Syncpoint state*—TP can respond to the sync point request.

- *Backed out state*—TP can respond to the "backed out" indication.

- *Deallocate state*—TP can deallocate the conversation.

APPC conversation states are clearly applicable to the client/server computing model. For example, in order to initiate a client/server interaction, the client must be in a Send state, while the server must be in the Receive state.

7.3.5   APPC/LU6.2 sessions

Conversations between transaction programs are carried over sessions between their respective logical units. Therefore, one of the principal functions of APPC/LU6.2 is to provide session services between communication partners.

Session allocation

A particular session is used by only one pair of conversing transaction programs at a time. In a multiprocessing, multiple-workstation environment, APPC/LU6.2 should allow for multiple concurrent transactions by supporting two or more sessions at a time, even with the same partner.

Logical units that can support parallel sessions (multiple concurrent sessions with the same partner) are called *parallel-session* LUs, even if only one such session is currently active.

There are some logical units, however, that can have only one active session at a time. Such LUs are called *single-session* LUs. Any session they support, regardless of whether it is with a single-session or with a parallel session LU, is called a single session. The session classification depends on the type of the participating logical units. All sessions between a pair of LUs are either single or parallel. In other words, a parallel-session LU6.2 can have one or more concurrent parallel sessions with one or more parallel-session LUs, and one single session with each single-session LU.

When a session is activated by an LU6.2, or a previously used session is freed, the LU6.2 places the session in a *session pool*. When a TP initiates a new conversation, LU6.2 allocates a session from the session pool, provided that one is available.

Thus, LU6.2 avoids the time and resource-consuming session activation process by allowing sessions to be reused by successive conversations. The configuration and size of the session pool is specified by an operator.

Who is first

When a session is allocated, each end of the session can try to start a peer-level conversation at the same time, thus creating a session contention. To resolve this contention, the *session contention polarity* is specified for each session. A session for which a local LU6.2 is designated to win an allocation race is called a *contention-winner* session, or *first-speaker* session.

A session that a local LU6.2 is designated to lose to its partner is called a *contention-loser* session. The contention-loser LU6.2 will then *bid* the contention winner to use the session. That is why contention-loser sessions are also called *bidder* sessions.

There are certain session characteristics that apply to the actual session activation/deactivation and usage. While these characteristics are beyond the scope of this book, descriptions of a primary/secondary LU, session pacing, and BIND requests deserve a more detailed examination.

Primary and secondary LU

When one LU6.2 activates a session with its partner, it does so by sending a BIND request message. The logical unit that sends the BIND request (activates the session) is called the *primary* LU (PLU). The LU that receives the BIND is called the *secondary* LU (SLU).

The same logical unit can be primary on one session and secondary on another. The PLU always has the first use of a session; that is, it can always initiate the first conversation on the session, regardless of the session contention polarity. The contention-winner LU repossesses its right to initiate conversations when the first conversation completes.

Pacing

One LU may send data to another LU faster than the receiver can process. To prevent that situation from happening, APPC/LU6.2 observes a *session-level pacing protocol*. At session activation time, communicating partners exchange the number and the size of the messages they can process at one time. The sending LU6.2 will not exceed the receiving LU acceptance limit until it receives an acknowledgment from the receiver that it is ready to receive another message.

BIND request

To activate a session between two LU6.2 units, a BIND request is sent from the PLU to the SLU. The BIND request carries the PLU's suggested session parameters that may be based on the PLU's implementation-dependent support or on the installation-specified values currently in effect.

The SLU receives the BIND and uses it to determine whether it can accept the requested session parameters. The SLU does not reject the BIND because of any incompatibility it may find with the parameters specified in the BIND. Instead, if the BIND format is valid, the SLU sends a positive response. This response includes a complete set of session parameters that can either match the ones sent on the BIND request, or be different. The BIND session parameters for which the SLU may choose different options are known as *negotiable* parameters.

Chapter

8

Client/Server and Middleware

Up to this point, the discussion of client/server architecture has concentrated on the characteristics of clients and servers as specialized nodes in a distributed computing environment. Client/server computing was defined as a specialized form of distributed cooperative processing. Five different general styles of client/server cooperative processing—remote presentation, distributed presentation, distributed application, remote data management, and distributed data management—were defined and analyzed.

One key characteristic of all these styles of cooperative processing is the fact that clients and servers are "separated" by sets of interfaces, and these sets vary from one style to another. The goal of this chapter is to analyze the architectural boundary between a client and a server and to define and explain a new layer of the client/server architecture known as *middleware*.

8.1 MIDDLEWARE—A NEW CLASS OF SOFTWARE

In client/server architecture, various application components or tasks are distributed between specialized client and server platforms, which cooperate to perform the desired application functions. Client/server interactions are defined as those in which a client initiates the interaction and requests a particular service from its "home" server. This server reacts to the client's request by either performing the desired service or routing the request to another server for the fulfillment of the request; irrespective of the final location of the service, the original or home server sends the response back to the client.

Looking closer, these interactions can be viewed as interactions between interconnected components of the client/server architecture. Each component provides an interface through which it communicates with other components. Two distinct classes of components can be defined:

- *Process components.* Typically, these are software components that actively perform some functions.

- *Resource components.* These provide the services requested by process components.

From the point of view of client/server interactions, an active resource component acts as a server, whereas the users of the resource component—process components—act as clients. Process and resource components, as well as clients and servers, enter into an association with each other for the purpose of communication. This association is the *connection* between a sender of information (request, message, etc.) and a receiver of that information. The client/server connections can be static or dynamic. Static connections are set up at compile or load time, or at system initialization time, and cannot be changed. A dynamic connection can be changed "in flight," at run time.

Whatever the nature of the connection, client/server interactions do not make any assumptions on the topology of the architecture. In principle, there is nothing to prevent a client and a server from existing on the same physical machine. Nevertheless, at a minimum, these interactions require:

- A common set of interfaces both clients and servers can use to communicate

- Various interprocess communication mechanisms that can be used by clients and servers alike

- Reliable and robust delivery facilities that can transport the interaction requests and responses over an appropriate medium between clients and servers

In very general terms, when clients and servers are physically located on separate, potentially remote nodes, client/server communications will have to be performed over a suitable network. Such a network could be a local area network (LAN) for a small workgroup or a wide area network (WAN) for geographically dispersed nodes. Traditional IBM Systems Network Architecture (SNA) networks, popular Transmission Control Protocol/Internet Protocol (TCP/IP) networks, public networks utilizing packet-switching protocols, or networks based on the standard Open Systems Interconnection (OSI) protocols could all be used for client/server communications.

In a distributed environment, various system resources (data, computing power, programs, etc.) are distributed across multiple locations. These resources utilize some kind of communication system to interact with each other. In this context, a communication system is a mechanism that allows the distributed resources to exchange control information and data. Communication systems may be visible enough for the end users to be aware of the network and protocols that provide actual resources interconnection. Obviously, such awareness can result in poor portability to other communication systems.

Conversely, client/server interactions can be isolated from the underlying interprocess communications and network protocols by implementing a *common set of interfaces and run-time facilities* which will allow client/server interaction to be developed and performed in a way totally transparent to application developers and end users alike. Since these common interfaces and run-time facilities are architecturally layered between clients and servers, they are collectively known as middleware.

8.1.1 Definition and functionality

The term *middleware* is used in many different ways. Conceptually, it is the glue that holds together the disparate systems in a distributed computing environment. Architecturally, it is a layer of the client/server architecture that resides between the client and the server, supports multiple communication and data access protocols and interfaces, and enables run-time client/server interactions. (See Fig. 8.1.)

The latter point is crucial and implies that whatever else the middleware may be, it is a run-time environment. It also means that middleware excludes development tools and systems management utilities unless they contain features that directly support applications at run time.

Middleware integrates application programs and other software components in a distributed environment which can be characterized by:

- Distribution of processing among multiple systems
- Interactions between dissimilar systems
- Ability to share resources between individual interconnected systems
- Multiple specialized and heterogeneous nodes and networks

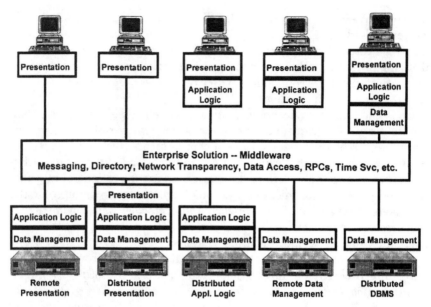

Figure 8.1 Middleware.

As a software layer, middleware is not intended to replace communication system functionality. It is architected to be a common software component that sits between clients and servers on top of the communication protocols and frees client applications from the need to know low-level communication protocols, which may include OSI transport layers, SNA LU6.2, TCP/IP, NetWare IPX/SPX, DECnet, etc. The middleware objectives specify that the traditional communication system functionality (discussed in detail in Chap. 5) is left to the underlying communication technology. This basic communication system has to support the following functionality:

- Network addressing
- Segmenting and blocking
- Network flow control
- Transmission synchronization
- Transmission priority
- Error control

The middleware design should take advantage of already available communication system functionality previously described. In order to integrate applications in a distributed environment and to take advantage of the functionality provided by communication networks, middleware provides an abstraction layer that, at a minimum, should enable:

- Node, service, and data location transparency

- Seamless interactions between application components via a set of common consistent APIs

- Scaleability and extensibility

- Reliability and availability

- Vendor, platform, operating system, and networking protocol independence

A single, common API may not be enough to support these requirements. Therefore, a middleware solution may consist of a complex set of APIs and functions designed to provide the following functionality:

- Client/server interactions support, which includes:

  Synchronous and asynchronous message delivery and processing

  Message queuing

  Dynamic and alternative message routing

  Deferred and guaranteed message delivery

  RPC

  Connection-oriented pipes and sockets

  SQL interactions

- Data translation and transformation services

- National language support

- Directory and naming services

- Broadcasting/multicasting

- Dynamic resource management

- Security and recovery

- Load balancing

- Application session management

This is not an exhaustive list of functions. Heterogeneous network environment support, for example, may require such additional middleware functionality as communication protocol stack normalization and context bridging.

8.1.2 Forces that drive middleware

There are several facts that can be identified as the driving forces behind the emergence and acceptance of middleware. Among them are:

- Proliferation of local area networks and workgroup computing created the system environment in which data appears on every platform, from the desktop to the enterprise server, and in which the end users want to be able to access data and applications using off-the-shelf software packages.

- Downsizing or rightsizing efforts are characterized by a significant client/server-based application development activity across multiple industries, which is balanced by the decline in large-scale mainframe applications development.

- The wide selection of software and hardware products available for the client/server implementations, coupled with the reluctance of corporate decision makers to rely on a single vendor for the hardware, operating system, communications, transaction managers, and DBMSs only emphasizes the heterogeneous nature of the applications destined for the client/server environment.

- This heterogeneity of the applications is enforced by the fact that the majority of mission-critical applications is still residing on corporate mainframes, thus necessitating cross-platform application interoperability.

- The need for interoperability, combined with the complexity of networking and data access protocols, result in high demand for the developer's skill sets covering an in-depth knowledge in communications, databases, and operating systems—a skill set traditionally not found in the average programmer.

To solve the skill-set problem, corporations should conduct extensive and expensive hands-on training and education for their employees on a continuous basis (because the technology continues to change rapidly). However, while the training and education of employees is essential to the organization's success on the road to a distributed client/server environment, the rapidly changing nature of the technology can be addressed more effectively by isolating application developers from the underlying and often transient technology expertise. Middleware is the means to achieve this isolation.

Under the client/server computing model, middleware has become many things to many people. The protocols that compose middleware span almost the entire scope of the OSI model, from the network protocols to distributed systems management and groupware applications. (See Fig. 8.2.)

8.1.3 Middleware computing models

Given the variety of styles of cooperative processing used by the client/server computing model, it is not surprising that the majority of the

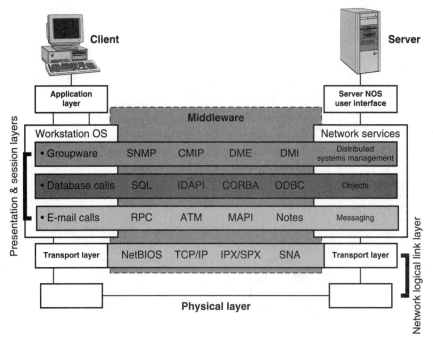

Figure 8.2 Middleware protocols.

interest in middleware is focused on its role in distributed cooperative computing.

On a high level, middleware can be classified into two major groups:

- Distributed logic middleware that supports some kind of program-to-program communication typical of the distributed application logic style of client/server cooperative processing (see Fig. 8.3)
- Data management middleware which connects an application or a DBMS on one node (e.g., a client) with a DBMS running on another node (e.g., a server), which satisfies the processing requirements of the remote and distributed data management styles of cooperative processing (see Fig. 8.4)

Other types of cooperative processing, namely remote and distributed presentation, can be supported by a subset of the distributed logic middleware.

These types of middleware can be implemented in a simple server-requester form applicable to most client/server implementations today. They can also be implemented in a more complex peer-to-peer computing model.

Server-requester middleware facilitates interactions between clients and server where a business application is partitioned between two or

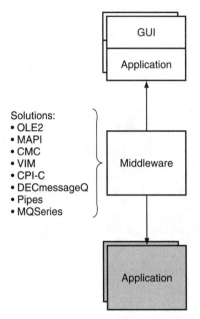

Solutions:
• OLE2
• MAPI
• CMC
• VIM
• CPI-C
• DECmessageQ
• Pipes
• MQSeries

Figure 8.3 Distributed logic middleware.

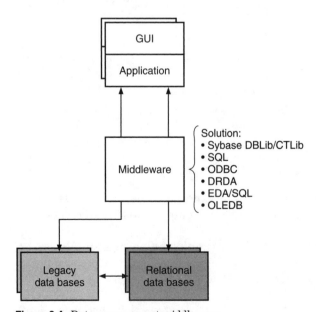

Figure 8.4 Data management middleware.

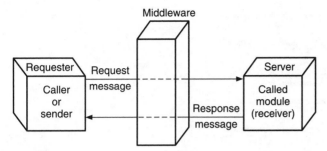

Figure 8.5 Server-requester middleware.

more computing platforms, and where each partition/platform has a pre-defined role within the application. In this model, the middleware receives the request messages from a client and routes them to an appropriate server using some agreed-upon mechanism and protocol (e.g., message queue, RPC, store-and-forward, asynchronous, synchronous, etc.). (See Fig. 8.5.)

In the peer-to-peer model, middleware supports multiple applications, each of which can perform independently of the other, acting either as a client or as a server at any given moment. (See Fig. 8.6.) Conversely, these peer-to-peer applications can all act together by exchanging messages and creating a business workflow. While, conceptually, the middleware functionality in this model does not change, the requirements of flexibility, scaleability, dynamic routing, and reconfiguration, including dynamic load balancing, become much more critical.

8.2 MIDDLEWARE TECHNIQUES

A client/server computing model corresponding to each of the cooperative processing styles can be supported by one or more cooperative processing techniques. Let's consider two basic, low-level techniques of cooperative processing communication that a client/server architecture can use:

- Remote procedure calls
- Messaging and queuing

These mechanisms can be used to support both the *distributed logic* middleware and the *database* middleware. Since these mechanisms provide a relatively low level of abstraction for client/server interactions, they are key to understanding the interoperability issues surrounding a vendor's efforts to dominate the middleware market.

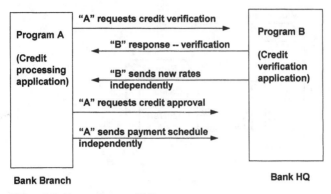

Figure 8.6   Peer-to-peer middleware.

8.2.1   RPC

A *remote procedure call* (RPC) is a mechanism by which one process can execute another process (subroutine) residing on another, usually remote, system, possibly running a different operating system. It is a generalization of the traditional and familiar programming paradigm—procedure call—that can be found in most programming languages. RPCs extend this paradigm from a single system to a network of systems. An RPC is a connectionless mechanism—the RPC connection exists only for the duration of the call. Theoretically, two successive RPCs to the same remote routine, identified by name, could be executed on different servers. Any parameters needed by a subroutine are passed between the original and the subroutine processes. The details of the transport mechanism used by the RPC are hidden from the RPC user. A specific RPC tool may support one or several different transport mechanisms. The main requirement for successful RPC implementation is the ability of a caller to find a server where the subroutine resides. One way to accomplish the search is to match the required subroutine name with those maintained in a special subroutine/server database. The entries in this database can be modified so that the target server for the subroutine can be assigned dynamically. This assignment can change from one invocation of an RPC to another.

Once the server is found, RPCs can authenticate the client and the server to each other, check their security privileges, and even automatically manage the server's concurrency. X/Open's Transaction Processing Work Group has specified extensions to the DCE RPC to support distributed transaction processing, and systems like Transarc's Encina follow that specification by extending basic RPC functionality to include transactional semantics. The resulting transactional RPCs can support the data integrity requirements of transaction processing. Finally, RPCs permit users to adopt the object-oriented design and programming methodologies as well. Indeed, the servers, with all their data and logic, can be considered as complex objects, while RPCs are just methods on those objects. With a well-defined interface specified in the Interface Definition Language (IDL), a server object can be utilized by multiple client applications in a distributed object-oriented heterogeneous environment.

Together, the RPC and its integrated services constitute a very powerful middleware that simplifies the development of client/server applications in a distributed computing environment. With the endorsement of X/Open and most major computer vendors, the Open Software Foundation's Distributed Computing Environment has become a strong candidate for the RPC industry standard to run applications over a heterogeneous network. In the context of a communication system role in a client/server environment, an RPC requesting a particular service from a resource component (server) is issued by a process component (client). The location of the resource component is hidden from the user (client). RPCs are highly suitable for client/server applications, usually providing developers with a number of powerful tools that are necessary to build such applications. These tools include two major components:

- A language and a compiler that simplify the development of distributed client/server applications by producing portable source code

- A run-time facility that allows distributed applications to run over multiple, heterogeneous nodes, thus making the system architectures and the underlying network protocols transparent to the application procedures

Among several RPC implementations and proposals competing for the role of standard RPC, DCE's RPC appears to be one of the strongest candidates that deserves closer examination. To develop a distributed, DCE-compliant client/server application, a developer creates an interface definition using the IDL. IDL syntax is similar to the ANSI C language with the addition of several language constructs appropriate for a network environment. Once the definitions are created, the IDL compiler translates them into a necessary communication code, or stubs, that are bound with the client and the server (see Fig. 8.7).

The stub on a client system acts as a substitute for the required server procedure. Similarly, the server stub substitutes for a client. The stubs are needed to automate otherwise manual operations: copy-

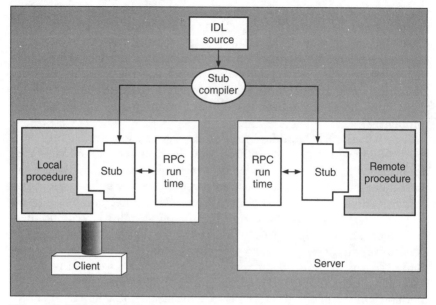

Figure 8.7 RPC implementation.

ing arguments to and from RPC headers, converting data as necessary, and calling the RPC run time.

RPC run time should have the following features:

- Transparency and independence from the underlying networking protocols

- Support for reliable transmission, error detection, and recovery from network failures

- Support for a common method of network naming, addressing, and directory services, while at the same time being independent of network directory services

- Multithreading support for parallel and concurrent processing and the ability to handle multiple requests simultaneously, thus reducing the time required to complete an application

- Portability and interoperability with various system environments

- Support for resources integrity and application security

Examples of RPCs are OSF RPC, Sun's RPC, Netwise RPC, IBM's OS/2 Distributed Program Link (DPL), and Sybase RPC. The DCE implementation of the remote procedure call is one of the most advanced and includes special semantics for network transport independence and transparency. The ISO X.500 standard is used to provide global directory services. DCE RPC uses Kerberos authentication and authorization to support security service, and POSIX-standard asynchronous threads to support concurrent and parallel processing. The latter allows both clients and servers to process multiple items at the same time. To sum up, RPCs can facilitate and even simplify the development of client/server applications in several ways:

- RPC hides the details of the underlying communications system, making applications development that much less complex and the application itself communication system independent.

- RPCs integrate network services for security, naming, and concurrency, which allows large-scale client/server applications to run effectively.

- RPCs support transactional extensions to provide additional data integrity requirements that business environments require.

- RPCs are mature and widely available on a variety of platforms and support communications across heterogeneous environments.

8.2.2 Messaging and queuing

Even though many businesses rely on RPCs for distributed heterogeneous computing, often the synchronous nature of the RPCs makes them less desirable for a number of business requirements. Indeed, the synchronous nature of the RPC forces the client to wait until the processing is completed on the server, which may be unacceptable for such applications as stock trading, for example. The answer lies in *message-oriented middleware* (MOM), which extends the synchronous process-to-process communications in a distributed environment by implementing a messaging model missing from the DCE. As the name implies, messaging is, in essence, a process of distributing data and/or control information through the use of messages. In this context, a message may contain data, control information, or both, and may be represented by data packets, streams of data, SQL strings, images, voice, and any other agreed-upon form. Different forms of messaging exist.

Many businesses are turning to message queuing for an answer to the challenges of distributed networking and interoperability. In general, *messaging* can be viewed as a waitless communication technique, where communicating partners do not wait for each other to exchange messages, without regard for the availability or accessibility of either. *Queuing,* on the other hand, is a connectionless communication technique, which allows communicating entities to save information until the intended recipient is ready to receive it. Thus, in queuing, communicating parties are not directly connected, and each entity can operate at its own speed, without regard or need for the synchronization. The only agreement between communicating partners is that they will fill and empty designated message queues.

Message queuing transfers data by using queues between each phase of the transfer process. As illustrated in Fig. 8.8, application A, for example, hands a message to the queue manager to be placed in the message queue. Application B can request messages from its queue manager. The queue manager should be aware of the address of the message destination, and in the case of a remote system, the message is given to a remote queue manager, to be in turn handed over to a requesting application.

Message queuing may be implemented using separate queues for message delivery and message processing, and typically supports asynchronous message processing (even though message delivery can be implemented over a conversational protocol such as APPC.

This simple asynchronous message-queuing technique differentiates itself from other forms of client/server communications in the following ways:

- Time independence enables communicating programs to run at different times: Messages can wait on a local queue for the remote system to become available before transmission.

- Structure flexibility means that no constraints are placed on the application structure and relationship: In addition to a one-to-one relationship, a message can be sent from one queue to a defined list of

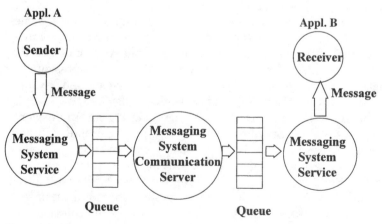

Figure 8.8 Message queuing.

other queues, thus creating a one-to-many relationship; conversely, a many-to-one relationship is also possible.

- Insulation from the underlying networking and communication mechanisms. Similar to RPCs, message queuing insulates applications from the complexities of the underlying transport by providing a relatively simple API to send and receive messages: The simplicity of the API allows it to remain consistent across platforms.

- A reduction in the number of networking connections results in a reduction in networking expenses, simpler application programming, and separation of application and communication environments.

- Sharing of message data streams may result in the ability to process messages concurrently and in load balancing.

- Separation of queue and application management promotes independent control of applications and queues, and supports event-driven application design (via trigger queues).

- Flexibility in designing information flow patterns allows, among other things, for the integration of new and legacy applications, and promotes new advanced application designs that can benefit from deserialization of processes (parallelism).

To sum up, using messaging and queuing for client/server interactions means that they never wait for each other, are not connected to each other, and do not even identify their communication partners.

Contrast this with more traditional conversational communication techniques, where communication requires a dedicated logical connection between partners as well as the identification of each partner by the other. Often called *pipes,* these various conversational implementations may support one or several concurrent transport mechanisms. The details of the supported transport mechanisms are hidden from the user, and these pipes impose minimal protocol and format restrictions on users. Basically, pipes provide facilities only to mark the boundaries between discreet messages, to determine the identity of the sender, and to perform verification of the receipt of a message. Conversational pipes implementations vary from very simple to such complex architectures as IBM's Advanced Program-to-Program Communications (APPC/LU6.2) and CPI-C.

Each of these communication mechanisms—messaging, queuing, and pipes—has its advantages. Combining these mechanisms into a hybrid message-passing model will provide support for synchronous and asynchronous message delivery (as in queuing), as well as synchronous and asynchronous message processing (as in messaging). Such a hybrid mechanism can be used by RPCs, distributed database management systems, transaction management systems, and message queue managers, thus providing a flexible and powerful foundation for virtually any type of middleware solution.

Examples of existing messaging products include Digital DECmessageQ, Pipes from Peer Logic, MQSeries from IBM, EzBridge Transact from Systems Strategies, CI from Covia Technologies, Message Express from Horizon Strategies, Entire from Software AG, and many others. Some of these products are discussed later in this chapter.

8.2.3 Message queuing and e-mail

Due to its asynchronous nature, messaging is widely used in e-mail applications. Applications which utilize e-mail fall into two broad categories which reflect the degree to which they exploit messaging:

- *Mail-aware* applications require basic messaging capability in order to function. An example is a forms-routing application that sends an expense report to a series of recipients and records their approval or disapproval.

- *Mail-enabled applications* require full access to all of the back-end messaging services, including the message-store, address-book or directory, and transport functions. These applications include e-mail clients, workflow automation programs, and report distribution systems.

Several important industry initiatives are underway to define standard interfaces to these. One of these initiatives is the Common Mail Calls (CMC) interface: an X.400 Application Program Interface Association (XAPIA) standard for cross-platform mail services. CMC was designed in part by such vendors as Lotus, IBM, Microsoft, and Novell, and users organizations such as RAM, AT&T, Bull, and France Telecom. CMC has been ratified by IEEE, CCITT, and X/Open and offers a simple (10 high-level functions) interface to basic mail services. Thus, it is appropriate for implementing simple mail-aware applications. These applications are typically concerned with the easy exchange of data files and simple messages.

Another notable initiative in defining standard e-mail APIs is Microsoft's Extended MAPI, which allows mail-enabled applications to more fully manage handling large volumes of complex messages and addressing with complex folder management requirements. MAPI is discussed in more detail later in this chapter.

8.2.4 RPC versus messaging

Obviously, each method—RPC or messaging—has its own advantages and disadvantages. Specifically, among RPC advantages are:

- Familiar programming paradigm
- Ease of use and understanding
- No need for new API
- Enabling technology for DCE
- Higher-level application than messaging, and ability to use messaging for transport
- Well suited for client/server computing model
- Standards-based (i.e., DCE RPC, OSI RPC)

RPC disadvantages include:

- Fundamentally synchronous (even though asynchronous RPC processing can be implemented via complex programming)
- Requires IDL precompilers

Similarly, messaging advantages include:

- Support for synchronous and asynchronous message delivery and processing
- Does not require both parties to be available all the time
- No need for precompilers
- Event driven in nature, well suited for client/server, peer-to-peer, and distributed object models

Among messaging disadvantages are:

- New programming paradigm
- Standards are still emerging
- Multiple, often incompatible APIs
- Lack of interoperability between various messaging vendors and products
- Lack of integration with DCE

The comparison between messaging and RPCs indicates that there is no clear winner. Therefore, the selection of the middleware technique should be based on application requirements, affinity to the existing system environment, availability of the products, available expertise, product time to market, and other business needs.

8.2.5 Data management middleware

As previously discussed, both RPCs and messaging middleware support a number of middleware requirements by providing a transparent and consistent application-to-application communication. A special case of middleware solutions addresses a relatively narrow class of application-to-database connectivity. Conversely, this form of middleware addresses a large number of business applications struggling with the interoperability and portability issues. Indeed, the problems of database connectivity are apparent in the differences among the programming interfaces, DBMS protocols, DBMS languages, and network protocols of disparate data sources. Even when data sources are restricted to relational DBMSs that use SQL, significant differences in SQL syntax and semantics must be resolved.

In the absence of a consistent way to connect front-end applications to various back-end databases, applications developers are forced to incorporate support for vendor-specific APIs in their applications. A common example is the use of Sybase DB-Lib and CT-Lib APIs (System 10) to access SYBASE SQL Server. Support for additional database systems requires that applications developers either build new applications or modify existing ones to accommodate diverse APIs—this is a very labor intensive and expensive process. It becomes quite obvious that a common approach to heterogeneous database access is required. This approach is a middleware solution that focuses on client/server SQL interactions.

Client/server SQL interaction

This is a mechanism for passing the Structured Query Language (SQL) requests and associated data from one process (usually a client) to another process (server). Client/server SQL is a special case of client/server interactions, applicable to distributed relational database applications. In this case, the server is a relational database server. It can reside on a different system (remote relative to a client), possibly running under a different operating system. The majority of the client/server products implemented to date are based on client/server SQL interactions. Both the messaging and the RPCs can be used for these interactions, and many different transport mechanisms are supported. And while the details of the transport mechanisms are hidden from application developers, client/server SQL interactions impose severe protocol and format restrictions on users. SQL syntax, functionality, and supported data formats are the reasons for these restrictions.

Client/server SQL interactions represent a connection-oriented mechanism. The connection here is made between the client (issuer of SQL requests) and the server. This connection is, in fact, a client/server conversation between partners.

The major drawback of client/server SQL interactions is its data-oriented nature. Indeed, a client/server architecture that implements only the SQL interactions mechanism is limited to those applications that are built on the relational data model (that does not mean that the database has to be relational; it only has to support SQL). This limitation does not make the database middleware solutions trivial—any application using a database middleware software expects it to at least:

- Support relational and nonrelational DBMSs with a consistent API
- Support multiple client and server operating systems in a heterogeneous distributed environment
- Support multiple network transport protocols
- Support database transactions
- Provide data type and data representation conversion
- Provide robust security
- Support consistent error handling

Several proposals from various standards organizations and vendor consortiums are trying to become de facto standards that address database middleware issues. Among them are the embedded SQL and call-level interface (CLI) standards from ANSI and SAG (SQL Access Group) and emerging standards like IBM's Distributed Relational Database Architecture (DRDA), Microsoft's ODBC, and OLEDB.

Another approach to solving the database middleware puzzle is to use database gateways. In this case, SQL translation, data conversion, and other essential functions are performed by a common piece of software—database gateway—which receives requests from clients and hands them over to a server for processing. Gateways "speak" both the client language and the server language, and do a translation or interpretation of the database interactions. Examples of gateways include Information Builders' EDA/SQL, TechGnosis SequeLink, SYBASE Open Gateways for CICS and DB2 (including MDI Database Gateway), and ORACLE SQL*Connect.

8.2.6 Distributed TP managers

Middleware is a run-time software layer that binds the client and the server applications into seamless but complex networked applications. The middleware glue facilitates the distribution of processing among multiple systems and interactions between dissimilar systems and provides the ability to share resources between individual interconnected systems, multiple specialized and heterogeneous nodes, and networks. Building applications requiring coordinated and responsive resource sharing in the distributed environment is difficult, time consuming, and error prone. This is partly due to the fact that large production systems are often supplemented by new distributed systems.

Another reason for the difficulty in building applications is the level of detail required by the programmer in constructing distributed networked applications. The solution is the enabling software that constructs a stable, platform-independent application environment—middleware. Functionally, distributed transaction managers like IBM's CICS are capable of providing that enabling layer not only in mainframe-based OLTP systems, but also in the new, distributed heterogeneous environment. Therefore, often TP managers are considered as a special class of middleware solutions, characterized by their ability to provide a consistent application-to-application interface in a distributed on-line transaction processing (OLTP) environment. In addition to interface consistency, TP managers as middleware solutions can typically support transaction routing, execution of remote functions (e.g., function shipping), transparent access to remote data, transaction integrity, security, manageability, and recoverability.

Although a detailed discussion on transaction managers can be found in Chap. 13, a list of available TP manager products may make the picture more complete. Several TP manager products are available today for use in distributed OLTP environments:

IBM's CICS

The ability to provide a Common Application Environment, good portability, and a strong and mature mechanism for transaction and function routing across systems make CICS an extremely popular tool. The CICS family of products includes CICS/ESA, CICS/VM, CICS/400 for AS/400 midrange systems; CICS/2 for the OS/2 operating system; and CICS/6000 for the AIX operating system (IBM's version of UNIX). The later is ported to non-IBM UNIX environments—HP-UX from Hewlett-Packard, and Solaris from Sun Microsystems—an indication that CICS has significant potential in the new distributed computing environment arena, especially as a means to provide mainframe coexistence for the new OLTP applications. In addition, since IBM's distributed CICS products are based on Transarc's DCE services and Encina Transaction Manager, the resulting relationship between DCE and CICS may assure DCE's leading role as the technology of choice for network communications.

The CICS system is very strong in its API, intersystem communications facilities, server-to-host interoperability, security, interprocess communications between servers, and scheduling. On the down side, CICS' historically centralized approach to transaction processing results in poor load balancing. CICS/6000 cannot distribute client requests to multiple replicated nodes and cannot manage all nodes from a central location—each of these nodes has to be managed independently.

TUXEDO

This is a TP manager from UNIX System Laboratories, a Novell company. The majority of TUXEDO installations are UNIX-based, although there is a version of TUXEDO that runs on IBM mainframes under the MVS/ESA operating system. TUXEDO is the least complex of these transaction managers and excels in performance, availability, and data-dependent routing. However, TUXEDO is not as strong as CICS on the host connectivity and server-to-server IPC. Lacking integration with the DCE affects TUXEDO security capabilities.

TOP END from AT&T/GIS

This is another TP manager aimed at UNIX. TOP END demonstrates a very high degree of load balancing and client and terminal interoperability (including support for DOS, Windows, OS/2, and 3270 clients). Among its strong features, TOP END is capable of integrating non-XA-compliant DBMSs and provides easy-to-use GUI interfaces for OLTP systems. On the negative side, TOP END is not very strong in host interoperability, application multithreading, and nested transactions. Similar to TUXEDO, TOP END does not use DCE security, which affects its security capabilities, as well as server-to-server IPC abilities.

Encina from Transarc

This is an advanced TP manager that employs transactional RPCs. Encina is ported to many UNIX environments committed to the OSF DCE and, in fact, provides underlying low-level TP services to the CICS/6000. Encina is excellent in multithreaded application support, nested transactions, durable queues, and transaction suspend/resume processing. Encina provides a high degree of distributed system capabilities and supports both server replication and routing across nodes, which enhances its availability. In addition, Encina is well integrated with the DCE, which results in strong security and server-to-server communications. On the down side, Encina lacks flexible priority schedule capabilities; its host connectivity is based on APPC/LU6.2, which makes the programming relatively complex; and its Structured File System–based file access is relatively slow.

8.3 MIDDLEWARE AND EMERGING STANDARDS

Among the most popular standards that are emerging to respond to the fast-growing middleware market, software vendors and IS organizations alike pay special attention to the OSF Distributed Computing Environment (DCE), Microsoft's Open Database Connectivity (ODBC),

OLEDB (an encapsulation of database access routines into Object Linking and Embedding) and Mail API (MAPI), and Common Object Request Broker Architecture (CORBA). Although promising, these standards are good examples of the lack of interoperability among several middleware solutions vying for marketplace dominance.

Let's look at these standards. DCE was discussed in Chap. 1, though not necessarily from a middleware perspective. From a complete middleware solution standpoint, one of the biggest issues with the DCE is its heavy reliance on RPCs and its lack of messaging support.

Microsoft's ODBC is a solution that focuses exclusively on vendor-independent data access. OLEDB is an encapsulation of database access into Object Linking and Embedding (OLE) and, as such, is an attractive approach aimed at integrating data access within the OLE paradigm, thus completely insulating the application from the data location and structure. MAPI, on the other hand, deals with the e-mail class of applications that are characterized by asynchronous message delivery. ODBC, OLEDB, and MAPI are described later in this chapter.

CORBA, briefly described in Chap. 1, is an object-oriented switching mechanism for the messages passed between objects. This mechanism, known as an object request broker (ORB), fits closely into the client/server architecture. While CORBA supports messaging, it is heavily focused on synchronous communications and, in fact, uses messaging in very much the same fashion as it would RPCs.

One possible middleware architecture based on open system standards could be that shown on Fig. 8.9.

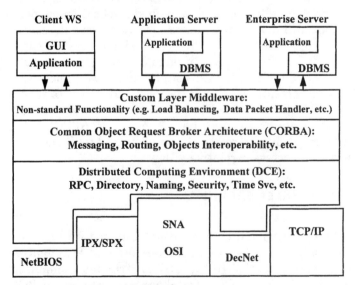

Figure 8.9 Possible middleware architecture.

Here, an application distributed across three-tiered hardware platforms sends data and service requests to CORBA's object request broker, which is responsible for all the mechanisms required to find the specific object implementation for this request, to prepare the object implementation to receive the request, and to communicate the request to the object. The interface used by the client application is completely independent of the service location and the object implementation. In other words, CORBA provides location-independent messaging to the specified object, residing on a known named server. The ORB uses DCE RPCs, distributed file system, directory services, time services, thread services, and security to deliver requests to the servers and services (object implementations). DCE supports various communication protocol stacks either natively or by employing a separate multiprotocol access layer similar to IBM's Multi Protocol Transport Network. The functionality missing from this architecture, but required by the extended enterprise client/server computing middleware component, is implemented in a separate "thin" architecture layer that sits on top of the CORBA.

8.4 MAJOR VENDOR'S MIDDLEWARE STRATEGIES

The importance and revenue potential of the middleware market is difficult to underestimate. A significant number of software vendors are competing for the market share by offering new and improved versions of their middleware solutions on an almost daily basis. Given the number and the dynamic nature of the products, it would be an almost impossible task to list all available and emerging middleware products. Therefore, this chapter provides a brief overview of the middleware strategy of major vendors—hopefully, those who help shape the market and standards in the middleware arena.

8.4.1 IBM

IBM has entered the middleware arena with a suite of products and strategic directions that has made a visible impact on the market. IBM offers middleware products that support:

- *RPC*—DCE RPC is available on OS/2 and AIX platforms and will be available on every platform where DCE is ported. Distributed program link, or DPL, is an RPC-like mechanism for any-to-any CICS applications.

- *Asynchronous messaging* (MQSeries products: message queue manager, or MQM, for variety of platforms)—These products support syncpoint participation, are rich in functionality, and are consistent across supported platforms, which include MVS/ESA, OS/400, VSE/ESA, OS/2, DOS, MS Windows, System/88, Stratus, and Tandem. MQSeries MQM products allow specific and nonspecific message retrieval, support message triggers, request/reply, reply-only, and request-only modes of communications, persistent and nonpersistent messages, parallel message processing, and user-written exits. For consistency, interoperability, portability, and ease of application development, applications communicate with the MQSeries products via a common message queuing interface, or MQI, which contains only 11 basic verbs (operations) that an application can use for messaging.

- *Synchronous messaging* (Common Programming Interface for Communications, or CPI-C)—It is based on IBM's established and popular Advanced Program-to-Program Communications protocol (APPC/LU6.2). CPI-C is endorsed by X/Open and OSI, which makes it a safe choice for synchronous messaging middleware.

- *Database middleware* (Distributed Relational Database Architecture, or DRDA)

- *Networking middleware* (Multiprotocol Transport Network, or MPTN)—This includes isolating applications from the networking protocol stack; for example, MPTN allows an APPC conversation to run over a TCP/IP network or to run TCP/IP Sockets over SNA (see Fig. 8.10)

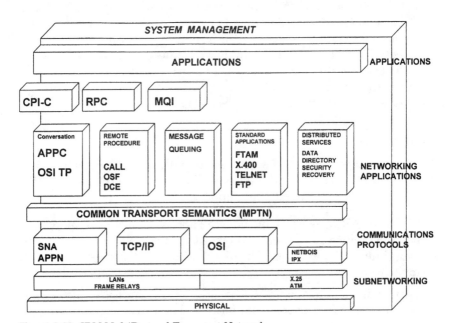

Figure 8.10 IBM MultiProtocol Transport Network.

8.4.2 Microsoft

Microsoft offers two middleware solutions: Vendor Independent Database Access and the Vendor Independent Store and Forward Messaging Interface.

ODBC

Open database connectivity (ODBC) is a core component of WOSA and Microsoft's strategic interface for accessing data in a heterogeneous environment of relational and nonrelational database management systems. Conceptually, the ODBC approach is similar to the familiar Windows print model, where a developer writes to a generic print interface and a run-time loadable driver maps the generic print logic to hardware-specific commands. ODBC provides an open, vendor-neutral way of accessing data stored in a variety of proprietary personal computer, minicomputer, and mainframe databases. By providing data access to a virtual relational DBMS, ODBC alleviates the need for independent software vendors and corporate developers to learn multiple application programming interfaces.

ODBC is based on the SQL Access Group's call-level interface (CLI) specification and, as a result, has broad industry support. It has undergone extensive industry technical review during the specification process. ODBC defines several conformance levels: from core ODBC, which guarantees database-independent access, to fully capable drivers, which exploit all of the functionality of a specific database server.

ODBC is SQL-based but can support SQL and non-SQL databases. It is communications protocol independent. ODBC consists of the SAG CLI specification plus enhancements for data typing, error handling, scrollable cursors, and performance optimizations.

With growing industry support, ODBC is quickly emerging as an important industry standard for data access for both Windows and Macintosh applications. Each application uses the same code, as defined by the ODBC API specification, to talk to many types of data sources through DBMS-specific drivers. A driver manager sits between the applications and the drivers. In Windows, the driver manager and the drivers are implemented as dynamic link libraries (DLLs).

The application calls ODBC functions to connect to a data source, send and receive data, and disconnect. The driver manager provides information to an application such as a list of available data sources, loads drivers dynamically as they are needed, and provides argument and state transition checking. (See Fig. 8.11.)

The driver, developed separately from the application, sits between the application and the network. The driver processes ODBC function calls, manages all exchanges between an application and a specific DBMS, and may translate the standard SQL syntax into the native

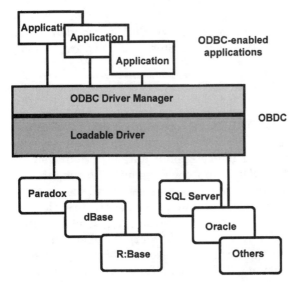

Figure 8.11 ODBC architecture.

SQL of the target data source. All SQL translations are the responsibility of the driver developer.

Applications are not limited to communicating through one driver. A single application can make multiple connections, each through a different driver, or multiple connections to similar sources through a single driver. And here lies one of the biggest advantages of ODBC: its ability to match client programming requirements to a variety of server DBMSs. ODBC provides applications that use multiple DBMSs with complex context management logic to control multiple connections and multiple SQL requests.

To access a new DBMS, a user or an administrator installs a driver for the DBMS. ODBC promises that a user does not need a different version of the application to access the new DBMS. In cases where this is true, ODBC provides a tremendous benefit for end users, as well as significant savings for organizations, in support and development costs.

Unfortunately, even ODBC is not perfect. For example, since practically all available DBMSs are different in their architecture and features that go far beyond simple SQL, ODBC provides pass-through functionality, so that application developers can issue native DBMS API calls whenever necessary. This, of course, renders application programs not portable from one DBMS to another.

Developers could avoid this trap by using ODBC drivers for a given DBMS, as is the ODBC intention. Notwithstanding the benefits of ODBC, development organizations and users should be aware of the drivers-quality issue. The ODBC driver for a given DBMS may conform to various ODBC SQL compliance levels (0, 1, 2, with level 0 conforming to SAG CLI). It may be developed by a third-party provider with not as detailed knowledge of the DBMS as the DBMS vendor itself. Finally, as new versions of DBMSs hit the market, ODBC drivers will have to track the changes very closely and accurately. To be prudent, organizations should carefully analyze the ODBC drivers before choosing ODBC for a mission-critical application.

OLEDB

Data access via OLE is a long-term Microsoft strategy. (See Fig. 8.12.) In this schema, Microsoft proposes to provide applications with data access using the same interfaces used for its popular Object Linking and Embedding technology. ODBC will still be used to access relational databases, with native OLE interfaces used for nonrelational data and application data linking (i.e., documents, e-mail, etc.).

OLEDB is intended to include updated ODBC components as well as business rules that cross different data types, a catalog for libraries, query and update capabilities across data providers, and a set of services for direct access to underlying components. Since OLEDB is an extension of the ODBC model rather than a new paradigm, the transition to OLEDB is designed to have minimum impact on the application architecture (see Fig. 8.13). To ease this transition, Microsoft plans to add a translator (code named *Kagera*) between OLEDB applications and ODBC drivers.

This approach will allow the creation of class libraries of reusable data access objects suitable for integration with procedural code as

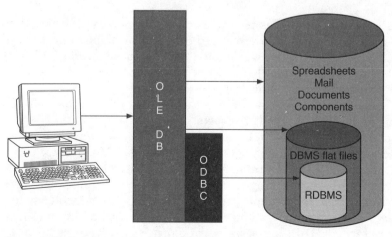

Figure 8.12 Data integration using OLE.

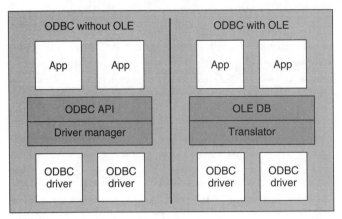

Figure 8.13 ODBC with and without OLE.

well as with GUI-based visual data controls. Coupled with Network OLE—distributed OLE capabilities codeveloped with Digital Equipment Corporation and based on Digital's Object Broker—the OLEDB integration of data access into the OLE will free application developers from the details of data location, structure, and even the technology. Such a uniform data access model will enhance application developers' productivity and facilitate component reuse.

MAPI

Microsoft's Messaging Application Programming Interface (MAPI), a client application interface, supports Common Mail Calls (CMCs), and simple and extended MAPI function calls. Similar to ODBC, MAPI is one of Microsoft's Windows Open Services Architecture (WOSA) facilities.

MAPI provides interfaces to transport, mail directory, and message store services. Simple MAPI provides 12 API calls to support basic mail capability. It also includes an optional common user interface (dialog boxes) to allow a consistent look between mail applications. The simple MAPI calls enable an application to send, address, and receive messages. Messages can include data attachments and Windows Object Linking and Embedding (OLE) objects.

Extended MAPI goes far beyond simple MAPI to provide greater interaction with the messaging services. Extended MAPI is an additional API set, intended for complex messaging-based applications such as advanced workgroup programs that use the messaging subsystem extensively. Such applications are likely to handle large and complex messages in large numbers and require sophisticated addressing features. Extended MAPI supports advanced message features such as *custom forms* and *smart forms*.

The MAPI architecture is based on WOSA with its two tiers: an API interface for client applications and an SPI interface for back-end mail service providers.

The MAPI Service Provider Interface (SPI) supports address book providers and message store providers. Independent transport providers are also supported. The Service Provider Interface for MAPI allows messaging service providers to work with MAPI applications.

MAPI message store. These message store capabilities are based on folders to organize messages. Folders contain messages, and messages can contain attachments. Folders, messages, and attachments all have properties such as the time sent, type (binary, integer), and so on. Folders are organized in a hierarchical tree, allowing applications to store messages in any subtree. In addition, wastebasket or outbox folders can be created. Table operations are provided to enable a user to scroll through the folder structure and to view the messages in each folder by subject or other property. Multiple folders can also be searched for specific information. Criteria can be entered to locate messages with particular properties such as subject, sender or recipient, or message text. Received messages can be modified and stored back in their folders.

MAPI address book. Address books, as defined by MAPI, are a collection of lists of message recipients. Each list is called a *container*. Recipients can be either a single user or a distribution list. Depending on the features of the service providers available on the network system, address books can be organized to have just a single container, a list of containers, or a hierarchy of containers. MAPI supports custom address-book providers. Even if multiple service providers are installed, MAPI allows access to the different service directories and provides a common interface to give the appearance of a single address book to the client application. MAPI also provides a specialized container in the address book called the *personal address book*. Users can store copies of frequently used addresses in this container and can also maintain entries for e-mail recipients who are not in the main address book of the underlying messaging system.

8.4.3 Digital

Digital Equipment Corporation is a major contributor to the OSF DCE. As such, Digital supports practically all forms of middleware. Among the more important products are the following.

- Digital RPCs are a port of the DCE RPC for VMS and Ultrix.

- DECmessageQ (DMQ) is a core component of Network Application Support. It is used in manufacturing, real-time data acquisition, finance, transaction processing, and health care applications. It consists of DMQ Client Library, Basic DMQ Server, and Transactional DMQ Server. DMQ provides a consistent API (11 verbs) and supports multiple queuing servers, synchronous and asynchronous message processing, message priorities, specific or "any" message retrieval, dead-letter queue. DECmessageQ supports OpenVMS, Ultrix (Digital variant of UNIX), HP-UX, SunOS, AIX, Windows/NT, MS Windows, OS/2 and Macintosh over DECnet, and TCP/IP.

8.4.4   Others

Of course, many other vendors are busy developing their middleware products to participate in this emerging and promising market. Among vendor products available today there are a few that are mentioned here for the purpose of illustration only. These references are not intended to be complete, but rather should give a reader an indication of how the market is moving toward an all-encompassing middleware solution.

ezBRIDGE Transact for MQSeries

This product resulted from the alliance between IBM and Systems Strategies Inc. ezBRIDGE provides a simple, robust example of the message-queuing mechanism. The message queuing interface of ezBRIDGE handles user application requests to read and write from the queuing system. The product supports a system administration facility and several communication protocols, including APPC/LU6.2, DECnet, and TCP/IP.

SYBASE Open Client/Open Server

This provides a variation of data management middleware that allows SYBASE clients to interact with multiple data sources in a consistent fashion.

PIPES Platform from Peer Logic

This supports MS Windows, OS/2, AIX, Ultrix, HP-UX, SunOS, NetWare, and MVS over TCP/IP, APPC, IPX, and NetBIOS. PIPES provides 12 API verbs implemented as C functions. It is a self-managing and self-healing platform, with automatic recovery from errors and the ability to reroute messages around failures. The PIPES Platform contains a distributed database of system information that is dynamic and automatically updates as the system changes. In addition, PIPES provides a hierarchical, logical naming service that enables true resource location independence.

8.5 MIDDLEWARE BENEFITS

A complete middleware solution will provide organizations with the following benefits:

- Consistent API across multiple platforms
- Platform, operating system, and network protocol independence
- Insulation of applications developers from the intricacies of the underlying network protocol stack
- Data location and possibly structure independence
- Enhanced source code portability and application interoperability
- Lower development and maintenance costs
- Reusability of application-to-application communication code
- Improved system availability and manageability by incorporating dynamic routing and load balancing into middleware functionality

Cooperative Processing and Data Management in Client/Server Environments

Traditionally, most large organizations developed applications to reside on central, mainframe computers. As a result, the data these applications access was also stored in central locations in corporate databases. However, the use of large, centrally located computers for such centralized application processing was becoming more and more expensive, especially when compared with the price-performance advantages of microcomputers. Today, businesses are becoming more and more interested in implementing distributed databases. Some of the reasons for doing this include:

- *Business's desire to reduce operating costs and to decentralize operations in order to be more competitive and more responsive to customer demands*
- *Advances in the area of distributed and client/server computing*
- *The availability of enabling technology for distributed processing, including products implementing distributed databases in a client/server architecture*

As a result, operational systems for most large organizations reside on a variety of platforms and use multiple-database products. Applications' and end users' data access requirements in such a widely heterogeneous and diverse environment are not easy to fulfill. Given the ever-pressing need to ensure high data availability, integrity, and currentness, distributed data management poses a challenge to developers and database administrators alike.

Chapter

9

Distributed Data Management

The discussion on centralized versus distributed data is largely dominated by the degree of data sharing and local autonomy required by an organization. The main purpose of distributed data management is the ability to access data distributed to multiple sites (network nodes) in a fashion transparent to end users. Given the complexity and relative inefficiency of existing solutions to provide end-user data access to the (often remote) locations at which data originates, distributed data management is also given the responsibility of keeping most data local to the sites that actually use it.

Ideally, a properly implemented distributed database allows each node to be configured to handle the amount of data residing at the node, as well as the multitude of user applications and a large number of concurrent users. As the number of applications and users grows, the corresponding data requirements grow as well. The resulting upgrades to a distributed environment tend to be less expensive than a corresponding centralized system upgrade and can often be implemented in a fashion totally transparent to end users.

Distributed data management is one of the styles of cooperative distributed processing implemented in the client/server architecture. Indeed, the client/server architecture offers an ideal solution to the requirements of distributed data management. Most of the client/server architecture implementations available today are implementations of distributed database management systems, or DDBMS. The distributed data management environment is characterized by two-way distribution:

- The data and DBMS are distributed among multiple nodes, including the node with the application logic.

- Data management functions are distributed between a front-end system (data manipulation logic and language, or DML) and the back-end server (database functions, or DBMS).

While one of the most popular variations of the client/server architecture, distributed data management deals with a lot of complicated issues, some of which have not been solved to date.

The issues of data distribution, methods of distributed data access, data integrity, consistency, and concurrency are described in this chapter.

9.1 WHY DATA DISTRIBUTION?

Distributed data management deals with data (databases) distributed among multiple nodes. Distributing data among multiple sites offers the following benefits:

- Placement of data closer to its source wherever appropriate

- Higher data availability by placing multiple copies of critical data at different locations, thus eliminating a potential single point of failure and enforcing local autonomy

- More efficient data access, thus improving data management performance

- Application load balancing as it relates to data access

- Facilitation of growth in applications and end-user demands

There are, of course, some drawbacks to distributing data. Among them are the complexity of the distributed data management and a relatively high potential for the loss of data synchronization. In fact, the decision on centralized versus distributed data is largely dominated by the degree of data sharing and local autonomy required by an organization—the higher the degree of data sharing, the more attractive is the option that includes centralized data storage. Obviously, centralized data is easier to monitor, manage, and control. However, organizations that are geographically dispersed and require a high degree of local autonomy, cannot be satisfied with centralized data solutions. Then data distribution becomes a viable alternative.

While the data distribution methods described in this section apply to any data model, be it sequential, hierarchical, networked, or relational, the relational data model makes the illustration of the data distribution methods easier to understand. Therefore, most of the examples deal with data organized in a relational data model. The following is a very brief and informal description of the relational data model.

9.2 RELATIONAL DATA MODEL

A relational data model views all data as organized in tables. Table rows represent records of data, while table columns (attributes) represent fields in the record. There are no duplicate rows in a given table, and the order of rows is not significant. Tables reflect facts and values of the real world. Therefore, each table contains data about some real fact. For example, a bank's individual CUSTOMER table contains data about noncorporate customers, while an EMPLOYEE table contains data about bank employees (see Fig. 9.1).

The column (or a combination of columns) that uniquely identifies a particular fact that the table is based on represents a unique *primary key* for this table. Typically, each table contains a primary key. For example, the CUSTOMER table may have a customer's social security number as the primary key (it is unique and it identifies customers). To eliminate data redundancy, designers perform the *normalization* process, which aims to put *all* data about the primary key in the same table where the key is defined.

To illustrate the relational data model, consider a bank application which deals with customers, employees, and checking and saving accounts. Let's look at the customer information. It consists of the customer's social security number, name, address, account number, and account information (balances, last deposits/withdrawals, etc.). All these data elements can be organized in one table. However, since a customer may have many accounts and several accounts may allow more than one customer (e.g., customer's spouse or children), such a table will contain a fair amount of redundant (duplicate) data. Redundancy can cause a data integrity problem when such a table has to be changed. After the normalization process is completed, the resulting, normalized relational customer-account data model consists of three tables: CUSTOMER, CHECKING (account), and SAVING (account), as illustrated in Fig. 9.1. Similar to the facts of the real world, all three tables should be related. For example, the CUSTOMER table may contain a column with the savings account number and another column with the checking account number.

It is important to note that the savings account number column in the CUSTOMER table must point to an existing savings account number (primary key) in the SAVING table. Otherwise, the customer will have a nonexistent savings account. The same logic applies to the checking account column in respect to the CHECKING table. Columns in one table that represent a reference to the matching primary key values in another table are called *foreign* keys. An example

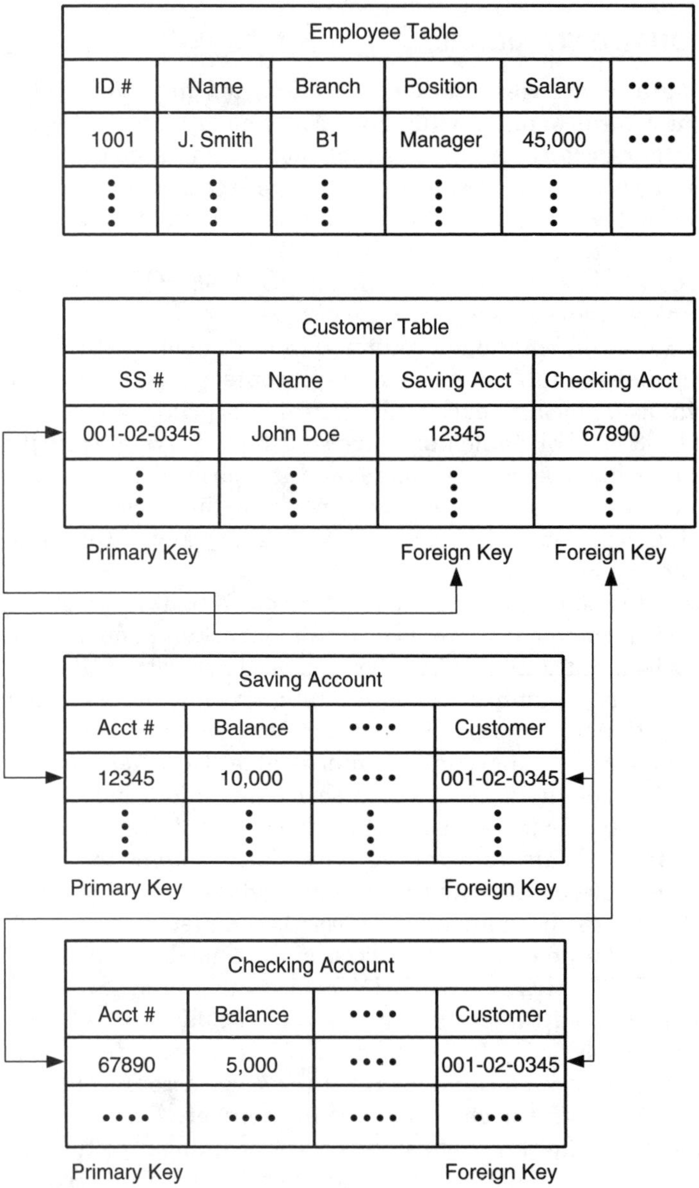

Employee Table					
ID #	Name	Branch	Position	Salary	••••
1001	J. Smith	B1	Manager	45,000	••••
⋮	⋮	⋮	⋮	⋮	

Customer Table			
SS #	Name	Saving Acct	Checking Acct
001-02-0345	John Doe	12345	67890
⋮	⋮	⋮	⋮

Primary Key   Foreign Key   Foreign Key

Saving Account			
Acct #	Balance	••••	Customer
12345	10,000	••••	001-02-0345
⋮	⋮	⋮	⋮

Primary Key   Foreign Key

Checking Account			
Acct #	Balance	••••	Customer
67890	5,000	••••	001-02-0345
••••	••••	••••	••••

Primary Key   Foreign Key

Figure 9.1 Relational data model.

of a primary key–foreign key pair is the social security number (SSN) column in the CUSTOMER table and the CUSTOMER_SSN column in the SAVING table, correspondingly. The relationship between primary and foreign keys presents an interesting problem when one (or more) of the related tables is updated. Consider, for example, that a row containing a primary key value, referenced by a foreign key, is deleted (e.g., a row of the CUSTOMER table with the SSN value equal to 101-22-3333). Then, the foreign key for this primary key (e.g., the CUSTOMER_SSN column of the SAVING table) either has to be changed to point to the existing primary key value or deleted. Otherwise, the corresponding savings account will lose its owner. Similarly, if a new row, containing a foreign key, is inserted (added) into the table, the value of the new foreign key must match one of the primary key values in the related table. These rules describe a special type of constraint that exists between primary and foreign keys: the *referential integrity* constraint.

Relational databases support the relational language *SQL (Structured Query Language)*. This language is used to formulate operations that define and manipulate data in relational form. The subset of SQL that defines data is called *Data Definition Language (DDL)*, while *Data Manipulation Language (DML)* supports data manipulation in the relational data model. SQL is the only means of providing access to data in a relational database. SQL contains only a handful of operators and appears to be easy to learn and use. This ease is deceptive and may be true for simple applications. To design a complex relational database and provide efficient data access to it, SQL requires a knowledge of relational algebra as well as an understanding of a particular RDBMS.

One of the main advantages of SQL and the relational data model is *nonnavigational* data access. In nonrelational database management systems, the user has to tell the DBMS not only *what* data is needed, but also *how* to get to it. The *how* is done by selecting a data access path and navigating along it in the physical implementation of the underlying data model. This navigation differs from one nonrelational database to another. For example, in the hierarchical data model a programmer uses the appropriate procedural DBMS language (e.g., DL/I) to move from top to bottom and from left to right to reach the desired data destination.

Relational DBMSs and SQL are based on the relational theory. Therefore, users familiar with the theory should expect to access data with fewer errors and fewer unpleasant surprises. Since users do not tell the RDBMS how to satisfy data requests, the database management system itself should be intelligent enough to figure out the best access path to the required data. By design, RDBMS provides for better data independence by isolating end users from the underlying physical structure of the database. SQL applications are, in theory, independent of a particular RDBMS implementation. A familiar tabular form of data representation, the relative simplicity of SQL, the lack of procedural data access coding, and data access portability across any RDBMS result in increased application developer productivity and are the main reasons for the wide acceptance of relational technology.

9.2.1 Evolution of SQL

Over the years, Structured Query Language has grown considerably in its scope and power. The first step toward SQL was the relational database model developed by Dr. E. F. Codd at IBM, who had proved that the logical operations of relational algebra can be used to extract any fact from the data organized into a relational database, and that no procedural code is required for such a task.

SQL has been endorsed by ANSI, whose X3H2 Database Standards Committee started its work on a relational language in 1981 and in 1986 produced its first standard—SQL-86. At that time, the SQL-86 standard was, in effect, the lowest common denominator to all SQL dialects then in existence. Vendor products and their efforts to move the standards process forward by establishing the SQL consortium (SQL Access Group, or SAG) resulted in the accelerated pace at which SQL was becoming more mature, powerful, and flexible. The current version of the standard—SQL-92—embraces the best features of many current vendor implementations, and goes even further. It includes advances in orthogonality, an extended JOIN syntax for the FROM clause, date and time data types, and many other features. Most database vendors are actively working on incorporating the SQL-92 standard into their database engines.

The work on the SQL enhancements continues today. The next version of the standard—SQL3—is an extension of SQL-92 that includes Massively Object-Oriented SQL Extensions (MOOSE). Despite the object-oriented extensions considered for SQL3, many still doubt that MOOSE will be accepted by the object-oriented world. One reason for this uncertainty is the difference in the object-oriented models used by the SQL3 and C++, SmallTalk, and other object-oriented languages. Another reason is that the Object Database Management Group (another vendor consortium) has published its own standard—a pure object-oriented database management system language, and not at all an extension to SQL-92.

Another SQL enhancement effort is related to multimedia. SQL Multi-Media (SQL/MM) proposals discuss extensions to handle free text, images, and geographical and spatial data. Even though SQL/

MM's future is uncertain, one fact remains certain: as business needs continue to grow and diversify, the relational model and SQL will have to continue to evolve to accommodate the ever-expanding scope of user requirements.

9.3 METHODS OF DATA DISTRIBUTION

There are several methods of distributing data in a distributed environment. Some of these methods are rather simple, while others may appear more complex. The important fact is that the method selected for data distribution affects the way the data can (and sometimes should) be accessed. It should be noted that the more complicated data distribution methods, while theoretically possible and implementable on a relatively small scale, may force such high demands on the state of the database and networking technology that not every organization will be able to afford it. In business terms, the most practical solution for a geographically dispersed organization may be the delivery of all data needed by a remote site to that site. The next sections will discuss these data distribution methods.

9.3.1 Manual extract

In a centralized, nondistributed environment, all data is concentrated in one central place (e.g., corporate databases on a mainframe). In a distributed environment, the data is distributed among multiple locations. Logically, however, distributed data still belongs to a centralized corporate data repository. Distributed data management environment designers must decide:

- *How* and *when* data should be taken from the conceptual, central repository for distribution

- *What* are the optimum locations for data element placement

The latter question involves various data access methods as well as network throughput characteristics. The former question, however, applies equally to any data location configuration and is dealt with in this chapter.

One of the simplest ways to distribute data is to allow the user to manually copy the data from one central location to other locations. This method of data distribution is called a *manual extract*. It is simple enough to be controlled by the user as requests for the data arrive at the data administrator.

For example, consider the bank application previously described. The central bank information repository is located in New York and contains all customer, checking, and savings account data in corresponding tables. In addition, it contains a currency EXCHANGE table.

In the distributed environment, bank branches maintain their own customer and account repositories corresponding to their customers (see Fig. 9.2). If a new branch is opened, the data administrator can make a complete or partial copy of the EXCHANGE table and load it in the EXCHANGE table for a given branch.

Such an operation can be performed as a manual extract. It can be done in one of two ways:

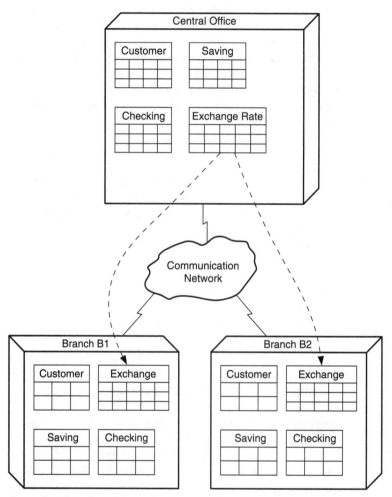

Figure 9.2 Distributed data—bank application.

- From the central site (then the extract is performed against the local table, and the load against the remote table)

- From the new branch (the extract is executed against the remote table, and the load against the local table)

In the case of the relational data model, extract and load can be done via appropriate SQL statements (e.g., SELECT and INSERT).

In fact, the manual extract would be satisfied by limiting each group of SQL statements (SELECTs and INSERTs) to a single data location (central site or new branch). More accurately, the manual extract can be performed by the remote request or remote transaction types of distributed data access. These and other distributed data access methods are described in the Sec. 9.5.

9.3.2 Snapshot

To automate the user-performed operations of the manual extract, the tasks of data distribution should be given to the DDBMS itself. As the requirements for data distribution increase in complexity, so do the intelligence, capability, and complexity of distributed DBMSs.

Among distributed data management tasks given to the DDBMS, *snapshot* processing is relatively simple. Imagine that the DBMS provides the capability of defining a "snapshot" copy of the desired table at the needed locations, as well as the frequency of the extract-load procedure. Using SQL, such definitions may look like:

```
CREATE SNAPSHOT <name>
         AS SELECT .. TIME <hh:mm:ss>, INTERVAL <hh:mm:ss>
```

In snapshot processing, the user may define which tables (and which columns in these tables) have to be used to create a snapshot. The time and frequency of the snapshot processing can also be specified by the user (for example, at midnight, or every six hours). Then, the DBMS will automatically perform all necessary actions. The tables and columns are specified in the SELECT clause, which lists the data elements (column names) and corresponding table names required to build a snapshot copy of the original table.

Snapshots are designed to distribute relatively static information that changes rather infrequently. For example, the currency EXCHANGE table is the ideal snapshot candidate, because changes to the exchange rates are, at most, done once a day. Although snapshots can be updated, no provision is usually made to take these updates back to the original source of data. Therefore, snapshots are typically limited to read-only access.

9.3.3 Replication

For those applications where the distributed data can be updated at multiple locations, snapshot processing is not sufficient. Such an application may require a copy of the same table to be maintained at multiple locations.

The DDBMS is capable of supporting an advanced data distribution method, *replication,* when this DDBMS can:

- Create and maintain copies (replicas) of a given table at multiple required locations

- Maintain data consistency among all replicas (either synchronous or asynchronous processing).

Clearly, replicating data to a remote location makes it more accessible to the remote parts of the organization and thus increases the degree of local autonomy. In the bank application example, let's assume that customers can transfer their accounts from branch to branch. If a customer record and relevant account information is not found in a given branch, the required information can be copied from the branch that used to maintain the customer and his/her accounts. In an extreme case, the entire CUSTOMER table could be replicated, with replicas placed at every branch. In order to be able to maintain accurate records, all replicas should have consistent information about customers and their accounts.

Synchronization of updates between all replicas is not the only problem that a distributed DBMS must solve. By definition of a true distributed DBMS, when multiple copies of the same table exist, applications that access this replicated data in a distributed environment should not be aware of the location of the replicas. Otherwise, applications have to be changed depending on the location of the systems on which they currently reside and on the number of replicas currently maintained. Indeed, if every branch of the bank maintains a Customer Balance Sheet program, the program should not be aware of the location of the CUSTOMER table replica it accesses.

Replication management, data consistency, and location transparency are among the tasks the Distributed DBMS should perform to be able to support distributed replicated data. Each of these requirements represents a serious design and implementation challenge. As demonstrated later in the book, some of these problems can be solved only by limiting the functionality of the access to distributed data or by changing the distributed model to a replicated database model, which often proves to be a more practical solution.

This section is not intended to provide all details on data replication, but rather considers the replication in the context of the distributed database technology. A detailed discussion on data replication can be found in Chap. 11.

9.3.4 Fragmentation

Besides table replication, distributed data requirements may include the need for row and column replication, where only particular rows and/or columns of a given table are replicated by the DDBMS. If only the subset of data that is subject to update is replicated, row/column–level replication may simplify data synchronization. In addition, from the data size perspective, it may be more efficient to replicate only parts (*fragments*) of the data. Data fragmentation, although it represents a special case of data replication, is the most complicated method of data distribution and also results in a lower degree of local autonomy. Fragmentation is best illustrated in the relational data model, where data tables can be fragmented either horizontally or vertically.

To illustrate horizontal fragmentation, let's expand the bank application by adding the EMPLOYEE table, which contains one row for each employee (see Fig. 9.3).

In a distributed environment, the EMPLOYEE table is to be distributed to different branches, based on the list of employees for every branch. To do this, the entire EMPLOYEE table is fragmented *horizontally* by creating subsets of employees—rows in the EMPLOYEE table. To illustrate vertical fragmentation, let's assume that the EMPLOYEE table contains employee medical history records, which can be viewed only by the centrally located medical department. These medical records represent a subset of the EMPLOYEE table columns. To distribute medical records (certain columns of the EMPLOYEE table) to the medical department, the EMPLOYEE table is fragmented

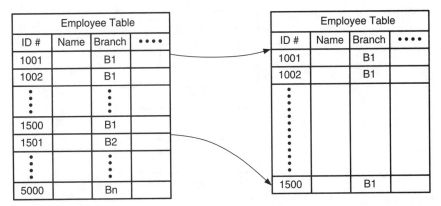

Figure 9.3 Horizontal fragmentation.

vertically, and the appropriate fragments are placed at desired locations (see Fig. 9.4).

Of course, both the horizontal and vertical fragmentation methods can be combined to obtain subsets of rows and columns to be distributed. Regardless of the method, fragmentation, by being more selective, allows only the needed data to be distributed physically close to where it is used.

However, the main drawback of fragmentation is the complexity of its implementation. It becomes evident in light of the application requirement of full transparent access to data in the distributed environment. Indeed, consider the EMPLOYEE table that is distributed by fragmentation (horizontally, vertically, or both). If a management

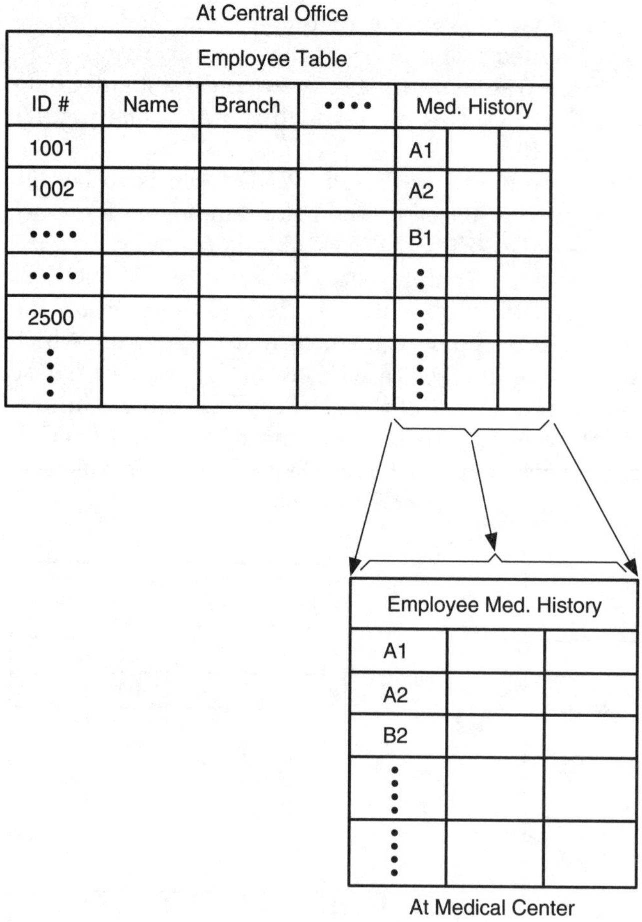

At Central Office

Employee Table						
ID #	Name	Branch	• • • •	Med. History		
1001				A1		
1002				A2		
• • • •				B1		
• • • •				•		
2500				•		
•				•		

Employee Med. History		
A1		
A2		
B2		
•		
•		

At Medical Center

Figure 9.4 Vertical fragmentation.

appraisal application requires access to all employee records in their entirety, such an application will have to access employee data in all branches of the bank and then combine it with the portion of the employee data kept at the medical department.

Employees can transfer from one branch to another, and branches can be merged into bigger branches. Therefore, the application should be able to access distributed data in a manner totally transparent from the data location and the fragmentation method. That can be achieved by viewing the fragmented data as residing in a single table. The alternative is to rewrite the application every time an employee is transferred.

Providing the perception of data being resident in a single table at a single site (location and fragmentation transparency) is one of the major challenges facing distributed DBMSs designers.

9.4 DISTRIBUTED DATA LOCATION ANALYSIS

Designers of distributed environments must decide which computing resources have to be distributed as well as at which locations. Decisions about data locations are among those required to implement a truly distributed environment.

Whenever the architecture defines a distributed computing model, it also has to provide a decision process that justifies a particular choice for data placement. Indeed, a distributed client/server system presents a number of opportunities for data placement (e.g., locally on a client, remotely on a server, remotely on a next-tier server, distributed among several platforms, etc.). When making a data placement decision, several factors need to be taken into account. For example, the following can influence a local data placement decision:

- It enables local autonomy.
- It minimizes network traffic (to/from server).
- Data is read only or read/write, small in size, and local in context (no need to keep a copy remotely).

Similar factors can be applied to data resident on a local (i.e., branch) server, especially if the data in question needs to be shared among this server constituency (workgroup). The factors that adversely affect the local data placement decision include:

- Cost of distributing or replicating data from a central site
- Cost of replication/distribution software

- Network bandwidth
- Cost, complexity, and availability of data management and synchronization
- Availability of a load/build window to create a local database
- Frequency and size of data movement
- Cost and complexity for data location, replication, and fragmentation transparency

These factors can be assigned weights, and then the decision on data placement can be calculated based on known access patterns weighted accordingly.

The following analysis is offered as an example of such a decision-making process. Assume that the distributed environment for the bank application consists of only two locations: the central site (location S1) and one branch (location B1). Assume further that the CUSTOMER table, kept in its entirety at the central site, is partially replicated (e.g., horizontally fragmented, as described in the previous section) in the branch B1 location. In order to maintain consistent customer information, every update to the CUSTOMER table at either location must be duplicated at another location, while read-only operations can be done locally. Remember, that S1 has all customer records and branch B1 maintains all the customer records it may need to retrieve.

Assume that the CUSTOMER table at location S1 contains 10,000 records, is read 2000 times, and is updated 500 times daily. The branch B1 CUSTOMER table contains 1000 records, is read 1000 times, and is updated 100 times (see Fig. 9.5, top).

If all customer data is placed at one particular location, all data access from another location must be sent over the network connecting these locations. If all customer data is placed at S1, then the data traffic from/to branch B1 would be equal to 1100 messages (1000 reads plus 100 updates). Conversely, if all customer data is placed at B1, the total traffic would be equal to 2500 messages (2000 reads plus 500 updates). This consideration appears to indicate that leaving customer data at the central site would be the best solution. However, it is easy enough to prove that distributing data between these two sites can be even more beneficial to the network traffic. Consider the matrix of possible data locations and the resulting traffic figures (see Fig. 9.5, bottom). Remember, that traffic results from reading data not found at the given location and from the need to keep the updated data synchronous with its copy.

Out of the three possible configurations (all data at S1, all data at B1, data is distributed between S1 and B1), the third configuration is

Operation	Location	
	S1	B1
Read	2,000	1,000
Update	500	100

Assignment of Read/Update Operations Between Locations

Configuration Number	Data at Location		Message Traffic
	S1	B1	
1	Y	N	1,100
2	N	Y	2,500
3	Y	Y	600

Figure 9.5 Data location analysis matrix.

optimum from the network traffic point of view (traffic equals 600 messages—500 updates from the S1 location plus 100 updates from the B1 location).

While not totally accurate, such an analysis can be expanded to include multiple data objects (e.g., SAVING table and CHECKING table), costs per transmission (especially if there is a choice of networks), cost and requirements for data storage, and other characteristics of data distribution.

The important conclusions of this analytical approach are:

- Regardless of the data distribution method, distributing data appears to be beneficial to the distributed system throughput.
- The placement of the distributed data can be decided based on the logical data and process (read/update) models and the number and characteristics of the available data locations.

9.5   DISTRIBUTED DATA ACCESS

When data is distributed among several locations, all or part of the data management logic must be also distributed to accompany the data. As was already discussed, at least some portion of the database processing logic (DBMS) must reside on the same system as the database itself.

Regardless of the data distribution methods employed, the data access provided by distributed DBMS must be performed in such a fashion that location of the data is transparent to users and applications. In fact, in a truly distributed database environment, users and applications should not be aware that the data is distributed.

Distributed data access, while required wherever data is distributed among several network nodes, is not only appropriate but absolutely necessary in the client/server architectures which support data distribution between clients and servers. Any client/server implementation that allows data (and a local DBMS) to be maintained on client systems as well as on the database server must provide for distributed data access.

Therefore, various types of distributed data access are discussed in terms of the client/server architecture where an application resides on the client workstation and issues data requests for either local (client-resident) or remote (server-resident) data. These types of distributed data access are described in the following in order of increasing capabilities, and the relational data model is used for the illustration. Note that some of the distributed data management issues were formulated by C. J. Date, one of the first designers of relational databases. These are C. J. Date's 12 Distributed Database Rules and are listed in App. B and discussed in more detail in Chap. 10.

9.5.1   Remote request

Consider a simple one-client/one-server environment. One of the simplest tasks that the client application can issue is a data request to the server. When an application issues a *single* data request to be processed at a *single* remote site, it is called a *remote request* (see Fig. 9.6).

In the case of the relational model, such a single request is a single SQL statement which refers to the data resident at a single remote site (server). Again, consider the bank application. If the CUSTOMER table is located centrally on Server 1 rather than distributed, (remote) bank branch B1 can issue a remote SQL request to read the customer's information. Such a request contains references only to the remote data. The distributed DBMS can support remote requests transparently if the DDBMS maintains data locations. Conversely, the DDBMS

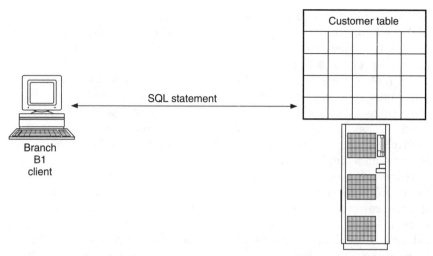

Figure 9.6 Remote request.

can support remote requests if the application specifies data locations. In the case of a relational DDBMS, a sample remote SQL request to retrieve New York customer data from the CUSTOMER table in the bank database (BANKDB) residing at remote Server 1 can be specified as follows:

```
SELECT * FROM SERVER1.BANKDB.CUSTOMER
    WHERE SERVER1.BANKDB.CUSTOMER.CITY = "New York"
```

Remote requests can be used to perform the manual extract method of data distribution. In the same scenario, when the CUSTOMER table is to be manually distributed to a local branch, the branch computer can issue a remote request for all customer data and can then copy the data into the local DBMS.

9.5.2 Remote transaction

The definition of a remote request can also be formulated from the point of view of transactions and logical units of work. A transaction can be defined as a sequence of predefined actions, performed on behalf of the application, that take a computing system and its resources from one consistent state to another in order to accomplish the desired business functionality. This predefined sequence of actions represents a *logical unit of work (LUW)* performed by a transaction. Therefore, a remote request can be redefined as a data processing *transaction* or logical unit of work, which consists of a *single* data request that refers to data residing at a *single* remote location (server). By definition of the LUW, when a remote request is completed successfully, the remote data is in a new, consistent state, and all work done in the remote request is committed.

A remote transaction capability allows a transaction to contain *multiple* data requests, all of which refer to data residing at a *single* (remote) location (see Fig. 9.7). If a remote request represents a simple, single-action logical unit of work, a remote transaction may consist of multiple actions, all dealing with the data at a single location and all comprising a single logical unit of work.

Therefore, a remote transaction is sometimes called a *remote unit of work (RUW)*. From the client/server architecture point of view, the remote transaction capability implies that the remote data is placed at a single server and accessed from a client workstation in a single logical unit of work. In the case of the relational data model, a remote transaction may consist of several SQL statements, each of which refers to data resident at a single remote site (server).

In the bank application example, the remote request to read customer information in the CUSTOMER table from any branch can be expanded by adding an update action. For example, a remote branch B1 (server B1) not only needs all the information about New York customers but also needs to update the branch table's POSTED indicator (both tables reside on server 1). Both of these actions represent a remote transaction that must be performed as one logical unit of work. If the application is required to specify data locations by using fully qualified table names, such a remote transaction may look like:

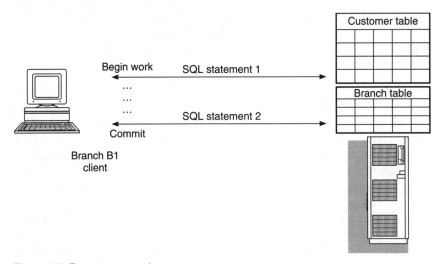

Figure 9.7 Remote transaction.

```
BEGIN WORK
SELECT * FROM SERVER1.BANKDB.CUSTOMER
  WHERE SERVER1.BANKDB.CUSTOMER.CITY = "New York"
UPDATE SERVER1.BANKDB.BRANCH
  SET POSTED_IND = 'YES'
COMMIT WORK
```

Note that the two SQL statements (SELECT and UPDATE) are surrounded by LUW brackets (BEGIN WORK and COMMIT WORK). Therefore, the remote unit of work illustrated here, will be successful only if both SQL statements are successful.

User-initiated remote transactions, similar to remote requests, can be used to perform the manual extract method of data distribution.

9.5.3 Distributed transaction

A distributed transaction capability allows a transaction to contain *multiple* data requests for data at *multiple* locations. Each of the requests refers to data residing at a *single* (remote) location, which may be *different* from the data location referred to by another request (see Fig. 9.8). A remote request represents a simple, single-action logical unit of work. A remote transaction is more complex and may consist of multiple actions, all dealing with the data at a single location. The distributed transaction, while still supporting the remote request/remote transaction limitation of a single location per data request, goes even further by allowing access to multiple locations within a single logical unit of work. In a client/server architecture, the distributed transaction capability implies that the data, distributed among multiple servers, can be accessed from a client workstation in a single logi-

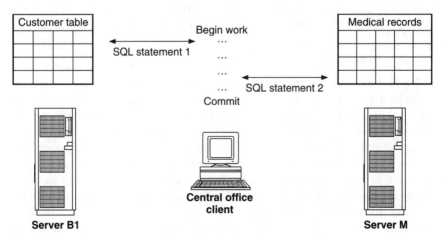

Figure 9.8 Distributed transaction.

cal unit of work. A distributed transaction represents a *distributed unit of work (DUW)*.

In the case of the relational data model, a distributed transaction may consist of several SQL statements, one for each data location among the available server locations.

In the bank application example, the central office (server 1) may need information about employees having advanced educational degrees (e.g., an MBA) who work at remote branch B1. Simultaneously, the central office may need the medical history of all employees of that branch. All medical records are kept at the medical department (server M).

Both of these actions represent a distributed transaction, since they deal with multiple locations in the same logical unit of work. If the application is required to specify data locations by using fully qualified table names, such a distributed transaction may look as follows:

```
BEGIN WORK

SELECT * FROM SERVERB1.BANKDB.EMPLOYEE
       WHERE SERVERB1.BANKDB.EMPLOYEE.EDLEVEL = "MBA"
SELECT * FROM SERVERM.BANKDB.EMPL_MED
       WHERE SERVERM.BANKDB.EMPL_MED.BRANCH = "B1"

COMMIT WORK
```

Note that, even though the two SQL statements deal with different data locations, they are surrounded by the LUW brackets (BEGIN WORK and COMMIT WORK). Therefore, the distributed unit of work illustrated here will be successful only if both SQL statements, executing at different locations, are successful. Similarly, if any one of the SQL statements fails, the entire logical unit of work is considered a failure.

9.5.4   Distributed request

The distributed request represents the most complex method of distributed data access. Distributed requests allow a transaction consisting of multiple requests to be processed by a distributed database server. A transaction consisting of *multiple* requests can be processed at *multiple* sites, and each request can reference data residing at *multiple* sites. To summarize, on the scale from simple to complex, a remote request represents a simple, single-action logical unit of work; a remote transaction represents a more complex unit of work that may consist of multiple actions, all dealing with the data at a single location; a distributed transaction allows access to multiple locations within a single logical unit of work; and, ultimately, the distributed request does not contain the single-site-per-request limitation. Each individual component of the distributed request can access data from multiple locations and, therefore, can be processed by multiple locations. Moreover, all actions performed within the distributed request constitute a single logical unit of work. In a client/server architecture, the distributed request capability implies that data can be distributed among multiple servers by either replication or fragmentation, and be accessed transparently from a client workstation in a single logical unit of work (see Fig. 9.9).

In the case of the relational data model, a distributed request may consist of several SQL statements, each referencing data located at multiple server locations.

In the bank application example, the central office (server 1) may need to report all employees who have advanced educational degrees, working at remote branch B1 (server B1) and, at the same time, the medical history of these employees, kept at the medical department (server M). In addition, the BRANCH table for branch B1, kept at the central site (server 1), has to be updated to indicate that the report has been done. Such a business requirement can be satisfied by:

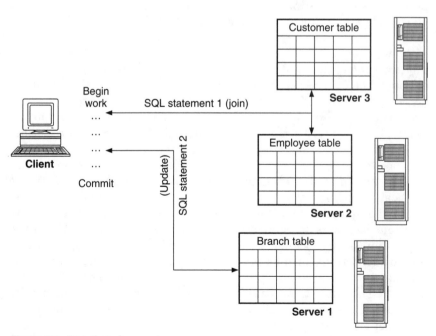

Figure 9.9 Distributed request.

- Joining the two tables—the EMPLOYEE table at location "Server B1", and the EMPL_MED table at location "Server M"
- Updating the BRANCH table at location "Server 1"

This is how such a distributed request may be coded in SQL:

```
BEGIN WORK

SELECT * FROM SERVERB1.BANKDB.EMPLOYEE B1,
            SERVERM.BANKDB.EMPL_MED M
    WHERE B1.EMPL_ID = M.EMPL_ID AND WHERE B1.EDLEVEL = "MBA"
UPDATE SERVER1.BANKDB.BRANCH
    SET REPORTED = "YES"
    WHERE SERVER1.BANKDB.BRANCH = "B1"

COMMIT WORK
```

Note that the first SQL statement joins two tables from two different locations, while the third SQL statement updates data at yet another location. And all these actions are performed as one logical unit of work, even though multiple physical DBMSs at multiple locations are involved. All four types of distributed data access are required to support a distributed DBMS. But only distributed request processing may be considered to support the concepts of a truly distributed database management system.

Remote requests and remote and distributed transactions all permit access to remote data, as well as allowing users to perform application (client) processing at locations different from the database (server) processing. Thus, these three types of distributed database processing all support some form of the client/server computing model. However, these three types of distributed database processing all impose restrictions on *how* the data should be accessed and *what* can be done by the application. In addition, remote request and remote and distributed transaction processing often require the application to know the physical location of the data. Ideally, the distributed request capabilities allow users to distribute data among multiple locations without applications having to know where the data is physically located. Therefore, distributed requests, by imposing no restrictions on the application's data access logic, support the complete cooperative client/server processing in a distributed computing environment. An example of such an environment is a fully distributed database application implemented in the client/server architecture (see Fig. 9.10).

Here, the DDBMS provides both data replication and fragmentation. Because data is closer to the applications using it, the DDBMS sup-

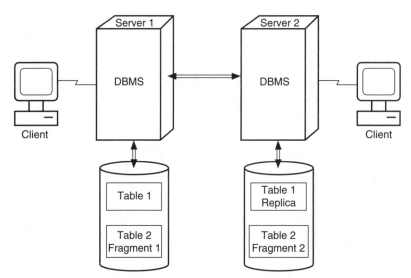

Figure 9.10 Distributed database in the client/server environment.

ports faster read-only operations and ensures data integrity when updates are performed on portions of the distributed data.

9.6   DATABASE TRANSACTION MANAGEMENT

A truly distributed database management system should support distributed requests by providing data location and fragmentation transparency to the applications and end users. However, the transparency requirements are only the beginning of a long list of features a distributed DBMS must have. One of the most important issues of the distributed DBMS is the integrity of updates applied to the distributed database. Distributed data integrity and consistency of databases are based on the previously mentioned fundamental concept of transactions. This means that a truly distributed DBMS is responsible for maintaining the database in either of the two consistent states: before the update transaction begins and after the update transactions executed *successfully*. Partially completed transactions should not be allowed.

Specifically, update data integrity is supported by the concept of database transaction management.

9.6.1   Database transactions

As applicable to distributed data management, the database transaction can be defined as a sequence of one or more data manipulation statements that together form an atomic, logical unit of work. Either all statements in the transaction will execute successfully or none of the statements will be executed. Formally, a database transaction should possess the following properties:

- *Atomicity.*   An entire transaction is either completed or aborted.

- *Consistency.*   A transaction takes databases from one consistent state to another.

- *Isolation.*   A transaction effect is transparent to other transactions, applications, and end users until the transaction is committed.

- *Durability.*   The changes to recoverable resources made by a committed transaction are permanent.

- *Serialization.*   As long as a transaction in progress depends on certain information, this information is locked to prevent any other transaction from changing it.

In general, a transaction, or logical unit of work, is said to be committed when it completes all processing successfully. A database transaction is committed when all data manipulation statements have been executed successfully. In this case, all changes made by the transaction to recoverable data become permanent. Transactions can be committed implicitly, by successfully terminating, or explicitly, by issuing special commitment statements.

If any of the data manipulation statements fails, the entire database transaction fails, and all partial changes to the database made before the data manipulation statement failure (if any) must be rolled back in order to bring the database to its before-transaction consistent state. In a relational database, a database transaction that consists of one or more SQL statements is committed when all SQL statements are completed successfully, and aborted if one of the SQL statements fails. SQL supports database transactions through two SQL transaction processing statements: COMMIT and ROLLBACK.

The ANSI/ISO SQL standard defines a SQL transaction model and the roles of the COMMIT and ROLLBACK statements. Most commercially available RDBMS products (for example, IBM's DB2) use this transaction model. Briefly, this transaction model specifies that a SQL transaction must automatically begin with the first SQL statement executed by a program or a user, and continues to execute the subsequent SQL statements until:

- A COMMIT statement *explicitly* ends the transaction successfully, making the changes to the recoverable data (e.g., databases) permanent.

- A ROLLBACK statement *explicitly* aborts the transaction, backing out (rolling back) uncommitted database changes.

- A program executing the transaction terminates successfully (*implicit* COMMIT), making the database changes permanent.

- A program executing the transaction terminates abnormally (*implicit* ROLLBACK), backing out all partial, uncommitted changes to the database.

When the transaction processing environment is localized (not distributed), and the only recoverable resource in question is a database, the DBMS itself can handle database transaction processing.

Usually, the DBMS uses a sophisticated transaction-logging mechanism. Before-the-change and after-the-change images of the changed database records, as well as COMMIT indications, are written in reliable, nonvolatile storage before the database record itself is changed and written back to disk storage.

The picture changes drastically as the environment becomes distributed and additional resources (e.g., databases, files, etc.) come into play.

9.6.2 Two-phase commit protocol

To better illustrate the complexity of database transaction management in a distributed environment, consider the bank application. Assume that the business requirements caused the SAVING_ACCOUNT table for all customers to be placed in the central office located in New York, while all checking account records reside at the checking processing center, located in Chicago. A money transfer (MT) transaction, which debits the savings account (in New York) and credits the checking account (in Chicago), deals with two physically remote databases and resource managers (DBMSs). As with any database transaction, the MT transaction starts with the first SQL statement to subtract the required amount from the saving amount value and proceeds to add this amount to the checking account. For example, the MT transaction may look as follows:

```
BEGIN WORK
    UPDATE SERVERNY.BANKDB.SAVING
        SET SAV_AMOUNT = SAV_AMOUNT - <money amount> WHERE
SERVERNY.BANKDB.SAVING.ACCT_NO = <customer account number>

    UPDATE SERVERCH.BANKDB.CHECKING
        SET CHK_AMOUNT = CHK_AMOUNT + <money amount> WHERE
SERVERCH.BANKDB.CHECKING.ACCT_NO = <customer account number>
COMMIT WORK
```

If both of these actions are successful, the transaction should commit the changes to the appropriate databases. If any one of the SQL statements fails, the transaction should abort and the changes made before the point of failure should be rolled back. Indeed, neither debiting the savings account without crediting the checking account nor crediting the checking account without debiting the savings account satisfies a business's or customer's requirements.

The DBMS at each of the processing sites can take care of the local COMMIT/ROLLBACK processing. The issue here is the coordination between the actions taken by multiple participants—in this case, the local and remote DBMS resource managers. That's where the transaction manager services become extremely important. These transaction services can be performed by a distributed DBMS itself or by a separate transaction processing manager (TPM), which then also becomes a participant in the transactions it manages. In order to decide whether to make the changes to the distributed databases permanent (i.e., to treat the COMMIT request as global) or roll them back, the DDBMS or TPM must follow a special set of rules, called the *two-phase commit* protocol.

The two-phase commit protocol is the process by which a *global commit* request is performed. It works as follows:

1. When an application attempts to commit a multiple-participant transaction, one of the participants is first designated as the *coordinator* of the two-phase commit process.

2. In phase one, which is called the *prepare phase,* the coordinator requests that all participants in a global transaction *prepare* to commit their local resources and signal their readiness back to the coordinator. Once the participant is prepared, its log file is marked accordingly and this participant can no longer attempt to abort the transaction.

3. If all participants are ready to commit, the coordinator brings the transaction into phase two—the *commit phase,* by broadcasting the COMMIT signal to all participants. At that point, all local resource managers commit their local recoverable resources.

4. If any of the transaction participants fails to prepare to commit, it notifies the coordinator. In this case, the coordinator broadcasts the ROLLBACK signal to all participants and the entire global transaction is rolled back.

Logging both the prepare and commit phases of the two-phase commit protocols allows all participants to determine the same outcome of the global, distributed transaction. It is either committed, thus placing the distributed resources into a new consistent state, or rolled back, nullifying the effects of the transaction as if it never happened. One of the better-known examples of the two-phase commit implementation is the transaction management performed by IBM's CICS in coordination with such resource management as DB2, VSAM, or IMS/VS.

9.6.3 Distributed two-phase commit

Complex distributed transaction processing applications may involve several transactions in different systems to be executed in order to perform the required application function. One way to accomplish this is to use the structured approach of the master-slave tree (see Fig. 9.11). There, the initial request starts the front-end transaction (master of the entire tree), which in turn starts another, remote transaction (its slave), which initiates its slave, etc.

This approach, while offering the least complicated design, causes this distributed transaction's synchronization points to involve all tree nodes. Unless the request for synchronization (either COMMIT or ROLLBACK) originates from the tree master, the synchronization is unlikely to succeed.

The tree master (transaction coordinator) must perform the following functions:

- Identify all participants involved in the transaction.

- Send PREPARE-TO-COMMIT (PTC) requests to all participants.

- Ensure that all participants successfully acknowledge the PTC request.

- Log the fact that all participants are prepared.

- Send the COMMIT request to all participants.

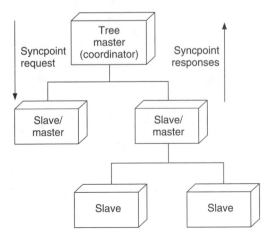

Figure 9.11 Master-slave tree.

- Ensure that all participants successfully acknowledge the COMMIT request.

- Log the fact that all participants have committed.

Logging of the commit phases is critical to transaction consistency and durability, i.e., implementation of a successful two-phase commit. Therefore, a transaction selected as the distributed transaction coordinator must be able to log the commit phases or interact with the transaction logging services provided by the transaction manager.

To support proper synchronization of the two-phase commit protocol, the transaction coordinator (tree master) should initiate the COMMIT process, and the synchronization signals should be propagated all the way down the tree. The COMMIT/ROLLBACK responses flow in the opposite direction, from the leaf nodes through the intermediate masters, to the tree master. The transactions should be designed in such way that if any of the transactions attempting to execute the COMMIT command (explicit or implicit) abends, that abend should be propagated to every other transaction in the tree, and all transactions should back out their protected resources.

The two-phase commit protocol is just one of a long list of distributed data management issues. RDBMS distributed query optimization, distributed DBMS administration, concurrency and locking, heterogeneous and homogeneous DDBMS implementation, access control (security), and other issues are described in the next chapters.

Designing a Distributed Data Management System

Distributed data and database management systems represent an interesting phenomenon. On the one hand, it appears to be one of the most popular, easily justifiable, and readily available implementations of the client/server architecture. On the other hand, distributed databases are among today's most complex and misunderstood technologies. This complexity and confusion are reflected in the variety of distributed data access standards as well as in the multitude of definitions and vendor implementations of distributed databases in the client/server environments.

The analysis of the methods for data distribution and access in the cooperative client/server environment was done in the previous chapter. It has already demonstrated the need for and complexity of such distributed DBMS features as data location, replication and fragmentation transparency, and distributed data integrity. The discussion of distributed database features, their analysis, and the issues the DDBMS designers have to deal with continues in this chapter.

10.1 DISTRIBUTED DATA DICTIONARY

The difficulty of the implementation of truly distributed databases becomes obvious when the DDBMS designers begin considering the ramifications of particular DDBMS requirements. The main problem unique to a distributed system in general is the need for global (centralized) knowledge about the entire system. Even from a communication point of view, it is difficult for one node to know everything about the rest of the network.

The problem becomes even more acute when the distributed system supports a distributed database. In this case, such a system, in addition to questions like "Where Is Node A?" and "Where Is Program B?," must have knowledge about the structure and location of every file, database, table, column, and their possible replicas. Moreover, there are other questions related to DDBMS processing that a distributed database system must solve. Questions like those of a distributed (two-phase) commit and of deadlock detection in a remote node are just a few examples.

Some of these questions can be answered by a *data dictionary, data directory,* and *system catalog*. The combination of data dictionary/directory/catalog plays an important role in the distributed system architecture. Each of these components performs its own critical function.

A typical database system keeps metadata—all necessary information about the resources it manages (data elements, attributes, entities, rules, indexes, statistics, etc.)—in a database *dictionary*. With the advent of the distributed DBMS, database dictionaries have been expanded to include references to remote data, control information about the network, and its nodes characteristics. Data location references are typically stored in database *directories*. In a client/server environment, database dictionaries and directories are usually kept at and maintained by the DBMS server. A successful implementation of such a metadata repository tool can bring several important business benefits to the organization. Among them are:

- Significant reduction in time spent on many projects through better communication and management of project requirements and requirements revisions

- Reduction in overall maintenance costs through improved capabilities to perform change impact analysis, particularly in cross-application maintenance situations

- Reduction in application system development costs through time savings resulting from automated information sharing among development tools

- Increased recognition of opportunities for cost savings from leveraging existing data and software

- Enabling the best-of-breed development tool environment which uses the data directory as a mechanism for storing and exchanging information

- Enhanced capabilities for locating data, performing change impact analysis, and identifying opportunities for data/process reuse
- Enhanced control and management of data and processes

Finally, let's consider a relational DBMS. In order to support non-navigational data access typical of RDBMSs, all pertinent information about the relational objects is usually kept in a set of internal, relational system tables called a system *catalog*.

Thus, the combined data directory/dictionary/catalog represents a critical focal point for all development and run-time data-related activities supported by a distributed database management system. As the name implies, in a distributed DBMS environment, the information from this metadata repository needs to be distributed as well. The need to distribute and maintain this critical information source has some very serious implications for the implementation of truly distributed databases.

If a repository is not distributed in a distributed database system, it is then "centrally" located. Every data request, regardless of the location of the requester, should be matched against a particular server-resident database repository in order to validate the request and to determine the location of the requested data.

One drawback of such an approach is obvious. A *centralized* metadata repository becomes a bottleneck for all data requests, as well as a strong candidate for being a single point of failure. Another reason for the distributed database dictionary/directory is the nature of distributed database systems. Again, consider the bank application example. Imagine that a centralized (nondistributed) database dictionary resides at the bank's New York headquarters. Every request for London customer data initiated by the London branch must first be routed to New York for validation and data location search, only to be returned back to London for processing—a practically unacceptable solution. If the repository was distributed between New York and London servers, however, such a request would be satisfied within the London branch. Such a distributed repository becomes *global*. It contains a global view of the distributed database. However, the global repository itself is a distributed database. As such, the distribution of the database dictionary/directory introduces a consistency problem. All those repository copies must be kept in sync even as data locations and network nodes characteristics change. Otherwise, a local copy of the data directory will point to a particular location at a specific node. If either the data has been moved or the node becomes unavailable, the data request could not be satisfied. As a result, the transaction, or even the entire system, may fail.

While the need for the data directory/dictionary is clear, its development, especially in a distributed client/server environment, is not a trivial task. Aside from the purely technical issues, the organizations embarked on the development of a distributed metadata repository have to deal with several organizational, operational, and administrative issues as well. Among these issues are:

- The need to synchronize logical data definitions with physical data structures

- The need for version control and change control tracking and management

- The impact of nonexistent, incomplete, or out-of-date documentation of legacy system, data structures, and processes on an organization's ability to document the existing and emerging data environment

- The effort required to obtain metadata information from historically paper sources and to reformat it for import into the data directory

In the ideal distributed database management system, the task of metadata repository synchronization is given to the DDBMS itself. Such an ideal distributed database system can be defined to satisfy the set of rules developed by C. J. Date.

10.2 C. J. DATE'S RULES AND DISTRIBUTED DATA MANAGEMENT ISSUES

In 1987, C. J. Date, one of the first designers of relational databases (together with Dr. E. F. Codd, the author of the relational theory), proposed 12 rules that a fully distributed database management system should follow (C. J. Date's Rules can be found in App. B). These rules do not represent absolute requirements. They were proposed only to bring some clarity to the heated debates on DDBMS. However, C. J. Date's Rules have become widely accepted as the working definition set and the criteria of a distributed database. Therefore, this chapter analyzes the requirements, features, feasibility, and associated issues of the distributed databases in terms of Date's 12 rules.

10.2.1 Rule 1—local autonomy

The first C. J. Date rule defines the DDBMS requirement for local autonomy. The rule states that in a truly distributed database environment, the sites (DBMS locations) should be autonomous, or independent of each other. This rule assumes that each site where a distributed database resides is characterized by the following:

- The local (for a given site) database is processed by its own database management system (DBMS).

- The DBMS at every site handles the security, data integrity, data consistency, locking, and recovery for its own database.

- Local data access operations use only local resources (e.g. local DBMS).

- Even though each site is independent of other sites for local operations, all sites cooperate in accessing distributed data from multiple sites in one transaction.

Date's first rule is quite logical, considering the architecture of the distributed database. For example, let's look at a distributed database environment implemented as client/server architecture (see Fig. 10.1).

This particular client/server implementation consists of three client sites connected to two database servers. This environment is designed to support an already familiar bank application where the client sites represent bank branches B1, B2, and B3. Each branch maintains a local (to a given branch) customer database, together with the local savings and checking account data, all managed by the local DBMS. Servers S1 and S2 represent the bank's data-processing centers that maintain the checking and the savings account databases accordingly for all customer accounts, as well as central copies (replicas) of all customer records.

For example, Date's first rule allows one of the branches to open customer accounts when another branch is closed, and even if one or both data-processing centers are not operational (e.g., they are undergoing

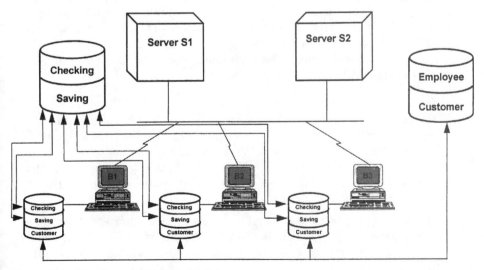

Figure 10.1 Client/server distributed database.

weekly maintenance). Moreover, each local transaction retains all database transaction properties of atomicity, consistency, isolation, and durability.

Conversely, violation of the first rule will force all bank branches and service centers to be on-line continuously, even if a customer decides to use a cash access machine in a local branch.

10.2.2   Rule 2—no reliance on a central site

Date's second rule is designed to complement the first rule. The second rule states that the truly distributed database system should not rely on a central site. It means that no one DBMS site (DBMS server) is more important and necessary than any other.

This rule dictates that a distributed DBMS environment should not be built to rely on one (and only one) particular site. Otherwise, such an arrangement could cause this central site to become the bottleneck for system throughput and performance. Also, one central site may become a single point of failure for the entire distributed system.

Date's second rule is sometimes misinterpreted to mean that a distributed DBMS should not have a central site even from the point of view of global control. On the contrary, even the example of a two-phase commit in a distributed transaction environment illustrates that there exists a need for a central coordinator to manage the distributed commit process. This logical central point may exist only for the duration of the distributed transaction, but exist it must.

Imagine a meeting of a group of people, all of whom are peers—equals—for the purpose of making a policy or a business decision. Even if everybody's vote on a decision has equal weight, there must be one person, assigned or elected only for the duration of this meeting, to conduct the meeting and announce the group/majority decision.

In a distributed database environment, Date's second rule can be implemented by the following technique:

- Each site should handle its own concurrency control, local database processing, and its own data dictionary/directory/catalog management. The latter implies that the dictionary is also distributed, probably by full replication, so that all data objects, both local and remote, are known to each site. Thus, in addition to the application processing, the DDBMS must keep the distributed dictionary/directory current among all sites.

- No one *central* site must be involved in every distributed transaction. In other words, if server S1 is chosen to be a central site, it does not have to participate in a customer inquiry initiated and executed at the client branch B1.

- A DBMS at any location (any DBMS server in the client/server architecture) can act as the distributed database manager, or DDM (e.g., the two-phase commit coordinator).

10.2.3   Rule 3—continuous operations

The third rule specifies that the distributed database system should never require downtime. The rule means that no planned database activity, including backing up and/or recovering databases, should require a distributed system shutdown.

For example, consider a distributed database environment supporting the bank application. Let's assume that one of the branches of the bank is located in London, England. The bank decides to perform routine maintenance of its databases (e.g., backup and reorganization) in the New York data-processing center (server S1) on the Friday of a long holiday weekend. Such an activity should not prevent the London branch from conducting its regular business.

Technically, continuous operations in the distributed database environment can be implemented by such DDBMS features as:

- Support for full and incremental (the data that has changed since the last backup) *on-line* backup and archiving. In other words, each database server should be able to back up its databases on-line, while processing other transactions.

- Support for fast (preferably, on-line) database recovery. One way of speeding the recovery is to keep a mirror image of the database available. Some database servers have a disk mirroring feature implemented in their hardware architecture. Some DBMSs implement software disk mirroring, thus providing DBMS fault resistance.

- Support for DBMS fault tolerance. Fault-tolerant DBMSs usually require fault-tolerant hardware.

10.2.4   Rule 4—data location independence

This rule describes a highly desirable—even critical—feature of a truly distributed database system. The rule defines a distributed environment where data is distributed among multiple sites, but users and applications are not aware of the fact that the data is distributed and should not need to know where it is.

Instead, a truly distributed DBMS that satisfies Date's fourth rule provides users and applications with a single image of the database, "local" to the user/application in its appearance and behavior. Therefore, the fourth rule is sometimes called the rule of data location transparency. In a client/server architecture, where a client application is typically remote to the DBMS server, support for the data location independence rule is extremely important.

Some implications of this rule have already been described in the discussion of the methods of data distribution (described previously). Consider what would have happened if the fourth rule was not implemented in the bank application. If a customer transferred all accounts from one branch to another, all programs dealing with this customer's accounts would have to be modified to reflect the new data location.

Moreover, lack of data location transparency would require every application to be aware of the location where this application (and every program) exists. Without data location transparency, the local data has to be distinguished from the remote data. Therefore, if an application has to be moved from one system to another, it would have to be changed accordingly. That's where the data dictionary/directory plays a critical role. To implement data location transparency, designers of the distributed DBMS could use the following approach:

- Users and applications should refer to data by its aliases.

- The distributed data dictionary/directory must maintain a table of data elements, their aliases, and their locations.

- The distributed DBMS should be able to automatically maintain and use this data dictionary, even when a particular data object has been moved from one location to another.

- In order for every user and application to perceive the distributed database as a single local database, the DDBMS must distribute (replicate) the data dictionary/directory to every site and maintain all replicas of the data dictionary/directory synchronized among all distributed system locations.

Often, data location transparency refers to data entities. In the case of the relational data model, the data location transparency rule deals primarily with the databases and tables. Indeed, it makes sense to keep New York customers in the CUSTOMER table in the New York branch of the bank, while the London branch keeps its customers in its own local table. In this scenario, the majority of data access operations deal with one location at a time (per transaction). Data access is usually done via remote requests or remote transactions (remote units of work) and rarely requires distributed tables to be logically combined into one conceptual table.

Many DBMS vendors today implement at least some degree of data location transparency by supporting remote requests/remote transactions that use different variations of the data dictionary/directory approach.

10.2.5 Rule 5—data fragmentation independence

As illustrated in the methods of data distribution, data can be divided into fragments. In the case of the relational data model, the table can be divided into horizontal or vertical fragments, which can be distributed among multiple locations. This method of data distribution is called *data fragmentation.*

Date's fifth rule specifies that in a truly distributed database, a table that has been fragmented must appear as a single table to users and applications. In other words, the fragmentation must be transparent to the users and applications.

Data fragmentation transparency is closely related to Date's fourth rule on data location transparency. However, if the data location transparency rule deals mostly with such objects as databases and tables, data fragmentation transparency handles the situation when a single table is broken into several portions, each of which resides at a different site (see Fig. 10.2).

The difficulty of supporting data fragmentation transparency is in the way the original table can be reconstructed from the fragments.

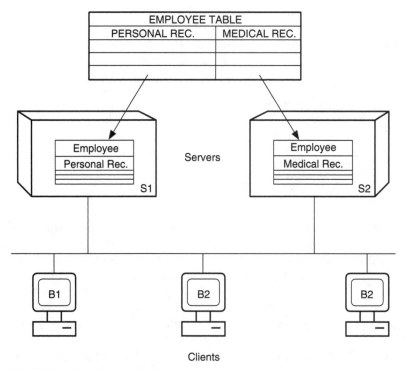

Figure 10.2 Data fragmentation.

Typical access to fragmented data may require the "logical" combination of data from two fragments into one unfragmented table. For example, if an EMPLOYEE table is fragmented into personal and medical fragments (each fragment at its own server location), an employee benefits department may need a complete, combined view of the employee record. Such a join between two fragments may look like the following:

```
BEGIN WORK
    SELECT * FROM SERVERB1.BANKDB.EMPLOYEE,
            SERVERM.BANKDB.EMPL_MED
    WHERE SERVERB1.BANKDB.EMPLOYEE.EDLEVEL = "MBA" AND
            SERVERM.BANKDB.EMPL_MED.BRANCH = "B1"
COMMIT WORK
```

When data from one table is distributed by fragmentation, data access to fragments may require conceptual table reconstruction. Depending on the type of fragmentation (vertical or horizontal), the operation the application may request from the DDBMS can be a join of two tables (as in the case of vertical fragmentation of the EMPLOYEE table just shown.).

Horizontally fragmented tables may be reconstructed using a SQL operation of UNION (e.g., the CUSTOMER table is horizontally fragmented into New York and London parts). A fragmented table reconstruction using the UNION operation may look like the following:

```
BEGIN WORK
    SELECT * FROM SERVERNY.BANKDB.CUSTOMER
    WHERE SERVERNY.BANKDB.CUSTOMER.BALANCE GREATER 10000

UNION
    SELECT * FROM SERVERUK.BANKDB.CUSTOMER
    WHERE SERVERUK.BANKDB.CUSTOMER.BALANCE GREATER 10000
COMMIT WORK
```

Data fragmentation transparency requires the implementation of data location transparency in the context previously described. But just using the data dictionary/directory is not sufficient to implement data fragmentation transparency. Regardless of the type of data fragmentation, access to the fragmented data may require data from multiple locations within a single transaction. The data access may be a distributed transaction or a distributed request. And that is in addition to the need to synchronize distributed database dictionaries!

As was illustrated previously, distributed transaction and distributed requests present several serious problems, among them the coordination of distributed updates, distributed data integrity, and consistency. Several DBMS products offer a degree of support for data fragmentation transparency. An example of these products is Sybase OmniSQL Gateway, which offers an interesting approach to data fragmentation.

10.2.6   Rule 6—data replication independence

Date's sixth rule expands the data location and fragmentation transparency requirements into the data distribution method of replication. The rule requires a distributed database system to be capable of updating replicated, redundant data transparently from applications and users. As the name implies, replicated data is a copy of data that exists elsewhere in the system (at other servers and even at some clients). Since the replicated data is one of the types of distributed data, Date's sixth rule requires the implementation of the data location transparency rule. But the data replication transparency rule has far-reaching implications.

In the bank application, an example of the replicated data may be a savings account database kept in its entirety in the savings account processing center (server S2, Fig. 10.1). Each branch (B1, B2, and B3) keeps its own subset of the SAVING (account) table for all local customers. For a given customer from branch B1, therefore, there exists a savings account record maintained at the customer's branch (client B1). At the same time, the exact copy of this record is kept at server S2.

If this customer withdraws money from the savings account, both the local (B1) and the remote (S2) copies of the database records must be updated. This is a classic case of the need to synchronize distributed resources. Such a synchronization can be done by employing the two-phase commit protocol with either a distributed transaction or a distributed request, or by using asynchronous messaging (see next chapter).

The need for the two-phase commit is clear when the implications of the unsynchronized updates are considered. If a customer withdrew all available funds and the local savings account record was updated (debited) but the central (S2) copy remained the same, the bank's books would show that the customer account had not been changed. Therefore, additional withdrawals (even from other branches, cash access machines, etc.) are possible. Thus, both update actions (local and remote account records) must either be committed or the transaction must be rolled back if any one of the updates fails.

The main issue in this scenario is not just the proper execution of the two-phase commit logic, but the need to perform such a synchronization *transparently* from the users and applications. Ideally, a Savings

Account Debit program should not be aware of the existence of other copies of the data it updates and may contain a simple single-site SQL update statement (using aliases), as follows:

```
UPDATE BANKDB.SAVING
    SET SAVINGS_AMOUNT = SAVINGS_AMOUNT - WITHDRAWL_AMOUNT
    WHERE BANKDB.SAVING.CUST_ACCT_NO = 12345
```

Therefore, the DDBMS itself should initiate additional updates within the now-expanded original unit of work. The DDBMS should conform to the two-phase commit protocol to ensure consistency between two copies of the savings account record. And all these actions should be performed automatically by the DDBMS without any user or application being aware of the replicated data. In effect, the DDBMS should transform the preceding update statement into something like the following:

```
BEGIN WORK
    UPDATE SERVERB1.BANKDB.SAVING
        SET SAVINGS_AMOUNT = SAVINGS_AMOUNT - WITHDRAWL_AMOUNT
            WHERE SERVERB1.BANKDB.SAVING.CUST_ACCT_NO = 12345
    UPDATE SERVERS2.BANKDB.SAVING
        SET SAVINGS_AMOUNT = SAVINGS_AMOUNT - WITHDRAWL_AMOUNT
            WHERE SERVERS2.BANKDB.SAVING.CUST_ACCT_NO = 12345
COMMIT WORK
```

Of course, the DDBMS is made aware of the existence of replicas by searching through the distributed database dictionary, which also must be kept synchronized among its own multiple copies.

As a result of adhering to Date's sixth rule, the DDBMS is becoming ever more complex and must perform increasingly involved, complicated tasks. Look at the task of adding records into the replicated table, for instance. Inserting rows will cause the DDBMS to enforce referential integrity constraints in a distributed environment, where multiple copies of the foreign keys must be checked against multiple copies of the primary key.

Another complicated issue is locking. Even though a detailed discussion of locking is beyond the scope of this book, it is a good illustration of the difficulty of the implementation of data replication transparency. Locking is the technique a DBMS uses to support consistency of data. While one transaction is updating a particular record or a group of records, the data being updated is held by an exclusive lock, i.e., it is locked from updates (and sometimes also from read access in order to prevent viewing of the inconsistent, "dirty" data) by any other transaction. In a distributed environment, where multiple replicas are to be updated, how should a DDBMS ensure that all copies of a given record are locked in every data location?

Furthermore, when two or more applications wish to exercise exclusive control over the same resources, such as database records that are already locked by these or other applications, these applications are in a deadlock. The DDBMS must resolve the deadlock condition, even though the locked resources reside in multiple remote nodes. Global deadlock detection is a serious problem the truly distributed database system should be capable of solving. Typically, a DDBMS detects and resolves deadlocks by keeping a timer and terminating a transaction that timed out waiting for a resource. In addition, some DDBMS products maintain a fixed, limited number of requests active at any given time in the system. Sometimes, a DDBMS employs a deadlock detection algorithm (e.g., terminate or interrupt the shortest-running task, terminate a task with fewer updates, etc.).

The complexity of the data replication synchronization forced database vendors to look for alternative solutions. In addition, the business requirements of many organizations make the synchronous nature of the two-phase commit protocol unacceptable for a number of applications. Instead, many business requirements give a higher priority to the need for a guaranteed delivery of data. Therefore, an alternative approach to data replication, suitable for business applications where the integrity of the replicas can be supported on an asynchronous, guaranteed-delivery basis, attracted a lot of attention.

10.2.7 Rule 7—distributed query processing

Date's seventh rule deals with the performance issues of the distributed database system. To fully understand these issues, let's look at how a query is processed in a nondistributed, centralized relational database (in a nonrelational DBMS, the performance of the query depends on the DBMS access path selected by a user or a program).

Remember that nonrelational DBMSs are navigational. That is, the access is directed by the user, and the DBMS itself follows the user directives.

A relational DBMS (RDBMS) provides for nonnavigational data access where users request *what* data they need, and not *how* to access it. Generally speaking, an RDBMS contains a navigational brain—an optimizer—that is "intelligent" enough to select the best access path for a given query totally transparent to the users and applications. Different RDBMS products offer different optimization techniques, which can be divided into two major classes:

1. Cost-based optimization
2. Rule-based optimization

Rule-based optimizers select an access path based on certain rules that the optimizer follows. For example, when a query to be processed is a join of two tables, the rule-based optimizer may decide that the table coded first (from left to right) in the SQL statement should be searched before the second table is read. The drawback of such an approach can be demonstrated in the following example. Suppose that the bank's central office (server S1) maintains a table of all bank employees and a table of managers. The query in question should look up all employees that are managers whose education level is MBA. Such a query may look like the following:

```
SELECT * FROM BANKDB.EMPLOYEE A,
         BANKDB.EMPL_MGR B
         WHERE    A.EMPL_ID = B.MGR_ID
         AND      A.EDLEVEL = "MBA"
         AND        B.EDLEVEL = "MBA"
```

Usually, there are more employees than managers. Assume that the EMPLOYEE table contains 100,000 rows and the managers table (EMPL_MGR) contains 1000 rows.

If rule-based optimization processes the left-most-referenced table first, the RDBMS will search 100,000 rows of the EMPLOYEE table to select all those with the education level of MBA and then compare them with the 1000 rows of the EMPL_MGR table. Obviously, such an approach is not very efficient.

Cost-based optimization selects the access path for a given query based on the estimated cost of the query processing. Typically, the optimizer calculates the cost in such units as the number of I/O operations and/or CPU cycles. A cost-based optimizer may take into account the number of rows needed to be processed to satisfy the query, the availability of indexes, and various statistical information about data organization, which are accumulated and maintained by the RDBMS in the *system catalog*. Such a catalog must be active, since any additions or deletions to the database (relational objects as well as data records) may change the statistical information.

When a cost-based optimizer processes the query described here, it can calculate the least expensive access path based on the row statistics. Therefore, the query processing should start from a smaller table (EMPL_MGR) and compare the selected managers to the list of employees whose education level is equal to MBA.

Performance becomes a major issue in *distributed* query processing. Indeed, imagine that the EMPL_MGR table and MANAGER table are distributed to two different locations. The size of each node's databases and relevant tables, the network speed, the processing, and I/O power of each node are then among the major factors that affect the performance of a distributed query. In client/server architecture, the DDBMS should maintain the list and processing characteristics of every available server.

In order to find the proper data location and obtain all necessary node characteristics and statistical information about remote databases, distributed query optimization requires access to a *global* database dictionary/directory/catalog. A global dictionary can be implemented by replicating all local dictionaries/catalogs on all nodes (database servers) where the query is performed. And to perform cost-based optimization based on real-time statistics, a truly distributed DBMS must maintain all dictionary replicas as current.

In distributed query processing, one DBMS server must provide the coordination of the optimization and synchronization efforts between all participating databases. Such a coordinator is usually called a *distributed data manager (DDM)*. It is elected dynamically by the DDBMS based on various criteria. In the client/server architecture, the DBMS server that receives the query first can be elected to be the DDM.

Date's seventh rule specifies that, in a truly distributed database system, the optimization must take into account not only local, but also global, factors, including distributed nodes and network characteristics.

Consider an example that illustrates the issues of the distributed query optimization and the role of the DDM. Assume that the bank's central office (server S1) maintains a table of all employees, while the processing center (server S2) holds a separate table of managers. The query in question should look up all employees that are managers whose education level is MBA. Here's how such a query can be processed in a truly distributed database system:

- The server that first receives the query is elected to become the DDM (in our example, it is server S1).

- The DDM knows that the tables in question reside at different locations (S1 and S2) and modifies the original query (see above) accordingly.

```
SELECT * FROM SERVERS1.BANKDB.EMPLOYEE A,
           SERVERS2.BANKDB.EMPL_MGR B
      WHERE A.EMPL_ID = B.MGR_ID      AND
            A.EDLEVEL = "MBA"         AND
            B.EDLEVEL = "MBA"
```

- The DDM accesses its own system catalog to assign costs to the local join component (EMPLOYEE table).

- The DDM connects to the remote server (S2) and accesses the S2 system catalog to assign costs to the remote components of the join (see Fig. 10.3).

- Based on the estimated costs and server characteristics, the DDM decides *where* the join is to be performed and *which* table is to be joined to the other.

- The DDM selects server S1 as the site for the join execution, since S1 is the more powerful server. The DDM decides that the smaller table (EMPL_MGR) will be joined to the EMPLOYEE table, since it requires fewer I/O operations and less network data movement between servers.

- The DDM initiates the selection of the proper rows from the smaller table and sends the filtered records (managers with the MBA degree) across the network to server S1.

Without distributed query optimization, the DDBMS may choose an extremely inefficient alternative—sending all 100,000 employee records to remote server S2 for selection and join, then sending the results back to S1. Clearly, joining data between two tables is the simplest possible case. Each additional table and/or database increases the number of choices for the optimizer and the complexity of the DDM. Therefore, a complete implementation of the distributed query

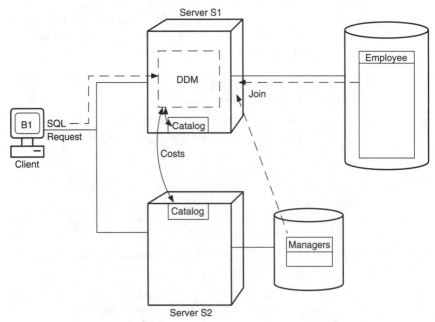

Figure 10.3 Distributed query processing.

optimization is a rather difficult task that only a handful of DBMS vendors attempt to undertake. In addition, remote data access standards, such as the Remote Data Access (RDA) standard from ISO and the full-function ANSI SQL standard, are still emerging. Products such as SYBASE, ORACLE, and INFORMIX, support Date's seventh rule with certain limitations, and even then the quality of optimization decreases as the complexity of the query grows.

10.2.8 Rule 8—distributed transaction management

Date's eighth rule is intended to provide data consistency, integrity, concurrency, and recovery in a distributed database system.

Updating a distributed database introduces a new set of complicated problems. Let's start with the distributed update complications that can cause different parts of the database to be out of sync if any one of the local updates fails. This situation was illustrated in the example of a money transfer operation in the distributed bank application. The two-phase commit protocol, which has been described in previous chapters, has to be used to guarantee consistency of the updated data.

Two-phase commit allows a COMMIT/ROLLBACK process to be implemented in a distributed environment (*distributed* COMMIT and *distributed* ROLLBACK). In essence, the two-phase commit protocol supports the atomicity, consistency, isolation, and durability of database transactions in a distributed environment. By supporting consistent rollback, the two-phase commit protocol also supports distributed database recovery from a transaction failure. However, the two-phase commit protocol requires a coordination of efforts between all participating parties during the prepare and commit phases of the process. The synchronization task is assigned to a transaction coordinator. A distributed data manager often acts as a coordinator.

In business, it is not always enough that the DDM can support the two-phase commit protocol. This support ideally should be intelligent and automatic, and should guarantee that the proper actions (COMMIT and/or ROLLBACK) will take place automatically on all protected resources of a distributed transaction, without user or application intervention. Some DDBMS vendors support an automatic two-phase commit protocol, while others offer a set of commands and procedures that allow applications and users to implement a two-phase commit protocol manually.

The distributed commit is not the only problem that the transaction management has to solve in a distributed environment. Among other issues are distributed locking, deadlock detection, local backup and global recovery, logging, administration, and security. Each one of these issues represents a complex DDBMS design problem in itself.

Some of these issues are discussed later in the book, while others are complicated enough to be beyond the scope of this book. The difficulty of distributed transaction management and the large potential scope of distributed transaction processing resulted in the emergence of the transaction management products developed by non-DBMS vendors. Indeed, if a distributed transaction involves resources other than DBMS-managed data, the distributed transaction manager is required to guarantee the integrity and synchronization of all protected resources. In addition, production-strength mainframe-based on-line transaction processing has demonstrated that the overall transaction processing management, availability, and robustness will benefit if the transaction management is separated from the DBMS code. Products such as IBM's family of CICS products, Encina from Transarc, and TUXEDO from Novell offer distributed transaction management solutions running on a variety of hardware and software platforms, and supporting a number of relational DBMSs via a set of standard interfaces such as the XA and ATMI standards from the X/Open.

10.2.9　Hardware, software, networks, and DBMS independence

Satisfying the desire for database management systems to work interdependently across networks is complicated by the fact that computing environments are increasingly heterogeneous. The next four of Date's rules—Rules 9, 10, 11 and 12—deal with the heterogeneous nature of distributed systems. These rules specify that a truly distributed database system should not depend on underlying hardware platforms, operating systems, networks, and even individual database management systems. The aim of the last four rules is to support the goals of open systems by allowing the implementation of distributed database systems in practically any networking environment, including existing networks, databases, and equipment.

Rule 9—hardware independence

Date's ninth rule states that distributed database systems should be able to run on different hardware platforms with all systems able to participate as equal partners. This rule allows designers to build a distributed environment that can consist of the computer systems from different vendors and different hardware architectures. This rule is essential to developers of client/server computing systems. The rule actually reinforces the notion of client and server specialization. And it is easy to picture a distributed database (e.g., ORACLE) in a client/server environment (see Fig. 10.4), where client B1 is an Intel-based personal computer, server S1 is a RISC-based machine (e.g., IBM's RS/6000), server S2 is a symmetric multiprocessor (SMP) from Sequent, and server S3 is an IBM mainframe. This is not at all an unusual situation. Therefore, many DDBMS vendors (e.g., Oracle, Sybase, Informix, CA/Ingres) support Date's Rule 9 by providing the DDBMS support for a wide variety of hardware platforms.

Rule 10—operating system independence

Date's Rule 10 supplements and expands Rule 9. The rule allows DDBMS designers to choose the hardware platform and at the same time not to be limited by a single operating system. Adherence to Rule 9 by itself does not guarantee support for multiple operating systems. This rule can be supported by selecting a DDBMS solution designed according to international and industrywide standards, i.e., designed to operate in an open systems environment.

Today, the marketplace offers DDBMS solutions designed for a particular operating system (e.g., IBM's DB2 for MVS, DB2/6000 for AIX, Microsoft's SQL Server for Windows/NT), as well as solutions for vari-

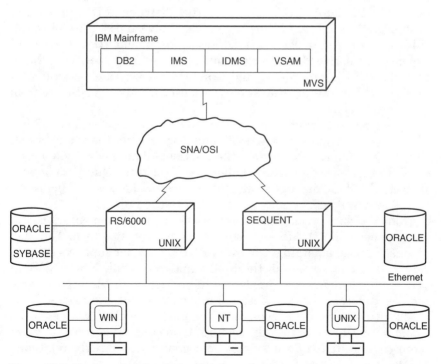

Figure 10.4   Hardware/software/network independence.

ous implementations of the UNIX operating system (e.g., SYBASE, INFORMIX, ORACLE). The client/server environment shown in Fig. 10.4 supports both Rules 9 and 10. Indeed, the ORACLE RDBMS shown here runs under MS/Windows, UNIX NT, and MVS.

Rule 11—network independence

Date's Rule 11 supplements Rules 9 and 10 by adding a requirement for the DDBMS not to depend on a particular network implementation and protocols. This rule is natural for any distributed network environment, especially a client/server environment. Adherence to the standards (OSI, ANSI, IEEE) allows many DDBMS vendors to support Rule 11. For example, the client/server architecture shown in Fig. 10.4 allows the ORACLE RDBMS to operate within an Ethernet LAN and across a wide area network (SNA/OSI).

Rule 12—DBMS independence

Date's rules discussed up to this point have been implicitly applied to distributed database systems where every node was supporting a "like," homogeneous DBMS. In other words, the intention of Date's Rules 1 through 11 appears to transform an existing database system (such as DB2, ORACLE, etc.) into a truly distributed DBMS. In fact, most DDBMS implementations available today support some of Date's rules only in a homogeneous DBMS environment. Date's Rule 12 expands the horizons of homogeneous data access by specifying that a truly distributed database should be able to interoperate with different kinds of databases, regardless of whether or not the DBMSs are from the same vendor.

The variation of homogeneous data access that satisfies Rule 12 is a distributed environment where all databases are not the same, but all support a common data model—the relational data model—via a common, standardized data access language—Structured Query Language. In fact, the data management middleware products like Microsoft's ODBC are designed specifically to satisfy Date's Rule 12.

From the data management perspective, the implementation of a heterogeneous DRDBMS environment is not a simple task. The SQL standard is still emerging. Not every RDBMS vendor supports the currently available version of the SQL standard in full. Every RDBMS vendor implements its product differently, with different name lengths, different return codes, and proprietary SQL extensions.

The situation becomes even more complicated when legacy nonrelational data is brought into the picture. Indeed, the real world is much more complicated than a single, homogeneous or strictly relational DBMS environment.

As illustrated in Fig. 10.4, a business enterprise may adopt the MS-Windows operating system and an ORACLE RDBMS for its client platform; ORACLE and SYBASE for the UNIX-based servers; and DB2, IMS, IDMS, and VSAM for the mainframe MVS platform. In fact, the majority of data today usually resides in legacy databases and files (i.e., IMS, IDMS, VSAM). This is true for many IBM and compatible mainframe sites. The problem of implementing a distributed DBMS in such an environment is complicated by the fact that each local DBMS speaks its own data access language and the translation of a SQL query, for example, into hierarchical IMS data access is not a trivial task. Sometimes, it simply cannot be done without rewriting a query or an entire application.

Driven by the real business need of heterogeneous data access, various middleware solutions from DBMS vendors are now emerging to address this issue. Almost every RDBMS vendor provides access to IBM's DB2 as well as to its own RDBMS (for example, by building DB2 mainframe gateways utilizing the Advanced Program-to-Program Communications protocol). Providing access to heterogeneous distributed data further complicates distributed DBMS issues of data integrity, locking, administration, and security. Notwithstanding the difficulties of heterogeneous data access, however, it is easy to see that support of Date's Rule 12 is a real business requirement for a truly distributed database system. The key to such a solution is support for the industry data access standards (Remote Data Access from the ISO; SQL from the ISO, the SQL Access Group, and ANSI; XA Interfaces from X/Open) and the maturity of various middleware solutions.

10.3   OTHER DISTRIBUTED DATA MANAGEMENT ISSUES

Even though they have become widely accepted as the working definition set and the criteria for a distributed database, Date's 12 Rules are not the perfect recipe for truly distributed database systems. However, adherence to Date's rules causes the designers of distributed database systems to solve other important, even critical, issues. Some of the issues and questions are briefly discussed in this section.

10.3.1   Administration

Database administration in a distributed environment can be a potential nightmare for database and system administrators and has to be designed with extreme care. Indeed, in a distributed database system where every node is equal, how does a DBA (database administrator) perform backups, recovery, creation/deletion of database objects, modifications at remote sites, change and version management, etc.? Ideally, a properly implemented DDBMS should provide a central database administration facility and tools for distributed DBA support. If distributed DBA administration features are not implemented, then the administration of the DDBMS can be performed by local DBAs. That means that additional highly qualified staff is required, and synchronization of the DBA's efforts must be controlled. Of course, a central DBA can travel to each remote site that needs DBA intervention. Obviously, it is not the most efficient or timely solution, especially if the remote sites are really remote—New York and Tokyo, for example! These are just a few issues that demonstrate the importance and complexity of database administration in a distributed environment. Some of these issues and solutions are discussed in more detail in Chap. 14.

10.3.2 Security

Data security may be defined as protection of data from deliberate or inadvertent disclosure, modification, or destruction. Data security can be implemented by utilizing access control, assigning users privileges for data access and data objects creation/deletion/modification, password protection, data encryption, and other similar techniques. Data security can be enforced and validated by maintaining active, on-line auditing. These data security techniques and methods must be expanded to be operational in a distributed database system. In a distributed environment, data security issues are closely related to administration issues and require a high level of coordination of efforts between all participating controllers. Among them are data administrators, security administrators, and network managers.

One of the security problems in a distributed environment is development of procedures that, for example, allow a user access to a table that is fragmented between three different nodes. At the very least, this user must be able to access the three network nodes and have access privileges to all three table fragments. If password protection is in effect, then all three nodes must recognize the same password. If the data is encrypted on one of the nodes, then the decrypting facility should be employed at this node to process the required data.

Of course, in a distributed database environment, especially in a client/server architecture that employs PCs as client systems, totally secured, critical data can be downloaded into an insecure PC environment—a security administrator's nightmare. The rule calling for each node to be responsible for the protection of its own data might not be sufficient in this case.

In a client/server environment, many vendors attempt to solve the security issues by placing all security procedures, rules, validations, and checking at the server itself. Then, the server becomes a place where all necessary security measures are implemented, including government standards of C1, C2, and B1 levels of security (discretional and mandatory access control, user verification and authentication, etc.). For example, the INFORMIX DBMS supports B1 mandatory access control security.

10.3.3 Currency control

Currency control issues can arise when a distributed database system is implemented according to Date's 12 Rules. It is an extension of the data consistency issues that present a potential problem when a database transaction updates two or more resources located at different sites. Database consistency issues may be solved by employing a two-phase commit protocol that makes database transaction atomic, consistent, isolated, and durable. Currency is not related directly to a single database transaction. Currency in a distributed database environment is a DDBMS state in which all related databases in a network are consistent relative to a version and/or date/time. Specifically, let's consider a distributed client/server architecture, as shown in Fig. 10.4. Assume that server S2 develops a serious hardware problem and has to be brought off-line. The distributed database environment (Fig. 10.4) is designed to satisfy Date's 12 Rules, and a failure of one node does not bring the system down. Moreover, any transactions that had been active when server S2 failed are rolled back, thus ensuring the data integrity and consistency. Let's further assume that server S2 keeps a management summary database of the bank account activity. This summary is continuously updated by certain transactions initiated from servers S1 and S3 and the client B1. It took 12 hours to repair server S2 and to bring it back on-line. However, the data that resides on server S2 is no longer current and, for some critical applications, may not even be useful. Now, the DDBMS, its administration, and currency control team must perform certain procedures that would bring the S2 database current. To do that, S1, S3, and B1 updates should have been captured and reapplied to server S2, for example. The point here is that currency control is a real issue, one of the many critical issues a truly distributed database system should be designed to handle.

Hopefully, the discussion of Date's rules has demonstrated the importance and complexity of a truly distributed database implementation. Several architectural activities are under way to define a road map toward a distributed heterogeneous database environment. For example, IBM offers an architecture that is designed to implement distributed data access across IBM system platforms: the Distributed

Relational Database Architecture (DRDA). IBM's DB2 family of products can take advantage of the DRDA to become one of the dominant players in this arena.

Among practical implementations of the distributed database management systems designed to operate in a heterogeneous environment are various data replication solutions, some of which are discussed in Chap. 11.

Chapter

11

Data Distribution and Data Replication

The main goal and advantage of distributed data management is the ability to share and access data located at multiple systems in a fashion transparent to end users, while keeping most data local to the locations that actually use the data. This chapter looks at two classes of distributed data management solutions: distributed database architecture and data replication architecture.

11.1 DATA DISTRIBUTION ARCHITECTURES

Distributed data management has been demonstrated as one of the styles of cooperative distributed processing often implemented in client/server architecture. In the context of client/server architecture, distributed data management operates in environments where the data and DBMS are distributed among multiple systems. Data management functions are distributed between a front-end system (data-processing logic, or DML) and the back-end server (database functions—DBMS). Distributed data management, already implemented in several client/server and distributed mainframe environments, deals with a lot of complicated issues, some of which have not been solved to date.

Some of the issues of distributed data management are being addressed by emerging industry standards, including the ANSI SQL standard, X/Open's XA architecture, ANSI and ISO distributed computing models, and the Remote Data Access (RDA) architecture. In addition to standards organizations, major DBMS vendors are also involved with distributed data management. Prominent among these vendor solutions is IBM's Distributed Relational Database Architecture (DRDA). DRDA is the IBM strategy to provide distributed data management and interoperability solutions for IBM-only and heterogeneous computing environments.

11.2 DRDA

Today, traditional customer loyalty to a vendor of choice is being replaced by a desire to reduce operating costs and to decentralize operations in order to be more competitive. Advances in the area of distributed and client/server computing and the availability of enabling technology for distributed databases in a client/server architecture force users to look very seriously into open systems, distributed computing, and distributed databases. These trends affect even a major vendor such as IBM. Given the challenges of open systems and facing increasing pressure for higher interoperability and openness from its customer base, IBM has focused on increased connectivity, network management, distributed database, and shared files services across computing platforms.

DRDA is a set of communications and interface protocols that IBM and other licensees follow to provide access and interoperability among applications and one or more remote relational databases. It is intended to satisfy the needs of applications requiring access to distributed *relational* data in IBM operating environments as well as in non-IBM environments conforming to DRDA. The DRDA goal is twofold. On the one hand, DRDA is designed to facilitate the development of new distributed and client/server applications within and across various IBM platforms. On the other hand, DRDA is intended to help migrate existing environments into the distributed and client/server world by leveraging investments already made in existing systems, networks, LANs, DBMSs, and transaction managers. It not only serves to link IBM's own disparate relational database management system products but has been embraced by independent software vendors (ISVs) as well. The intention is that products from other systems vendors will interoperate with IBM database products without complicated gateways.

IBM has formally published the DRDA specifications and licensed related technologies to other systems vendors. IBM has committed to track the progress of the emerging ISO Remote Data Access (RDA) standard and make DRDA interoperate with RDA if it finds market acceptance.

11.2.1 DRDA overview

DRDA is designed to provide the necessary connectivity to and from relational database management systems (RDBMS) that can operate in homogeneous (like) and heterogeneous (unlike) system environments. In the DRDA framework, heterogeneous environments span IBM MVS, VM, OS/400, OS/2, and AIX platforms, and any non-IBM RDBMS products that conform to DRDA (see Fig. 11.1).

By limiting its reach to relational databases, DRDA can standardize on a single data access language—the Structured Query Language (SQL)—as the common language that all applications must use to access distributed relational data.

From a structural point of view, DRDA is built on other architectures—architectural building blocks. These building blocks represent the following IBM architectures:

- Distributed Data Management architecture (DDM)
- Logical Unit Type 6.2 (APPC/LU6.2) architecture
- SNA Management Services Architecture (MSA)

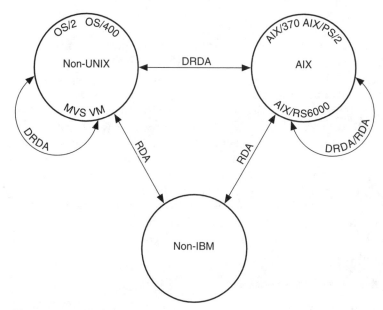

Figure 11.1 DRDA environments.

- Formatted Data Object Content Architecture (FD:OCA)
- Character Data Representation Architecture (CDRA)

DRDA ties these architectural blocks together into a common protocol that supports the distributed cooperation typical of distributed databases and client/server environments. While a detailed description of each of these architectures is beyond the scope of this book, the first two components, DDM and APPC/LU6.2, deserve a closer look. DDM architecture defines the functions and the commands that make up DRDA and needs to be described in more detail. APPC/LU6.2 architecture was discussed in previous chapters and will be analyzed here in the context of DRDA connectivity. It is safe to say, though, that both DDM and APPC/LU6.2 architectures are the cornerstones of the Distributed Relational Database Architecture.

Role of SQL

SQL is the standard language for data access in relational database management systems. In IBM system environments, SQL is adopted as the standard language within Systems Application Architecture. Due to its consistency, SQL enables distributed data access across various relational database management systems. SQL allows users to define, retrieve, and manipulate data in a distributed relational database environment. In the context of DRDA, such an environment can comprise interconnected DB2 systems—DB2/MVS, DB2/VM, DB2/2, and DB2/6000, as well as any non-IBM RDBMS that conforms to DRDA rules and protocols.

DRDA supports SQL as the standard application programming interface (API) for execution of applications. DRDA uses SQL to define logical connections (flows) between applications and a relational database management system. Program preparation processes use these flows to *bind* SQL statements to a target RDBMS. DRDA specifies that applications use SQL to access an RDBMS. If the requested data is remote, the DRDA requires that a special mechanism be used to determine where the data resides and to establish connectivity with the target remote RDBMS. In SQL, an application can use the SQL CONNECT statement to establish connectivity with the named RDBMS.

DRDA uses the term RDB_NAME to represent the name of the target relational database. To support subsets of data managed by an RDBMS (data fragmentation), DRDA allows each subset to be known by a separate RDB_NAME.

DRDA as the connection architecture

A distributed environment, including a client/server environment, is characterized by a collection of (possibly specialized) nodes intercommunicating over a network. Such an environment requires a connection architecture that defines specific flows, protocols, and interactions that are designed to support the intent and results of distributed data management. DRDA is the architecture that provides the necessary connections between applications and an RDBMS in a DRDA-supported distributed environment.

Even though DRDA's intent is to allow connection between IBM and non-IBM products, DRDA is primarily designed for IBM system environments and uses appropriate IBM communication architectures to describe:

- What information should flow between participants (clients and servers in a client/server computing model) in a distributed relational database management system (DRDBMS)
- Responsibilities of all DRDBMS environment participants
- When the interactions (flows) should occur

In other words, DRDA provides the formats and protocols required for data access in a distributed database system. However, DRDA does not provide the application programming interface for applications accessing data in a distributed RDBMS environment.

The distributed database processing formats and protocols supported by DRDA depend on the type of distributed database processing supported by the distributed database system.

There are four types of distributed database processing. They were described in previous chapters as remote request, remote transaction (remote unit of work), distributed transaction (distributed unit of work), and distributed request.

In the DRDA terminology, the four types of distributed database processing are called degrees of distribution. DRDA defines three degrees of distribution of database processing:

- *Remote unit of work* (RUW). Includes the remote request and remote transaction types of distributed database processing, and is described in the current level of DRDA.
- *Distributed unit of work* (DUW). Equivalent to the distributed transaction type of distributed database processing.
- *Distributed request.* The same for DRDA and non-DRDA definitions. This is highest degree of distribution.

Within the framework of the remote unit of work, an application program running on one system can use SQL to access relational data at a remote system. SQL is provided by and executed at this remote system. This model is symmetrical—an RDBMS running on a system where an application is executing can be accessed by applications running on other remote systems.

As was illustrated previously, the remote unit of work limits data access to a single RDBMS per unit of work, even though an application may perform multiple SQL statements within this transaction. Typically, all processing performed within a remote unit of work is committed (or rolled back) by the application at the end of the transaction. From the client/server point of view, the DRDA remote unit of work defines connections between an application process residing on a client system with the application/DBMS server.

That is in contrast to the distributed unit of work or a distributed request, where the commit/rollback process needs to be coordinated between multiple units of work executing at multiple locations (two-phase commit protocol). This coordination may be handled by a transaction manager (TPM) or by one of the DUW DBMS participants. DRDA defines the responsibilities of participants in the distributed unit of work and the distributed request, as well as formats and protocols required by a transaction coordinator. For example, DRDA can be used to define interconnections between two or more RDBMSs, which can be homogeneous (i.e., two DB2/MVS systems), IBM heterogeneous (i.e., DB2/MVS and DB2/6000), or a mix of IBM and non-IBM products, as long as all participants support DRDA.

The DRDA model describes connections between application processes and server processes (application servers and DBMS servers) that support the application's requests. Therefore, the DRDA model can be described in general terms of the client/server architecture. However, since the DRDA model emphasizes the interactions between different processes irrespective of the platform they are running on, the server/requester computing model can be used to describe DRDA protocols and functions more accurately. The DRDA server/requester computing model is illustrated in Fig. 11.2.

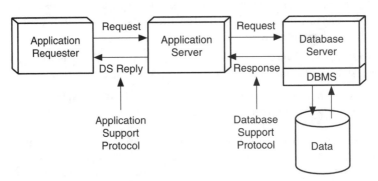

Figure 11.2 DRDA computing model.

In this model, DRDA defines three major components: application requester (AR), application server (AS), and database server (DS). To support connections among an application client process (application requester), application server, and RDBMS server, DRDA provides two types of connection protocols and three basic types of functions. The connection protocols provided by DRDA are:

- *Application Support Protocol,* which provides the connection between application requester (AR) processes and application servers (AS)

- *Database Support Protocol,* which provides the connection between application servers (AS) and database servers (DS)

DRDA defines the server/requester relationship among AR, AS, and DS as follows:

- The application requester (AR) supports the application end of the DRDA connection by requesting services from the application server (AS).

- The application server supports the DBMS end of the DRDA connection by requesting data services from the database server (DS) and delivering the DS replies back to the AR.

For each of the DRDA components, DRDA provides the following basic functions:

- *Application requester functions* include SQL support and program preparation services from applications. These functions correspond to those client functions of a client/server architecture that deal with issuing source SQL statements.

- *Application server functions* support AR requests by transforming them into calls to the RDBMS and routing these calls to the appropriate DBMS servers. These functions correspond to the data-processing logic portion of the distributed application in a client/server environment.

- *Database server functions* support requests received from application servers (AS). In a client/server architecture, these functions correspond to the database processing functions performed by the DBMS portion of an application on the server system.

These DRDA functions can be implemented on separate systems. Or all functions can be implemented in a single system—a mainframe, for example—if an application is running on a mainframe and accessing DB2 data. Or some of the functions can be performed on a single system, while the rest of the functionality is placed on a different system.

11.2.2   DRDA and DDM

IBM's Distributed Data Management (DDM) architecture provides a conceptual model for building common data management interfaces that are used for data exchange between homogeneous (like) and heterogeneous (unlike) systems. DDM commands, parameters, objects, and messages constitute the DDM data stream, which accomplishes the data interchange between various systems. DDM describes the common data interchange interfaces for various data models, including the relational data model. There are more DDM commands, parameters, objects, and messages than DRDA requires to implement a distributed relational database management system. Thus, DRDA uses an appropriate subset of DDM in its references and definitions.

DDM architecture

DDM architecture makes possible the sharing and accessing of data between different computer systems by providing a common language and a set of rules that enable different systems to communicate and share data. DDM architecture allows developers to build cross-system data management functionality into new as well as into existing systems. DDM architecture is designed to satisfy the following objectives:

- Standardize data management facilities for new system development.
- Provide data interchange among different systems.
- Increase efficiency of data exchange among homogeneous systems.

The DDM components that allow the architecture to achieve these objectives include:

- *Data Connectivity Language.*   It is a DDM-provided vocabulary of terms and set of rules (a language grammar) for accessing data from remote files and relational databases.
- *Standardized data structures.*   These are file models that describe how data is organized and managed within a file.
- *Standardized data access methods.*   These are mechanisms that provide a consistent way of accessing data stored in a file.
- *Standardized relational database model.*   It is a description of data organization within a relational database (RDB).
- *Standardized Structured Query Language Application Manager.*   It is a mechanism that provides a consistent way of requesting SQL services from a relational database.

The main goal of DDM components is to allow applications and users to access data without concern for where the file or the RDB is located.

In terms of Date's 12 Rules for a truly distributed database system, one of the DDM goals is to provide data location transparency. DDM architecture is designed to be independent of an underlying system's hardware architecture and its operating system. In other words, DDM is designed to satisfy the hardware and operating system independence requirements specified by Date's distributed database rules.

DDM architecture can also be viewed as a language that is used for data exchange between different computer systems. The DDM language is composed of the *vocabulary,* which contains DDM words (defined terms, such as "class" and "object"); *grammar,* which describes the word order and rules which the words have to obey; and *protocols,* which are sets of rules used to ensure the proper exchange of data between two interconnected systems.

DDM benefits

As the architecture designed to allow the sharing and accessing of data between different computer systems, DDM is designed to provide significant benefits to applications, users, and businesses. These benefits are better illustrated by the example of the bank application (see Fig. 11.3).

The bank's central office keeps the master copies of all customer and account records on its mainframe system (server S1). The central office is connected to two bank branches, B1 and B2. A balance report pro-

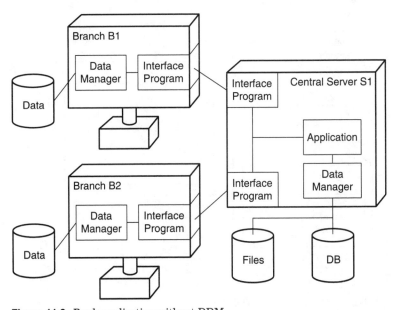

Figure 11.3 Bank application without DDM.

gram runs at the central office (S1) and needs to access both branches (B1 and B2) in order to verify the balances. Without DDM, this application would require two interface programs to allow access to two different, heterogeneous systems. But with DDM implemented on each system, the following benefits can be obtained:

- The development, programming, and maintenance costs are reduced since DDM provides all necessary interfaces (see Fig. 11.4).

- Data redundancy can be reduced if DDM-supplied shared data access is preferred to data replication; e.g., all customer records can be kept at the central office, thus helping to prevent a potential loss of data integrity.

- DDM provides for data location transparency by supporting the local data management interface (LDMI). DDM LDMI can handle requests for the data stored locally by passing them to the local DBMS or file system, while routing remote data requests to DDM to handle communications and necessary data access at remote locations.

- DDM improves data integrity in non-RDB environments by providing various file- and record-locking commands.

- DDM provides better resource management by facilitating shared data load balancing between multiple available storage devices.

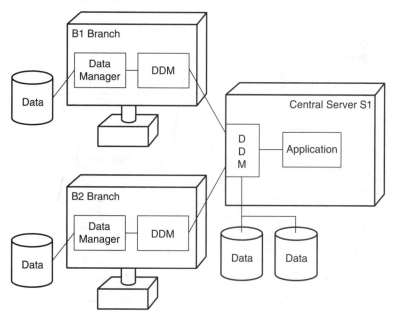

Figure 11.4 Bank application with DDM.

- The importance of standardization for open systems has already been discussed in considerable detail. By providing standard access methods, language, communication protocols, commands, and messages, DDM helps ensure the connectivity, portability, and interoperability of applications and systems.

DDM components interactions

DDM architecture is designed to provide data sharing and data exchange between two interconnected systems. In this context, DDM differentiates between the source system (the system containing the application program that requests data from a remote system) and the target system (the system that contains data requested by the source system). To support data exchange between the source and the target systems, DDM architecture defines two types of components:

- *DDM data management services.* It is the software that performs bidirectional request-reply conversion. An application's data requests, directed to application files or relational databases, are translated into DDM commands, and DDM reply messages are translated into data formats that applications can use. Typically, DDM data management services on each system (source and target) consist of the Local Data Management Interface (LDMI) and a DDM server.

- *DDM communications manager.* It is the software that handles the communications protocols and procedures necessary to exchange data with another, interconnected system. DDM architecture includes specifications for the use of IBM Systems Network Architecture's Advanced Program-to-Program Communications (APPC/LU6.2), even though other communications facilities could also be used.

The basic DDM components interactions are the interactions between requestors and servers shown in Fig. 11.5.

1. The application program on the source system requests data from a DDM-supported data management facility (files or RDBMS) by sending a data request to the local data management interface (LDMI). LDMI determines whether the requested data is stored locally or on the remote system.

2. If the data is on the local system, the LDMI sends the request to the local data manager (LDM) for processing.

3. If the requested data is located on the remote system, LDMI routes the request to the source DDM server, which translates the request into DDM commands and gives it to the source communications manager.

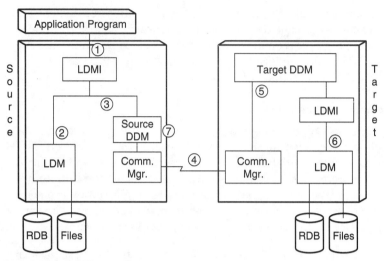

Figure 11.5 DDM components interactions.

4. The source communications manager transmits the request to the target communications manager.

5. The target communications manager gives the request to the target DDM server, which interprets the DDM commands, locates the requested file or RDBMS, translates the DDM commands for the target's LDMI, and requests the execution of the appropriate data management function.

6. The LDM of the target system retrieves the data and sends it back through the target LDMI to the target DDM server. The DDM server translates the reply into DDM form and gives it the target communications manager, which sends it back to the source communications manager.

7. The source DDM server receives data from the source communications manager and translates it into the format required by the source's LDM. In turn, the source LDM passes the data to the application program.

In addition to these steps, there are many other important tasks the DDM components must perform. Among them are resource management tasks (e.g., locating and locking resources, translating DDM data and commands), communications tasks (e.g., initiating and terminating communications, negotiating connectivity, controlling the flow of requests and replies), and common tasks (error handling and recovery, checking authorization).

DDM relational database models

The DDM relational database model consists of a single-system model and a distributed system model. Both models describe a relational database (RDB), which represents data as a collection of tables and employs the Structured Query Language. A single-system RDB model contains a SQL application manager (SQLAM) that provides a consistent method (interface) for requesting SQL services from an RDB (see Fig. 11.6). The SQLAM uses other system services (i.e., dictionary, directory, security manager, or SECMGR), to access the RDB and present the data returned by the RDB to the application.

In a distributed RDB model, DDM specifies that SQLAM services need the assistance of SQL agents and the communications manager (CMNMGR). According to the DDM definitions, the SQLAM, agents, and CMNMGR are to be split between the source and the target systems (see Fig. 11.7). The distributed RDB components are physically connected via corresponding CMNMGRs, even though logical connectivity exists between the application (source) and the RDB (target) as well as between source and target SQLAMs and agents.

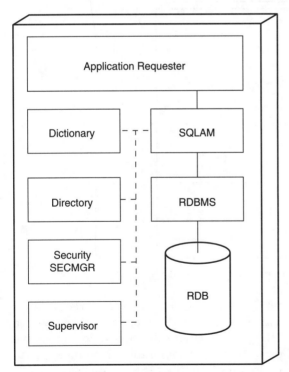

Figure 11.6 DDM single-system relational database model.

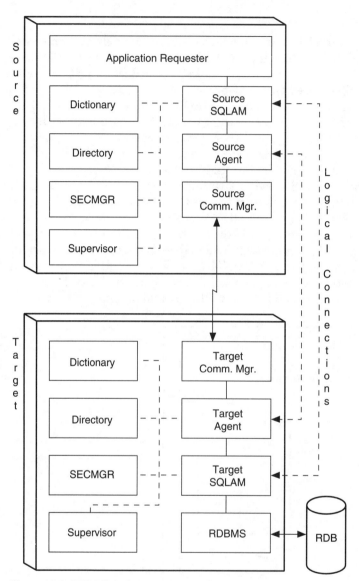

Figure 11.7 DDM distributed relational database model.

In this model, the source SQLAM receives application requests for SQL services from the RDB, uses source directory to determine the location of the required RDB, and routes the request to the source *agent*. The source agent uses the source communications manager to send requests to and receive replies from the target system.

DDM does not describe the internal functions (logging, locking, etc.) of the RDB. However, DDM defines that in the distributed RDB model both source and target SQLAMs must cooperate to efficiently process SQL queries. DDM allows for multiple queries to be processed simultaneously and requires source and target SQLAM to perform all necessary bidirectional data conversions if the source and target systems use different data representation.

11.2.3 DRDA processing model

The DRDA processing model describes the interchanges required between applications and a remote relational database (RDB) to implement a distributed relational database management system. DRDA uses an appropriate subset of DDM architecture (namely, its RDB model) and the APPC/LU6.2 architecture to support the following functions:

- Establish and terminate a connection between an application and a (remote) RDB.

- Bind the application's embedded (static) SQL statements and host language variables to an RDB.

- Execute these bound SQL statements as well as dynamic SQL statements on behalf of the application and return results to the application.

- Maintain a consistent logical unit of work between an application and a remote RDB.

The DRDA processing model describes these functions in terms of commands and command replies, as well as in terms of the correct flows of these commands and replies.

The DRDA processing model is shown in Fig. 11.8, and its processing flows are described as follows.

1. An application contains previously bound (to the remote RDB) SQL statements, that are transparent to the location of the target (remote) RDB. The remote RDB is represented by the local source SQLAM, residing on a source system (application requester, or AR), which is called whenever the application issues a SQL statement. Note that calls to the SQLAM interface are generated by the program preparation process and may be different in each DRDA implementation.

2. SQLAM checks the SQL request's parameters and translates it into DDM commands. It does so by using the DDM function models stored in the dictionary. SQLAM is also responsible for any required data representation conversion. SQLAM passes generated DDM commands to the source *agent*. The function of the

agent is to represent a requester to a server by interfacing with other DRDA managers.

3. The source agent receives the DDM commands, parameters, and data objects, and routes them to the DDM communications manager. It also keeps track of each command until the reply to it is received.

4. The DDM communications manager (CMNAPPC) uses APPC/LU6.2 protocols to communicate with the remote system. CMNAPPC receives DDM commands and objects, and creates DDM data streams for commands and data objects. Then, CMNAPPC invokes the local source system's LU6.2 facilities.

5. The LU6.2 of the application requester establishes an LU-LU session with the remote system (AS) and sends the request through the network to its partner LU6.2 over an LU6.2 conversation. AR and AS LU6.2 facilities utilize APPC protocols to maintain the conversation between the AR and AS intact, as well as to support session and conversation error recovery.

6. When the AS's LU6.2 receives the data, the target DDM communications manager decomposes the DDM data stream into original commands, parameters, and data objects, and passes them on to the target agent.

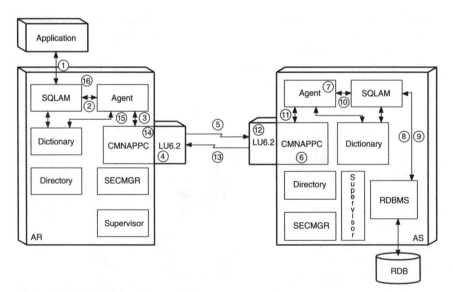

Figure 11.8 DRDA processing model.

7. The agent validates commands and parameters, and returns error messages (if any) to the DDM communications manager. If a command is valid, it is packaged together with received data objects and passed to the target's SQLAM.

8. The target SQLAM transforms DDM commands into calls to the supported RDBMS. All necessary data conversion from the AR format into the AS format is also performed here.

9. The target RDB processes calls from the SQLAM and returns any data, codes, and messages back to the target SQLAM.

10. The AS's SQLAM transforms received responses into DDM commands, parameters, and data objects, and sends them to the target agent. All necessary AS-AR data representation conversion is also performed here.

11. The target's agent checks the received data, assigns proper correlation identifiers to it, and sends it to the target communications manager.

12. The AS's communications manager creates a DDM data stream and invokes the target's LU6.2, which is still in session with its partner (the AR's LU6.2).

13. The target LU6.2 sends replies over the network to its partner LU6.2 as a response to the conversation request initiated by the AR's LU6.2 facilities. APPC/LU6.2 protocols maintain a conversation between the AR and AS intact, as well as provide for session and conversation error recovery.

14. The AR's CMNAPPC invokes its LU6.2 to receive the reply, decomposes the data into DDM commands, parameters, messages, codes, and data objects, and passes it to the source agent.

15. The agent verifies the receipt of the data against the commands sent to the AS and passes it to the source SQLAM.

16. The SQLAM converts the DDM data formats into the SQL-compliant representation and returns the reply to the application.

The DRDA processing model described here employs several DRDA managers—the SQL application manager, communications manager, agent, supervisor, security manager, and directory and dictionary managers. Most of these managers' functions have already been described. However, DRDA managers not described as part of the DRDA flows also play an important role in DRDA processing model, as follows.

■ The DRDA supervisor manages various managers within a particular operating environment—the resources manager, directory manager, dictionary manager, and security manager.

- The DRDA security manager ensures that the application requester, represented by its agent, accesses only those resources and managers it has been authorized to access, and only in the authorized fashion. The security manager works with the LU6.2 communications facilities, which perform all necessary requester's identification and verification, and with the RDBMS, which performs user's authorization to objects and operations with the RDB.

- The DRDA directory manager (DIRECTORY) maps the names of managers and their managed objects to their locations.

- The DRDA dictionary manager (DICTIONARY) provides interfaces to object descriptions (including valid DDM commands and messages) that are stored in the dictionary.

Conclusion

The Distributed Relational Database Architecture is the connection architecture for IBM's relational database management system products. DRDA is designed to provide the necessary connectivity to and from relational database management systems operating in homogeneous and heterogeneous system environments. DRDA can be used today to build a distributed database system in environments that are supported by the IBM DB2 family of products as well as by any non-IBM RDBMS products that conform to DRDA. This very brief description of DRDA features and protocols, and its relationship to other architectures demonstrates the complexity of distributed data management environments. It confirms the importance of database management systems and access methods, file and relational data models, and communication architectures, protocols, and components. Finally, DRDA demonstrates the power and convenience of the client/server computing model for building distributed computing environments.

11.3   OVERVIEW OF DATA REPLICATION

Distributed database processing and methods of data distribution, discussed in Chap. 9, are a good theoretical answer to the data distribution problem. DRDA is a good example of a well-thought-through distributed data architecture. It is also a demonstration of the complexity of a distributed database system. Indeed, while the ideal of a truly distributed DBMS compliant with all 12 rules of distributed DBMS processing is appealing, the reality of implementing remote updates and a distributed two-phase commit across an ever-increasing number of network nodes proved to be technically challenging and often impractical.

The alternative approach to a distributed database is based on data replication—a process of creating and managing copies of data for read and write access at the locations the data is needed the most. Replication appears to be embraced by the majority of DBMS vendors today.

11.3.1 History of data replication

The history and the role of data replication in distributed database management systems was briefly discussed in Chap. 9. This section revisits for the purpose of completeness some of the points made earlier.

Simple data replication has been employed for years. One of the simplest ways to distribute data is to allow the user to manually copy the data from one central location to other locations. This method of data distribution is called a *manual extract*. It is simple enough to be controlled by the user as requests for the data arrive at the data administrator. Manual extracts are frequently used for the replication of flat files and small database environments. To automate the user-performed operations of the manual extract, the tasks of data distribution are sometimes given to the distributed DBMS itself. Among distributed data management tasks given to a distributed DBMS, *snapshot* processing is relatively simple.

For those applications where the distributed data can be updated at multiple locations, snapshot processing is not sufficient. Such an application may require a copy of the same table to be maintained at multiple locations—thus, data replication (introduced in Chap. 9). Data replication methods have evolved from simple table-size synchronous replication to fragmentation, asynchronous replication in one direction, asynchronous bidirectional replication, and to heterogeneous bidirectional replication.

11.3.2 Replication technology and architecture

Data replication is based on the relational database technology, and the majority of the available replication solutions are designed to work with the relational databases as both data source and target environments. Some replication systems recognize the realities of legacy data stores and provide the means to replicate data from certain nonrelational sources.

A typical data replication architecture is shown in Fig. 11.9.

The architecture for data replication consists of the following major components:

- Data source
- Data capture component
- Captured data staging/queuing area

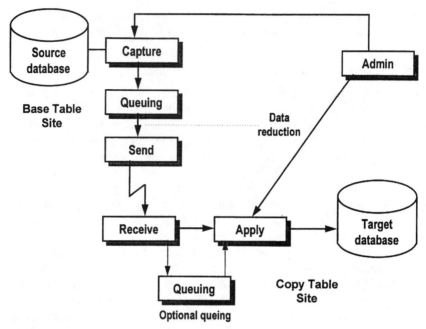

Figure 11.9 Typical data replication architecture.

- Sender/receiver
- Apply component
- Received data staging/queuing area
- Data target

Some of these components are optional, and a given replication system behavior is determined by the way these components are implemented. In fact, data replication systems can be classified based on the treatment of data sources and targets, replication techniques, timeliness, and the mechanism the system uses to capture and propagate the changes.

Data sources and targets

From the data source/target point of view, data replication can be implemented as either a *full refresh* or a *change propagation* model. The full refresh model refers to the mode where the entire source file is used to create replicas at remote sites. The change propagation model, as the name implies, accepts only changes to the source data and propagates these changes to defined target databases. Each approach has its pros and cons: full refresh contains relatively simple logic, but could be impractical for large data sizes; change propagation can solve large data size issues, but at a cost of higher complexity.

Techniques

There are two major classes of replication techniques: *peer-to-peer* and *subscriber-publisher*. In peer-to-peer replication, also known as *bidirectional* or *symmetric* replication, any of the servers which hold replicas of data may change the data. At replication time, these changes are reflected on other copies of the data (Fig. 11.10).

Peer-to-peer replication strategies require more careful planning since they must have a method of handling replication conflicts—situations where the same data item was changed on more than one of the replicas. To manage update conflicts, a designer of the peer-to-peer replication system should ask questions like:

- What happens if transactions arrival is reversed?
- Are transactions independent?
- Can transactions occur on the same data at two locations?

There are several conflict resolution techniques. One way to resolve update conflicts is to avoid them by design. To this end, designers use data partitioning, time slicing for allowable updates, and authorization schema to limit updates to known predefined users. A conflict resolution

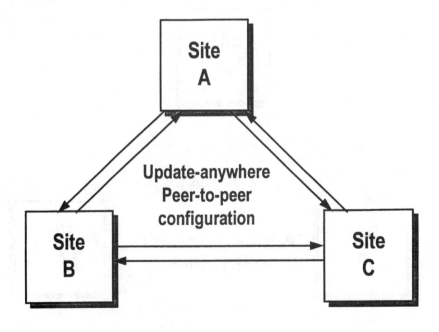

Figure 11.10 Peer-to-peer replication.

technique might be to automatically determine the winner (e.g., accept the most recent change for the replicated copy) and back out the loser.

Subscriber-publisher replication (also called master-slave) relies on one central copy owned by the publisher, called the *primary copy*. Changes made to the primary copy are then replicated to subscribers at specified times or on the occurrence of specified events. Changes made to a subscriber's local database are not generally replicated to the publisher (see Fig. 11.11).

Subscriber-publisher replication is based on a well-known model: a publisher (the source of the original data) replicates the data (or its fragments) to the requesting subscribers on a periodic basis. Typically, the roles of subscriber and publisher do not reverse, although a subscriber can become a publisher to other subscribers. An example of this replication model is a situation where a user (subscriber) maintains a local copy of data (replica) on the client system, with the original data source residing on the server; if the local data is changed by the subscriber, it will be reconciled with the server at a later time via a special process. A similar model can be implemented between servers placed at different geographical locations to maintain a "hot" backup site.

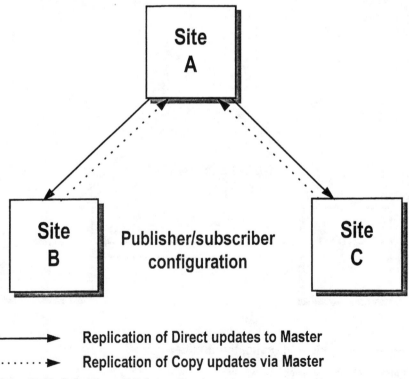

Figure 11.11 Subscriber-publisher replication.

Timeliness and consistency

Data replication is also classified by the timewise nature of the way data is replicated. The two forms of replications are synchronous and asynchronous replication models. *Synchronous* replication adheres to the change propagation model—it propagates changes at or near the real time the change was made. Such schemes are often implemented with database triggers and the multisite coordinated update (two-phase commit, or 2PC) capabilities of a DBMS and/or a transaction manager. Clearly, although synchronous replication enforces synchronization of replicas, this model becomes unsuitable for the full refresh operations and systems that maintain large amounts of redundant (replicated) data across a large number of sites.

Asynchronous replication operates on the store-and-forward messaging and queuing principle discussed in previous chapters as message-oriented middleware: changes to data are logged and then applied at predefined intervals. Both full refresh and the change propagation models are supported by asynchronous replication.

Closely related to timeliness is the notion of replication consistency. *Consistency* refers to the level of confidence that the data in various replicas are, in fact, identical at any given point in time. *Tight consistency* demands that all copies of the data are 100 percent consistent at all times. Synchronous replication is an example of this type of replication, and the two-phase commit is required for its success: indeed, all data must be updated at the same time. *Loose consistency* implies that various copies of data may not be consistent at any given time, but immediately following replication all replicas will be 100 percent consistent. An asynchronous replication model is an example of loose consistency.

Change capture and propagation mechanism

The two main approaches to capture changes in replication models are the DBMS log capture and using SQL in the form of triggers and/or stored procedures. The first technique requires less processing overhead, especially if it is done in a nonintrusive fashion, so that the performance does not suffer. This technique, however, may generate significant network traffic. The database procedure approach may reduce network traffic by building batches or packets of changes but at the price of performance impact on the replication and the entire DBMS.

Replication update conflict

Update conflict occurs when the replication system allows applications to commit competing, potentially incompatible updates to two or more replicas. Typically, the update conflict is detected when those conflicting updates are replicated to other replicas, although it is possible that the conflict is detected when a distributed application attempts to access and reconcile data from the affected replicas. There are two general classes of update conflicts:

- *Intratable* conflicts are detectable within the scope of a single table.
- *Intertable* conflicts cannot be detected within the scope of a single table.

Existing replication architectures combine options from all four groups. For example, there are peer-to-peer synchronous and asynchronous replication systems that are built upon database triggers and support both full refresh and change propagation modes, as well as subscriber-publisher asynchronous replication systems that read DBMS logs to obtain changes.

The majority of DBMS vendors support at least one model of data replication. When building a distributed client/server environment, data replication should be considered in preference of a distributed DBMS in most cases where the two-phase commit protocol is not appropriate. Data replication is also recommended as a solution for mobile computing that is characterized by disconnected or intermittently connected users.

11.4 REPLICATION SYSTEM REQUIREMENTS

In general, a well-designed replication system should conform to a number of technical requirements as listed following. These requirements are implemented at various degrees in a number of replication products discussed later in this chapter.

- *Heterogeneous database support.* A typical distributed client/server environment comprises multiple database products (for example, DB2/MVS, ORACLE, and Watcom for the mainframe, UNIX server, and the workstation correspondingly). The data that is originated on a mainframe may have to be replicated to servers and even workstations, which implies the need for heterogeneous database replication.

- *Guaranteed delivery.* Any replication system has to guarantee the delivery of subscribed changes to be of any use.

- *Performance.* A replication system should be able to satisfy a host of business requirements. For example, if business transactions processed in Japan have to be replicated before 8 A.M. EST in the United States, the replication system should be capable of delivering the necessary data to the replicated sites in time.

- *Push / pull mode.* A replication system should be flexible enough to support both modes of operations. Installations that maintain tight control over the replication system may wish to use a *push* model, which will replicate data to remote sites without their direct involvement; conversely, installations that require a high degree of local autonomy may elect the *pull* model, where the replicated site initiates the replication process when it's ready to process the data.

- *Asynchronous replication.* A well-designed replication system should support this mode of replication in addition to synchronous replication. In general, asynchronous replication supports nonblocking transactions and provides for better performance, higher availability, and autonomy, while maintaining integrity and consistency among replicas.

- *Flexible capture and apply capabilities.* A full-function replication system should be able to replicate any data, at any time, anywhere, in a continuous fashion or as a scheduled job. The capture and apply capabilities should be capable of supporting optional data enhancements (aggregates, joins, subselects, etc.).

- *Flexible replication strategies.* A replication system of choice should support replication to single and multiple targets. The latter should be supported directly or via a hierarchical replication.

- *Optional bidirectional capabilities.* A replication system may provide the option of supporting peer-to-peer, symmetric replication. This mode of replication is the most complex and often results in update conflicts. Therefore, a facility to detect and resolve the conflicts is mandatory. However, bidirectional replication improves local autonomy and availability and, in general, may simplify data distribution across heterogeneous databases.

- *Efficient administration and management facility.* A replication system may be extremely robust and efficient, but difficult to administer. Therefore, a full-function, graphical, centrally controlled administration and management facility can be the determining factor in selecting one replication solution over another.

11.5 REPLICATION BENEFITS

The following is a short list of the benefits of data replication:

- Local data access for performance and availability
- Faster response times for DSS and OLTP
- Local autonomy
- Reduced network traffic

- Reduced host processing

- High availability—fault tolerance, continuous operations

- Application migration and downsizing—maintain consistent databases, support coexistence of data and applications, enable staged migration

- Support for data warehouse—keep data warehouse current, accurate, in sync with operational data, add value through data enhancement/enrichment (standards, conversions, historical data)

11.6 IMPLEMENTATION EXAMPLES

This section is intended to take a closer look at the approaches that several DBMS vendors have chosen for their products.

11.6.1 SYBASE Replication Server

Many SYBASE users have taken advantage of the SYBASE Replication Server™, which has been available for several years. Sybase has chosen a loose consistency publisher-subscriber model for its Replication Server. SYBASE Replication Server supports selective replication of subsets of rows satisfying a selection criterion.

All updates are performed on the primary copy (source) before they are asynchronously sent to the replicated sites. Remote sites are created using the Replication Command Language to *subscribe* to that site. The client application updates the primary data server, which can be either a SYBASE SQL Server or any other database that can support a changed data agent (for example, SYBASE supports replication from DB2/MVS).

In the case of the SQL Server, the log transfer manager (LTM)—a change capture component of the SYBASE Replication Server system—reads the SQL Server transaction log to capture changes in the primary data. Captured changes are given to a local replication server, which checks for the subscription sites. As soon as the change unit of work is completed, the local replication server sends the necessary information to the remote replication servers at subscribed sites. Remote replication servers update the replicated copies upon receiving the changes.

All updates have to come through the primary sites. When a remote application needs to update its replica, a remote stored procedure is invoked at the primary site. This invocation can be synchronous or asynchronous.

Asynchronous stored procedures are used by remote sites to update data indirectly. Applications generate asynchronous transactions by executing special *replicated* stored procedures at the remote site. A replicated procedure and its parameters are transmitted asynchronously to the replication server at the primary site, where the procedure is executed, thus triggering a normal flow of replicated updates.

Note that if these procedures fail, they are queued at the primary site, and the DBA's intervention is required to correct the problem and reexecute the transaction.

The SYBASE Replication Server provides a management tool—Replication Server Manager (RSM)—which is a graphical system administration tool designed specifically to support the replication system. The replication system administrator can use RSM to determine the health of the system at a glance. Icons can be arranged on the desktop to represent each site in the replication system. The overall health of the system can be determined by the color of the icons. For example, red means that the component is down, green means active, yellow means suspect or hung, etc. Status colors can be modified using an RSM options window.

Overall, SYBASE Replication Server is a robust and reliable data replication solution.

11.6.2 IBM data propagator

IBM supports data replication and controlled data redundancy through its Data Propagator set of products. Data Propagator/ Relational (DPROP/R) can propagate data from DB2 to DB2 residing on any supported platform. DPROP/R is well suited for massive amounts of data that can be replicated from DB2 databases. DPROP/R has a unique two-stage architecture that consists of:

- *Capture* component—executes at the data source

- *Apply* component—executes at either source or the target

The capture component places changes to the source data in the staging tables (change data tables, or CDTs), that contain before and after images of data, the change operation, and the intent sequence which is used to serialized multiple updates within the transaction. In addition, the change tables contain a unit-of-work ID that links the change table to the UOW table. The capture component posts all committed transactions in the UOW table, thus enabling the system to replicate only committed changes.

The apply component contains the intelligence to select the right data source, varying from the change data tables to the original source itself. Apply pulls changes from the source or change tables at preset intervals. The pulling approach means that the target database is autonomous from the source data and thus is responsible for its data recovery. One of the apply component's most important features is its ability to transform data before copying it to the target. The apply component can perform any SQL operation on the source data, including aggregations, joins, and subselects. This feature is very useful for data warehouse applications (discussed in Chap. 15).

IBM provides a management system to clean up used resources (i.e., CDT and UOW tables), to define replication sources, targets, and transformation rules.

Data Propagator/Non-Relational (DPROP/NR) is a tool for propagating nonrelational data. It supports direct propagation of changes from IMS to DB2/MVS (asynchronously) and from DB2 to IMS (synchronously). Another component—DataRefresher—can refresh data from any MVS source to a variety of targets, including different versions of DB2.

Overall, IBM provides one of the most flexible data replication solutions available from any vendor.

11.6.3 Oracle Symmetric Replication

The original release of Oracle 7 provided an extract utility called Table Snapshot, which relied on user-written code for replicating transactions. In addition to the Snapshot, Oracle provides the Symmetric Replication feature, 'hat supports two types of replication:

- *Multiple Master* replication synchronizes full copies of tables at multiple sites. Each of these copies acts as a master, including the ability to be updated. The update changes to a given master are broadcast to all other copies—cascading changes from one master to another is not supported. This peer-to-peer replication model can result in update conflicts, which Oracle resolves by analyzing the flow of updates between sites; Oracle supplies a number of standard conflict resolution routines, which include "Apply the latest changes," "Apply all changes as additions," "Apply the maximum value" (for ascending sequences), etc. In general, conflict resolution may result in removing the change from the target.

- *Updateable Snapshot,* an extension to the original Table Snapshot, allows updates to snapshot copies to be sent back to the master table. All changes then flow from the master to the snapshots, and all conflict resolutions occur at the master—a model similar to SYBASE Replication Server. Table Snapshots extract data from the source by defining the target structure. In other words, a SQL statement is used to define a snapshot, which could be a subset of rows and columns, enhanced by aggregates and joins. Snapshots are refreshed (rebuilt) as complete table updates or changes only (fast refresh), both as background processes.

Oracle does not use the publisher-subscriber model to set up replication. A system administrator defines objects to be replicated as data, stored procedures, packages of stored procedures, etc., at the master definition site. This schema is then copied to all sites participating in the replication. Any changes to the schema are sent to all master sites for the system to work properly.

Oracle uses stored procedures, triggers, and packages of stored procedures to capture changes—this is different from Sybase's and IBM's approaches. The procedures and triggers are generated automatically from the replication schema.

Symmetric replication uses one of two methods to send changes:

- Row-level replication sends data changes to the other sites as a collection of INSERT, DELETE, or UPDATE statements, and before and after images for all changes.

- Procedural replication is invoked when a trigger makes the originating update; in this case, a replicated version of the trigger or a stored procedure at the other site is invoked. The advantage of the method is the reduction in network traffic, since only the procedure name and its parameters need to be sent to the replicated site. Of course, this method will not work if the "replicated" stored procedure does not apply to the replicated database (for example, it references another, not replicated, table).

11.6.4 Microsoft SQL Server Replication

Microsoft has made replication an integral part of its SQL Server 6 product. SQL Server 6 replication supports homogeneous replication, with the ODBC-compliant targets planned for the future. Similar to SYBASE, SQL Server 6 replication is based on the primary site strategy. All data at replicated targets is read-only and is subscribed to— SQL Server 6 follows the publisher-subscriber model. The data published from each table is an *article,* and can be a row and column subset of the original. Articles can be grouped together to create publications. Publications are replicated as a unit of work, which helps ensure data integrity constraints. Updates to replicas are performed by transactions consisting of SQL INSERT, DELETE, and UPDATE statements. A server that requests an article is a subscriber. When defining a subscriber, an administrator can specify replication latency and the number of transactions in the batch—both become tuning parameters for the replication system.

SQL Server 6 replication reads data changes from the log—there is a log reader task that runs continuously and captures log changes while they are still in memory. This design clearly minimizes negative impact on the transaction performance and throughput. A scheduling and execution facility (SQL Scheduler) runs a distributed task for each distributed subscriber database. The SQL Scheduler can run continuously to minimize the latency, or in a timed batch mode, which improves replication for large databases and narrow network bandwidth.

The SQL Server 6 Replication is integrated with the SQL Server performance monitor to display important replication-related statistics graphically.

11.6.5 Others

The products discussed here are not the only ones. Other software vendors provide versions of data replication solutions. Among them are Praxis, Trinzic Corporation's InfoPump, CA/Ingres's Replicator, and a popular groupware product—Lotus Notes. These products take different approaches to replication, from simple snapshot replication to complex bidirectional replication with multisite updates and update conflict resolution.

The availability and variety of the replication products indicate that data replication technology has become an acceptable, and often a desirable, solution for distributed data systems.

Chapter

12

DBMS Architecture and Implementations for the Client/Server Environment

Database management systems are the information backbone of today's organizations. Current technology and business requirements make it increasingly clear that distributed systems will play a major role in the advanced computing environments of today and of the future. Client/server computing, network computing, and peer-to-peer computing are just several examples of such environments. As these environments assume mission-critical roles in the enterprise, several trends affecting the DBMS technology are becoming evident. One of these trends forces the DBMS technology to enable the development and support of distributed environments, while another trend is driving the complexity and the sheer volume of the data toward the next generation of DSS and OLTP applications: data warehousing and on-line complex processing (OLCP). A clear indication of this trend can be found in the advancements in the area of commercial high-performance computing, in the amount and types of data that organizations are trying to process on the emerging client/server platforms, and in the general high level of expectations developers and users alike place on the client/server distributed DBMS. These new OLCP-capable database management systems can provide businesses with a quantum leap in the ability to *understand,* not just process, huge amounts of data. This understanding will allow organizations to obtain strategic competitive advantage by managing the business more efficiently, recognizing and adapting to trends, avoiding mistakes and bad business decisions, and providing customers with answers and value-added information directly, in a common, integrated platform.

Up to this point in the book, the emphasis was on the general theoretical criteria of an ideal distributed relational DBMS, formulated by C. J. Date in his 12 distributed RDBMS rules. Alternative approaches to data distribution, such as data replication, were shown to become practical means to implement distributed client/server environments.

Today, evaluating and choosing a database management system is steadily becoming one of the first system decisions MIS managers must make. And, with the OLCP requirements extending the scope of Date's rules and steadily pushing the limits of the traditional RDBMS technology, the task of selecting an appropriate DBMS becomes even more critical. Therefore, this chapter is intended to discuss some practical, technical RDBMS implementation trends and features that client/server RDBMS designers and users alike should be aware of.

12.1 IMPLEMENTATION TRENDS AND FEATURES OF CLIENT/SERVER DISTRIBUTED RDBMS

The volume of information flowing through enterprises has grown tremendously over the last several years. Until recently, enterprise databases could store only characters, numbers, and dates in a well-structured DBMS. Today, technology enables businesses to store large amounts of information, especially unstructured information. New infrastructures are being developed to allow virtually any authorized user to access this information (i.e., the World Wide Web).

The database world is changing considerably:

- New DBMS technologies are replacing accepted architectures—for example, data replication instead of two-phase commit. Replication is easier to understand and far easier to implement than two-phase commit protocols. Replication can be used for various applications, including

  —Populating data warehouses

  —Remote backup and fault tolerance

  —Mobile computing and support of disconnected clients

  —Local access of information

- New data types—text, image, voice, animation, multimedia, full-motion video—not only need to be stored and retrieved, but new applications like video-on-demand impose new demands on DBMS technologies.

- Databases grow steadily in size, and the support for very large databases (VLDB) presents new technical challenges.

- The need for load balancing between systems requires new capabilities from distributed DBMSs.

- Several key technologies are maturing and will be used extensively during the coming years, such as parallel DBMS functions.

- The relational DBMS is being extended to coexist with other models, such as object databases.

Distributed relational database systems make special demands on the database logical and physical design, and on the database management system architecture and functionality as well. At the very least, a distributed RDBMS must:

- Maintain data integrity by providing local and global locking mechanisms, and by supporting database commit/rollback transaction integrity.

- Automatically detect deadlocks and perform transaction and database recovery.

- Be intelligent enough to optimize data access for a wide variety of application requests.

- Have an architecture that is capable of taking advantage of the high-powered platforms it runs on.

- Overcome the traditional DBMS bottleneck—input/output (I/O)—by tuning the DBMS engine and I/O subsystem to achieve high data throughput and high I/O rates.

- Provide support for optimum space management, which is especially important if the underlying platform is a resource-constrained microcomputer.

- Support database security and administration facilities for distributed data/application locations, preferably from a single, centralized location.

And all this must be done by a distributed RDBMS reliably and within acceptable performance and throughput parameters, especially in multiuser distributed on-line transaction processing and complex data warehousing environments.

Therefore, even if every distributed DBMS implementation is designed to support some or all of C. J. Date's 12 distributed database rules, the users must take a close look at the actual technology of a given product. It is important to see how each particular rule is implemented, regardless of the hardware platform. At the same time, it is as important to understand how a DBMS can take advantage of a particular hardware/software platform, and what advanced features (if any) a given DBMS product offers to satisfy and possibly exceed customer expectations. In this respect, it is important to understand how a selected RDBMS is engineered for the one or more of the increasingly popular hardware architectures (see Chap. 4 for more details):

- Shared-memory symmetric multiprocessors (SMPs)

- "Shared-nothing" distributed-memory massively parallel processors (MPPs) and loosely coupled *clusters*

This is not an insignificant consideration. Granted, these emerging high-performance computing solutions appear more expensive than traditional uniprocessors. But in return, they promise an unprecedented scaleability for higher performance and throughput. And that scaleability is extremely important today, when client/server applications are pushing the capacity and performance of network servers to their engineered limits. In fact, these new DBMS technologies pusue two goals: speed-up (an ability to execute the same request on the same amount of data in less time) and scale-up (an ability to obtain the same performance on the same request as the database size increases).

Moreover, the key here is to achieve *linear* speed-up and scale-up—doubling the number of processors cuts the response time in half (linear speed-up) or provides the same performance on twice as much data (linear scale-up).

So, let's examine some key requirements for a database server architecture that have to be considered for the implementation of complex mission-critical distributed systems.

12.1.1   Relational DBMS architecture for scaleability

In a distributed multiuser client/server environment, a database management system resides at the database server and should be architected as a server component of the client/server computing model. As such, the DBMS server should be designed to receive and process a variable number of concurrent database requests from multiple remote users.

Scaleability

The server RDBMS should process client requests efficiently, and the performance and throughput characteristics of the RDBMS should not change as the number of concurrent users, database size, etc., grows. To maintain these characteristics, additional computing resources (e.g., CPU, memory, disks) may have to be added to the system at a relatively small incremental cost, with a *predictable* effect on the system and *without changing the application or administrative practices*. This property of the system is often referred to as the system's *scaleability*. There are two approaches to achieve scaleability:

1. The external approach, which increases the number of servers in the environment and lets multiple server systems run concurrently to share the workload. Loosely coupled systems running distributed databases support external scaleability. More often than not, this approach requires additional administrative support.

2. Internal (in-system) scaleability implies a single system that can be scaled up by adding a computing resource such as a faster CPU, or more CPUs, or more memory, etc., to the existing server platform. This approach should not require additional software components as scale goes up and, therefore, should not require a change in administrative practices.

Both types of scaleability dictate that an RDBMS should be able to effectively use all available computing resources, thus supporting an incremental approach to capacity planning. In effect, from a capacity planning perspective, a truly scaleable RDBMS is equivalent to a *free hardware upgrade*.

Internal scaleability is the focus of this discussion, since today it is achievable on multiprocessor machines—SMPs, MPPs, and clusters. These multiprocessor platforms allow the addition of processors without changing either the applications or the administrative process. To provide scaleability, a server RDBMS architecture should support:

- *Extensibility*—The DBMS should not be specialized for a particular system configuration (e.g., a certain number of processors) and should automatically take advantage of the new configuration, without the need for reinstall: this can be achieved by a sophisticated task-scheduling algorithm that can assign new tasks to additional resources in a load-balanced, predictable fashion, and by dividing large tasks (e.g., complex database queries) into a set of small subtasks that can be performed in *parallel*. By definition, a parallel scaleable RDBMS provides predictable extensibility. The principles of a parallel scaleable DBMS are discussed later in this chapter.

- *Limitation-free architecture*—If a DBMS has built-in architectural limitations (limits on the number size of supported tables, number of concurrent connections, etc.), it will not scale, regardless of how well it can parallelize tasks and operations.

- *Application transparency*—An application should not be aware of the platform architecture, configuration, and the changes to the platform implemented to achieve the next level of performance and throughput. Ideally, migrating from one platform to another (e.g., from an SMP to an MPP) should not require application changes, even though the DBMS itself may have to adapt to a new processing model (in this case, from a shared-memory model to a distributed-memory model).

Multithreading

Operating in a limited-resource environment (server system) under the control of an operating system, the DBMS designers can follow different strategies to achieve server efficiency.

One strategy is to create an operating system server process (task) for every DBMS client, which typically results in, among other things, additional operating system overhead (e.g., context switching) and additional CPU and memory requirements (see Fig. 12.1).

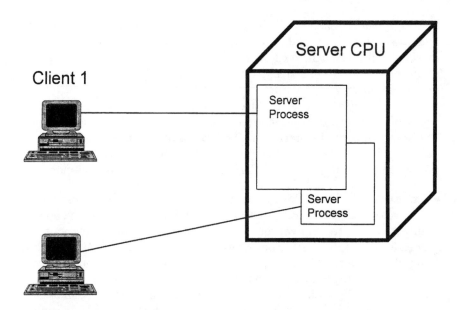

Figure 12.1 Single-threaded architecture.

A unit of context management under the control of a single process is called a *thread*. A thread can be either implemented within the server process or via operating system services. We will call this a *single-threaded* architecture.

A considerably more efficient approach is to launch a separate thread for each separate task (like a client connection supported by a server). Such a "lightweight" task can be controlled by the DBMS server rather than the operating system (see Fig. 12.2). In principle, threads can clone themselves and thus perform concurrent tasks.

Threads do not incur operating system overhead after being launched. A true multithreaded architecture provides a high degree of resource sharing (e.g., threads can share memory space with other threads) and tends to make system performance more stable with respect to the number of users and additional server functionality. In general, a multithreaded DBMS server architecture is preferable to a single-threaded one. A multithreaded database server can manage all the resources needed by the RDBMS itself (including buffers, disk I/O, locking, and logging), which essentially makes it a special-purpose operating system dedicated to the DBMS operations by scheduling threads execution.

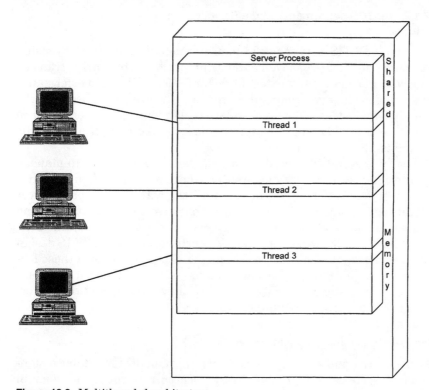

Figure 12.2 Multithreaded architecture.

The multithreaded scheduler can be either *preemptive* or *non-preemptive*. Non-preemptive threads execute until they give up control of the CPU or until a specified time interval (time slice) has expired, and therefore an "unfriendly" thread can block every other one from running. This approach imposes some requirements on the operating system and DBMS design, as well as some limitations on the system scaleability.

Preemptive threads can be interrupted by a scheduler when another thread requires the processor and satisfies some requirements (e.g., new thread's priority, thread class, the state of the current thread) imposed by the scheduler to initiate the switch-over. Preemptive thread scheduling is effective for database servers that must share resources between a DBMS and non-DBMS applications.

Among UNIX-based RDBMS server implementations, the SYBASE SQL Server is one example of the multithreaded server architecture. The latest release of the SYBASE SQL Server extends the concept of the multithreaded architecture to symmetric multiprocessing hardware platforms.

12.1.2 RDBMS performance and efficiency features

Relational DBMS server performance is usually measured by using standard benchmarks as well as some proprietary application transaction mix. Because many external factors affect RDBMS performance (operating system environment, hardware platform, etc.), benchmarks usually demonstrate some particular small aspect of the performance picture as a whole and can be unreliable as a predictor for any specific environment or configuration.

Clearly, a well-designed database server should be able to manage appropriate resources transparently from the application and use these resources efficiently. For example, the way the database server allocates and manages the system and shared memory, and the locking strategy in effect, all determine some overall performance characteristics of the RDBMS. However, there are certain relational DBMS design features that quite definitely affect its performance. Some of these features are applicable to the performance of the individual database engines, while others—such as global optimization—affect the performance of the entire distributed database system.

Server-enforced integrity and security

Data integrity and security are critical requirements for database management systems. Integrity features, such as referential and domain integrity, assure the accuracy and consistency of data, while database security refers to authorization and control of data access. Integrity and security can be implemented in several different ways. For example, integrity constraints and security procedures can be included in every application. In the client/server computing model, it may mean duplication of the relevant code on every client running these applications. However, the more efficient approach would call for the implementation of the integrity and security features centrally, directly at the DBMS server level. Such DBMS server architecture will provide for higher application reliability, reduced development and maintenance costs, and increased database security.

Global optimization

As was discussed in the previous chapters, the performance of a relational DBMS is largely determined by the capabilities of the query optimizer. C. J. Date's seventh distributed database rule specifies that in a truly distributed database system, the optimization must take into account not only local, but also global factors, including distributed nodes and network characteristics.

Typical cost-based optimization selects the access path for a given query based on the estimated cost of the query processing. Usually, the optimizer calculates the cost in such units as the number of I/O operations and/or CPU cycles, and takes into account the number of records needed to satisfy the query, availability of indexes, and various statistical information about data organization. These statistics are accumulated and maintained by the RDBMS in its internal system catalog. Optimization becomes even more critical in distributed query processing. Indeed, consider an application that attempts to join two database tables that are distributed to two different locations.

The size of each node's databases and relevant tables, the network speed, and the processing and I/O power of each node are among the major factors that affect the performance of a distributed query. The distributed (global) query optimization requires access to a global database directory/catalog in order to obtain necessary node characteristics and statistical information about the remote databases.

Without global query optimization, a distributed relational DBMS may perform extremely inefficiently. Such a system may send all the records of the bigger table to another, remote, location, for selection and join, and then send the results back. As the complexity of the queries exceeds the two table join requirements, each additional table and/or database increases the number of choices for and the complexity of the optimizer.

Therefore, an efficient implementation of global query optimization is a rather difficult task that only a handful of RDBMS vendors attempt to undertake. Products like INFORMIX and Ingres support global optimization with certain limitations, and even then the quality of optimization decreases with the complexity of the query.

Parallel relational DBMS processing

A special case of global query optimization is the query optimization in distributed-memory parallel systems (clusters and MPPs). Often, it is referred to as *parallel query processing.* Generally speaking, parallel RDBMS processing offers the solution to the traditional problem of poor RDBMS performance for complex queries and very large databases. Intuitively, it is quite clear that accessing and processing portions of the database by individual threads in parallel (instead of monolithic, sequential access of the entire large database) can greatly improve the performance of the query. This is especially important for data warehousing supporting complex decision support systems (DSS) and batch processing.

Types of parallelism

Database vendors started to take advantage of parallel hardware architectures by implementing multiserver and multithreaded systems designed to handle large numbers of client requests efficiently. This approach naturally resulted in *interquery parallelism,* where different server threads (or processes) handle multiple requests at the same time. Interquery parallelism has been successfully implemented on SMP systems, where it increased the throughput and allowed the support of more concurrent users. However, without changing the way the DBMS processed queries, interquery parallelism was limited— even though multiple queries were processed concurrently, each query was still processed serially, by a single process or thread. In other words, if a query consists of a table scan and join and sort operations, then this would be the order in which these operations execute, and each operation would have to finish before the next one could began.

To improve the situation, many DBMS vendors developed versions of their products that utilized *intraquery parallelism.* This form of parallelism decomposes the serial SQL query into lower-level operations such as scan, join, sort, and aggregation (see Fig. 12.3, Case 1). These lower-level operations then are executed concurrently, in parallel. By dedicating multiple resources to processing, a single request can be processed faster. Operations other than queries—INSERTs, DELETEs, UPDATEs, index creation, database load, backup, and recovery—can also be parallelized and thus speeded up.

Parallel execution of the tasks within SQL statements (intraquery parallelism) can be done in a number of ways:

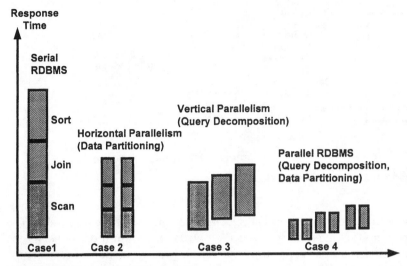

Figure 12.3 Types of DBMS parallelism.

Horizontal parallelism. This means that the database is partitioned across multiple disks, and parallel processing occurs within a specific task (i.e., table scan) that is performed concurrently on different processors against different sets of data. Indeed, if the entire database is partitioned into a number of smaller segments, each located on its own (logical) device, then the total query can be decomposed into an equal number of subqueries, all running in parallel against a corresponding partition of the database.

The resulting execution time is significantly reduced in comparison with a sequential query (Fig. 12.3, Case 2). Obviously, this approach requires a multiprocessor server. However, as illustrated in Fig. 12.4, with shared I/O, processor-based parallelism does not reduce a traditional DBMS bottleneck—I/O. It is only logical, then, that the multiprocessor server and a parallel RDBMS should benefit from the server architecture that supports parallel I/O. As illustrated in Fig. 12.5, additional performance improvements can be achieved by placing data partitions on separate physical devices (preferable, connected via separate I/O buses). The optimizer can partition the query based on the data partitioning rules (e.g., key ranges, hash algorithms).

Vertical parallelism. This occurs among different tasks—all component query operations (i.e., scan, join, sort) are executed in parallel in a pipelined fashion. This approach requires a much higher level of sophistication from the DBMS engine. It assumes that the database engine can decompose the query based on its functional components (in

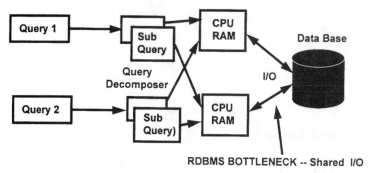

Figure 12.4 Shared I/O bottleneck.

our example, scan, join, and sort). Once decomposed, the query components can start executing in parallel, with a minimum delay between
the execution steps (vertical parallelism). Ideally, as database records
are processed by one step (e.g., scan), they are *immediately* given to the
next step (e.g., join), thus eliminating the wait time inherited in
sequential query processing. In this case (Fig. 12.3, Case 3), the query
decomposer and the optimizer can allocate different query components
to available processors from the processor pool.

Hybrid approach. Finally, parallel scaleable RDBMS can employ a
combination approach, where the query decomposer and the optimizer
can partition the query both horizontally (based on the data-partitioning algorithm) and vertically (based on the functional decomposition of
the query). The hybrid approach can result in the highest utilization of
computing resources available in a database server and will provide for
the best scaleability, performance, and throughput of the DBMS (see
Fig. 12.3, Case 4).

The ability to decompose and process large queries in parallel is
applicable to on-line transaction processing as well. In OLTP and especially OLCP environments, parallel query processing can supplement

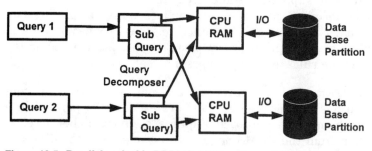

Figure 12.5 Parallel scaleable RDBMS, MPP, and parallel I/O.

an overall multithreaded approach where individual threads can be executed on separate processors. In other words, to take full advantage of the parallel hardware architectures and to achieve high performance of complex queries in a very large database (VLDB) environment, a relational RDBMS should be able to balance the workload of individual threads across multiple processors and decompose a complex query into multiple subqueries that can be executed in parallel.

Several major DBMS vendors offer various degrees of availability of parallel query processing, frequently coupled with a particular platform on which the query decomposer was developed. Most prominent among them are ORACLE with the Parallel Query and Parallel Server Options (version 7 and above), INFORMIX On-Line Dynamic Scaleable Architecture (version 7 and above), and SYBASE Navigation Server.™

Additional material on parallel database management systems can be found in Chap. 16.

Locking granularity

Locking preserves data integrity by preventing multiple updates to the same records simultaneously. Some servers permit manual locking, but, in reality, automatic locking in a database management system is imperative. The importance of locking becomes especially clear in a parallel RDBMS environment, where multiple users execute various steps of complex queries across multiple data partitions.

Users or processes that are locked out from access must wait until the required data is freed (locks are released). When this happens, the user's response time and, thus, a perception of DBMS performance suffer. For instance, table-level update locks, as a rule, result in poor performance. While locking, in itself, preserves data from corruption, it could limit the number of users simultaneously accessing the RDBMS.

If a DBMS locks an entire database for each user, then the DBMS becomes, in effect, a single-user DBMS. Therefore, the size of locks the RDBMS can impose on a database (locking granularity) becomes very important.

Ideally, the RDBMS should lock only those records that are being updated. The smallest level of granularity in commercial databases is the *row* level. Row-level locking implies that the database can use a lock granularity of a single row. This means that multiple users can simultaneously update different rows on the same page. Each user locks only the row on which the operation is performed and does not interfere with other users in the same page. Row-level locking permits the highest degree of concurrency by allowing users not to lock each other out. For example, ORACLE and INFORMIX RDBMS support row-level locking. The disadvantage of row-level locking is its significant overhead. Also, since each lock requires a certain amount of memory and/or disk space, depending on the design, the number of locks imposed on a database may be limited by the amount of available space. Some RDBMS servers can *escalate* locks from one level (e.g., row) to a higher level (e.g., data page or a table), and release lower-level locks when their number exceeds the user-defined limit. For example, IBM's DB2 supports lock escalation.

The next level of locking granularity is the *page* level. Thus, when one user updates a row, the entire page is locked and other users are blocked from updating, and sometimes even reading, rows in that page. Page-level locking introduces moderate overhead at the cost of reduced concurrency.

Table-level locking means that the database can lock an entire table at a time. This level is useful for locking a table for batch updates, locking out users for maintenance or reporting, etc.

Finally, *database*-level locking means that the entire database can be locked with a single command. Obviously, this level of locking practically eliminates concurrency.

Deadlock detection

Locking is associated with another performance problem: *deadlocks*. A deadlock occurs when program A locks a record that program B needs, and program B locks the record that program A needs. Each program must wait until the other completes, which is impossible. Thus, a deadlock (sometimes known as a "deadly embrace") has occurred. The DBMS server should automatically detect deadlocks and use appropriate algorithms to resolve them. As with global optimization, deadlock detection becomes much more complicated in a distributed environment. The time criterion might not be sufficient, since network delays and slow response time may be confused with a lock at a remote site. A truly distributed RDBMS server should be capable of resolving "distributed" deadlocks, even though the majority of the available DBMS implementations use some simple, time-out-based rules to resolve deadlocks.

Clustered indexes

Indexes usually represent separate data structures (e.g., various B-tree structures) that contain record keys and pointers to the corresponding records. Indexes can be used to access records directly by the key values and can also guarantee uniqueness of the keys (if the keys are defined as unique). Indexes should be constantly maintained—kept in sync with the key values of the records when the data is updated, added, or deleted. Even though index maintenance can negatively affect RDBMS performance, lack of indexes could result in serious performance degradation in direct (by full or partial key) data access. In this respect, clustered indexes are most important. Clustered indexes are usually built on a primary (as opposed to foreign) key, require the data to be sorted in ascending or descending key order, and are also sorted in the same order as the data (see Fig. 12.6). Thus, clustered indexes can significantly improve record search and sequential retrieval in key order by reducing the required number of input/output operations.

Note. Some RDBMS products (e.g., Ingres, Gupta) reduce or completely eliminate index I/O by supporting *hash indexes,* where records can be found by a key stored at locations calculated by a special algorithm. Hash indexes facilitate direct access and can coexist with indexes in the same RDBMS.

In addition to clustered indexes, some RDBMS products support *clustered tables.* Tables are said to be clustered when they are stored close to each other on disk, based on a commonly used join key. Clustered tables help speed up the data access if two tables are always accessed by the same join key.

A relational database management system's optimizer can improve the access path by automatically determining whether an index should be used for a given query. That is because index I/Os also consume resources and affect performance. Advanced optimizers, such as the one found in DB2, maintain index statistics and can actually determine whether a clustered index is still clustered after heavy insert/delete activity, before the decision is made to use the index. Despite the importance of clustered indexes, to date only a few products support them (for example, SYBASE, ORACLE and IBM's DB2).

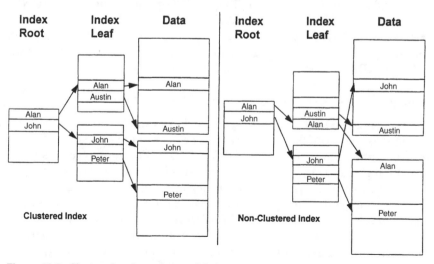

Figure 12.6 Clustered and nonclustered indexes.

Dirty reads

Some RDBMS products support a fast read mode without data integrity where the database system can scan the data as it currently exists on disk or in memory, regardless of whether the data has been committed or not. Even though dirty reads offer measurable performance advantages, their use has to be balanced against the potential exposure to inaccurate data.

Asynchronous I/O

RDBMS input/output is potentially a source of performance bottleneck. Properly designed database management systems should minimize the number of actual physical disk I/O and spread the cost of I/O operations across many users. One technique that facilitates reduction in the number of disk accesses is asynchronous I/O.

This technique involves overlapping I/O operations with other work the RDBMS server has to perform. In this case, the server does not wait for the completion of the I/O. Such an overlapping can be improved even further when the data is updated in shared buffers and the data writes are forced to disk only when the data buffers are full. The consistency of data in this case is guaranteed by write-ahead logging to a shared transaction log. In IBM system environments, asynchronous I/O is frequently implemented on an operating system level, as well as by a DBMS itself (e.g., DB2). UNIX-based databases, however, must be designed to implement asynchronous I/O. ORACLE, SYBASE, and INFORMIX all offer asynchronous I/O capabilities in UNIX environments.

In addition to asynchronous I/O, the I/O performance of the UNIX file systems can be improved by using *raw I/O*. RDBMS products such as SYBASE SQL Server use raw devices to bypass UNIX file system buffering schema and often offer much higher performance than that of the UNIX file systems and buffer managers.

Stored procedures

Stored procedures are collections of SQL statements and flow-control directives (e.g., IF, THEN, ELSE, etc.) that are parsed, verified, compiled, bound, and stored at the DBMS server. Stored procedures allow for the input and output parameters, user-declared variables, and conditional execution, typical of any programming language. Stored procedures can call other procedures and can be executed on remote relational DBMS servers. Stored procedures not only enhance the efficiency and flexibility of SQL, but also dramatically improve RDBMS performance. Indeed, due to the nonnavigational nature of SQL, the access path selection is performed by the relational DBMS optimizer when a SQL statement is bound (parsed, verified, etc.). This process is resource intensive—the corresponding instruction path length may be measured in several thousands of machine instructions. If it has to be performed every time a SQL statement is executed, the resulting performance will be greatly decreased (this type of SQL access is called *dynamic* SQL).

The SQL statements are *static* when they are parsed, verified, compiled, bound, and stored in the RDBMS server before they are executed or the first time they are executed. If SQL statements are static, the consecutive executions will be done at much smaller expense and, therefore, more rapidly. Some RDBMS systems (e.g., DB2) implement static SQL in such a way that the SQL statements are parsed and compiled before the execution, during the program preparation process. The resulting objects are stored in appropriate RDBMS libraries (i.e., database request modules and DB2 plans), from which they can be recalled. Other products (e.g., SYBASE SQL Server) parse and compile SQL statements the first time they are executed and may store the results in memory (usually, in a shared-procedure cache). Of course, even though there is no need to recall procedures from the libraries, one drawback of the latter technique is the possibility of the compiled stored procedure being paged out in a very active environment.

Regardless of the implementation technique, stored procedures improve the performance of SQL statements by eliminating costly pre-processing overhead. They also reduce network traffic by eliminating the need to send lengthy SQL statements from applications to RDBMS servers. In a typical UNIX-based client/server environment, for example, a stored procedure can be processed in one-fifth the time it takes to process a single embedded SQL command.

Cursor support

Cursors are programming constructs that allow applications to process the returned result set one record at a time. The result set can be derived from executing a single or multiple SQL queries in a single database connection. The record-at-a-time processing is typical of and required by OLTP systems. All RDBMS cursor implementations permit at least unidirectional (forward) access of the result set. Some RDBMS products also allow backward scrolling, which is useful for many retrieval applications.

12.1.3   DBMS connectivity

Heterogeneous data access

An advanced RDBMS implementation should be able to support the distribution of applications and data over networks and, as such, should be able to interconnect with like (homogeneous) and unlike (heterogeneous) systems and databases. Homogeneous connectivity is often built into the relational database system itself. Some distributed RDBMS products even offer distributed data consistency by supporting two-phase commit protocols.

Heterogeneous databases are much more difficult to interconnect—data structure, access, language can all be different, dissimilar. A traditional approach to heterogeneous DBMS connectivity is to build gateways that allow foreign database management systems to look like the native DBMS from an application's perspective. Sometimes, gateways allow third-party software vendors' programming tools and foreign databases to access data in the selected DBMS. However, because of the difference in heterogeneous DBMS architectures and supporting environments (e.g., SYBASE SQL Server on a UNIX server and DB2 on IBM MVS mainframes), gateways do not provide for seamless data access. Gateways may involve connection between different networks (i.e., Ethernet and SNA), different communication protocols (i.e., TCP/IP and APPC), different data representation (i.e., ASCII and EBCDIC), etc. Therefore, gateways are rarely used to support database transactions that span multiple heterogeneous environments, where all data consistency is guaranteed by a distributed heterogeneous two-phase commit protocol. Such implementations will require a cross-platform transaction manager that can interface with all participating heterogeneous databases. Such TP managers are being designed within the guidelines of the open systems. For example, X/Open has proposed XA interfaces for open systems TP managers, and the OSF Distributed Computing Environment, among other products, has selected these interfaces for its TP manager.

Nevertheless, today gateways solve a critical need to interconnect new and existing RDBMSs. Gateways play an important role by providing access to heterogeneous systems, especially when critical business data and legacy applications all reside on an organization's mainframes. Almost all gateways available today offer access to IBM's DB2. Better gateway implementations use Advanced Program-to-Program Communications (APPC/LU6.2) to provide real-time read-write access to mainframe data. Some gateways, such as MDI Database Gateway, OmniSQL Gateway, and Net/Gateway from Sybase, are DBMS extensible, and allow UNIX-based RDBMS to interactively access *any* mainframe data available via CICS/MVS (IBM's transaction monitor for IBM mainframes).

Middleware

As was discussed in Chap. 8, generalized access to heterogeneous databases is probably a function of the middleware layer of the advanced client/server architecture. Some middleware solutions include ODBC from Microsoft and DRDA from IBM. An emerging trend in middleware is to use asynchronous messaging and queuing mechanisms.

Remote procedure calls

If gateways represent one of the most popular ways to access heterogeneous data from one hardware/software platform to another, server-to-server and client-to-server RDBMS connectivity is best supported via the mechanism of remote procedure calls (RPCs). Remote procedure calls represent a connectionless mechanism by which one process can execute another process residing on a different, usually remote, system, possibly running a different operating system. Any parameters needed by a subroutine are passed between the calling and called processes. A database RPC is a clearly defined request for a service or data issued over a network to an RDBMS server by a client or another server. Unlike traditional remote procedure calls, database RPCs (e.g., SYBASE RPC) can call stored procedures and allow the DBMS server to return multiple records (rows) in response to a single request. Since database RPCs eliminate the need for a client to send lengthy SQL statements and to receive individual records separately, they greatly reduce network traffic. In addition, RPCs can help implement heterogeneous DBMS connectivity by solving the language incompatibility problems. One system can call a remote procedure on another system without concern to the remote system's language syntax.

12.1.4 Advanced RDBMS features

Database triggers and rules

Advanced relational DBMS implementations should provide users with the ability to initiate (trigger) certain user-defined actions based on a particular data-related event. *Triggers,* which can be viewed as a special type of stored procedure, are often used to implement referential integrity constraints. For example, a user may attempt to insert data into or update a table field which represents a foreign key (see discussion on referential integrity in previous chapters). The appropriate trigger can be designed to check the new field value against the values of the primary key. Similarly, delete actions can be controlled (e.g., prevented or cascaded) using user-developed delete triggers. In general, triggers can call other triggers or stored procedures and are powerful tools for application development. Centrally located on the server (in SYBASE SQL Server, for example), triggers can improve RDBMS performance, although they require programming efforts, especially when implementing referential integrity.

Dictionary-based declarative referential integrity implementations are preferable to those using triggers. Declarative referential integrity provides better documentation and clarity by using standard, nonprocedural SQL statements to define referential integrity constraints. For example, DB2 and SYBASE both support declarative referential integrity.

If triggers are often used to support referential integrity, RDBMS rules are used to implement user-defined domain constraints. For example, a database rule may say that the state code must be one of the approved two-character codes: NY, NJ, or CA.

Products that support database-resident rules facilitate the development of applications by implementing many business rules centrally as RDBMS rules. CA/Ingres and SYBASE SQL Server are just two examples that implement RDBMS-resident rules.

Support for complex data types

Today, business requirements often include the need to support multimedia—in particular, image applications. Ideally, an RDBMS should also support special, sometimes user-defined, data types often stored as BLOBs (binary large objects). These represent very large (up to several gigabytes) fields that are used to store images, spatial coordinates, graphics, long text documents, and even audio recordings. Ideally, the RDBMS should be capable of not only storing and retrieving BLOBs, but it should make complex data types available through the use of standard SQL like any other data element (i.e., query by image content, or QBIC). Several RDBMSs (e.g., INFORMIX, Illustra, and SYBASE) provide complex data types support. In addition, some RDBMS vendors and standards groups, such as the SQL Access Group, are working on SQL extensions that allow manipulations of complex data types from SQL statements. Conversely, object-oriented DBMSs (OODBMSs) are probably even better suited to handle this problem.

Graphical front-end development tools

Users of distributed RDBMSs all demand an advanced graphical suite of application development tools. Today, users can see two trends in the front-end tools for DBMS application development. Some RDBMS products (like INFORMIX, Gupta, and ORACLE, to name just a few) integrate graphical application development tools as an integrated solution. Oracle even offers computer-aided software engineering (CASE) tools to facilitate application development. Other RDBMS vendors rely on third-party front-end tool vendors to supply application development tools that can construct applications efficiently for a given RDBMS. Examples of such tools are JAYCC, Uniface, and Neuron Data. Intimate knowledge of the underlying database system often results in better application performance when integrated front-end/DBMS solutions are used. On the other hand, independent front-end tool vendors often offer better and more open graphical user interfaces (GUIs) and allow users to be more flexible about choosing the best database management system. Whatever the case, front-end tools must be considered when selecting an RDBMS. More discussion on application development tools can be found in Chap. 17.

On-line analytical processing (OLAP) and multidimensional databases (MDDB)

Often, system designers and users like to differentiate operational databases, designed for OLTP applications, from data warehouse databases, designed to support decision support systems (DSS). Aside from purely operational consideration (availability, multiuser support, etc.), databases designed for DSS should easily lend themselves to support ad hoc analytical queries. Sometimes, the analytical needs appear to exceed the two dimensions (rows and columns) of the classical relational data model. This multidimensional on-line analytical processing may employ multidimensional DBMS to allow users to:

- View data from many different viewpoints.
- Easily switch from one viewpoint to another.
- Drill down into the data with a parent-child relationship between the data points.

A detailed discussion of OLAP tools and multidimensional databases can be found in Chap. 16.

Object-oriented DBMS

The object-oriented approach continues to grow in acceptance. Object-oriented analysis and design and object-oriented programming are becoming a desired and preferred way of developing applications rapidly and efficiently due to the ability to reuse application code and entire business objects. The need for and the benefits of object-oriented database management systems (OODBMSs) are the driving forces that result in developing a new database system model—OODBMS. Therefore, while OODBMS discussions are beyond the scope of this book, a few comments should be made for the purpose of completeness. The development of the new OODBMS follows two major approaches: extending the relational model to accommodate object concepts and building radically different, nonrelational database systems.

The first approach is defined in the "Third-Generation Database System Manifesto" (1990), pursued by many vendors (including traditional RDBMS vendors) and is facilitated by the ANSI SQL committee and SQL Access Group (SAG) working toward the object-oriented extensions to SQL (SQL3).

The second approach is promoted by OODBMS vendors and Object Database Management Group, or ODMG, that believe that the relational data model is not suited for the object-oriented approach. Their efforts are focused on developing a common set of standards for OODBMS, a set that is probably quite different from the one being developed by ANSI.

It is a fair assumption that both approaches will eventually result in an OODBMS model that will incorporate the best features of both worlds. Some OODBMS products on the market today, such as Gem-Stone from Servio Corporation and ObjectStore (Object Design Inc.), are examples of the new generation of object-oriented database management systems that provide access to objects through the applications written in C, C++, and SmallTalk. Others, such as Matisse (ADB Inc.), Objectivity/DB (Objectivity), and UniSQL (UniSQL Inc.), support object databases through the standard SQL interfaces, including ODBC. Many established RDBMS vendors (i.e., Oracle, Sybase, Informix) plan to implement object extensions in the next versions of their products.

12.2 DBMS RELIABILITY AND AVAILABILITY

The key factors affecting DBMS availability are:

- *Robustness*—The ability to reduce the affects of any particular failure, coupled with the ability to recover from failures automatically

- *Manageability*—the ability to administer a DBMS on-line, often from a remote site.

Although availability is critical to any DBMS model (relational, nonrelational, object), the following discussion will focus on how these factors affect the design of a relational database system.

12.2.1 Robustness, transactions recovery, and consistency

A database transaction treats one or more SQL statements as a single unit of work, which is the atomic unit of database recovery and consistency. Consistency in RDBMS prevents simultaneous queries and data modification requests from interfering with each other and prevents access to partially changed and not yet committed data.

An RDBMS should provide for automatic database consistency by implementing the proper levels of locking, validating logical and physical database consistency, and supporting two-phase commit protocols.

Consistency checking should be performed automatically during transaction and database recovery. There are two major types of recovery: transaction recovery from a system/application failure and system recovery from a media failure.

Transaction recovery means that, in case of system or application failure, all committed changes must be made permanent—committed data must be written to a database device (disk). At the same time, all data affected by this transaction but not yet committed is recovered (rolled back) to the pretransaction state completely and automatically. The direction of the recovery process is backward, from the point of failure to the last point of consistency.

In the case of media failure (i.e., disk crash), an RDBMS must be designed to perform point-in-time recovery, which includes restoration of the lost data using the most current backup and forward recovery of data to the specified point-in-time or to the point immediately before the media failure. Transaction logs are usually used to store changes to the database and perform recovery procedures: before-change image (for backward recovery) and after-change image (for forward recovery). Often, an RDBMS uses an automatic checkpoint mechanism to maintain the currency of the transaction log. The majority of the database products available today support various degrees of database consistency and recovery.

Shared log files

Technically speaking, the mechanism a DBMS employs to ensure the integrity of database transactions is database *logging*. DBMS logging requires that every change to the database be automatically written to the database log file. These change records can be used by the DBMS to recover from an in-flight transaction failure (ROLLBACK) and for the point-in-time forward recovery. Advanced RDBMS implementations allow one physical write to the log file to contain the COMMIT/ROLLBACK information for several transactions. The resulting reduction in log I/O improves RDBMS update performance, allows for the efficient use of resources, and facilitates multiuser support.

On-line backup and recovery

The database backup and recovery mechanisms should be able to operate dynamically, on-line, while the RDBMS server continues to operate. Indeed, in a multiuser, multidatabase environment, a backup of one database should not prevent users from accessing other databases, even on the same physical system. That is especially true when many organizations authorize database owners to be responsible for backing up their databases and corresponding transaction logs. On-line recovery should allow a database to recover automatically from an application or transaction failure (i.e., perform automatic rollback) and support a forward recovery procedure. On-line backup and recovery should be a mandatory feature for RDBMS products selected for real-time, OLTP environments (e.g., banking, brokerage, ticket reservation, air traffic control).

Fault tolerance

While backup and recovery are important availability features, a database management system concerned about their robustness must also employ hardware and software measures typically found in fault-tolerant systems. Hardware fault-tolerance requires a physical system implementation where all (or the majority of the components) are duplicated, so that when one component fails, the "hot" standby takes over immediately. Among the fault-tolerant measures found in DBMSs are the ability to work with RAID (redundant array of inexpensive disks) devices DBMS server clustering with automatic failover, disk mirroring, and duplexing. In addition to protecting from failures, these measures often help optimize I/O performance.

Disk mirroring

There are several vendors that supply hardware fault-tolerant solutions (e.g., Tandem and Stratus computers). Unfortunately, these solutions are rather expensive and lock RDBMS developers and users into a particular vendor or product. Several RDBMS vendors offer software-based fault-tolerance by providing disk mirroring for transaction logs and/or databases. For example, SYBASE SQL Server supports disk mirroring for either the transaction log or the database itself.

Mirroring a transaction log protects against the loss of any committed transaction (see Fig. 12.7), while mirroring a database guarantees continuous operation in the event of media failure. Indeed, mirroring a database means nonstop recovery (see Fig. 12.8).

Disk mirroring requires availability of a separate physical disk drive device on an RDBMS server and actually duplicates all writes to the primary device on the mirror. Disk mirroring has an added advantage that both disks—the primary and the mirror—are available for read operations. Some RDBMS products take advantage of this fact by routing read requests to the disk drive that provides better response time.

12.2.2 RDBMS administration

Relational DBMS administration for high availability has two aspects: remote administration and on-line administration.

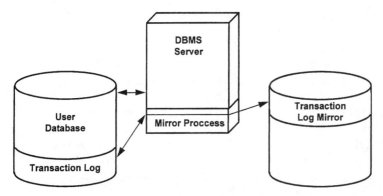

Figure 12.7 Disk mirroring—minimum guaranteed configuration.

Remote administration

Users looking for a distributed RDBMS solution should want the selected RDBMS to support database administration (DBA) functions from any site. Database administration includes installing the database system software, managing disk storage, creating and managing database objects, performing backup and recovery, providing database security, managing database users and their permissions and privileges, controlling database and table access, monitoring and tuning system performance, and determining and solving system problems. In a distributed environment, these tasks may have to be done at each database location. Thus, users should require that RDBMS vendors provide database administration facilities that allow limited DBA staff to perform the necessary administration functions rapidly, conve-

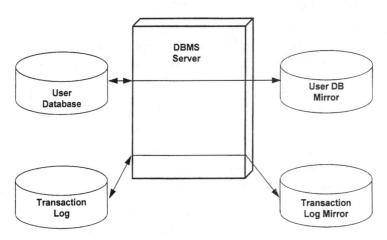

Figure 12.8 Disk mirroring on multiple disks.

niently, and from any (preferably centralized) location. Indeed, if remote database administration is not available, an organization has to face two unattractive choices: send DBAs to the database location as the need arises or maintain qualified DBA personnel at each location. If a network contains hundreds or even thousands of nodes, either choice becomes economically unfeasible.

Most RDBMS products available to date, especially products that operate in UNIX-based environments, provide at least some degree of remote database administration. Noticeable among them are solutions that are based on the Tivoli Management Environment (TME) framework. Examples can be found in such database implementations as ORACLE, SYBASE, and INFORMIX.

On-line administration

Administrative tasks such as performance tuning, resource management, database recovery, and archiving often interfere with the RDBMS availability requirements. On-line administration implies continuous operation of the DBMS irrespective of the administrative actions taken against it. For example, traditional RDBMS administration tasks, such as initiating a backup, adding a new user, modifying a user profile, and creating database objects, should be performed on-line, without stopping the database system and interrupting ongoing activities.

To be fair, remote database management should be considered as part of a larger distributed systems management issue, discussed in more detail in Chap. 14.

12.3   CLIENT/SERVER RDBMS SOLUTIONS

There are several DBMS products designed to work in client/server environments based on various hardware and operating system platforms. To demonstrate how the architectural and design features previously discussed apply to the major RDBMS products, the following discussion focuses on some of these products—SYBASE, ORACLE, INFORMIX, CA/Ingres, DB2/6000, and Microsoft SQL Server.

12.3.1   SYBASE

Sybase's client/server architecture is a proven solution for integrating heterogeneous data and applications. Some particular strengths of SYBASE SQL Server are:

- 32-bit multithreaded architecture—SYBASE implements multithreading in the engine, and does not use operating system threads.

- Dynamic (on-line) backup / continuous operations—Sybase published the benchmark results rating the Backup Server at 45 GB/h.

- Database triggers and stored procedures, with trigger self-recursion.

- Server-enforced business rules and referential integrity.

- Support for user-defined data types.

- Cost-based optimization.

- ANSI standard SQL support.

- Clustered indexes.

- Cursor support.

- Asynchronous I/O.

- Multilevel locking.

- Operating system support—UNIX, Windows NT, OS/2, VMS.

- Access control, security, and remote database administration—SYBASE supports *role-based* security and database auditing by roles; stored procedure executions can be limited by roles.

SYBASE supports software disk mirroring and provides integrated graphical application development environment—*PowerBuilder*.

Distributed databases are supported by remote procedure calls (RPCs) and remote stored procedures, gateways, and open client/server interfaces that are based on the ISO Remote Database Access (RDA) protocol. Data location transparency and programmable two-phase commit for multisite updates are enhanced via the use of RPCs.

The Open Client is a programmable interface which manages all communications between clients and the SQL Server. SYBASE Open Server provides a consistent method of receiving SQL requests or RPC from SYBASE applications and passing them to a non-SYBASE application.

For heterogeneous (relational, nonrelational databases and files) data access, SYBASE provides the Open Connectivity solutions which include MDI Gateway and OmniSQL Gateway that allow a SYBASE application to access non-SQL Server data, including legacy (mainframe) data available through CICS.

The follow-on to SYBASE SQL Server 4.x was a major product release called SYBASE System 10. System 10 does not refer to just the SQL Server but to an entire family of products. For example, OmniSQL Gateway, Replication Server, and Navigation Server are components of the System 10 release. Other examples include systems management tools to manage local and distributed client/server environments. Among these tools are:

- Enterprise SQL Server Manager (ESSM)—a graphical systems management tool for distributed DBMS that is based on the Tivoli Management Environment (TME) framework.

- SQL Server Monitor—a graphical tool used to monitor SQL Server performance. Up to 300 parameters can be monitored concurrently.

- SQL Debug—a source-level debugger for Transact-SQL code.

- Other systems management features include support for the system's estimation of storage space allocation, reports on the status of integrity constraints, and threshold violation by database segment. The system can determine when to rebuild the index following the sort order change. SYBASE also supports chargeback statistics per user based on CPU and I/O usage.

Virtual server architecture

SYBASE SQL Server design is based on Sybase's Virtual Server Architecture (VSA), which allows it to utilize coarse-grain parallel processing features on symmetric multiprocessing (SMP) systems. SQL Server can be run as a single process (does not utilize SMP) or as multiple cooperating processes.

Asynchronous I/O

The SQL Server engine uses an asynchronous device I/O on platforms that support it. SQL Server allows the user to partition a physical device into several logical devices. Each logical database device uses a separate thread, providing asynchronous I/O capability even within one physical device.

Because a separate thread is used for each logical device, the SQL Server can write concurrently to different database devices. The asynchronous I/O capability also allows for nonserial writes within mirrored devices. This means that the system can queue up writes immediately to both sides of mirrored devices. Without asynchronous I/O, the system would have to wait for each write to finish before starting another.

Client-side asynchronous I/O

Client applications can benefit greatly from the use of asynchronous programming capabilities. Asynchronous applications are designed to make efficient use of time by performing other work while waiting for server operations to complete. The new Open Client Client-Library (CT-Library) provides programmers with a set of routines for asynchronous programming. These asynchronous I/O capabilities allow client applications to use one connection for multiple actions.

Replication

Sybase has implemented data replication services as a variant of the publisher/subscriber model. The replication processing and control logic are built into a separate product called Replication Server. Replication Server keeps copies of data up-to-date at multiple sites providing client applications with access to local data instead of remote, centralized databases. The Replication Server provides reliable data and transaction delivery despite network failures and automatically synchronizes data after failure. Replication Server has an open architecture allowing organizations to build a replicated data system from existing systems and applications. Systems can be expanded incrementally as the organization grows and business requirements change.

Parallel query processing

Sybase has implemented parallel query processing as a separate product called SYBASE MPP (previously known as Navigation Server). SYBASE MPP provides high-speed access to large volumes of data by partitioning the data across multiple SYBASE SQL Servers and by using parallel concurrent access to multiple processors.

SYBASE MPP product is designed to provide support for very large database (VLDB) environments that are typical for data warehousing. SYBASE MPP is designed to handle thousands of users, very high transaction rates, and complex decision support applications. More details about SYBASE MPP can be found in Chap. 16.

The query optimizer

SYBASE SQL Server supports both syntax-based and cost-based optimization. Syntax-based optimization is based on the form of the SQL expression. The advantage of syntax-based optimization is low overhead on the server. With cost-based optimization, statistics are kept on the database tables. The optimizer makes use of the statistical data to determine the best plan for the execution of a particular query.

Performance improvements in SYBASE System 11

SYBASE System 11—the long-awaited follow-on to SYBASE System 10—addresses many of the performance and scaleability issues of System 10. Some of the System 11 improvements include:

- Multiple buffer choices—named variable size buffer caches for improved I/O performance
- Increased data I/O size (blocks up to 16 KB)
- Parallel log writes

- Improved "cache hit ratio" for enhanced SMP performance
- Parallel data partitioning (data can be added to several partitions concurrently)
- Parallel lock manager (concurrent control to several types of transaction locks)
- Multiple network engines eliminate System 10 single network engine (Engine 0) limitation
- Update-in-place (System 10 performs updates as a combination of delete and insert operations)
- Nonblocking ("dirty") reads
- Optimizer enhancements for subquery processing (typical in decision support applications)

12.3.2 ORACLE

Oracle is one of the largest RDBMS vendors. The ORACLE RDBMS is available on practically every hardware platform and every operating system. Starting with version 7, ORACLE provides parallel query processing capabilities and, as such, is the first commercial RDBMS that is available on several SMP and MPP platforms. ORACLE offers not just a relational database management system, but the entire suite of integrated software tools, including an Integrated Computer Aided Software Engineering (I-CASE) toolset. Some of the strongest features of ORACLE RDBMS are:

- Hardware and system software portability
- Wide communication protocol support
- Distributed processing capabilities
- Parallel query processing
- Active data dictionary
- SQL support:
  —Procedural (PL/SQL)
  —SQL precompiler support
  —ANSI SQL support
  —Extended SQL support (SQL*Plus)

ORACLE front-end tools include SQL*FORMS graphical tools for application development, SQL*ReportWriter, and SQL*Menu products.

The ORACLE RDBMS offers standard SQL implementation with several useful extensions and two programming interfaces: low-level ORACLE Call Interface and embedded SQL with SQL precompilers.

The ORACLE RDBMS offers sophisticated concurrency control, row-level locking, contention-free queries, event-related triggers, and asynchronous I/O. In addition, ORACLE supports shared databases via its Global Cache system, where multiple ORACLE instances residing on multiple systems can share the same database located on a shared disk. Beginning with version 7, the ORACLE RDBMS supports cost-based optimization, clustered indexes, stored procedures, database triggers, disk mirroring, server-enforced integrity constraints, BLOB data types, on-line backup/recovery, and on-line, remote database administration.

The ORACLE distributed RDBMS implementation is facilitated by the SQL*Net and SQL*Connect products. These components allow ORACLE to support distributed queries and updates, data location transparency, site autonomy, heterogeneous DBMS access, and network independence. Oracle's SQL*Net is a heterogeneous network interface and supports DECnet, TCP/IP, SNA LU0, LU2 and APPC/LU6.2, Novell's IPX/SPX, Named Pipes, NetBIOS, X.25, OSI, Async, and Banyan Vines, to name just a few. The Oracle SQL*Connect heterogeneous DBMS connectivity facility supports access to DB2, SQL/DS, and VAX RMS.

One of the most important components of the ORACLE RDBMS is its active data dictionary, which is a set of read-only tables containing information about the database and database objects (tables, views, indexes, synonyms, sequences, and clusters). The data dictionary provides information about user names, user privileges, table constraints, column default values, primary and foreign keys, object space allocation, and audit data, and is, in fact, a database reference guide for all database users.

As mentioned before, ORACLE was the first commercial RDBMS that successfully ventured into the high-performance scaleable commercial computing arena with the support of very large databases. To that end, ORACLE's architecture uses simulated multithreading, with one server process used for each concurrently executing user request, but allowing users to share a set of processes. Incoming processes are dispatched to a server process assigned from the process pool, with both the number of servers and dispatchers tunable by the system administrator. One drawback of this approach is that the entire process (and not a lightweight thread) can be blocked waiting for the I/O, memory, or other system resources. The shareability of the server processes can result in what Oracle calls *artificial deadlocks*. These occur when a server process acquires an exclusive lock needed by other servers, but then is released from the current user and is used by another user. If no other server is available to process SQL statements holding the lock, ORACLE will attempt to start another server from the limited pool. If the maximum number of servers is reached, a DBA must intervene to resolve the conflict. Despite these drawbacks, ORACLE uses process switching to facilitate its port to an SMP or MPP architecture. An add-on Parallel Server Option (PSO) for loosely coupled clusters and MPP, together with the Parallel Query Option (PQO), are designed to take advantage of SMP and MPP architectures by allowing separate instances of ORACLE to run on individual processors, while sharing access to database files. Oracle solves the critical issue of memory and cache management in multiprocessor environments by implementing a global lock manager and the GigaCache system, which provide for cache coherency and in-cache data integrity.

More information on ORACLE's PSO and PQO can be found in Chap. 16.

12.3.3   INFORMIX

The INFORMIX On-Line Dynamic Server (available starting with release 6) is a completely reengineered RDBMS product based on the INFORMIX Dynamic Scaleable Architecture (DSA). The INFORMIX On-Line Dynamic Server offers a number of fully integrated advanced features at no extra cost. Among them are:

- True multithreaded architecture
- Distributed DBMS capabilities
- Symmetric multiprocessing (SMP)
- Parallel disk I/O and utilities
- Hot standby support
- Multiprotocol network support
- Parallel query processing
- Table partitioning
- Partition-level backup and restore
- Support for large databases

INFORMIX Dynamic Scaleable Architecture supports multiple concurrent threads, which are scheduled based on resource availability independently of the mechanism used by the platform's operating system. The scheduler itself is non-preemptive, and assigns tasks from the multiple, different priority *ready queues* on a FIFO basis. The architecture supports two additional queue types: the *wait queue* (where threads waiting for an event such as resource availability are placed) and the *sleep* (inactive threads) queue.

INFORMIX On-Line Dynamic Server SMP support is provided via the true multithreading feature of the DSA. In essence, although it looks like a single server to the user, the DSA schedules multiple virtual processors, each of which runs multiple threads by context switching. A virtual processor is assigned to a particular CPU and belongs to one of the processor classes. The number of virtual processors can be altered dynamically by users for some classes and automatically by the system for other classes.

Parallel disk I/O, parallel utilities, and parallel query processing features are integrated into the DSA, which divides each atomic database operation into multiple concurrent threads. In addition, each database operation is data-flow driven, and begins its processing as soon as input data is available. In turn, the output of each database operation is fed to the next operation for processing. This approach allows concurrent threads to be assigned in parallel to sort, merge, scan, join, selection, and projection operations (see Case 3 in Fig. 12.3)—vertical parallelism. Similarly, this architecture allows different tasks to run in parallel—horizontal parallelism (as in Case 4, Fig. 12.3). The latter can benefit from data partitioning supported by the DSA in three modes: index key partitioning, hash partitioning, and expression partitioning (partitions are established based on a SQL expression).

To achieve the highest levels of scaleability and performance, Informix announced its support for loosely coupled clusters and MPP systems in the Release 8 Extended Parallel Server (XPS). Other INFORMIX On-Line features include software disk mirroring, on-line backup and recovery, asynchronous parallel I/O, flexible monitoring facilities for the configuration information and DBMS activity, and cost-based optimization. INFORMIX On-Line supports binary large objects (BLOBs) for image, graphics, voice, and large text objects. In fact, INFORMIX is so efficient in multimedia applications that it is often chosen as the underlying DBMS for commercial image systems. INFORMIX distributed database support includes distributed cost-based optimization, data location transparency, and distributed queries. For heterogeneous DBMS connectivity, Informix uses third-party software vendors to implement its gateway strategy. With the acquisition of Illustra, Informix has expanded its server capabilities to support complex and user-defined data types and functions, and data access through the Web.

Overall, INFORMIX On-Line offers an innovative server architecture, relatively few hardware/software requirements, an impressive software development tool (New Era), and excellent performance.

12.3.4 CA/Ingres

The OpenIngres/Intelligent Database (Computer Associates) offers advanced relational database technology for both OLTP and decision support system (DSS) UNIX-based environments. CA/Open Ingres RDBMS, referred to as Ingres in this section, consists of three components: a relational DBMS server, a knowledge management facility, and an object management facility. The Ingres RDBMS server is a robust, high-performance multidatabase, multithreaded database management system that includes cost-based optimization, hashed tables, asynchronous I/O, and stored procedures.

Ingres multithreaded architecture is well suited to either single-processor or multiprocessor, especially symmetric multiprocessor (SMP) computers. Ingres RDBMS features include:

- ANSI standard SQL support
- Parallel database query implementation
- Referential integrity
- Multilevel locking
- Support for very large databases and binary large objects
- Integrated graphical application development environment (Windows 4GL)
- Access control, security, and remote database administration
- On-line backup/recovery

The knowledge management facility allows users to create and store triggers that enforce referential and domain integrity, implement server-enforced business rules, and control resource utilization.

The Ingres Event Alerts feature can be used to create applications that dynamically respond to business requirements.

The Ingres RDBMS allows users to define their own data types, functions, and operators that enhance the base functionality of SQL, simplifies application development, and increases programmer productivity. For the application developers, Ingres offers a 4GL product called Application-By-Form (ABF), graphical Windows4GL, an application generator called Vision, visual programming tools, embedded SQL (ESQL), and forms-based query utility (Query-By-Form).

Ingres supports distributed database access with such products as Ingres/Gateways, Ingres/Net, and Ingres/Star. Ingres/Gateways provide the capability to access such databases as Oracle RDB/VMS, IBM's DB2, SQL/DS, and IMS (the latter is for read-only). Ingres/Net connects Ingres applications across such networking protocols as DECnet, Async, SNA, TCP/IP, and OSI. Ingres/Star provides distributed Ingres RDBMS capability by supporting distributed cost-based optimization, multisite update with automatic two-phase commit, and data location transparency.

By combining Ingres RDBMS with Ingres/Net, Ingres/Star, and Ingres/Gateways, users can implement distributed client/server environments across different networks, platforms, and database management systems.

12.3.5 IBM

Advances in client/server architecture and distributed computing, the emergence of open system standards, and wide acceptance by users of open system goals continue to change the computing environment and information systems market directions and trends.

One of the most noticeable changes in the computer industry today is that the market for traditional mainframe and even minicomputers is shrinking, while the market for microprocessor-based solutions and local area networking is expanding. These market changes and customer demands for the availability of distributed, open, client/server products have led IBM to accept and embrace the client/server computing architecture and ideas of interoperability and support for open systems. As a result, IBM extended the range of available services by providing connectivity, network management, distributed database, shared files, presentation services, mail exchange, and common languages not only among its operating environments—MVS, OS/2, and AIX—but also interoperability among multiuser, multivendor systems. In the context of distributed data management, however, this chapter will briefly discuss a relatively new addition to the DB2 family: DB2/6000 for AIX (Advanced Interactive eXecutive operating system—IBM's version of UNIX). Starting with version 2, DB2/6000 provides many of the features that were missing from the first version of the product and even adds a number of features not available from such established RDBMS industry leaders as Oracle, Informix, and Sybase. The code base for this version is a consolidation of the code of DB2/6000 v.1 for AIX and DB2/2 for OS/2, and is used for DB2 implementations under Windows NT, HP-UX, Sun Solaris, Siemens-Nixdorf's Sinix, and OS/2.

Summary of features

DB2/6000 supports:

- Nested triggers and stored procedures that can operate on a row or a statement level
- Check constraints, used to embed business rules into the database and enforce domain integrity
- User-defined data types
- User-defined functions (UDF)

- Relational extenders—function libraries that can be added to the database to extend its object orientation
- Visual development language
- Support for database partitions
- Support for raw devices on all UNIX versions
- Support for object-oriented programming and VisualAge (a variant of SmallTalk) programming language
- Support for multimedia applications by providing features that facilitate image storage and manipulation
- Enhancements in query optimization, performance, and scaleability
- A suite of data warehousing and connectivity products that includes:
  —DataGuide—an information catalog (metadata) facility
  —DataJoiner—a tool that allows a single query to access heterogeneous data sources (including DB2, SYBASE, ORACLE, IMS, and VSAM)
  —DataPropagator—a data replication system that supports relational and nonrelational (e.g., IMS) systems
  —Visualizer—an end-user data access tool with graphical query and charting capabilities

Access to host data

One of the clear advantages of DB2/6000 is its transparent access to distributed corporate data. This connectivity is based on IBM's Distributed Relational Database Architecture (DRDA). DB2/6000 uses Distributed Database Connection Services/6000 (DDCS/6000), an implementation of the DRDA Application Requester (AR) for the AIX platform. Using DDCS, DB2/6000 can directly participate in the distributed unit of work with any DRDA-compliant RDBMS, including DB2/MVS, SQL/DS (VM and VSE), and Database Manager for OS/400.

In addition to providing direct connection to these RDBMSs, DDCS can act as a gateway for remote database clients, including DOS, MS Windows, AIX, and OS/2 clients using TCP/IP and SNA APPC/LU6.2 protocols.

Transaction management

DB2/6000 provides full transactional support in compliance with X/Open's XA transactional interfaces. As XA-compliant resource manager, DB2/6000 can participate in the CICS-controlled two-phase commit. In addition, since CICS/MVS APIs are supported by CICS/6000, a mainframe COBOL/CICS/DB2 application can be easily ported to an

AIX platform running CICS/6000 and DB2/6000. DB2/6000 can support other XA-compliant transaction managers, including Transarc's Encina.

Administration

DB2/6000 administration and management is facilitated by the Database System Monitor, which allows the gathering of real-time statistical information for the entire DBMS, individual databases, tables, and applications. DataHub is an IBM database administration tool that provides remote administration of heterogeneous database management systems and unattended database operations. Visual Explain is an easy-to-use tool for analyzing and tuning SQL statements. Database Director is a bundled client-side software that aids in database administration. It allows a DBA to define databases and specify their locations. Once the location directory is complete, access to the database is transparent to users and applications, regardless of the database location.

DB2/6000 Backup and Recovery is an integrated facility that supports on-line backup operations. Parallel backup of table spaces is supported in version 2. Database restore and forward recovery procedures are also supported. Remote backup to MVS and VM systems is supported via Adstar Distributed Storage Manager (ADSM). Other administration tools provide graphical support for database configuration, directory management, recovery, and user and user group security.

Application development

As already mentioned, DB2/6000 supports nested triggers and stored procedures, referential and domain integrity, user-defined data types, and user-defined functions (UDFs). UDFs allow developers to define any function that is invoked from a standard SQL statement similar to built-in scalar and aggregate functions. For example, a user may define a function called DISTANCE that calculates a distance from the destination based on current coordinates. Such a function may be invoked as part of a standard SELECT statement. DB2/6000 supports and provides relational extenders which are function libraries that can be added to the database to extend its object orientation. IBM provides extenders to handle text, image, video, audio, and fingerprint data.

The development environment includes a visual development language that is similar to Visual Basic with extensions that support used-defined functions and stored procedures. Object-oriented VisualAge and graphical VisualGen (a GUI builder) are components of the DB2 application development environment. Multimedia application support includes tools such as Ultimedia Manager and Ultimedia

Query that facilitate image storage and manipulation. DB2/6000 BLOBs can be up to 2 GB in size, and several BLOB columns can be defined in a single table. DB2 provides functions that support searching BLOBs for text or images (query by image content, or QBIC) and concatenation to other text BLOBs. In addition, users can define their own functions (UDFs) to perform various operations on multimedia data.

Additional DB2/6000 application development support includes a rich set of APIs and software developer's toolkits that provide static and dynamic SQL, declarative referential integrity, ODBC, call-level interface (CLI), SQL precompiler, and embedded SQL from C, C++, FORTRAN, COBOL, and REXX programs. The ANSI-standard SQL support is extended to include a subset of the ISO/ANSI SQL3 standard—compound SQL statements and the VALUE scalar function. The compound SQL allows application developers to group several SQL statements into a single executable block. The VALUE function returns the first non-null result from a series of expressions.

An application development tool—DB2 Stored Procedure Builder—is used to develop clientside GUI applications, server-based stored procedures, and user-defined functions.

Performance and scaleability

Many RDBMS performance-enhancement features are incorporated into the DB2/6000 design. Among them are row-level locking, highly advanced cost-based query optimizer, buffer manager, stored procedures, and triggers. DB2/6000 supports database partitions via table spaces that segregate storage for data, indexes, and binary large objects (BLOBs). Table spaces may span devices; they can be extended and backed up without stopping the database. All UNIX versions of the product support raw devices for improved I/O performance.

DB2/6000 advanced optimization techniques include support for recurring SQL (useful for optimization and routing problems, such as finding the best route for delivery trucks or airplanes), and the ability to rewrite complex queries as a series of simpler ones—a very valuable feature for ad hoc client/server applications. Query speed-up technologies include big-block reads (the ability to read several disk pages in a single I/O operation) and a read-ahead feature, whereby data pages are read in anticipation of their use.

DB2/6000 is designed for scaleability by supporting symmetric multiprocessing and distributed memory systems (MPPs). By incorporating parallel query processing into DB2/6000, it can achieve significant performance levels running on the SMP systems from IBM, HP, and Sun, as well as on shared-nothing systems like IBM SP-2.

12.3.6 Microsoft

Before the breakup with Sybase in 1994, Microsoft offered its version of SQL Server which was based on SYBASE SQL Server version 4.2. That version of the product has successfully penetrated the market for small database servers. Its integration with Windows NT and GUI-oriented administration tools reduced the learning time and offered good price-performance, low cost of ownership, and an easy migration path to the UNIX-based SYBASE SQL Server product.

However, now the two companies, Sybase and Microsoft, follow different development paths, and their products, although still named "SQL Server," are diverging in features, interfaces, and architecture. This section will briefly discuss Microsoft's SQL Server version 6.0, originally code-named SQL Server 95.

SQL Server 6 has confirmed Microsoft's intention to replace the Sybase process and memory management architecture in favor of an approach optimized for Windows NT. Although this approach limits SQL Server 6 to a single operating system (Windows NT), it makes a lot of sense from Microsoft's point of view to leverage robust and scaleable Windows NT services rather than include them in the database engine. For example, SQL Server 6 uses Windows NT threads. The threads are scheduled by the Windows NT scheduler and can share the same address space, all without incurring the overhead associated with thread creation and dispatching. The number of threads is configurable using a single system parameter. SQL Server 6 offers many new and improved features. Several features of MS SQL Server 6 are covered as follows.

Scaleability and parallelism

One of the more interesting features of SQL Server 6 is Parallel Data Scan. With Parallel Data Scan, SQL Server 6 launches multiple NT threads for reading data from disk to memory in parallel. The DBMS performance is improved significantly since Parallel Data Scan increases the probability that required data pages are already in memory (clearly, this feature can especially benefit SMP systems with a large memory and good disk striping capability). However, the retrieved rows of data are still processed sequentially, via a single thread, which significantly reduces the potential benefit of Parallel Data Scan. In fact, the SQL Server 6 parallelism is limited, and it does not apply to operations such as sorting, filtering, and SQL statement parsing. SQL Server 6 determines when to perform the Parallel Data Scan based on the disk access pattern and not on the decision by the optimizer.

Built-in replication

SQL Server 6 has built-in replication capabilities that are not an add-on product but are part of the core engine. SQL Server 6 replication supports homogeneous replication, with ODBC-compliant targets planned for the future. Similar to SYBASE, SQL Server 6 replication is based on the primary site strategy. All data at replicated targets is read-only and is subscribed to—SQL Server 6 follows the publisher/subscriber model. SQL Server 6 replication reads data changes from the log—there is a log reader task that runs continuously and captures log changes while they are still in memory. This design clearly minimizes negative impact on transaction performance and throughput.

SQL Server 6 replication is integrated with the SQL Server performance monitor to display important replication-related statistics graphically.

SQL Scheduler

This is a scheduling and execution facility that runs a distributed task for each distributed subscriber database. The SQL Scheduler can run continuously to minimize the latency or in a timed batch mode, which improves replication for large databases and narrow network bandwidth.

Distributed management

SQL Server 6 offers a graphical capability to manage multiple SQL Servers from a single management workstation. This capability is built on 32-bit OLE objects called distributed management objects (DMOs). DMOs encapsulate all SQL Server management functions such as starting and stopping the server, accessing system catalog and stored procedures, managing devices and databases, managing publications and subscriptions for the replication services, handling alerts, and running Transact-SQL commands (SQL Server programming language). Microsoft supplies a management application—SQL Enterprise Manager—that uses DMOs to provide a graphical easy-to-use management environment.

Administration

In the area of database administration, SQL Server 6 improves both performance and productivity. Specifically, SQL Server 6 offers improved versions of such utilities and commands as backup and recovery, indexing, database consistency checking, and even updating optimizer statistics. Backup and recovery can be performed in parallel, by striping the backup across multiple devices and by loading the database from multiple devices. Also, SQL Server 6 supports backup over Named Pipes, which enables backups on remote systems or via a third-party backup product. Another attractive feature is the ability to preview information in the dump file prior to loading it into a database. Both backup and restore (DUMP and LOAD commands) are automatically logged in the Windows NT event log.

Cursors

SQL Server 6 provides very attractive and frequently requested serverside cursors, which can improve network performance by allowing data manipulation without returning rows to the client system. And what's more, these cursors support forward and backward (bidirectional) scrolling. The cursors can be engaged via API calls to the DB-Library for C and the ODBC SQL Server driver.

Among other features are:

- Integrated Visual Basic for Application (VBA) macro language for automated operations
- Event notification
- Mail and messaging integration

The list of features is much longer than this section of the book indicates. Suffice it to say that Microsoft's SQL Server is an advanced relational database management system that is closely integrated with Windows NT and capable of providing cost-effective and functionally rich solutions.

Transaction and Systems Management in Client/Server Environments

Transaction processing is the backbone of daily business activities throughout organizations and industries. Major governments and such industries as transportation, communications, distribution, financial services, manufacturing, and retailing rely on transaction processing systems to manage mission-critical information. Today, transaction processing technology is becoming increasingly important because of the computer industry direction to perform on-line transaction processing (OLTP) on open, distributed systems and in the client / server architecture.

The client / server computing model which can be viewed as a special case of cooperative processing, facilitates the development and implementation of networked, distributed environments. Indeed, linking multiple computers together through a communications network allows users to access and share all available distributed resources, while at the same time effectively distributing the computing workload. From a client / server architecture perspective, the workload distribution between clients and servers may allow clients to manage input, output, and presentation functions, some application logic functions, and even certain local data access functions. Servers, on the other hand, perform the database access functions and common shareable application functions. Most important, the servers' role is to perform workload distribution and management, synchronization, and control of access to centralized resources based on clients' requests. As a result, the cost effectiveness of the computing environment is maximized and the environment itself becomes flexible, scaleable, and reliable.

Workload distribution, synchronization of client / server interactions, and management of resource access are the functions of transaction, systems, and workflow management that are described in this and following chapters.

Chapter

13

Distributed Transaction Processing

Traditionally, transaction processing has been performed on centralized systems, typically running proprietary operating systems. Naturally, such centralized (nondistributed) transaction processing has
been supported, often quite successfully, by transaction monitors
native to the underlying mainframe hardware and operating systems.
The last several years have been characterized by the advent of distributed heterogeneous computing architectures and open systems,
often based on the UNIX operating system. As a result, transaction
processing is evolving to satisfy two complementary goals:

- On the one hand, providing support for the traditional, nondistributed transaction management in the new, open systems environment

- On the other hand, providing a focal point for a distributed, enterprise-wide transaction processing system

Needless to say, a transaction processing system that satisfies both
requirements will enable users of proprietary TP monitors to take
advantage of distributed environments and open systems while protecting and leveraging the users' investment in existing proprietary TP
systems. Such a transaction processing system will allow customers to

choose freely among various vendor products. It will support nondisruptive growth of systems and applications and will allow sharing of computing resources among customers and service suppliers across a worldwide open enterprise.

Let's follow the evolution of transaction processing by taking a closer look at the concepts of distributed transaction processing and DTP implementations.

13.1 DTP CONCEPTS

To illustrate the emerging TP management trends, the definition and properties of transactions described in the previous chapters can be expanded to include the concepts of distributed transaction processing (DTP).

13.1.1 Transactions

A transaction can be defined as a sequence of predefined actions performed on behalf of the application. A transaction takes a computing system and its resources from one consistent state to another in order to accomplish the desired business functionality. Transactions possess the following ACID properties:

- *Atomicity*—The entire sequence of actions (Logical Unit of Work) must be either completed or aborted. The transaction cannot be partially successful.

- *Consistency*—A transaction takes a computing system and its resources from one consistent state to another.

- *Isolation*—A transaction's effect is not visible to other transactions until the transaction is committed.

- *Durability*—Changes made by the committed transaction are permanent and should tolerate system failures.

We can also expand these ACID properties by adding another—*serialization*—which means that as long as a transaction in progress depends on certain information, this information is locked to prevent any other transaction from changing it.

These transaction properties have been illustrated in the previous chapters in the example of database transactions.

13.1.2 TP monitors

By supporting these transaction properties, transaction processing, as the name implies, deals with the execution and control of transactions and provides users with on-line, near-instantaneous access to many types of information. Computer systems that support on-line transaction processing (OLTP) are typically called *transaction processing monitors,* or *TP monitors.* Transaction management and support can also be considered as one of the services provided by the data access middleware. There are several misconceptions regarding transaction management:

- It is used only for mainframe CICS applications.

- Its usefulness is limited to the two-phase commit protocol.

- It implies synchronous communications.

- There is no need for it since modern DBMSs provide all TP monitor functionality.

In fact, a strong case can be made for the use of TP monitors when downsizing existing OLTP applications to a distributed client/server environment.

In addition, services and benefits provided by the new generation of transaction managers are desirable even for non-OLTP types of applications, such as e-mail, decision support, and office workflow management. These services include:

- Guaranteed delivery of application-to-application messages across similar or dissimilar operating systems

- Synchronous and asynchronous message delivery

- Automatic scaleability with application replication

- Reduced server workload by multiplexing and managing client transaction

- Transaction management, including two-phase commit across heterogeneous DBMSs, applications, or other resources

- Simplified system administration by leveraging TP monitors' built-in ability to balance workload, collect system statistics, and monitor performance and throughput

- Increased application availability by providing for application and DBMS recovery and restart

- Reduced application complexity by insulating application developers from the knowledge of low-level synchronous and asynchronous middleware primitives such as CPI-C, APPC, Sockets, RPCs, and message queuing

Therefore, transaction managers are often considered a special class of middleware solution, characterized by its ability to provide consistent application-to-application interfaces in a distributed cooperative processing environment. In addition to interface consistency, transaction managers typically support transaction routing, execution of remote functions (e.g., function shipping), transparent access to remote data, transaction integrity, security, manageability, and recoverability.

The management scope of a transaction manager exceeds that of a modern DBMS. In fact, a full-function TPM ensures the ACID properties (atomicity, consistency, independence, durability) of all transactions irrespective of whether they affect a single DBMS, heterogeneous DBMS environment, or non-DBMS data. The way transaction manager accomplishes this is defined in X/Open's DTP Reference Model (discussed in the next sections).

In a nondistributed environment, TP monitors perform their functions by running on the same system where the application functions, presentation functions, and database management systems reside. Therefore, the resources that the TP monitor must manage are local, and appropriate interprocess communications mechanisms can be used to control and coordinate all participants in a transaction. However, when the business logic functions and, therefore, the work they are designed to do are distributed among several systems, the role of the TP monitor must be expanded to manage transactions affecting multiple systems in a distributed transaction processing environment (DTP).

Even though each distributed node performs its share of the work in its portion of the still atomic "local" transaction (with all its local transaction properties intact), distributed transaction processing requires a new concept of distributed atomicity, consistency, isolation, and durability. These new distributed transaction properties are provided by new distributed transaction processing managers (TPM).

13.1.3   Distributed transaction processing

Distributed transaction processing is the evolution of traditional, centralized transaction processing into the world of open distributed computing. The result of this evolution is the creation of *enterprise transaction processing,* in which the entire enterprise is involved in the execution of business transactions under the control of the *enterprise transaction management.*

In distributed transaction processing, a business transaction that is executed across a network of distributed systems actually comprises multiple participants—"local" transactions. Every local transaction is executed on its own system, under the control of a distributed transaction manager. The communication between participants in distributed transaction processing is synchronous. Each transaction can be designed in such a way that its processing depends directly on the results of the processing performed by the other. In a DTP environment, synchronization (consistency) points taken by one transaction can be coordinated with the corresponding synchronization points in the other. So, all changes made to local and remote resources can be committed or rolled back synchronously.

To illustrate this important point, consider the infamous funds transfer problem. A customer of the central bank wants to transfer funds from his/her checking account into the savings account. The checking account resides in the checking accounts database in New York City, while the savings account is handled by the data processing unit located in Des Moines, Iowa.

In the conventional way of thinking, the New York branch will submit a transfer (delete) request to the New York home office data processing department via a home office transaction program. At the same time, the transfer (add) request is wired to Des Moines to be processed by the nightly batch program. Such a transfer will probably take place overnight. However, in today's fast-moving business environment, such slow batch processing may not be appropriate. In a real-time OLTP environment, two different transactions should take place practically simultaneously. What will happen if either one of these transactions fails? Will the customer get an unexpected credit to his savings account without reducing his/her checking, or will a certain amount be debited from the checking account without being credited on the savings side?

Without distributed transaction management to provide for the consistency and integrity of resources, the results of such a transaction could be unpredictable. Enterprise-wide distributed transaction processing should be managed to ensure that the funds are either transferred successfully or the transfer should not take place.

Conceptually, an enterprise distributed transaction processing (EDTP) environment should support the local transaction processing manager (TPM) on each distributed node. At the same time, EDTP should provide for a global, logically centralized TP coordinator (manager) that can communicate with and control each of its participant TPMs.

This concept can be illustrated in the example of a three-tiered client/server OLTP computing environment (see Fig. 13.1). Here, the client workstations may perform local transactions under the control of a local TPM. Concurrently, they may participate in a workgroup transaction coordinated by a server TPM. Conversely, servers may participate in a distributed transaction spanning multiple servers and/or in a global transaction initiated and coordinated by a host TPM.

All these distributed transactions must be coordinated, and all participating transaction monitors must be integrated into a "centralized"

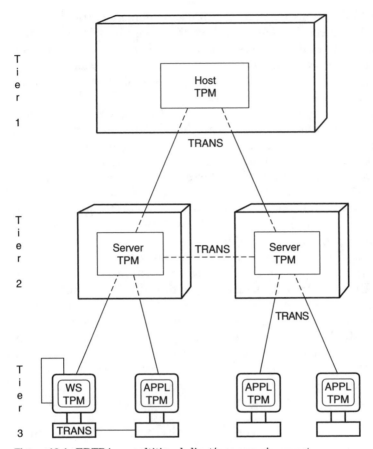

Figure 13.1 EDTP in a multitiered client/server environment.

distributed TP manager. The key to such integration is the existence of a common Transactional Application Programming Interface (TP-API), which is understood by all participants—transaction managers and resource managers (e.g., database). Implementations of these APIs are based on two major cooperative processing techniques: Advanced Program-to-Program Communications (based on IBM's SNA LU6.2 protocols) and remote procedure calls (RPCs).

Despite considerable technical difficulties, some vendors offer proprietary implementations of such APIs to tie together even single-vendor, homogeneous environments (e.g., IBM's CICS/MVS and CICS/6000 intercommunication via APPC/LU6.2).

However, the importance of common APIs between transaction managers and resource managers (RMs), as well as the complexity of their implementation, becomes even more obvious in an open systems environment. Various distributed transaction processing standards are being developed by international standards organizations. For example, the X/Open organization developed its DTP TPM/RM interface standard—the XA interface.

Once these standards are completed, software vendors can incorporate DTP APIs into their products (transaction managers, resource managers), to make an open distributed transaction processing environment a reality.

13.2   X/OPEN DISTRIBUTED TRANSACTION PROCESSING MODEL

Modern transaction managers are designed to comply with the X/Open Distributed Transaction Processing Reference Model (see Fig. 13.2), that is incorporated in the X/Open Portability Guide (XPG4). In this model, the standard interfaces employed by a transaction manager include X/Open's XA and TX interfaces for communication with resource managers and application programs.

The X/Open DTP Reference model contains three software components:

- An application program (AP)

- Resource managers (RMs) such as databases and file systems that provide access to shared resources

- A transaction manager (TM) that assigns global identifiers to transactions, monitors their progress, and manages the transaction integrity protocols and recovery from failures

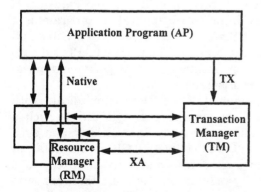

Figure 13.2 X/Open Distributed Transaction Processing Reference Model.

As part of this reference model, an interface between a transaction manager and resource managers such as a DBMS or a file system is defined through the XA specification and provides for transaction control by using such constructs as *transaction begin*, *transaction commit*, *transaction abort*, *transaction end*, etc.

XA includes the concept of global and branch transactions. A global transaction accomplishes a unit of work as seen by an end user or an application. One global transaction may cause several branch transactions to occur, each performing a particular function (i.e., update a resource file, insert a record into a database, etc.), possibly in association with a particular resource manager.

13.3 OVERVIEW OF CICS

Among the various proprietary solutions available today, IBM's Customer Information Control System (CICS) family of transaction processing monitors is an example of a successful transaction monitor implementation that supports distributed transaction processing.

CICS is one of the most popular TP monitors on the market today. Started originally as a System/370 product, CICS is now available on all IBM system platforms and many non-IBM platforms (i.e., CICS/9000 is available for HP-UX).

As a system designed to support on-line transaction processing and real-time communication between users, computer programs, and data resources. CICS was a natural choice to be the first System/370 product to implement the APPC/LU6.2 communication protocol. CICS support for Common Programming Interface for Communications (CPI-C) provides CICS users with a high-level consistent interface (API) to the LU6.2 session services.

The CICS API facilitates application developers in building distributed applications designed to work in a distributed transaction processing environment. This documented application programming interface is provided by the CICS family of TP monitors (CICS) on all of their supported platforms. The common documented API and supporting CICS facilities allow programmers to write portable applications across all supported environments.

In a multiple-system environment, CICS can communicate with other systems that have suitable communication facilities. Such a cross-system communication partner can be another CICS system, such as CICS/ESA, CICS/2 (OS/2), CICS/400 (OS/400), CICS/6000 (AIX), or IMS/VS system (version 1.3 or later). Most important, however, CICS can communicate with any system or workstation that supports APPC/LU6.2 protocols. This last feature makes CICS an ideal choice for implementing a client/server computing environment across platforms that support APPC/LU6.2 application programming interfaces.

13.3.1   CICS intercommunication methods

To describe CICS intercommunication methods, consider the most popular CICS implementation under a mainframe IBM operating system: MVS/ESA. In general, there are two ways in which a local CICS system can communicate with other (remote) systems: *intersystem communication* (ISC) and *multiregion operation* (MRO).

Multiregion operation

MRO is designed for CICS-to-CICS communications by enabling CICS systems that run in the same host but are located in different address spaces to communicate with each other. MRO does not support communications between CICS and non-CICS (such as IMS/VS) systems. SNA networking facilities and access methods (ACF/VTAM) are not required for MRO, and all data transfers between address spaces are handled by either a CICS-supplied interregion communication program (IRC) or by MVS cross-memory services (XMS).

Intersystem communication

Communication between systems residing in different locations implies the existence of a network linking these locations. Such communication also requires some sort of a communication access method to provide the necessary communication protocols. The CICS implementation of intersystem communication is, in fact, an implementation of IBM's Systems Network Architecture. The SNA access method—ACF/VTAM—is used to provide the necessary communication protocols for ISC. The principal protocol used for ISC is APPC/LU6.2, even though SNA LU6.1 protocols are also available for certain connections.

   Note.   Intersystem communication via ACF/VTAM can be used between systems in the same host processor. In this case, the application-to-application facilities of ACF/VTAM are used.

   There are three basic forms of ISC: ISC within a single processor (intrahost ISC), ISC between physically adjacent processors, and ISC between physically remote processors. From the CICS point of view, intrahost and interhost ISC are indistinguishable. Compared with MRO, ISC offers a wide variety of configurations for both local and remote systems, including the APPC-based client/server computing model. Therefore, the discussion that follows is concentrated on the CICS intersystem communication facilities. (See Fig. 13.3.)

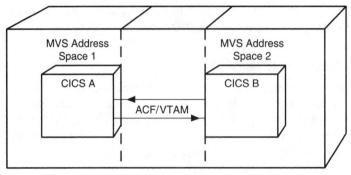

ISC Within Single Host

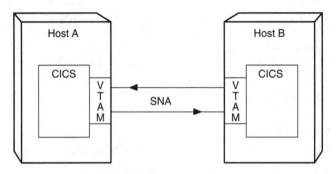

ISC Between Hosts

Figure 13.3   CICS intersystem communications.

13.3.2   CICS intercommunication facilities

CICS intersystem communication (ISC) provides four basic types of intercommunication facilities: CICS function shipping, asynchronous processing, CICS transaction routing, and CICS distributed transaction processing (DTP). For completeness, a brief description of these facilities is provided, even though these facilities are not universally available for all forms of CICS intercommunication.

CICS function shipping

This facility is available only for CICS-to-CICS intercommunication via MRO or ISC LU6.1 and LU6.2 links. Function shipping is designed to enable an application program running in one CICS system to access a resource owned by another CICS system.

The remote resource can be a file or DL/I database, a transient data queue, or a temporary storage queue. Application programs that access remote resources can be designed and coded as if the resources were local to the system in which the application is to run. CICS handles the function shipping by passing a request from a local system to a special transaction in the remote system known as a *mirror transaction*. CICS supplies a number of mirror transactions, each of which corresponds to a particular function.

Asynchronous processing

This facility enables a CICS transaction to distribute the required processing between systems in an intersystem communication environment by initiating a transaction in a remote system and passing data to it. The reply does not have to be returned to the task that initiated the remote transaction, and no direct correlation can be made between a request and a reply (other than the application-provided code). The processing is thus called *asynchronous*. It differs from synchronous distributed transaction processing, in which a session is held by two transactions for the period of a conversation between them, and requests and replies can be directly correlated. Asynchronous processing is available via MRO or ISC LU6.1 and LU6.2 links. (See Fig. 13.4.)

CICS transaction routing

This facility is available only for CICS-to-CICS intercommunication via MRO and ISC LU6.2 links. It enables a device (terminal) that is owned by one CICS system to initiate a transaction that is owned by another CICS system. For ISC links, the two systems can be connected via LU6.2 protocols only. CICS supplies a special relay program which provides the communication mechanism between the local terminal and the remote transaction.

As with function shipping, the intricacies of the actual communication are handled by CICS itself, and an application can be designed in a way that makes it transparent that the terminal is connected to another CICS system.

CICS distributed transaction processing

This is the CICS facility that enables a CICS transaction to communicate with a transaction running in another system for the purpose of distributing the required processing between two or more systems in an intercommunication environment. The other system can be another CICS connected via MRO, ISC LU6.1, and LU6.2 links, IMS/VS connected via LU6.1 links, or any other system supporting APPC/LU6.2 protocols. (See Fig. 13.5.)

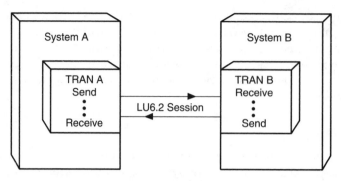

Synchronous Processing

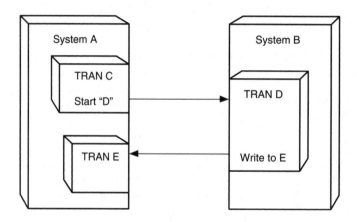

Asynchronous Processing

Figure 13.4 CICS synchronous and asynchronous processing.

Synchronous CICS DTP communication using APPC protocols means that a session is acquired and held by two transaction programs for the duration of a conversation between them. The transactions have exclusive use of the session, and the messages that pass between transactions as part of the conversation can be directly correlated. Each transaction can be designed in such a way that the processing depends directly on the results of the processing performed by the other.

13.3.3 Front-end and back-end transactions

To start a distributed transaction, a front-end transaction must initiate a conversation with its partner (back-end transaction) over a ses-

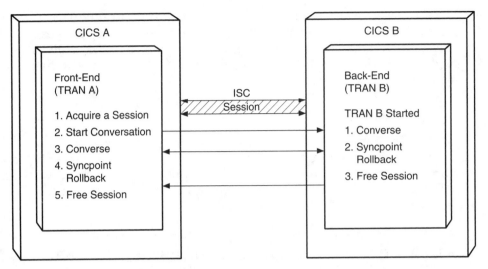

Figure 13.5 Distributed transaction processing.

sion between logical units (LU-LU session). So, the first action the front-end transaction should perform is to acquire an LU-LU session to the required remote system by issuing an ALLOCATE command to CICS (and its LU6.2). The front-end transaction specifies the name of the remote system as a parameter of the ALLOCATE command.

After the session has been allocated, the front-end transaction should initiate a back-end transaction. For LU6.2 sessions, CICS APPC API provides a special command—CONNECT PROCESS—which the front-end transaction must issue before the first SEND or CONVERSE. On its conversations with the back-end transaction, the front-end transaction must specify what conversational resource (conversation-id) it is using. This conversation-id is supplied by LU6.2 when the session is allocated, and it must be used by the front-end transaction on every command it issues for that conversation. The exceptions to this rule are CICS SYNCPOINT and ROLLBACK commands that apply to every conversation this transaction is involved in.

While in conversation, the front-end and back-end transactions exchange messages by issuing SEND, RECEIVE, or CONVERSE CICS commands. The state of the conversation at either end of the link is determined by the previous state and the most recently executed command. The front-end transaction always starts in the Send state, the back-end in the Receive state. The conversation follows the LU6.2 half-duplex flip-flop protocol. The state change can be initiated only by a transaction in the Send state by issuing the CONVERSE or SEND commands, even though it can be requested by the transaction in the Receive state.

Specifically, a transaction in the Receive state can use the ISSUE SIGNAL command to request a change of direction (change of states). Irrespective of the current state, a transaction can issue ISSUE ERROR and ISSUE ABEND commands to inform its partner that an error has occurred.

13.3.4 Syncpoints

APPC/LU6.2 protocols define the way in which synchronization of distributed processes can be performed. LU6.2 architecture supports three synchronization levels: NONE, CONFIRM, and SYNCPT. CICS APPC supports all three synchronization levels. They can be specified on the CONNECT PROCESS command:

- Level 0 (NONE) indicates that no synchronization is possible.
- Level 1 (CONFIRM) indicates that LU6.2 SYNC_LEVEL (CONFIRM) is selected. As defined in the LU6.2 architecture, confirmation exchanges are supported. CICS APPC API supplies special commands (e.g., SEND CONFIRM, ISSUE ERROR, ISSUE ABEND) to implement this protocol.
- Level 2 (SYNCPT) corresponds to the LU6.2 SYNC_LEVEL (SYNCPT). This means that in addition to the confirmation exchanges, full CICS syncpointing (SYNCPOINT and SYNCPOINT ROLLBACK commands) is available for distributed transaction processing.

The maximum synchronization level available on the session must be agreed on by both ends of the session and is determined at the session BIND time. The synchronization level for a particular conversation over that session is specified in the CONNECT PROCESS command, even though it cannot exceed the maximum allowed for the session.

Synchronization level 2 conversations support and participate in the syncpointing activity also known as the two-phase commit protocol. The two-phase commit process consists of two distinctive portions: the *prepare* phase and the *commit* phase. Typically, during both phases of the commit process, the response of every application involved in the transaction is written to that application's permanent log. This ensures that the data managed by the application is correctly updated even in the event of a system failure.

CICS commit actions are called *syncpoints*. CICS syncpoints are implemented by APPC/LU6.2 protocols and, according to the two-phase commit rules, include a designation of one of the distributed transaction participants as the coordinator. The coordinator is in charge of coordinating the phases of the two-phase commit. The CICS syncpoints are initiated and coordinated by any one of the transactions connected by the level 2 conversations when it issues the SYNCPOINT or SYNC-POINT ROLLBACK command. These commands always apply to all level 2 conversations held by a transaction. However, CICS APPC API supplies a special command (ISSUE PREPARE), that requires the conversation-id and allows individual conversations to be prepared for the syncpointing activity.

The CICS transaction that initiates the syncpoint is called the *syncpoint initiator*. It must be in the Send state when the SYNCPOINT command is issued. All transactions that receive the syncpoint request are in a Receive state relative to the syncpoint initiator and are called *syncpoint slaves*. For the syncpoint slave, the normal response to a syncpoint request is to issue the SYNCPOINT command.

However, in the distributed transaction processing environment, the slave may hold level 2 conversations with other transactions. Therefore, it must participate in the distributed syncpoint (distributed commit process). The slave becomes the syncpoint initiator for these transactions and must ensure that it is in the Send state in relation to its slaves before SYNCPOINT commands can be issued.

In the terminology of the two-phase commit protocol, during the first, *prepare* phase, the initiator's SYNCPOINT command sends the Prepare-To-Commit (PTC) request to its first slave. PTC requests are then propagated down the syncpoint tree. The slaves exchange positive Request Commit (RC) responses when they are ready to commit. Once all slaves but the *last* answered with the RC, the initiator starts the second, *commit* phase, by sending the RC to its last slave. At that point, the Committed (CTD) responses are exchanged between the syncpoint tree nodes as the resources are being committed (see Fig. 13.6).

While the syncpoint activity is in progress, one of the slaves may detect an error. The syncpoint request is then rejected. The rejecting slave can use the SYNCPOINT ROLLBACK, ISSUE ERROR, or ISSUE ABEND commands to answer with a negative response.

In a CICS environment, the ISSUE ERROR command, issued in response to a syncpoint request, causes the syncpoint initiator to abort, thus initiating a rollback among participating transactions (CICS dynamic transaction backout). The ISSUE ABEND command goes even further by causing the syncpoint initiator to abend the conversation. Therefore, the recommended negative response to a syncpoint request is the SYNCPOINT ROLLBACK command. This command can be issued regardless of whether the transaction is in a Send or Receive state. When issued, it causes the current logical unit of work to roll-back unconditionally. The rollback request (RB) is propagated to all level 2 conversational partners of the transaction. The syncpoint tree,

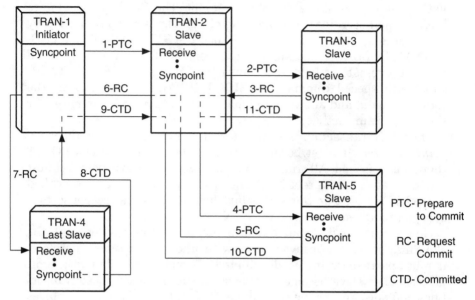

Figure 13.6 Distributed syncpoint.

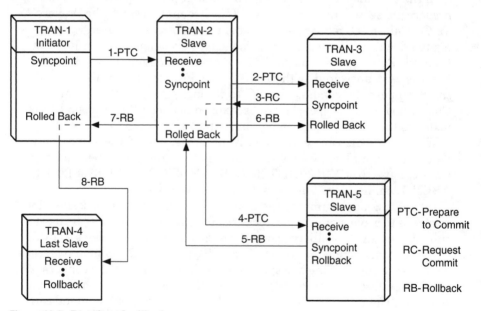

Figure 13.7 Distributed rollback.

shown in Fig. 13.7, illustrates how a negative response from TRAN-5 is affecting the entire distributed unit of work.

By supporting APPC/LU6.2 Level 2 synchronization, CICS ensures the atomicity, consistency, isolation, and durability of transactions in a distributed transaction processing environment.

13.3.5 CICS distributed two-phase commit

Complex distributed transaction processing applications may involve several transactions in different systems to be executed in order to perform the required application function. One way to accomplish this is to use the structured approach of the master-slave tree (see Fig. 13.8). There, the initial request starts the front-end transaction (master of the entire tree), which in turn allocates a conversation with another remote transaction (its slave), which initiates its slave, etc.

In a CICS environment, this approach, while offering the least complicated design, involves multiple LU6.2 sessions. As a result, the synchronization points in that distributed transaction can involve all tree nodes. Unless the request for synchronization (either commit or backout) originates from the tree master, the synchronization is unlikely to succeed.

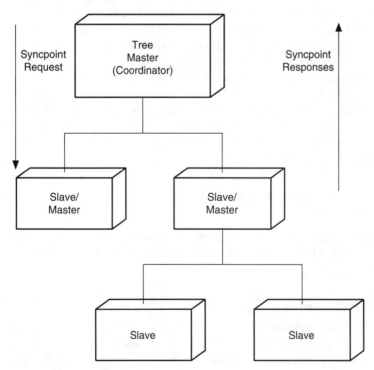

Figure 13.8 Master-slave tree.

The tree master (transaction coordinator) must perform the following functions:

- Identify all participants involved in the transaction.
- Send Prepare-to-Commit (PTC) requests to all participants.
- Ensure that all participants successfully acknowledge the PTC request.
- Log the fact that all participants are prepared.
- Send the Commit request to all participants.
- Ensure that all participants successfully acknowledge the Commit request.
- Log the fact that all participants have committed.

Logging of the commit phases is critical to transaction consistency and durability, i.e., implementation of a successful two-phase commit. Therefore, a transaction selected as the distributed transaction coordinator (a syncpoint initiator) must be able to log the commit phases or interact with the transaction logging services provided by the transaction manager. Notice that CICS logging is supported by CICS automatically. To support proper synchronization of the two-phase commit protocol, the transaction coordinator (tree master) should initiate the commit process, and the synchronization signals should be propagated all the way down the tree. The syncpoint responses flow in the opposite direction, from the leaf nodes through the intermediate masters, to the tree master. The transactions should be designed in such way that, if any of the transactions attempting to execute the SYNCPOINT command (explicit or implicit) abends, that abend should be propagated to every other transaction in the tree, and all transactions should back out their protected resources.

13.4 TRANSACTION MANAGEMENT SOLUTIONS

This section focuses on the discussion of open OLTP products that include Novell's TUXEDO, Transarc's Encina, and TOP END from AT&T GIS.

13.4.1 TUXEDO overview

Novell's TUXEDO technology is the most well-established of the self-proclaimed "open" OLTP products brought to market in the last few years. It enables commercial-grade transaction processing in distributed computing environments. TUXEDO has been endorsed by systems suppliers such as Amdahl, Bull, Data General, ICL, Olivetti, Pyramid, and Unisys as their strategic UNIX transaction technology and by other systems suppliers such as Digital and Stratus as an available option for their customers. TUXEDO supports popular relational database management systems (RDBMSs) that follow the X/Open interface standard. TUXEDO follows the X/Open DTP model, which, in fact, was originally based primarily on the TUXEDO design itself.

13.4.2 TUXEDO architecture

TUXEDO developers took into consideration all important characteristics of the OLTP architecture. Indeed, a typical OLTP environment is characterized by:

- A large number of relatively short interactions
- Many users
- Large shareable databases
- High availability and recoverability
- Transaction management to satisfy business needs

To make OLTP environments more efficient, designers attempt to reduce overhead per interaction and per user; provide resource shareability; use robust, high-performance DBMS; prioritize transactional activity; and ensure reliability, integrity, availability, and security of transactions. All these OLTP issues can be addressed by an enhanced client/server architecture (see Fig. 13.9).

This enhanced client/server model provides such benefits as high performance, efficiency, data and process location transparency, robustness, and scaleability. For instance, clients may request services from servers by calling a particular server process. TUXEDO intercepts these requests and routes them to the appropriate server transparently to the application. Service locations and descriptions are handled by the Name Server. For example, as shown in Fig. 13.9, the first and the last clients request the same service. The TUXEDO Name Server decides where the required service resides and, in the case of multiple locations, even routes requests in such a way that the workload balance is ensured.

TUXEDO expands the enhanced client/server model by employing modular architecture and incorporating standards-based interfaces and protocols for communications and interactions with resource managers.

TUXEDO is positioned as a key component in a three-tiered USL distributed model, termed *enterprise transaction processing* (ETP). ETP consists of desktop devices (PCs or technical workstations) on industry-standard LANs, distributed departmental systems or servers

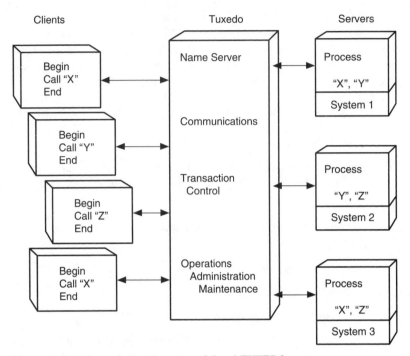

Figure 13.9 Enhanced client/server model and TUXEDO.

on LANs or WANs, and proprietary mainframes connected to the first two tiers by WANs based on proprietary protocols. In this model, TUXEDO acts as the glue that connects the three tiers together by providing transaction, communications, and administrative services.

TUXEDO ETP consists of:

- System/T—the base TP monitor
- System/Q—the queuing service enhancement to the monitor
- System/WS—the client software for intelligent workstations and PCs running DOS, Windows, and OS/2
- System/Host—the interface to MVS/CICS TP applications
- System/D—a proprietary TP-oriented data management system

These components can be purchased fully integrated or separate. Separate, they can be integrated with other front ends, database systems, and network programming interfaces in a systems supplier's or ISV's OLTP product.

System/T provides such facilities as the Name Server; communications manager; transaction control; and operations, administrations, and maintenance (OA&M) to control client/server interactions. System/D includes server applications and their interfaces for database access and access to remote applications.

The TUXEDO transaction manager and resource manager employ such standard interfaces as the Application Transaction Manager Interface (ATMI) and X/Open XA interfaces for communication with resource managers.

ATMI provides client/server communications, including service location transparency, load balancing, priority processing, network independence, context-sensitive routing, and transparent data representation conversion.

The ATMI and XA interfaces provide for transaction control by using such constructs as "transaction begin," "transaction commit," "transaction abort," "transaction end," etc. TUXEDO's openness in respect to resource managers is derived from its conformance to X/Open's DTP Reference Model, which specifies the resource manager–to–transaction manager interfaces (XA).

System/T is a mature, widely available product. Until 1991, it was a traditional, terminal-based TP product that ran on UNIX time-sharing systems. During 1990 and 1991, USL reengineered the product to reflect the emerging popularity of the client/server model. While workstation and mainframe-connectivity capabilities were added at that time, System/T retained its ability to support character-oriented terminals. A System/T enhancement, System/Q provides administrative support for reliable message queuing of transaction calls, which facilitates OLTP in less reliable wide area networks and workflow processing on a WAN or LAN.

The System/WS and System/Host components were the first to push open OLTP beyond the UNIX environment and into desktop (MS-DOS, Windows, OS/2, as well as UNIX) and IBM CICS systems. The System/WS component uses Novell's TCP/IP-based LAN Workplace product to interface DOS, OS/2, and Windows desktops. System/Host provides ASCII-to-EBCDIC translation of TUXEDO file types. It supports LU6.2 connectivity and CPI-C functions to enable developers to write gateways to other proprietary OLTP products.

System/D provides a high-performance, networked database designed specifically for OLTP. In addition, TUXEDO works with other popular UNIX databases.

13.4.3 TUXEDO distributed transaction management

The TUXEDO ATMI allows the transaction manager to define and support global transactions. A global transaction is a transaction that allows work that may involve more than one resource manager and span more than one physical location to be treated as one logical unit of work.

Global transactions may be composed of several local transactions, each accessing a local resource manager (a database, a file, etc.) under the control of the local TUXEDO TPM (see Fig. 13.10).

A given local transaction may be either successful or unsuccessful in completing its work. A global transaction is treated by the TUXEDO transaction manager as a specific sequence of events comprising all local transactions. Both the global and local transactions are characterized by the previously described transaction's properties of atomicity, consistency, isolation, and durability.

Global transactions are defined to the TUXEDO TPM using ATMI primitives. The TUXEDO transaction manager provides a directory service—Name Server—which contains all service locations on the system. Name Server is used by the TUXEDO TPM to provide service location transparency in a global transaction. Once a global transaction is defined, the TUXEDO System TPM is responsible for managing its status and ensuring that its atomicity, consistency, isolation, and durability are preserved. In other words, in a distributed transaction processing environment, TUXEDO TPM coordinates global transactions by:

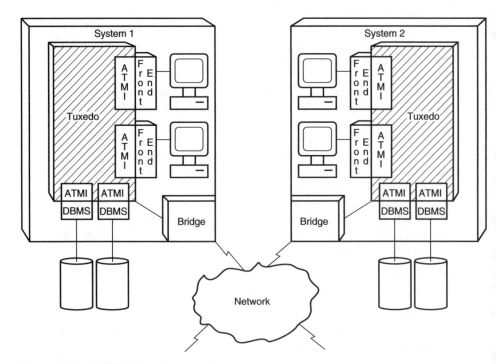

Figure 13.10 TUXEDO distributed architecture.

- Creating transaction identifiers
- Tracking the status of all participants
- Executing the two-phase commit algorithm by acting as the coordinator for all participating resource managers
- Detecting and resolving global deadlocks
- Coordinating transaction recovery

Resource managers participating in a global transaction must also adhere to the interoperability standards. In fact, all major UNIX DBMS vendors have adopted the strategy of building XA-compatible interfaces. This strategy allows their DBMSs to work with and benefit from such standard-oriented TPMs as TUXEDO. From the network interoperability point of view, TUXEDO uses the UNIX System V Transport Layer Interface (TLI), which supports TCP/IP, NetBIOS, OSI protocols, BSD socket interfaces, and APPC/LU6.2, thus isolating the TUXEDO System from the underlying network technologies.

13.5 ENCINA

Transarc's Encina is a DCE-based client/server transaction monitor, queuing service, data management product, and distributed computing toolkit. Like TUXEDO, it is basically a source-code product designed primarily for incorporation into system-supplier and independent-software products.

Transarc also sells binary versions of Encina for Sun. IBM, which owns a share of Transarc, sells the Encina toolkit as an open system OLTP product and also markets CICS/6000, a UNIX-based version of its CICS/ESA product. CICS/6000 uses the CICS front end familiar to thousands of programmers and users, and the underlying Encina technology.

13.5.1 Encina architecture and components

Encina technology is built on the basis of the three-tiered client/server architecture and principles of extreme modularity. As a result, Encina components can be used to build distributed transaction managers, resource managers, or integral parts of other systems. Conformance to such open system standards as X/Open interfaces ensures that Encina modules will interoperate with other open system standards-compliant systems. This standards compliance will support interoperability among a large number of heterogeneous systems across networks.

Encina components are designed to work together with the Distributed Computing Environment (DCE). Encina provides DCE with its

AFS Distributed File System. The components (see Fig. 13.11) are designed to perform some specific client and/or server functions and interact with each other to support full-featured TP managers, resource managers, or other distributed systems.

These components can be grouped into the client and server components. They consist of the Encina TP Monitor, the Recoverable Queuing Service (RQS), the Structured File Service, the Peer-to-Peer Communications (PPC) service (includes support for the CPI-C protocol and the PPC Gateway/SNA), and the Encina TP Toolkit.

RQS

Encina's Recoverable Queuing Service extends the value of queues by combining queueing with transactions. It means that transactional ACID properties are preserved:

- RQS enqueue operations are performed as part of the transactional unit of work.
- After the enqueueing transaction commits, queue elements stored in the RQS will not be lost or become corrupted.
- RQS dequeue operations are also transactional—if the dequeueing transaction fails, the dequeued element will be placed back in the queue as part of the rollback process.

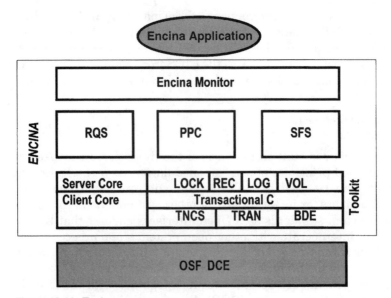

Figure 13.11 Encina components.

Because of their transactional nature, RQS queues can be used to partition complex and long-running operations that must be completed with guaranteed integrity into a number of smaller pieces that can be processed independently. Additionally, because there is no synchronous dependency between enqueueing and dequeueing processes, RQS enables Encina applications to operate asynchronously even if the applications use synchronous TRPC to process queue entries.

PPC

This service extends the APPC/LU6.2 and CPI-C support with the standard programming interface that enables Synclevel 2 (syncpoint) communications for both SNA and TCP/IP networks. This enables two-phase commit synchronization across heterogeneous applications. The PPC Gateway/SNA provides Synclevel 2 support between Encina Monitor applications and the mainframe. The PPC support is bidirectional and allows Encina Monitor applications to act as both clients and servers in distributed systems.

SFS

This service provides an integrated-record-oriented file system that offers entry-sequenced, relative, and key-index access to records.

Encina Toolkit

This provides low-level basic services that are divided into client and server components, and perform functions such as the beginning and ending of a transaction, exceptional conditions handling, and transactional RPCs. For the server side, the Toolkit enables the construction of recoverable servers, provides for full transaction integrity, and supports archiving and backup. The Toolkit includes:

- TNCS Services—transactional communications which include transactional RPCs (based on HP/Apollo's NCS) and a run-time library for the asynchronous communications needs of TRAN.

- TRAN Services—distributed transaction services which provide an optimized two-phase commit, isolated recovery, communication and operating system interfaces, nested transactions, and heuristic outcome support. In addition, TRAN supports a general TP interface which includes RPCs and peer-to-peer communications, TRAN-to-TRAN communications, and X/Open's XA interfaces.

- The Base Development Environment (BDE) allows for operating system portability and supports POSIX-style threads and process synchronization, signal handling, time and alarm services, and dynamic storage allocation.

- Transactional C—C language libraries which support transactional applications, threads of control, locks, recoverable variables, and prepare/commit/abort operations.

- LOG Services provide for stable reliable data storage with archiving support (possibly to tape), common-log storage, and administrative support.

- REC Services provide for undo/redo logic and administrative support, buffer management, and physical/logical logging of changes for committed data.

- LOCK Services provide for transactional shared, exclusive, and intentions locks.

- VOL Services provide support for large file disk management, data storage on multiple volumes with reduced disk fragmentation, and support for high concurrency of access, fast sequential retrieval, and disk mirroring.

13.5.2 Encina Monitor features

The Encina Monitor supports a three-tiered client/server computing style. The Encina Monitor's applications encompass client, application server, and resource manager components. The Encina Monitor:

- Provides an application-oriented infrastructure on top of OSF's DCE that simplifies development, provides an application execution environment, and enables a single system image for arrangement of Encina Monitor applications

- Integrates powerful failure management mechanisms, including distributed transactions, into the DCE framework

- Extends transactional connectivity to a wide range of resources including relational databases, mainframe applications, and queuing products

- Provides support for the concurrency and parallelism opportunities in DCE-based distributed systems

One of the key Encina features is the extension of the remote procedure calls into transactional RPCs, or TRPCs. TRPCs are supported by the Encina distributed transaction services, which manage distributed (global) transactions and use an advanced synchronization protocol—the "presume-abort" protocol. Clients define the beginning and the end of business logic that should be performed as a transaction. Then, instead of using DCE RPCs to call application servers, the application invokes the TRPC that invokes transactions on a network as if they (transactions) were local and performs all updates to the server automatically as a part of a global transaction that spans all resources accessed from inside the client's transaction statement.

All updates are either completed as a unit (Encina issues an automatic commit), or rolled back automatically if a failure occurs. The TRPC invocation is contained within a distributed transaction. All necessary transaction processing, including state information, is delivered over an existing client/server RPC connection totally transparent to users and applications. To create a TRPC, the developer simply has to create a transactional IDL (TIDL) file (similar to DCE RPC IDL file), run the Encina Monitor's TIDL generator, and link the resulting code stubs with the application program.

Another important feature of the TRPC is its support of the DCE authentication and security all the way down to the RPC level. Other basic features of the Encina Monitor include the following.

- Use of an object-oriented paradigm to encapsulate both the code and data in the server process is enabled. Therefore, multiple servers or multiple instances of the same server can operate on each distributed node.

- Support for nested transactions, which are transactions that can invoke other transactions and assemble results, is provided. Nested transactions help isolate failures within a transaction. Failing transactions are retried automatically and transparently to users. Thus, system reliability is improved. Nested transactions help utilize multiple servers on a network, therefore improving transaction throughput and data availability. Nested transactions are supported by nested commits, logging, and recovery, which Encina TPM accomplishes with logical locks and complex atomicity functions.

- Support for a distributed and/or mirrored logging increases system reliability and availability in a distributed environment is provided.

- Node management utilities permit authorized users to install servers on remote nodes. Servers can be started, stopped, and restarted dynamically, without interruptions to user access.

- Support is provided for user-defined and abstract data types directly within client core and server core components, without participation of an advanced DBMS.

- Support for the X/Open XA interfaces between the Encina Monitor and XA-compliant resource managers (e.g., RDBMSs) is provided.

- Support for the *heuristic outcome* allows Encina Monitor to work with other transaction protocols. In a heterogeneous distributed environment, heuristic outcome support allows individual sites to recover from failures even if they cannot communicate with the rest of the nodes

- Coordinator migration allows transactions to originate on workstations or PCs without sacrificing transaction reliability. The transaction coordinator's responsibilities can be automatically migrated from a local PC to a more reliable server system.

- There is support for dynamic load balancing across application servers. This load balancing is combined with priority scheduling of the application servers and repetitive, nested access to resource managers within a transaction.

The Encina system administration environment is based on the concept of cells. In the Encina model, a network of computing systems can be organized into multiple cells—regions of autonomous control. Cells can be managed separately by individual *cell managers,* and yet can share information across cells. The Encina Cell Architecture, shown in Fig. 13.12, is highly scaleable and provides global connectivity and local configuration autonomy.

A cell manager maintains a cell configuration database and provides configuration services, load monitoring, centralized logging of exceptional conditions, audit trail, performance statistics, and debugging information.

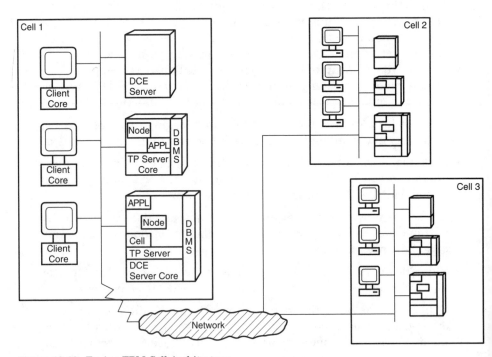

Figure 13.12   Encina TPM Cell Architecture.

Cell managers control application servers' start-up and shutdown, maintain access control lists, and provide the authorization services for users and client registration services. To perform the start-up and shutdown services, a cell manager requests these services from an appropriate node manager, which is responsible for the actual node start-up/shutdown as well as for the server process failure reporting.

13.6   TOP END

TOP END (AT&T GIS) is a suite of OLTP products providing distributed transaction management in networks of NCR 33xx, 34xx, 35xx, 3600 UNIX servers and systems, and other UNIX systems. TOP END is part of NCR's Open Cooperative Computing Architecture (OCCA).

13.6.1   TOP END features

From the client/server architecture standpoint, TOP END is a server that divides functions between separate processing components (systems, servers, and workstations) that can be positioned for greatest efficiency and replicated for concurrency and autonomy. TOP END follows the X/Open DTP model and a host of other standards. In addition, TOP END has extended the DTP model by offering support for communications resource managers. The extension allows either an RPC package or OSI module to act like a DTP-model resource manager.

TOP END offers the maximum amount of data integrity by separating the transaction management and application execution functions.

The goal of TOP END is to provide mainframe-class OLTP on open systems. To be a serious player in this arena, TOP END was designed to incorporate systems administration tools and availability/recovery functionality. Security is dynamic and lets users authenticate and authorize passwords across the network.

TOP END is scaleable in performance. It is designed to provide a consistent computing environment from portable workstations to large enterprise systems capable of handling tens of thousands of transactions per second (TPS). TOP END uses parallel processing to scale up to enterprise-level systems.

From the open system portability point of view, all TOP END ports are designed to meet the following criteria:

- Feature content remains the same across all platforms.

- All ports and TOP END interoperate with each other.

- Applications written to the TOP END APIs can be ported without changes to the TOP END interfaces.

- The administration software works in a heterogeneous environment.

TOP END supports both character-based terminals and DOS, Windows, OS/2, as well as UNIX workstations as clients. TOP END supports automatically initiated, multistep, multiapplication, and background transactions from multiple, geographically distributed nodes. The transactions can access multiple databases. TOP END uses two-phase commit processing to provide the necessary integrity. It can automatically and dynamically replicate OLTP applications on multiple servers based on workload requirements. After replication, TOP END balances the workload between servers. It provides a flexible framework for the development, execution, and management of enterprise-wide, mission-critical client/server applications.

13.6.2   Top End components

TOP END components (see Fig. 13.13) include server, client, administrative, and development software organized logically into:

- *Application components*—user-written and ISV- or NCR-supplied applications.

- *Client/server integration software*—begins and ends distributed transactions, interfaces to resource managers, and communicates with clients, servers, and peers in the network.

- *Transaction management*—for process control, transaction and communications services, network interface, and security.

Client connectivity options are achieved via:

- *Log-In Client,* a graphic user interface to TOP END for character-based terminal users

- *Personal Computer Support,* a DOS-based front-end processor to TOP END for DOS PC connection via RS232 or TCP/IP protocols

- *Remote software modules* that facilitate the use of a graphical user interface (GUI) to TOP END for DOS, Windows, OS/2, and UNIX workstation users, primarily on wide-area networks

- *IBM 3270 Terminal Services*

TOP END tools include:

- Administrator's graphical application for management of component start-up and shutdown, auditing and recovery, activation of communications links, automatic distribution, etc.

- Administrator's Windows-based application that provides system definition and generation; format management software that lets developers easily create and customize screen layouts

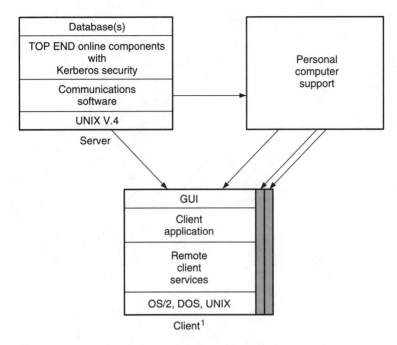

¹Login client software available for direct character-based terminal

Figure 13.13 TOP END components and interrelationships.

- Application development facilities that include support for COBOL, C, C++, and the Timer service.

TOP END provides developers and users with component independence. Applications can deal with clients and servers via a non-TOP END component designed for that purpose and simply use TOP END to ensure two-phase commit. Conversely, an application could simply use TOP END's client/server interaction features for workload balancing and security and let another application handle two-phase commit.

Systems Management in a Client/Server Computing Environment

The client/server computing model represents a special case of cooperative distributed processing. As such, client/server computing must solve multiple issues relevant to a distributed cooperative processing environment. Among them are the basic issues of the distribution of the presentation, application, database logic, and data across network-connected systems. Making all these distributed components of the client/server architecture work together in a cooperative fashion is what the client/server computing environment is all about.

So far, the focus of this book has been directed at the issues of the distribution of application components and data between clients and servers, and on the cooperative processing interactions performed by clients and servers. However, one critical, but often forgotten, issue of client/server architecture and distributed computing deserves special attention. This is the issue of distributed systems management for client/server systems.

14.1   SYSTEMS MANAGEMENT

The client/server computing model is more complex, more labor-intensive, and, in most instances, more expensive than the traditional mainframe-centric model. Its management is always a challenge.

14.1.1   Overview of distributed systems management

To enable the development and deployment of mission-critical applications into these new environments a new, integrated approach to systems management has become necessary. This new approach should not be confused with a simple migration of a centralized systems management model into a distributed environment.

Popular network systems management tools are inadequate to manage distributed client/server environments and applications. Indeed, network management has traditionally dealt with polling, monitoring, and handling emergency situations. Systems management was oriented to managing one expensive resource (typically a mainframe), keeping it operational to be shared among many users. That is why the systems management discipline is evolving from a resource shared among many users to one addressing the management of many local resources shared among users.

The new distributed systems management model integrates solutions for the daily monitoring, resource planning, system administration, change management, operations, performance, and other initiatives needed to maintain effective productivity in a distributed, networked computing environment. In fact, distributed systems management applications are object-oriented, since the resources they manage are modeled as objects. The scope of distributed systems management is broad and includes management of distributed databases, applications, operating systems, processes, and, ultimately, multimedia environments.

One of the problems associated with distributed systems management is the difficulty of its cost justification. The real impact of distributed systems management becomes obvious only when it does not work—then, both the end users and information systems organizations are affected.

As a discipline, distributed systems management examines the issues concerned with proactive management of distributed resources and the policies and organizational infrastructure necessary to support distributed resources. It includes the technology, people, and processes that an organization uses to manage the effective daily operations and productivity of the distributed client/server computing system.

14.1.2 Complexity management

A distributed client/server environment may be composed of heterogeneous systems connected via a network. Each of these systems may be acting as either a client, a server, or both. When an existing business enterprise undergoes a transition from a centralized hierarchical architecture to a distributed client/server architecture, a three-tiered computing model, as shown in Fig. 14.1, is often used as the blueprint of such rearchitecture project.

Consider the three-tiered environment shown in Fig. 14.1. Let's assume that the corporate headquarters are responsible for the overall management of the environment, as well as for the development, purchase, installation, and maintenance of all the software running on every node of the network. It means that every client workstation, for example, runs a set of programs provided by a corporate division located possibly thousands of miles away. After the initial installation of the software across all platforms, the corporate management is facing an interesting challenge—what to do with the software maintenance and upgrades. When a new version of an application program is available, how will it be delivered and installed at every client and server? Should the new version be put on a magnetic diskette and mailed to every end user? And if so, are the end users capable of installing new software without disrupting their existing environment? What if one of the users (or one group, for example) has not received the latest software version? Can they continue to use their workstations? These and similar questions should be answered by a new distributed systems management system.

As client/server becomes a mainstream computing model, the environment grows ever more complex. The increase in system complexity can be attributed to the following:

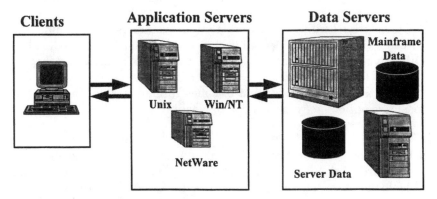

Figure 14.1 Three-tiered architecture.

- *A growing number of systems components*—even well-managed environments tend to become unmanageable as the number of components grows.

- *A growing number of system users*—client/server applications and databases that are manageable when supporting a small number of users can become unmanageable as the user population grows.

- *Systems and platform heterogeneity*—client/server applications deployed across heterogeneous platforms raise the total complexity of a system by orders of magnitude. A need to support and manage a multitude of platforms, operating systems, network protocols, and database management systems, often from different vendors, presents an additional level of complexity enforced by a weakness of cross-system management tools.

- *Large-scope distribution*—the farther apart the system components are, the harder it is to configure, manage, and troubleshoot the environment.

As the scope of client/server projects becomes more enterprise-wide, the complexity of these projects can grow so much that they become impossible to manage, often despite the amount of money or labor a company throws at the project.

Symptoms of an unmanageable system include severe, unpredictable performance swings; increased difficulty in correctly identifying system problems and performing real-time system monitoring; and lack of verifiable configuration information.

Systems that are manageable may not remain manageable. By replacing simple load modules with collections of components, thus increasing the system's complexity, a company can cause a system to cross the manageability threshold and thus become unmanageable. Similarly, a system can become unmanageable by scaling applications across a larger user population.

One of the leading indicators that a system is approaching the threshold of manageability is that the system becomes less predictable. Other symptoms are that the system becomes less reliable and that its response time degrades.

When a client/server system becomes unmanageable, there are at least two options to restore the manageability:

- Scale back the deployment to a manageable range.

- Reduce overall complexity by eliminating other dimensions—i.e., standardizing on a single LAN management product, restricting deployment to a narrow range of workstation configurations, or shutting off some of the application's functions.

The architectural reason for the management complexity of the client/server environment is based on the fact that all client/server components are interconnected and cooperate with each other. As discussed earlier in the book, this cooperation is made possible by placing correct software components on each of the tiers, making sure that all software versions are current and synchronized with each other, and ensuring that they are installed and configured properly. In other words, a *systems management framework* has to be in place that can provide systems management control stations with reliable and timely information about failed components, and preferably, can proactively find out which of the components is about to fail.

14.2 DEFINITION AND SCOPE
OF DISTRIBUTED SYSTEMS MANAGEMENT

The scope of a distributed systems management framework is beyond traditional network management, which often concentrates on managing network devices and does not necessarily enable help-desk staff to troubleshoot an application or a printing problem. In fact, one of the core systems management issues of client/server computing is focusing on solving a slew of problems that often face the *user* of a client/server system. For example, the client/server systems management functionality must help resolve applications-related problems like "My application is not running," or "I can't print documents from WordPerfect." These problems are often exacerbated by the simple fact that frequently client systems are physically remote from a site where the appropriate expertise or a help desk resides.

To resolve these problems requires expanding the scope of systems management beyond the network devices and connections by getting inside systems and applications. Let's define systems management as *the ability to control the interconnected computers and applications on the network.* Note that this definition goes beyond network management tools that are based on event-processing technologies. Tools like HP OpenView, IBM NetView/6000, and SunNetManager are examples of network management tools that were often positioned as systems management integration platforms.

Indeed, the network management framework provides a good foundation on which distributed systems management can be built. Its architecture is well positioned to be expanded to integrate additional functionality.

As the need for integrated systems management tools and their scope continues to grow, these tools have been repositioned to reflect the more global nature of distributed systems management. This repositioning is reflected in additional functionality and even in new names (i.e., HP AdminCenter, IBM SystemView, Sun Solstice).

It becomes increasingly evident that two general classifications of management tools are required to implement effective and scaleable systems management solutions. These general disciplines can be defined as:

- *Event-based disciplines* such as network management, which support timely reactions to events that occurred on the network

- *Configuration-based disciplines* such as change management, inventory management, and software distribution that, although extremely important, are designed to support management tasks that do not require the "timely" reaction typical of the event-based management system

Of course, this classification is general, and some distributed systems management functions such as performance management and distributed systems administration appear to span both disciplines, although the analysis of these functions can help classify them into an appropriate category. In fact, there is an undeniable need for each category tool to be aware of the other group activities. For example, the event-based tools need to be aware of events related to configuration activities, and the configuration-based tools should be able to share or pass events such as SNMP (Simple Network Management Protocol) alerts. Furthermore, event-based tools can trigger a configuration activity that is required after processing of a given event.

14.3 DISTRIBUTED SYSTEMS MANAGEMENT FUNCTIONS

Together, the distributed systems management functions include the following categories:

- *Problem detection, analysis, and resolution.*   Includes functions that enable systems administrators and help-desk personnel to be alerted when a device or application fails. In addition, they need to be able to determine what went wrong and how to resolve the problem, even if it occurred at a remote site. Ideally, the goal of systems management is to avoid problems whenever possible and resolve them when they occur.

- *Asset management.*   This includes automated inventory discovery and software auditing.

- *Security management.*   This includes user profile definition, verification, authorization, and authentication.

- *Distributed hierarchical storage management.* As the amount of data managed at distributed locations grows, some historical data may be migrated from a fast-access device to a slower and less expensive one. Whenever the migrated data needs to be accessed again, it would have to be found in the archive and recalled back to the fast-access device for processing.

- *Backup and recovery of distributed data and applications.* Clearly, in a distributed client/server environment, data has to be backed up to prevent the loss of valuable information. In case of data loss or system software corruption, both the data and the software have to be recovered from a reliable source.

- *Software distribution, configuration, and change management.* The distributed client/server computing model implies that applications are distributed across clients and servers, and across networks. These distributed applications need to be configured easily and consistently. In addition, the systems management solution should support inventory management, version control, security, and software distribution (e.g., a new release of an application code or a version update of the MS Office suite of products).

- *Performance management.* This includes performance trends analysis and threshold event management. A distributed client/server environment often consists of heterogeneous networked components that cooperate with each other to perform designated functions. Part of the required functionality includes a particular level of performance. When response time slows, user perception is often similar to that of the application failure or network outage. The reasons for the performance degradation are often complex and may be related to the network, LAN O/S, disk, or application. The systems management should enable systems administrators to pinpoint the sources of the problem and help tune the system to the specified levels of performance.

- *Remote database management.* This includes functions that allow users to manage remote databases from a single central console (i.e., database administration, including user setup and DBA activities; database operations, including performance monitoring, tuning, backup, and restore; and integration with systems and network management platforms such as HP's SNMP-compliant OpenView and the Tivoli Management Environment or TME).

A graphical presentation of these systems management functions appears in Fig. 14.2.

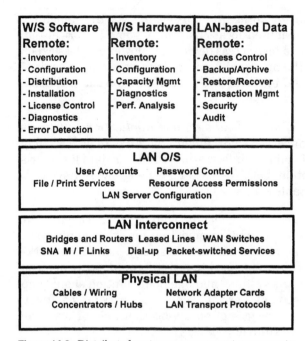

W/S Software Remote:	W/S Hardware Remote:	LAN-based Data Remote:
- Inventory	- Inventory	- Access Control
- Configuration	- Configuration	- Backup/Archive
- Distribution	- Capacity Mgmt	- Restore/Recover
- Installation	- Diagnostics	- Transaction Mgmt
- License Control	- Perf. Analysis	- Security
- Diagnostics		- Audit
- Error Detection		

LAN O/S
User Accounts   Password Control
File / Print Services   Resource Access Permissions
LAN Server Configuration

LAN Interconnect
Bridges and Routers   Leased Lines   WAN Switches
SNA M / F Links   Dial-up   Packet-switched Services

Physical LAN
Cables / Wiring   Network Adapter Cards
Concentrators / Hubs   LAN Transport Protocols

Figure 14.2   Distributed systems management components.

14.4 SYSTEMS MANAGEMENT MECHANISMS

A high-level view of distributed systems management consists of the hierarchy of systems that are managed by an integrated set of systems management applications residing on a centrally located systems management station (see Fig. 14.3).

Clearly, this model does not rely on or require a single management station, or, for that matter, a single systems management system. A hierarchy of both may be required, especially when the number, size, and complexity of managed systems is high. In this case, a manager-of-managers structure can be employed to provide various degrees of management details designed to solve a particular set of problems.

Most systems management packages available today employ one or more mechanisms and protocols for retrieving information from managed systems. These include:

- *Polling.* The user of the systems management system sets up a polling interval. The management station issues a request to each managed system, usually on a round-robin basis, asking for updated data. The agent software in each managed system then responds by

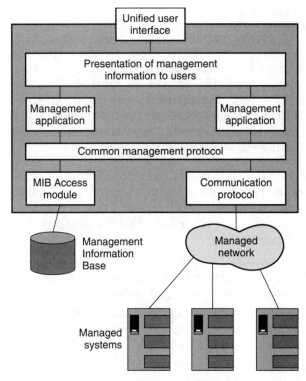

Figure 14.3 Systems management station model.

transmitting all current data. The main drawback of polling is that it can consume a fair amount of network bandwidth, thus reducing the capacity for normal production network traffic. With polling, most systems management applications will "deduce" that there is a problem simply from the fact that a managed system stopped responding.

- *Alerts.* Agent software in the managed system monitors data values on its own and compares new data with thresholds that have been preset by the systems manager. If the threshold is exceeded, then the agent will issue an alert across the network notifying the management station about the event. Alerts, or *traps,* can put more management responsibility (and processing) on the managed system rather than on the management station. A serious drawback of alerts is their inability to notify its management station when the managed system crashes. Nevertheless, alerts are useful when the bandwidth is limited and when the management process is focused on the exceptional reporting.

14.5 DISTRIBUTED SYSTEMS MANAGEMENT REQUIREMENTS AND FRAMEWORK

As already mentioned, distributed systems management is more than a set of stand-alone applications. Indeed, simple functions, such as backup, restore, and inventory management, can be handled by shrink-wrapped application packages available on the market today. But in order to attack complex issues, true systems management must satisfy at least the following requirements.

- *A holistic system view for resolving cross-product problems.* A holistic approach to distributed systems management includes tasks such as inventory/asset management, software distribution and license management, backup and restore, problem troubleshooting and tracking, and performance tuning.

- *Performance.* A distributed systems management has to be able to support high performing management applications and should not adversely affect the performance of managed systems.

- *Scaleability.* A successful distributed systems management framework must easily grow and manage many resources without sacrificing response time and throughput.

- *Security.* This requirement is a cornerstone of system administration. The distributed systems management framework has to enforce proper authority, protect resources and promote privileges, enable concurrent distributed execution under a single, high privilege level (i.e., a root authority in UNIX).

- *Conformance to standards.* This is key to ensure that management applications can interoperate with other applications and can function across heterogeneous platforms and operating systems. Specifically, managing systems as objects requires a certain degree of synergy with the Object Management Group's Object Request Broker and services (CORBA).

- *Policy.* These are rules placed on the system that allow administrators to customize applications at run time.

- *Fully distributed architecture.* This aims to isolate application developers from the knowledge of system location and network devices. Message-based communications is one method of providing location transparency, facilitating interoperability.

- *Extensibility and heterogeneity.* A distributed systems management framework must support easily defined extended functionality for site-specific needs, and must be capable of supporting highly diverse (heterogeneous) environments.

- *Reliability.* A systems management framework must be able to deliver reliable management applications and robust exception-handling capabilities.

- *Internationalization.* The scope of distributed systems management spans national borders, and similar management applications may have to be administered in several environments and several languages.

In order to satisfy these requirements, organizations can adopt one of three approaches:

- *Point solutions.* Individual products are used to solve individual problems; each of the products may be functionally rich, but managing and supporting a number of disparate systems management tools from different vendors could be difficult and expensive.

- *Integrated solutions.* Large, complex applications combine the functionality of multiple point solutions. This may be very effective, but these applications tend to be rather monolithic and difficult to manage, and are provided by a single vendor which could adversely affect an organization's ability to chose from the best-of-breed and leverage multiple-vendor solutions for the best price.

- *Framework-based solutions.* Similar to the integrated approach, but without its disadvantages, a framework-based systems management environment is a combination of point solutions, all of which comply with a chosen management framework.

Framework solutions are often based on a set of well-defined APIs that are used to glue all management applications. A variation to an API-based frameworks is a repository-based framework, where a relational database is used to integrate systems management applications. For example, a performance monitoring tool collects performance data and deposits this information into a repository. A reporting tool can retrieve this information from the repository and display it on a management console. Using an RDBMS-based repository allows for tighter application integration without the complications of API-based frameworks.

An example of a systems management framework that satisfies the systems management requirements listed here has been defined by the X/Open Systems Management Work Group. It states that a successful systems management framework must be cohesive and object-oriented, which enables and promotes the development of interoperable management applications. This framework (see Fig. 14.4) comprises a set of multiple-level services and interfaces including:

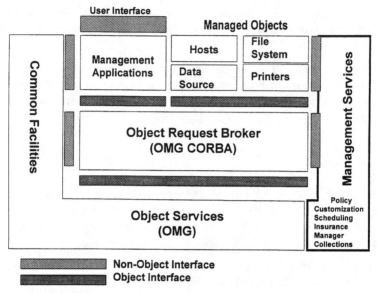

Figure 14.4 X/Open Systems Management Reference Model.

- Management applications
- Managed objects
- Services such as communications, data storage, security, OMG object services, management services (customization, scheduling, collections, policy)

The object request broker (ORB) is at the center of the distributed systems management framework, and provides fundamental mechanisms that allow objects to make and receive requests regardless of their locations (more details on the OMG and CORBA can be found in Chap. 1).

The ORB-based X/Open Systems Management Framework is an example of an architecture designed to build fully functional distributed systems management systems. This framework is the foundation of the Tivoli Management Environment (TME), SYBASE Enterprise SQL Server Manager (ESSM), and other successful systems management solutions. TME and ESSM are discussed later in this chapter.

14.6 SOFTWARE DISTRIBUTION REQUIREMENTS

One visible component of distributed systems management is electronic software distribution, which is designed to help users distribute programs and files in their environments. In the context of distributed systems management, software distribution, configuration, installation, and management is well beyond the capabilities of a distributed DBMS that is primarily concerned with data distribution issues.

Let's examine the complexity of the software distribution, configuration, installation, and management environment through the following example. A multinational organization with branches in New York, Chicago, Los Angeles, Paris, London, and Tokyo has implemented a distributed client/server computing environment that comprises an IBM mainframe acting as the enterprise server, UNIX-based middle tier servers, and a population of heterogeneous (client) workstations that include a number of UNIX variants as well as Microsoft's Windows and Windows/NT platforms. Client applications include Watcom DBMS and Microsoft Office suite (for Windows and NT clients), ORACLE RDBMS and an in-house developed business application. Servers support both the development and operational environment by running ORACLE RDBMS. A corporate mainframe is the residence of the corporate data warehouse distributed among several DB2/MVS databases. A wide area network connects all mainframes and servers, while all client workstations are attached to their servers via local area networks (see Fig. 14.5).

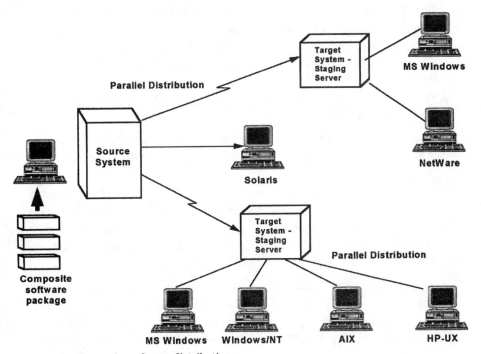

Figure 14.5 Enterprise software distribution.

Corporate management has decided that since all users are connected on the network, any and all changes to the software used by the servers and end users will be distributed electronically, over the network.

Let's assume that the business application program has been upgraded, and the new version is available at the corporate headquarters. The new version of the program requires an additional 20 MB of the hard disk space and a special driver which has to be specified in the CONFIG.SYS file (if the new program has to be installed under MS Windows). To distribute a simple program change like this to all end users, the software distribution system should support several complex requirements. Among them are the ability:

- To know the configuration of each client workstation. The configuration data includes the amount of available disk space and memory, number of disk drives, drive name where MS Windows software is installed, etc.

- To know the current version of the program installed, so that the distribution/installation software can save the previous version and restore it if the new version does not work properly.

- To schedule the distribution/installation job at a time when users are not using the system. For example, if the CONFIG.SYS file has been changed, the PC has to be rebooted for the changes to take effect.

- To provide technical support utilities for those clients that need it. For example, a utility can be distributed to make a backup copy of the existing configuration and to print installation and/or upgrade notes.

- To provide remote management support for the recipient nodes as well as for the network.

- To provide the required level of security while distributing information, so that unauthorized access and tampering with the distributed software is prevented.

- To be "smart" enough to rely on the underlying networking protocols for transport, notification, and optimum network routing selection.

- To take advantage of and be integrated with the distributed DBMS software as well as with the distributed transaction management in a distributed client/server cooperative processing environment.

And, most important, a software distribution system should provide users with a single view of the distributed environment. The *single system image* should be supported even in a heterogeneous distributed environment, where disparate networking protocols interconnect different hardware platforms running different operating systems and different database management systems. In other words, an ideal software distribution system should be designed to operate in an open systems environment.

Fortunately, many software packages available today can operate over standard network protocols, can build and maintain the inventory of hardware and software assets, distribute software packages, control company's license limits when the software is duplicated for the distribution (this function is called *software metering*), and can even help troubleshoot the environment.

The inventory packages alone are extremely useful—they can help systems administrators negotiate purchases by providing rundowns of past purchases and calculating the cost of software and hardware upgrades. These packages can even check the memory, disk space, and software interrupt addresses of workstations remotely, often by running a collection agent on each managed system at start-up time.

In short, a software distribution system can automate a lot of labor-intensive tasks such as installation, configuration, inventory, and update of commercial and internally developed applications as well as text, data, and systems files.

14.7   REMOTE DATABASE MANAGEMENT

Remote database management is a component of distributed systems management that is targeted specifically to solve complex problems of database management over the network. The goal of remote database management is to allow users to manage remote databases from a single central console. The functions necessary for efficient off-site database management include:

- Database administration, including user setup and DBA activities
- Database operations, including performance monitoring, tuning, backup, and restore
- Advisory tools for analyzing systems and applications
- Integration with systems and network management platforms such as HP's SNMP-compliant OpenView and the Tivoli Management Environment (TME)

In addition, a remote database management solution should:

- Manage enterprise-wide multivendor (heterogeneous) database environments
- Perform unattended remote database management functions

- Provide data replication functionality for full refresh and change propagation
- Be scaleable from a small to very large and widely distributed environment

In fact, a number of vendors—Informix, Legent, Oracle, BMC, and Sybase—recently announced products that include this functionality and will allow users to manage remote databases from a central site.

The building blocks of current remote database management are the Tivoli Management Environment (TME) and the Simple Network Management Protocol (SNMP). SNMP's formats can't handle the complex information flow that remote database management requires. Tivoli's TME, on the other hand, is capable of handling even the most challenging database management problems.

For example, Informix and Sybase designed their products within Tivoli's TME, and Oracle provides event notification through the Tivoli console. In addition, Legent's tool integrates database, network, system, and application operations through SNMP-based consoles, Oracle's operations functions are SNMP-console-based, and all products can report problems through SNMP consoles.

The remote database management system addresses a major obstacle users face in widespread client/server application deployment. User benefits include:

- *Cost-effective use of expensive database management skills.* Without these new products, the only option users have is putting people on-site to manage distributed databases. This solution is error prone and costly as companies deploy large numbers of databases.
- *Consistent database policies.* Consolidating database management responsibility in the hands of fewer people will result in greater coordination across disparate databases.
- *Effective problem resolution.* Integrating database management with systems and network management is the best way to diagnose problems stemming from interrelated client/server components—and to recover from a failure.

14.7.1 Database systems management examples

IBM DataHub

IBM's solution for remote database management is called DataHub, a suite of database management tools that includes:

- DBA tools for UNIX platforms for heterogeneous UNIX DBMS management

- DBA tools for the DB2 family of DBMS
- DB2 Performance Monitor (supported on MVS, AIX, and OS/2)
- DB2 Visual Explain (supported on AIX and OS/2)
- DB2 Estimator (runs under MS Windows)

DataHub uses the concept of software agents resident on managed systems. Called *Watchdogs,* these agents perform individual checks for database and operating system threshold violation. Watchdogs provide for adjustable threshold value definitions, maintain adjustable timers, and take corrective actions defined in the DataHub central database. Among supported alert actions are user notification and/or launch of predefined system tasks (i.e., an operating system script, SQL script, DataHub command). Watchdogs operations are rules-based, and include simple if-then rules, more complex boolean logic rules, and trends-based rules (e.g., IF CPU USAGE EXCEEDS 75% LAUNCH . . .).

DataHub manages such DB2 utilities as Reorg, Copy, Backup/Recover, Load/Unload, and Runstats. In addition, DataHub is a focal point of control for the IBM data replication system, including Capture and Apply (MVS, AIX, OS/2, OS/400, SunOS, and Solaris), ORACLE and SYBASE replication targets (via DataJoiner), and Data Propagator Non-Relational for IMS and VSAM.

DataHub's future platforms include parallel versions of the DB2 family of DBMSs: DB2 for HP-UX, DB2 for Solaris, DB2 for NT, and all major UNIX-based relational database management systems.

SYBASE Enterprise SQL Server Manager™ (ESSM)

The SYBASE Enterprise SQL Server Manager (ESSM) is a remote database management tool designed for the efficient control of heterogeneous DBMS environments. Specifically, ESSM allows administrators to perform the following operations on remote servers:

- Configure database servers.
- Monitor server status and performance levels.
- Start and stop servers.
- Manage server space utilization.
- Administer users and ensure security.
- Manage server and database objects such as devices, databases, dump devices, segments, etc.
- Schedule and perform backup and recovery operations.
- Use existing and new database administration scripts.

ESSM can perform these operations to individual servers as well as to groups of servers, thus streamlining DBA operations and maximizing their productivity.

ESSM is based on the Tivoli Management Environment (TME) framework, which is discussed later in this chapter. Since the TME is based on the open systems standard—the X/Open Systems Management Reference Model—the ESSM can be used seamlessly together with other TME-based third-party tools. Furthermore, ESSM has provisions to support SNMP and thus can provide management information to a number of systems management tools such as HP OpenView, IBM NetView/6000, and Sun Solstice.

ESSM is a highly scaleable product and, for example, allows distribution of database configuration changes to multiple servers in a single step, all using a single ESSM component: ESSM Profile Manager.

ESSM supports automatic event detection and notification by employing software agents on each managed system. Administrators can be alerted whenever a predefined event has occurred. Agents collect server statistics on server status, user connections, aggregate device I/O, database lock usage, network communications, and segment space available. Events can be handled by agents by triggering predefined responses, which in addition to notifications include event logging and/or an execution of a specified program.

14.8   SYSTEMS MANAGEMENT SOLUTIONS

This section will briefly discuss a number of general-purpose systems management solutions that are available in the marketplace.

14.8.1   Microsoft Systems Management Server

Microsoft's Systems Management Server (SMS) is one of the most powerful products for managing PCs on corporate networks. SMS provides inventory, remote management, software distribution, and network monitoring functions in a single package.

SMS complies with the Management Information Format (MIF) standard of the Desktop Management Task Force (DMTF). SMS implements a distributed client/server model by including a primary site server system that requires Windows NT and Microsoft SQLServer 6.0 or higher. This primary site can be connected to target systems directly or via secondary servers over LANs or WANs. Clients and supported protocols include DOS, Windows and Windows NT, OS/2, and Macintosh, with the LAN support including NetWare, LAN Manager (Microsoft), LAN Server (IBM), and Pathworks.

SMS supports remote-control features, including remote reboot, file transfer, dial-up support, and on-line chat mode, which must be enabled by users themselves so that they can control security. SMS remote control features include support of DOS and Windows systems over LAN and WAN (IPX, NetBEUI, ISDN, X.25, and IP).

One of the most powerful tools in the SMS arsenal is the Microsoft Network Monitor, which captures network packets of any kind, even from remote nodes, and graphically selects, filters, and displays them. A TCP/IP-like ping facility is included for testing network connections. SMS administrators can retransmit captured packets for problem determination. In addition to the network packet analyzer tool, SMS network management features include network statistics, SNMP support, configurable alarms for notification of systems administrators, and job scheduling.

SMS provides a GUI front end that can graphically display a site's domain tree structure, making it easier to find a particular system. There is a query facility that can find a given machine by name.

SMS obtains and stores a great deal of information about each system under management and can either produce a report or a graphical representation of the system assets. In fact, SMS provides hardware detection for all DMI-defined devices and can also detect about 2500 software applications.

SMS provides a powerful software distribution mechanism, which uses the notion of *software packages*. Each package to be installed is defined and scheduled as a job to be run on selected systems. All these actions can be done through a point-and-click GUI front end. SMS performs file compression and staged transmission of packages to avoid network saturation. SMS supports full software install, remote batch editing of INI files, file update and replacement, and a powerful scripting language.

Software license monitoring and metering functions include site license support, software suite licensing, time-based restrictions, workstation agent software, configurable notification for network administrators, and WAN support.

Among the disadvantages are the week-long training requirement and a great deal of planning and understanding, from the network topology to system tuning. Also, SMS does not directly support software metering.

14.8.2   The Tivoli Management Environment

The Tivoli Management Environment (TME) was designed specifically to provide a secure, robust, and cohesive environment for managing complex enterprise-wide client/server resources. The core technology of the TME architecture is an OMG/CORBA-compliant object request broker, and the TME architecture is based on the X/Open Systems Management Reference Model (see Fig. 14.4). Tivoli's object-oriented distributed platform offers an efficient way to provide management scaleability for enterprise systems management as well as isolate management applications from the heterogeneous nature of distributed client/server computing. TME applications interoperate via a consistent interface and present users with a common GUI-based look and feel. TME controls the costs of distributed systems management by letting systems administrators manage and control users, systems, databases, and applications from a central location. TME applications allow users to automate and delegate routine, time-consuming tasks, enabling users to control the distributed environment from a central location. For example, a central TME administrator can:

- Distribute software to remote locations.
- Manage the configuration of users, desktops, and servers.
- Change access privileges.
- Install and update applications.
- Automate operations.
- Monitor resources and services.
- Perform job scheduling.

These functions are performed by a suite of well-designed products composing the TME:

- Tivoli/Admin simplifies the process of user and system administration, automated management of configuration parameters, secure delegation of administrative tasks, and centralized control of UNIX and PC systems.
- Tivoli/Enterprise Console is a management automation application that collects, processes, and automatically initiates corrective actions to system, application, network, and database events. Built-in event correlation facilitates problem isolation and identification.
- Tivoli/Courier automated the software distribution process, and installs and updates applications and software in a coordinated, consistent manner across heterogeneous platforms.
- Tivoli/Sentry performs intelligent local monitoring of system resources, initiates corrective action, and alerts administrators of potential problems.
- Tivoli/Workload is an automated application for job scheduling in client/server environments. It provides real-time job control, exten-

sive alarm and monitoring services, and fault resistance for distributed computing environments.

- Tivoli/Print is an efficient print manager application that simplifies and automates printer management tasks such as assignment and queuing of print jobs throughout the network.

In addition, TME product strategy provides for easy customization and extensive flexibility by using standard APIs, including TME Toolkits, and integrated third-party applications.

Tivoli supports a number of UNIX variants, including AIX, HP-UX, SunOS, and Solaris. Tivoli Event Adapters support generic SNMP protocols and management systems environments including HP Open-View, IBM NetView, SunNet Manager, and Windows NT.

Note. Expanding its systems management scope to include distributed applications, in 1995 Tivoli announced an open specification for application management. Specifically, the new application management functionality includes a set of APIs to be used by application developers as well as tools vendors. These Application Management Specifications (AMS) allow TME to handle software distribution, inventory, dependencies, event monitoring, and administration for applications that incorporate them. To demonstrate its commitment to the AMS, Tivoli has found a development tool partner, PowerSoft, who, in a joint effort with Tivoli, announced plans to embed AMS into the PowerBuilder Enterprise. As a result, PowerBuilder Enterprise developers can enable TME management merely by supplying required information.

14.8.3 Other systems management solutions

Of course, there are many other systems management solutions available on the market today. While a detailed analysis of all these tools is beyond the scope of this book, a brief discussion on available functionality is valuable to provide readers with a snapshot of the market.

Frye Utilities for Networks

Frye Computer Systems (Boston, Mass.) has long been popular with NetWare administrators. Frye Utilities for Networks is a set of integratable components that can perform a number of distributed systems management functions across a variety of LAN and WAN networks:

- NetWare Management which displays server and network statistics
- NetWare Early Warning System which notifies administrators of problems based on configurable parameters

- NetWare Console Commander, which runs unattended scripts at the NetWare console

- Statistics Display Rack, which graphically displays real-time network statistics using MS Windows

- Node Tracker which displays statistics on network traffic

- Software Metering and Resource Tracking, which meters and audits the use of software

- Software Update and Distribution System, which can perform remote software installation and uninstall, and supports external compression programs to reduce network traffic

- LAN Directory, which performs hardware and software inventory

The following paragraphs briefly describe the major features of Frye Utilities for Networks.

Workstations and networks supported. Clients and protocols supported include DOS, Windows, and OS/2, with network support including NetWare, LAN Manager (Microsoft), LAN Server (IBM), Vines, Pathworks, and WAN.

Software distribution. Frye Utilities for Networks supports full software install, remote batch editing of .INI files, file update and replacement, configurable standard file sets, software uninstall feature, and a powerful scripting language.

Inventory management. Frye Utilities for Networks provides hardware detection for about 700 items and can also detect about 8000 software applications, both on clients and servers.

Software license monitoring and metering. Frye Utilities for Networks software license monitoring and metering functions include site license support, license waiting list, software suite licensing, and configurable notification for network administrators.

Network management. Frye Utilities for Networks network management features include network statistics, the ability to replicate user information across servers, configurable alarms for notification of systems administrators, a built-in virus scan, network packet analyzer tools, and job scheduling.

In short, Frye Utilities for Networks provides administrators with an a la carte selection of utilities that are characterized by rapid response time, low system resource requirements, and excellent reporting facilities.

Among the disadvantages of this tool are poor support for ad hoc queries and limited platform support—most utilities run only on DOS.

Saber LAN Management System

This systems management package is a mature set of programs that work together from a common window. Saber bundles its LAN Workstation Management product with Saber Enterprise Application Manager, Saber Server Manager, and ReachOut Remote Control software (Ocean Isle Software, Vero Beach, Fla.). Saber supports systems inventory, software distribution, metering, remote control, and network management over multiple network protocols.

The following paragraphs briefly describe major features of the Saber LAN Management System.

Workstations and networks supported. Clients and protocols supported include DOS, Windows, and Macintosh, with network support including NetWare, LAN Manager (Microsoft), LAN Server (IBM), Vines, Pathworks, LANtastic, and WAN.

Software distribution. The Saber LAN Management System supports full software install, remote batch editing of .INI files, file update and replacement, configurable standard file sets, a task recording and replay function, a powerful scripting language, and WAN support for software distribution.

Inventory management. The Saber LAN Management System provides hardware detection for about 50 items on clients and can also detect about 1000 software applications, both on clients and servers.

Software license monitoring and metering. Saber's software license monitoring and metering functions include site license support, license waiting list, software suite licensing, configurable notification for network administrators, workstation agent software, and WAN support.

Network management. Saber's network management features include network statistics, SNMP support (currently only for Macintosh), configurable alarms for notification of systems administrators, optional help-desk support, and job scheduling.

Remote-control features. Saber's remote-control features include support of DOS and Windows systems and file transfer support over IPX, NetBEUI, FTP, and IP.

In short, Saber provides a full-feature set of mature systems management products and good vendor support. Saber is less intuitive to use than many other packages. For example, Saber relies extensively on command arguments in DOS and .INI settings in Windows.

Norton Administrator for Networks (NAN)

This is an excellent general package for inventory, software distribution, metering, and network management. It is easy to set up and use, it works with many network protocols, and, significantly, it is integrated with HP's OpenView. All NAN features are available from a single, very intuitive console window.

The following paragraphs briefly describe major features of Norton Administrator for Networks.

Workstations and networks supported. Clients and protocols supported include DOS, Windows, OS/2, and Macintosh, with network support including NetWare, LAN Manager (Microsoft), LAN Server (IBM), Vines, Pathworks, LANtastic, and WAN.

Software distribution. NAN supports full software install, remote batch editing of .INI files, file update and replacement, configurable standard file sets, a task recording and replay function, a software uninstall feature, a powerful scripting language, and WAN support for software distribution.

Inventory management. NAN provides hardware detection for about 260 items on clients and can also detect about 1500 software applications.

Software license monitoring and metering. NAN's software license monitoring and metering functions include site license support, license waiting list, software suite licensing, configurable notification for network administrators, time-based restrictions, workstation agent software, and WAN support.

Network management. NAN network management features include network statistics, configurable alarms for notification of systems administrators, optional help-desk support, and job scheduling.

Remote control. NAN remote-control features include integration of pcAnywhere software into the NAN console. NAN remote control supports DOS and Windows systems, dial-up, file transfer over IPX, NetBEUI, TCP/IP, and across WAN.

14.9 NETWORK MANAGEMENT

A network management framework consists of several building blocks. Among them are *agents* (software components that reside on managed systems and interact with network system manager), the *manager* (the heart of the network management system), and *management information protocols* that transport management information in a specific format (i.e., SNMP, CMIP).

In addition, network management includes the following functional areas:

- *LAN administration.* This includes configuring LAN servers, adding new users, applications, and peripherals.

- *Physical LAN management.* This entails managing LAN connections (wiring, adapter cards, and concentrators/hubs), analyzing LAN protocols, and monitoring LAN devices.

- *Management and configuration of LAN devices.* This comprises fault, configuration, and performance monitoring of routers and bridges.

- *Transmission link management.* This includes managing wide area leased lines, dial-up, and X.25 services for data communications as well as WAN switches such as T1 multiplexers.

- *Performance management.* This includes measuring the response time and general well-being of the network. It also proactively models and automatically reroutes network traffic.

- *Fault management.* This function detects and isolates problems in network communications and protocols.

- *Security management.* This controls access to data, and protects against unauthorized modifications of data and eavesdropping on the network.

- *Accounting.* Measures and logs network usage and performs billing, budgeting, and accounting verification.

These areas reflect the view that the physical, tangible entities like routers, bridges, cables, etc. are the domain of network management, which can be considered as a complementary set of management disciplines that together constitute enterprise distributed systems management. A key requirement of network management is the gathering and displaying of information from devices on a network. This process typically includes MIB browsers (SNMP), CMIP (OSI), IP discoverers, and event monitors.

Simple Network Management Protocol (SNMP) was originally designed to manage network devices and operations in a centralized fashion, which complicated management of large distributed systems. SNMP relies on the Management Information Base (MIB) structures to tell its agents what information to collect and store. SNMP version 1 has limited security provisions, which allows a third-party software to observe the SNMP traffic and act as a manager. SNMP Version 2 adds security capabilities, supports multiple managers, and facilitates manager-to-manager interactions. Today, SNMP has emerged as one of the most popular protocols for systems management. It has been employed by more than half of all available systems management packages, including all major vendor solutions. Indeed, SNMP-based management systems are capable of monitoring *any* resource defined in a MIB, and nothing mandates or limits the type of actions taken in response to events.

To successfully meet all network management requirements, different network management vendors created their products based on SNMP-based framework (see Fig. 14.6).

There are a number of robust and function-rich network management systems on the market today. Systems like IBM NetView/AIX, HP OpenView, and CA Polycenter all grow from a relatively simple suite of network management applications to solutions capable of solving enterprise-wide problems. Let's briefly look at one of the network management system products that exemplifies the capabilities of the network management framework.

14.9.1   IBM SystemView

This is a full-featured network management system that has adopted a process, rather than tools, orientation. Under SystemView, management becomes repeated tasks that can be automated. For example, if a critical application stops unexpectedly, the resolution process might involve restarting the software, restoring data, notifying the administrator, and logging the interruption. The task metaphor drives the user interface which appears as a hierarchical file tree called the *launch panel,* rather than a screen full of icons.

SystemView offers functionality spanning six areas critical to managing a heterogeneous enterprise:

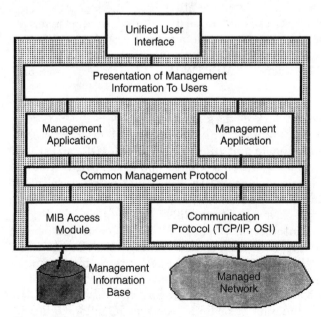

Figure 14.6 Network management station model.

- Change management
- Configuration control
- Operations
- Problem resolution
- Performance monitoring
- Business administration

The actual execution of these activities is handled by 22 previously disparate tools that have been integrated.

As a result, SystemView represents a platform that:

- *Solves multiple problems from a common console.* This will help users that had to implement a different tool from a different vendor for each management application.
- *Leverages existing investments.* SystemView supports all of the existing NetView Association third-party tools out of the box.
- *Provides ease-of-use.* This is a key criterion for the design of the integrated user interface in SystemView. All tools share a common look and feel, thus lowering training and support costs.
- *Is positioned for object-oriented implementation.* SystemView plans include the incorporation of CORBA infrastructure services and an integrated data model without forcing users to endure repeated tool migrations.

14.10 WORKFLOW MANAGEMENT

Due to increasing pressure to stay competitive, organizations are looking at the fundamental way they do business. Business processes, from the department to the enterprise, are being evaluated with the goal of using LAN-based PCs to make the process more efficient. Workflow applications are the method used to automate these processes.

14.10.1 Workflow management overview

Workflow software enables organizations to automate the business process by breaking it into discrete tasks and sending each task to a worker within the flow for processing. Tasks can be sequential where they must be done in the specified order, or in parallel where the tasks can be done as other tasks in the workflow are also being done. As each worker receives the task as it flows through the organization, the data associated with that task is available to the worker. Rules can be set up to describe how the tasks should flow through an organization.

These rules are dynamic—they change as the business requirements dictate.

An example of how workflow might operate is the hiring of an employee in a human resource application. Hiring an employee touches many parts of a company. Information about the employee (name and address information, photo ID, payroll deductions, insurance data) needs to be collected and routed to the correct departments for processing. Each department may have its own procedures and policies when hiring a new employee. The automation and coordination of these processes can be automated and tracked by a workflow application.

The workflow applications can be broken into three categories:

- *Production workflow* involves complex, highly structured processing activities, such as loan applications, engineering change orders, product development, and insurance claims. Production workflow is task-driven. The output of the workflow is most often the product itself. Activity-driven workflow can involve the same people who repeatedly perform the same tasks, sending work to the next person in the flow for approval or processing. Production workflow is enterprise-wide and involves sophisticated routing and work-in-process reporting. An example of a production workflow application is the SmartStream Series from D&B Software.

- *Administrative workflow* involves simple, form-intensive tasks such as check requests, purchase orders, and personnel procedures. A typical administrative workflow procedure might be a purchase order approval or travel and expense report procedure. Administrative workflow typically uses e-mail as a communications mechanism. The main purpose of the administrative workflow is to automate the approval cycle and route forms to the appropriate person. Lotus Notes or Microsoft Exchange could be used to write these administrative workflows.

- *Ad hoc workflow* is composed of repetitive, unstructured processes that may involve different people with each transaction. Workflows are temporary and can be initiated by the end users themselves. Typical ad hoc workflow processes are product documentation, sales proposals, receivable assessments, and product evaluations. For example, an ad hoc workflow team may be set up across departments to assess company-wide downsizing.

A workflow that starts as an ad hoc workflow may evolve over time into an administrative workflow if it becomes a typical task used by other people and groups. Similarly, administrative workflows may become production workflows if they become involved in a complex, enterprise-wide process.

14.10.2 Workflow architectures

There are several architectural models that workflow applications can fit into. These models are based on the client/server architecture, and reflect various styles of client/server computing (described in Chap. 2).

- *Mail-based workflow* uses the inherent capabilities of an e-mail system to build the application. This architecture is appropriate for document-based applications. The client holds all the rules and data, as well as performing all the processing. Without a server, management of workflow (i.e., to find the status of a process) is impossible. Since all rules are stored on the client, maintaining them across an enterprise is difficult.

- *Shared database workflow* also uses an e-mail system to build the application. All processing is still done on the client, but the data is stored on a document server. This makes management and update of rules easier. An example of this implementation is Lotus Notes.

- *Client/server workflow* allows flexibility with some processing on the client and some on the server. Rules and data are stored on the server. In addition, rules are executed on the server. This allows integration of other applications that are server-based. A number of monitoring and management applications are available for this architecture. For example, Action Technology has a tool that allows users to build client/server workflow applications.

6

Client/Server—Mature Architecture

The first generation of client/server systems has brought data to the desktop, often as an implementation of decision support systems (DSS) and executive information systems (EIS). Unfortunately, not all of this data was easy to understand, and as such, was not very useful to end users. In addition, these applications were focused on presenting data to high-level executives. To improve the information content of the data and to empower knowledge workers of today and tomorrow, the latest hot technologies that have emerged on the client/server arena are focused on filtering unnecessary data and presenting the valuable information in a user-friendly, intuitive, and easy-to-understand way. Among these technologies are data warehousing, metadata repositories, on-line analytical processing (OLAP), and data mining. These technologies are the manifestation of the maturity of the client/server computing model and its applicability to a wide variety of business problems.

The discussion of these technologies consists of two parts—a general overview of data warehousing and some of the integrated solutions available today from a number of vendors and vendor alliances is the subject of Chap. 15, with in-depth analysis of data warehousing technologies, tools, and some vendor products presented in Chap. 16.

Data Warehousing

The 1990s are the decade when organizations are beginning to recognize the strategic use of data as an entirely different discipline from operational use. Operational database systems have been traditionally designed to meet mission-critical requirements for on-line transaction processing and batch processing. In contrast, strategic data usage is characterized by on-line ad hoc query processing or batch intelligence-gathering functions for decision support.

A data warehouse is the means for strategic data usage. It is not the same as a decision support system (DSS). Rather, a data warehouse is an environment with integrated data of improved quality to support many DSS applications and processes within an enterprise. Data warehousing improves the productivity of corporate decision makers through consolidation, conversion, transformation, and integration of operational data, and provides a consistent view of an enterprise.

In short, data warehousing is a blend of technologies aimed at effective integration of operational databases into an environment that enables strategic use of data. These technologies include relational and multidimensional database management systems, client/server architecture, metadata modeling and repositories, graphical user interfaces, and much more.

15.1   THE NEED FOR DATA WAREHOUSING

The data warehouse is an environment, not a product. It is an architectural construct of information systems that provides users with current and historical decision support information that is hard to access or present in traditional operational data stores. In fact, the data warehouse is a cornerstone of the organization's ability to do effective information processing that, among other things, can enable and *share* the discovery and exploration of important business trends and dependencies that otherwise would have gone unnoticed. In principle, the data warehouse can meet informational needs of knowledge workers, and can provide strategic business opportunities by allowing customers and vendors access to corporate data while maintaining necessary security measures.

There are several reasons why organizations consider data warehousing a critical need. These drivers for data warehousing can be found in the business climate of a global marketplace, in the changing organizational structures of successful corporations, and in the technology.

From a *business perspective,* in order to survive and succeed in today's highly competitive global environment, business users demand business answers mainly because:

- Decisions need to be made quickly and correctly, using all available data.

- Users are business domain experts, not computer professionals.

- The amount of data is doubling every 18 months, which affects response time and the sheer ability to comprehend its content.

- Competition is heating up in the areas of business intelligence and added information value.

In addition, the necessity for data warehouses has increased as organizations distribute control away from the middle management layer that has traditionally provided and screened business information. As users depend more on information obtained from information technology systems—from critical-success measures to vital business-event-related information—the need to provide data warehouse for the staff to use becomes more critical.

There are several *technology reasons* for the existence of data warehousing. First, the data warehouse is designed to address the incompatibility of informational and operational transactional systems. These two classes of information systems are designed to satisfy different, often incompatible requirements. At the same time, the information technology infrastructure is changing rapidly, and its capabilities are increasing, as evidenced by the following:

- The price of MIPS continues to decline, while the power of microprocessors doubles every two years.

- The price of digital storage is rapidly dropping.

- Network bandwidth is increasing, while the price of high bandwidth is decreasing.

- The workplace is increasingly heterogeneous from both the hardware and software viewpoints.

- Legacy systems need to be and can be integrated with new applications.

15.2 OPERATIONAL AND INFORMATIONAL DATA STORES

Corporations have a variety of on-line transaction processing systems (e.g., financial, order entry, work scheduling, and point-of-sale systems) which create operational data. Operational data focuses on transactional functions such as bank card withdrawals and deposits. This data is part of the corporate infrastructure; it is detailed, nonredundant, and updateable; and it reflects current values. It answers such questions as "How many gadgets were sold to customer number 123876 on September 19?"

Informational data, on the other hand, is organized around subjects such as customer, vendor, and product. It focuses on providing answers to problems posed by decision makers, such as "What three products resulted in the most frequent calls to the hotline over the past quarter?" Informational data is often summarized, is redundant to support varying data views, and is nonupdateable. In an operational system, a single data record can change constantly, while decision support requires that the record be stored as a series of snapshots of instances of that record over time.

Informational data is obtained from operational and external data sources (including any or all applications, databases, and computer systems within the enterprise). Since operational data is fragmented and inconsistent (for example, names and addresses for customers might be handled differently on each system), it must be "cleaned up" to conform to consistent formats, naming conventions, and access methods in order for it to be useful in decision support.

Data warehousing is designed to provide an architecture that will make corporate data readily accessible and usable to knowledge workers and decision makers. This differs from the operational systems which:

- Are organized by application
- Support daily business processing on a detailed transactional level
- Are update intensive
- Use current data
- Are optimized for high performance
- Access few records per transaction, often using direct access by primary key
- Support a large number of relatively short transactions
- Support a large number of concurrent users

While the majority of informational and operational databases use the same underlying relational DBMS technology, the following characteristics of information data illustrate its difference from operational data:

- *Data access*—tends to be ad hoc vs. predefined, structured access
- *Data model (schema)*—reflects end-user analysis needs, while operational data model is normalized to support ACID properties
- *Time base*—recent, aggregated, derived and historical data, while operational data tends to be current data or a snapshot of recent data
- *Data changes*—informational data changes are mostly periodic, scheduled batch updates, while operational data is subject to continuous high-frequency changes
- *Unit of work*—informational data is queried, while operational data is subject to concurrent update, insert, delete
- *Records range accessed per transaction*—millions for informational data vs. tens for operational
- *Number of concurrent users*—typically, hundreds for informational vs. thousands for operational
- *Transaction volume*—relatively low for informational data vs. high for operational
- *Types of users*—analytical, managerial vs. clerical, operational users; frequently, a user of the operational data is another system
- *Number of indexes*—often many complex, compound vs. few, simple

These differences between the informational and operational databases are summarized in the following table.

	Operational data	Informational data
Data content	Current values	Summarized, archived, derived
Data organization	By application	By subject
Data stability	Dynamic	Static until refreshed
Data structure	Optimized for transactions	Optimized for complex queries
Access frequency	High	Medium to low
Access type	Read/update/delete	Read/aggregate
	Field-by-field	Added to
Usage	Predictable	Ad hoc, unstructured
	Repetitive	Heuristic
Response time	Subsecond to 2–3 s	Several seconds to minutes

15.3 DEFINITION AND CHARACTERISTICS OF DATA WAREHOUSE

Data warehouse can be viewed as an information system with the following attributes:

- It is a database designed for analytical tasks, using data from multiple applications.

- It supports a relatively small number of users with relatively long interactions.

- Its usage is read-intensive.

- Its content is periodically updated (mostly additions).

- It contains current and historical data to provide a historical perspective of information.

- It contains a few large tables.

- Each query frequently results in a large result set and involves frequent full table scan and multitable joins.

A formal definition of the data warehouse is offered by W. H. Inmon:

> *A data warehouse is a subject-oriented, integrated, time-variant, non-volatile collection of data in support of management decisions.*

In other words, a data warehouse combines:

- One or more tools to extract fields from any kind of data structure (flat, hierarchical, relational, or object; open or proprietary), including external data

- The synthesis of the data into a nonvolatile, integrated, subject-oriented database with a metadata "catalog"

There are a number of other terms related to the data warehouse. Following are some informal definitions of these terms:

- *Current detail data*—data that is acquired directly from the operational databases, and often represents an entire enterprise. The current detail data is organized along subject lines (i.e., customer profile data, customer activity data, demographics data, sales data, etc.).

- *Old detail data*—represents aged current detail data or the history of the subject areas; this data is what makes trend analysis possible.

- *Data mart*—an implementation of the data warehouse where its data scope is somewhat limited compared to the enterprise-wide data warehouse; a data mart may contain lightly summarized departmental data and is customized to suit the needs of a particular department that owns the data; in a large enterprise, data marts tend to be a way to build a data warehouse in a sequential, phased approach; a collection of data marts composes an enterprise-wide data warehouse; conversely, a data warehouse may be construed as a collection of subset data marts.

- *Summarized data*—data that is aggregated along the lines required for executive-level reporting, trend analysis, and enterprise-wide decision making; summarized data volumes are much smaller than current and old detail data.

- *Drill-down*—the ability of a knowledge worker to perform business analysis in a top-down fashion, traversing the summarization levels from highly summarized data to the underlying current or old detail; for example, if highly summarized geographical sales data indicates a reduction in sales volumes in North America, an analyst can drill down into the state, county, city, and even the address of the sales offices with the worst sales records.

- *Metadata*—one of the most important aspects of data warehousing; it is data about data, and contains the locations and descriptions of warehouse system components; names, definitions, structure and content of the data warehouse and end-user views; identification of authoritative data sources (systems of record); integration and transformation rules used to populate the data warehouse; a history of warehouse updates and refreshments; metrics used to analyze warehouse performance vis-à-vis end-user usage patterns; security authorizations, etc.

While users' needs from a data warehouse will differ from company to company, similarities will exist. The following classification defines and describes some data warehouse attributes:

- A data warehouse provides a mechanism for separating operational and informational processing, with information being the domain of the warehouse. Since the warehouse is populated by data created by the operational environment, the flow of information is usually one way, from the operation data stores to the data warehouse.

- A holistic perspective that eliminates the vertical, line-of-business orientation of the operational data and provides an integrated perspective across the enterprise. The data warehouse is designed to help resolve inconsistencies in data formats, semantics, and usage across multiple operational systems.

- Part of a warehouse's function will include processing the data from its raw form in the operational databases. Data warehouse procedures include aggregating, reconciling, and summarizing data to make it more relevant and useful for users.

- The data content of the warehouse is a subset of all data in an organization. Even though the warehouse contains data originating from the operational environment, the contents of the warehouse are unique. Within the informational landscape, however, the warehouse should be considered as a universal set of all data emanating from inside and outside the company.

- Collecting data throughout the enterprise can result in an overwhelming amount of information. An effective means to navigate through the data maze can make a big difference as to whether the warehouse is used.

- Frequently, data from outside the company contributes to the decision-making process. Incorporating external data and mapping it to the appropriate applications are important data warehouse functions and should be transparent to the user.

- Automating the data extraction and the required frequency of updates needs to be the warehouse's responsibility. Often, subsets of informational data need to be replicated for remote sites. Since data consolidation needs to precede replication, the warehouse becomes a logical place for the consolidation to occur. Monitoring the data replication process to ensure that remote sites are synchronized with events at the central site also falls under the purview of the warehouse solution.

Although these attributes are normally associated with a data warehouse, they may not be immediately required by an organization's data warehouse implementation. But planning ahead for future needs will result in a data warehouse solution that is flexible.

15.4   DATA WAREHOUSE ARCHITECTURE AND COMPONENTS

The data warehouse architecture is based on a relational database management system server that functions as the central repository for informational data. In the data warehouse architecture, operational data and processing are completely separate from data warehouse processing (see Fig. 15.1).

The source data for the warehouse is the operational applications. As the data enters the data warehouse, it is transformed into an integrated structure and format. The transformation process may involve conversion, summarization, filtering, and condensation of data. Because data within the data warehouse contains a large historical component (sometimes from 5 to 10 years), the data warehouse must be capable of holding and managing large volumes of data as well as different data structures for the same database over time.

15.4.1   Data warehouse components

This section discusses the five data warehouse components illustrated in Fig. 15.1.

1. Data sourcing, cleanup, transformation, and migration tools

A significant portion of the data warehouse implementation effort is spent extracting data from operational systems and putting it in a for-

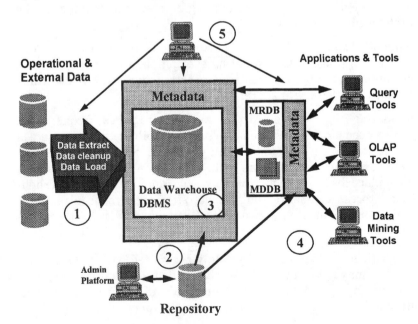

Figure 15.1 Data warehouse environment.

mat suitable for informational applications that will run off the data warehouse.

The data sourcing, cleanup, transformation, and migration tools perform all of the conversions, summarizations, key changes, structural changes, and condensations needed to transform disparate data into information that can be used by the decision support tool. This component produces the programs and control statements, including the COBOL programs, MVS job control language (JCL), UNIX scripts, and SQL data definition language (DDL) needed to move data into the data warehouse from multiple operational systems. It also maintains the metadata. The functionality includes:

- Removing unwanted data from operational databases
- Converting to common data names and definitions
- Calculating summaries and derived data
- Establishing defaults for missing data
- Accommodating source data definition changes

The data sourcing, cleanup, extract, transformation and migration tools have to deal with some significant issues, as follows:

- *Database heterogeneity.* DBMSs are very different in data models, data access language, data navigation, operations, concurrency, integrity, recovery, etc.
- *Data heterogeneity.* This is the difference in the way data is defined and used in different models—homonyms, synonyms, unit incompatibility (U.S. vs. metric), different attributes for the same entity, different ways of modeling the same fact.

These tools can save a considerable amount of time and effort. However, significant shortcomings do exist. For example, many available tools are generally useful for simpler data extracts. Frequently, customized extract routines need to be developed for the more complicated data extraction procedures. The vendors prominent in this arena include Prism Solutions, Evolutionary Technologies Inc. (ETI), Vality, and Carleton.

2. Metadata repository

Metadata is data about data that describes the data warehouse and is used for building, maintaining, managing, and using the data warehouse. It includes:

- Source data description
- Transformation descriptions, i.e., the mapping method from operational databases into the warehouse, and algorithms used to convert/enhance/transform data

- Warehouse object and data structure definitions

- Data warehouse operational information, i.e., data history (snap-shots, versions), ownership, extract audit trail, usage data

Equally as important, metadata provides interactive access to users to help understand content, find data. One of the issues dealing with metadata relates to the fact that many data extraction tools' capabilities to gather metadata remain fairly immature. Therefore, often there is a need to create a metadata interface for users, which may involve some duplication of effort.

Metadata management is provided via a metadata repository and accompanying software. Metadata repository management software can be used to map the source data to the target database, generate code for data transformations, integrate and transform the data, and control moving data to the warehouse. This software, which typically runs on a workstation, enables users to specify how the data should be transformed, such as data mapping, conversion, and summarization.

The ability to do the extracts periodically and to refresh and update the synthesized data is key. The maintenance of the information catalog of metadata (data about the data) is critically important.

In some data warehouse architectures, the metadata repository is also known as a *dictionary* or *encyclopedia*. Examples of such repositories include Prism Solution's Directory Manager, Platinum Repository, and Rochade from REO.

3. Warehouse database technology

The data warehouse itself is almost always based on the relational database management system (RDBMS) technology. However, a warehouse implementation based on traditional RDBMS technology is often constrained by the fact that traditional RDBMS implementations are optimized for transactional database processing. Certain data warehouse attributes, such as very large database size, ad hoc query processing, and the need for flexible user view creation including aggregates, multitable joins, and drill-downs, have become drivers for different technological approaches to the data warehouse database. These approaches include:

- Parallel relational database designs that require a parallel computing platform, i.e., a symmetric multiprocessor (SMP), massively parallel processors (MPP), and/or clusters of uni- or multiprocessors. (The discussion on this technology started in Chaps. 4 and 12, and continues later in the next chapter.)

- An innovative approach to speed up a traditional RDBMS by using new index structures to bypass relational table scans. (This is also discussed in more detail in the next chapter.)

- Multidimensional databases (MDDB) that are based on proprietary database technology or implemented using already familiar RDBMS. MDDB is designed to overcome any restrictions placed on the warehouse by simple rows and columns. This approach is tightly coupled with the on-line analytical processing (OLAP) tools, and from the data warehouse components viewpoint is bundled with the data query, reporting, analysis, and mining tools (see no. 4).

4. Data query, reporting, analysis, and mining tools

The principal purpose of data warehousing is to provide information to business users for strategic decision making. These users interact with the data warehouse using front-end tools, which are either purchased or developed internally. Many of these tools require an information specialist, although many end users develop expertise in the tools. Both dynamic and preplanned analysis are enabled in a high-performance environment because joins, summations, and periodic reports are preplanned and results are usually moved to servers as close to end users as possible for immediate access.

The end-user tools area spans a number of components. For example, all end user tools use metadata definitions to obtain access to data stored in the warehouse, and some of these tools (e.g., OLAP tools) may employ additional/intermediary data stores (i.e., a multidimensional database). These additional data stores play a dual role—they may act as specialized data stores for a given end-user tool or just be a subset of the data warehouse covering a specific subject area—e.g., a data mart.

For the purpose of this discussion let's divide these tools into three main groups:

- *Data query and reporting tools.* These are easy-to-use, point-and-click tools that either accept SQL or generate SQL statements to query relational data stored in the warehouse. Some of these tools proceed to format the retrieved data into easy-to-read reports, while others concentrate on the on-screen presentation. These tools are the preferred choice of the users of business applications such as segment identification, demographic analysis, territory management, and customer mailing lists. As the complexity of the questions grows, these tools may rapidly become inefficient.

- *On-line analytical processing (OLAP) tools.* These tools are based on the concepts of multidimensional databases and allow a sophisticated user to analyze the data using elaborate, multidimensional, complex views. Typical business applications for these tools include product performance and profitability, effectiveness of a sales program or a marketing campaign, sales forecasting, and capacity planning. These tools assume that the data is organized in a multidimensional model which is supported by a special multidimensional database (MDDB) or by a relational database designed to enable multidimensional properties (multirelational database, or MRDB). A detailed discussion on OLAP and multidimensional databases is presented in the next chapter.

- *Data mining tools.* These tools are focused on the area of analysis that deals with predictive modeling and discovering previously unknown facts, patterns, and dependencies in the data. A detailed discussion on data mining is presented in the next chapter.

5. Data warehouse administration and management

Data warehouses tend to be as much as four times as large as related operational databases, reaching terabytes in size depending on how much history needs to be saved. They are not synchronized in real time to the associated operational data but are updated as often as once a day if the application requires it.

In addition to the main architectural components already described, almost all data warehouse products include gateways to transparently access multiple enterprise data sources without having to rewrite applications to interpret and utilize the data.

Furthermore, in a heterogeneous data warehouse environment the various databases reside on disparate systems, thus requiring internetworking tools. Although there are no special data warehousing internetworking technologies, and a typical data warehouse implementation relies on the same communications software as messaging and transaction processing systems (i.e., NetWare, TCP/IP protocols, products that use DCE technology), the need to manage this infrastructural component is obvious.

To summarize, managing data warehouse includes:

- Security and priority management
- Monitoring updates from multiple sources
- Data quality checks
- Managing and updating metadata
- Auditing and reporting data warehouse usage and status (for managing the response time and resource utilization, and providing chargeback information)
- Purging data

- Replication, subsetting, distributing data

- Backup and recovery

- Data warehouse storage management (i.e., capacity planning, hierarchical storage management or HSM)

15.4.2 Data warehouse access and client/server architecture

From the end-user perspective, the data warehouse represents a source of data, access to which is provided by the end-user query, reporting, analysis, or mining tools. In other words, the data warehouse can be viewed as an information server to its clients—end users using front-end tools. Let's consider two client/server models that apply to data warehouse access.

Two-tiered data warehouse architecture is based on the first generation of client/server architecture and demonstrates the same characteristics (discussed in detail in Chap. 2). Specifically, it is a "fat" client model, where client system functions include user interface, query specification, data analysis, report formatting, data access, and resource-consuming aggregation. The data warehouse server performs data logic, data services, and file services, and maintains metadata (see Fig. 15.2).

The two-tiered architecture lacks the scaleability and flexibility of the multitiered model. Multitiered data warehouse architecture reflects the multitiered client/server model (see Fig. 15.3).

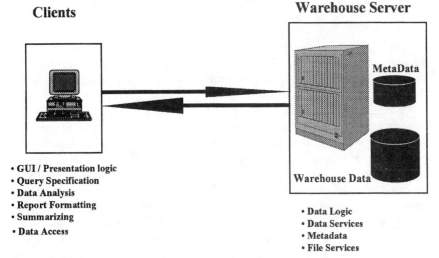

Clients

Warehouse Server

MetaData

Warehouse Data

- GUI / Presentation logic
- Query Specification
- Data Analysis
- Report Formatting
- Summarizing
- Data Access

- Data Logic
- Data Services
- Metadata
- File Services

Figure 15.2 Two-tiered data warehouse architecture.

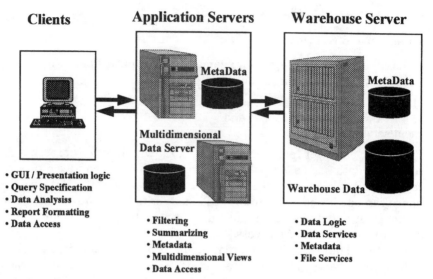

Clients   **Application Servers**   **Warehouse Server**

- GUI / Presentation logic
- Query Specification
- Data Analysis
- Report Formatting
- Data Access

- Filtering
- Summarizing
- Metadata
- Multidimensional Views
- Data Access

- Data Logic
- Data Services
- Metadata
- File Services

Figure 15.3 Multitiered data warehouse architecture.

This architecture solves the scaleability and flexibility issues of the two-tiered data warehouse. Application servers can be data-mart-specific, perform data filtering, aggregation, and data access; support metadata; and provide multidimensional views. A client system is left with GUI, query specification, data analysis, report formatting, and specialized data access.

15.5 BUILDING A DATA WAREHOUSE

15.5.1 Approach

The information scope of the data warehouse varies depending on the business requirements, business priorities, and even the magnitude of the problem. The subject-oriented nature of the data warehouse means that the nature of the subject determines the scope (or the coverage) of the warehoused information. Specifically, if the data warehouse is implemented to satisfy a specific subject area (i.e., human resources), such a warehouse is expressly designed to solve business problems related to personnel. An organization may choose to build another warehouse for its marketing department. These two warehouses could be implemented independently and be completely stand-alone applications, or they could be viewed as components of the enterprise, interacting with each other, and using a common enterprise data model. As defined earlier, the individual warehouses are known as *data marts*. Organizations embarking on data warehousing development can choose one of the two approaches:

- *The top-down approach* means that an organization has developed an enterprise data model, collected enterprise-wide business requirements, and decided to build an enterprise data warehouse with subset data marts.

- *The bottom-up approach* implies that the business priorities resulted in developing individual data marts, which are then integrated into the enterprise data warehouse.

The bottom up approach is probably more realistic, but the complexity of the integration may become a serious obstacle, and the warehouse designers should carefully analyze each data mart for integration affinity.

15.5.2 Organizational issues

Most Information Systems (IS) organizations have considerable expertise in developing operational systems. However, the requirements and environments associated with the informational applications of a data warehouse are different. Therefore, an organization will need to employ different development practices than the ones it uses for operational applications.

The IS department will need to bring together data that cuts across a company's operational systems as well as data from outside the company. But users will also need to be involved with a data warehouse implementation since they are closest to the data. In many ways, a data warehouse implementation is not truly a technological issue; rather, it should be more concerned with identifying and establishing information requirements, the data sources to fulfill these requirements, and timeliness.

15.6 DESIGN CONSIDERATIONS

To be successful, a data warehouse designer must adopt a *holistic* approach—consider *all* data warehouse components as parts of a single complex system, take into the account *all* possible data sources and *all* known usage requirements. Failing to do that may easily result in a data warehouse design that is skewed toward a particular business requirement, a particular data source, or a selected access tool.

In general, a data warehouse's design point is to consolidate data from multiple, often heterogeneous sources into a query database. This is also one of the reasons why a data warehouse is rather difficult to build. The main factors include:

- Heterogeneity of data sources, which affects data conversion, quality, timeliness

- Use of historical data, which implies that data may be "old"
- Tendency of databases to grow very large

Another important point speaks about the experience and accepted practices. Basically, the reality is that the data warehouse design is different from traditional OLTP. Indeed, the data warehouse:

- Is *business* driven (not IS driven, like in OLTP)
- Requires *continuous* interactions with end users
- Is *never finished,* since both requirements and data sources change

Understanding these points allows developers to avoid a number of pitfalls relevant to data warehouse development and justifies a new approach to data warehouse design—a business-driven, continuous, iterative warehouse engineering approach.

In addition to these general considerations, there are several specific points relevant to the data warehouse design.

15.6.1 Data content

One common misconception about data warehouses is that they should not contain as much detail-level data as operational systems used to source this data in. In reality, however, while the data in the warehouse is formatted differently from the operational data, it may be just as detailed. Typically, a data warehouse may contain detailed data, but the data is cleaned up and transformed to fit the warehouse model, and certain transactional attributes of the data are filtered out. These attributes are mostly the ones that are used for the internal transaction system logic, and they are not meaningful in the context of analysis and decision making.

The content and structure of the data warehouse is reflected in its *data model.* The data model is the template that describes how information will be organized within the integrated warehouse framework. It identifies major subjects and relationships of the model including keys, attributes, and attribute groupings. In addition, a designer should always remember that decision support queries, due to their broad scope and analytical intensity, require data models to be optimized to improve query performance. In addition to its effect on query performance, the data model affects data storage requirements and data loading performance.

15.6.2 Metadata

As already discussed, metadata defines the contents and location of data (data model) in the warehouse, relationships between the operational databases and the data warehouse, and the business views of the warehouse data that are accessible by end-user tools. Metadata is searched by users to find data definitions or subject areas. In other words, metadata provides decision support-oriented pointers to warehouse data, and thus provides a logical link between warehouse data and the decision support application. A data warehouse design should ensure that there is a mechanism that populates and maintains the metadata repository, and that *all* access paths to the data warehouse have metadata as an entry point. To put it another way, the warehouse design should prevent any direct access to the warehouse data (especially updates) if it does not use metadata definitions to gain the access.

15.6.3 Data distribution

One of the biggest challenges when designing a data warehouse is the data placement and distribution strategy. This follows from the fact that as the data volumes continue to grow, the database size may rapidly outgrow a single server. Therefore, it becomes necessary to know how the data should be divided across multiple servers and which users should get access to which types of data. The data placement and distribution design should consider several options, including data distribution by subject area (e.g., human resources, marketing), location (e.g., geographical regions), or by time (e.g., current, monthly, quarterly). The designers should be aware that, while the distribution solves a number of problems, it may also create a few of its own—for example, if the warehouse servers are distributed across multiple locations, a query that spans several servers across LAN or WAN may flood the network with a large amount of data. Therefore, any distribution strategy should take into account all possible access needs for the warehouse data.

15.6.4 Tools

A number of tools available today are specifically designed to help in the implementation of a data warehouse. These tools provide facilities for defining the transformation and cleanup rules, data movement (from operational sources into the warehouse), end-user query, reporting, and data analysis. Each tool takes a slightly different approach to data warehousing and often maintains its own version of the metadata which is placed in a tool-specific, proprietary metadata repository. Data warehouse designers have to be careful not to sacrifice the overall design to fit a specific tool. At the same time, the designers have to make sure that all selected tools are compatible with the given data warehouse environment and with each other. That means that all selected tools can use a common metadata repository. Alternatively, the tools should be able to source the metadata from the warehouse data dictionary (if it exists) or from a CASE tool used to design the warehouse database. Another option is to use metadata gateways that translate one tool's metadata into another tool's format. If these requirements are not satisfied, the resulting warehouse environment may rapidly become unmanageable, since every modification to the warehouse data model may involve some significant and labor-intensive changes to the metadata definitions for every tool in the environment. And then, these changes would have to be verified for consistency and integrity.

15.6.5 Performance considerations

Although the data warehouse design point does not include subsecond response times typical of OLTP systems, it is nevertheless a clear business requirement that an ideal data warehouse environment should support interactive query processing. In fact, the majority of end-user tools are designed as interactive applications. Therefore, "rapid" query processing is a highly desired feature that should be designed into the data warehouse. Of course, the actual performance levels are business-dependent and vary widely from one environment to another. Unfortunately, it is relatively difficult to predict the performance of a typical data warehouse. One of the reasons for this is the unpredictable usage patterns against the data. Thus, traditional database design and tuning techniques don't always work in the data warehouse arena. When designing a data warehouse, therefore, the need to clearly understand users' informational requirements becomes mandatory. Specifically, knowing how end users need to access various data can help design warehouse databases to avoid the majority of the most expensive operations, such as multitable scans and joins. For example, one design technique is to populate the warehouse with a number of denormalized views containing summarized, derived, and aggregated data. If done correctly, many end-user queries may execute directly against these views, thus maintaining appropriate overall performance levels.

15.7 TECHNICAL CONSIDERATIONS

A number of technical issues are to be considered when designing and implementing a data warehouse environment. These issues include:

- The hardware platform that would house the data warehouse
- The database management system that supports the warehouse database

- The communications infrastructure that connects the warehouse, data marts, operational systems, and end users

- The hardware platform and software to support the metadata repository

- The systems management framework that enables centralized management and administration of the entire environment

Let's look at some of these issues in more detail.

15.7.1 Hardware platforms

Since many data warehouse implementations are developed into already existing environments, many organizations tend to leverage the existing platforms and skill base to build a data warehouse. This section looks at the hardware platform selection from an architectural viewpoint—what platform is best to build a successful data warehouse from the ground up.

An important consideration when choosing a data warehouse server is its capacity for handling the volumes of data required by decision support applications, some of which may require a significant amount of historical (e.g., up to 10 years) data. This capacity requirement can be quite large. For example, in general, disk storage allocated for the warehouse should be 2 to 3 times the size of the data component of the warehouse to accommodate DSS processing, such as sorting, storing of intermediate results, summarization, join, and formatting.

Often, the platform choice is the choice between a mainframe and non-MVS (UNIX or Windows NT) server.

Of course, a number of arguments can be made for and against each of these choices. For example, a mainframe is based on a proven technology; has large data and throughput capacity; is reliable, available, and serviceable; and may support the legacy databases that are used as sources for the data warehouse. The data warehouse residing on the mainframe is best suited for situations where large amounts of legacy data need to be stored in the data warehouse. A mainframe system, however, is not as open and flexible as a contemporary client/server system and is not optimized for ad hoc query processing. A modern server (nonmainframe) can also support large data volumes and a large number of flexible GUI-based end-user tools, and can relieve the mainframe from ad hoc query processing. However, in general, non-MVS servers are not as reliable as mainframes, are more difficult to manage and integrate into the existing environment, and may require new skills and even new organizational structures.

From the architectural viewpoint, however, the data warehouse server has to be specialized for the tasks associated with the data warehouse, and a mainframe can be well suited to be a data warehouse server. Let's look at the hardware features that make a server—be it a mainframe, UNIX-based, or NT-based—an appropriate technical solution for the data warehouse.

To begin with, the data warehouse server has to be able to support large data volumes and complex query processing. In addition, it has to be *scaleable,* since the data warehouse is never finished as new user requirements, new data sources, and more historical data keep being incorporated into the warehouse and as the user population of the data warehouse continues to grow. Therefore, a clear requirement for the data warehouse server is the scaleable high performance for data loading and ad hoc query processing as well as the ability to support large databases in a reliable, efficient fashion. Chapter 4 briefly touched on various design points to enable server specialization for scaleability in performance, throughput, user support, and very large database processing.

An important design decision when selecting a scaleable platform is the right balance between the number of processors in a multiprocessor system and the I/O bandwidth. Typically, when a hardware platform is sized to accommodate the data warehouse, this sizing is frequently focused on the number and size of disks. As important is a proper allocation of processors to efficiently handle all disk I/O operations. If this allocation is not balanced, an expensive data warehouse platform can rapidly become CPU bound. Indeed, since various processors have widely different performance ratings and thus can support a different number of disks per CPU, data warehouse designers should carefully analyze the disk I/O rates and processor capabilities to derive an efficient system configuration.

15.7.2   Data warehouse and DBMS specialization

To reiterate, the two important challenges facing the developers of data warehouses are the very large size of the databases and the need to process complex ad hoc queries in a relatively short time. Therefore, among the most important requirements for the data warehouse DBMS are performance, throughput, and scaleability.

The majority of established RDBMS vendors has implemented various degrees of parallelism in their respective products. Although any relational database management system—such as DB2, ORACLE, INFORMIX, or SYBASE—support parallel database processing, some of these products have been architected to better suit the specialized requirements of the data warehouse.

In addition to the "traditional" relational DBMSs, there are databases that have been optimized specifically for data warehousing, such as Red Brick Warehouse from Red Brick Systems. The DBMS features designed to satisfy the high-performance and scaleability requirements of a data warehouse are briefly discussed in Chap. 12. The next chapter looks into the DBMS characteristics for performance and scaleability from the data warehouse viewpoint.

15.7.3 Communications infrastructure

When planning for a data warehouse, one often neglected aspect of the architecture is the cost and efforts associated with bringing access to corporate data directly to the desktop. These costs and efforts could be significant, since many large organizations do not have a large user population with direct electronic access to information, and since a typical data warehouse user requires a relatively large bandwidth to interact with the data warehouse and retrieve a significant amount of data for the analysis. This may mean that communications networks have to be expanded, and new hardware and software may have to be purchased.

15.8 IMPLEMENTATION CONSIDERATIONS

A data warehouse cannot be simply bought and installed—its implementation requires the integration of many products within a data warehouse. The caveat here is that the necessary customization drives up the cost of implementing a data warehouse. To illustrate the complexity of the data warehouse implementation, let's discuss the logical steps needed to build a data warehouse:

- Collect and analyze business requirements.
- Create a data model and a physical design for the data warehouse.
- Define data sources.
- Choose the database technology and platform for the warehouse.
- Extract the data from the operational databases, transform it, clean it up, and load it into the database.
- Choose database access and reporting tools.
- Choose database connectivity software.
- Choose data analysis and presentation software.
- Update the data warehouse

When building the warehouse, these steps must be performed within the constraints of the current state of data warehouse technologies.

15.8.1   Access tools

Currently, no single tool on the market can handle all possible data warehouse access needs. Therefore, most implementations rely on a suite of tools and internally developed applications. The best way to choose this suite includes defining different types of access to the data and selecting the best tool for that kind of access. Examples of access types include:

- Simple tabular form reporting
- Ranking
- Multivariable analysis
- Time-series analysis
- Data visualization, graphing, charting, and pivoting
- Complex textual search
- Statistical analysis
- Artificial intelligence techniques for testing of hypothesis, trends discovery, definition, and validation of data clusters and segments
- Information mapping (i.e., mapping of spatial data in geographical information systems)
- Ad hoc user-specified queries
- Predefined repeatable queries
- Interactive drill-down reporting and analysis
- Complex queries with multitable joins, multilevel subqueries, and sophisticated search criteria

In addition, certain business requirements often exceed existing tool capabilities and may require building sophisticated applications to retrieve and analyze warehouse data. These applications often take the form of custom-developed screens and reports that retrieve frequently used data and format it in a predefined standardized way. This approach may be very useful for those data warehouse users who are not yet comfortable with ad hoc queries.

There are a number of query tools on the market today. Many of these tools are designed to easily compose and execute ad hoc queries and build customized reports with little knowledge of the underlying database technology, SQL, or even the data model (i.e., Impromptu from Cognos, Business Objects, etc.), while others (e.g., Andyne's GQL) provide relatively low level capabilities for an expert user to develop complex ad hoc queries in a fashion similar to developing SQL queries for relational databases. Business requirements that exceed the capabilities of ad hoc query and reporting tools are fulfilled by different classes of tools—OLAP and data mining tools. The technology behind these tools is discussed in the next chapter.

15.8.2   Data extraction, cleanup, transformation, and migration

As a component of the data warehouse architecture, proper attention must be given to data extraction, which represents a critical success factor for a data warehouse architecture. Specifically, when implementing data warehouse, several selection criteria that affect the ability to transform, consolidate, integrate, and repair the data should be considered:

- The ability to identify data in the data source environments that can be read by the conversion tool is important. This additional step may affect the timeliness of data delivery to the warehouse.

- Support for flat files, indexed files (e.g., VSAM) and legacy DBMSs (e.g., IMS and CA-IDMS) is critical, since the bulk of corporate data is still maintained in data stores of this type.

- The capability to merge data from multiple data stores is required in many installations. Using data replication technologies (see Chap. 11) helps—a data-change capture facility provides the functionality of reading log data to obtain only the changed data to be transferred. This reduces the amount of data that must be loaded into the data warehouse for periodic updating of the data warehouse.

- The specification interface to indicate the data to be extracted and the conversion criteria is important.

- The ability to read information from data dictionaries or import information from repository products is desired. This can reduce the amount of specification effort required.

- The code generated by the tool should be completely maintained from within the development environment.

- Selective data extraction of both data elements and records enables users to extract only the required data.

- A field-level data examination for the transformation of data into information is needed. For example, a user-exit feature is important for users who may need to perform more sophisticated operations on the data than can be achieved using the facilities provided with the tool.

- The ability to perform data-type and character-set translation is a requirement when moving data between incompatible systems.

- The capability to create summarization, aggregation, and derivation records and fields is very important.

- The data warehouse database management system should be able to perform the load directly from the tool, using the native API available with the RDBMS; alternatively, the system should support the capability to create a flat file and then use the load utility provided by the RDBMS.

- Vendor stability and support for the product are items that must be carefully evaluated.

Vendor solutions

Some vendors have emerged that are more focused on fulfilling requirements pertaining to data warehouse implementations as opposed to simply moving data between hardware platforms.

The extraction tools described in the following illustrate three separate approaches to the warehousing extraction function. Prism markets a primarily model-based approach, while Information Builders markets a gateway approach. SAS products could handle all the warehouse functions, including extraction. Other extraction tools are Evolutionary Technology's Extract Tool suite and Carleton's Passport gateway.

Prism Solutions. Prism Warehouse Manager maps source data to a target database management system to be used as a warehouse. Warehouse Manager generates code to extract and integrate data, create and manage metadata, and build a subject-oriented, historical base. The standard conversions, key changes, structural changes, and condensations needed to transform operational data into data warehouse information are automatically created. Prism Warehouse Manager can extract data from multiple source environments, including DB2, IDMS, IMS, VSAM, RMS, and sequential files under UNIX or MVS. Target databases include ORACLE, SYBASE, and INFORMIX. Prism Solutions has strategic relationships with Pyramid and Informix.

Carleton's Passport. Passport is positioned in the data extract and transformation niche of data warehousing. The product currently consists of two components. The first, which is mainframe based, collects the file/record/table layouts for the required inputs and outputs and converts them to the Passport Data Language (PDL). The second component is workstation-based and is used to create the metadata directory from which it builds the COBOL programs to actually create the extracts. The user must transfer the PDL file from the mainframe to a location accessible by Passport. The metadata directory is stored in a relational database, currently DB2/2 with others coming soon. The product itself runs on Windows and OS/2. The Windows version shows a graphical representation of the workflow that operates using the standard expand, collapse, drill-down, etc., metaphor. Carleton's Passport can produce multiple output files from a single execution of an extract program. Carleton is partnering with Sybase on the integration of Passport with SYBASE Open Client and Open Server.

Information Builders Inc. The EDA/SQL family of products provides SQL access to and a uniform relational view of relational and nonrelational data residing in over 60 different databases on 35 different platforms. EDA/SQL implements a client/server model that is optimized for higher performance. EDA/SQL supports copy management, data quality management, data replication capabilities, and standards support for both ODBC and the X/Open CLI. IBI's product is the component of almost every systems supplier's legacy data access strategy, including Amdahl, IBM, Digital Equipment, HP, and Bull, as well as many database and tool vendors.

SAS Institute Inc. SAS begins with the premise that most mission-critical data still resides in the data center and offers its traditional SAS System tools as a means to serve all data warehousing functions. Its data repository function can act to build the informational database. SAS Data Access Engines serve as extraction tools to combine common variables, transform data representation forms for consistency, consolidate redundant data, and use business rules to produce computed values in the warehouse. SAS views serve the internetworking and refresh roles, and SAS's reporting, graphing, and decision support products act as the front end. In addition to interacting with SAS System databases, SAS engines can work with hierarchical and relational databases and sequential files.

15.8.3 Data placement strategies

As a data warehouse grows, there are at least two options for data placement. One is to put some of the data in the data warehouse into another storage media, e.g., WORM, RAID, or photo-optical technology. The data selected for transport to the alternate storage media is detailed and older and there is less demand for it. The bulk storage can be handled either by the data warehouse server or another server used exclusively for handling the bulk storage media.

The second option is to distribute the data in the data warehouse across multiple servers. Some criteria must be established for dividing it over the servers—by geography, organization unit, time, function, etc. Another factor in determining how data should be divided among multiple data warehouse servers is the pattern of usage, such as what data is accessed and how much data is accessed, and any joins, sorts, or other processing that occurs after the data is accessed. However the data is divided, a single source of metadata across the entire organization is required. Hence, this configuration requires both corporate-wide metadata and the metadata managed for any given server.

Data replication

Where most users require only a small subset of the corporate data, using data replication or data movers to place only the data that is relevant to a particular workgroup in a localized database can be a more affordable solution. In many cases, often only a small portion of the data a company collects will be relevant. Many companies use data replication servers to copy their most-needed data to a separate database where decision support applications can access it. Replication technology creates copies of databases on a periodic basis, so that data entry and data analysis can be performed separately. Thus, end users' ad hoc queries and analytical processing are prevented from competing with operational applications for server resources.

Database gateways

Aside from the high cost of development, many data warehouse solutions require the use of a database gateway. While traditional gateway technology provides LAN users with the ability to easily access small amounts of mainframe data, it is not optimized for moving large files. Networks can be slowed by multiple concurrent user requests for similar data through a gateway. Because gateway queries are not predictable, the DBMS cannot be tuned for gateway access. Gateway access for decision support will often compete with production applications for resources.

15.8.4 Metadata

A frequently occurring problem in data warehousing is the problem of communicating to the end user what information resides in the data warehouse and how it can be accessed. The key to providing users and applications with a road map to the information stored in the warehouse is the metadata. It can define all data elements and their attributes, data sources and timing, and the rules that govern data use and data transformations. Metadata needs to be collected as the warehouse is designed and built. Since metadata describes the information in the warehouse from multiple viewpoints (input, sources, transformation, access, etc.), it is imperative that the same metadata or its *consistent* replicas are available to all tools selected for the warehouse implementation, thus enforcing the integrity and accuracy of the warehouse information. The metadata also has to be available to all warehouse users in order to guide them as they use the warehouse. Even though there are a number of tools available to help users understand and use the warehouse, these tools need to be carefully evaluated before any purchasing decision is made. In other words, a well-thought-through strategy for collecting, maintaining, and distributing metadata is needed for a successful data warehouse implementation.

An interesting approach to metadata repository management is offered by Prism's Directory Manager. This product is designed to integrate and manage all metadata definitions throughout the warehouse environment. The Directory Manager can:

- Import business models from CASE tools (Bachman, ADW, IEF, and any other CDIF-compliant CASE tools)

- Import metadata definitions from the Prism Warehouse Manager (the transformation and extraction component of the Prism product suite)

- Export metadata into catalogs/dictionaries/directories of many DSS access tools

- Create flexible customized views based on end-user requirements using graphical front-end application

In other words, Prism Directory Manager appears to be able to solve the problem of creating and managing a unified metadata repository to support the entire data warehousing environment.

15.8.5   User sophistication levels

Data warehousing is a relatively new phenomenon, and a certain degree of sophistication is required on the end user's part to effectively use the warehouse. A typical organization maintains different levels of computer literacy and sophistication within the user community. The users can be classified based on their skill levels in accessing the warehouse. For example, let's define three classes of users:

- *Casual users.*   These users are most comfortable retrieving information from the warehouse in predefined formats and running preexisting queries and reports. These users do not need tools that allow for sophisticated ad hoc query building and execution.

- *Power users.*   In their daily activities, these users typically combine predefined queries with some relatively simple ad hoc queries that they create themselves. These users can also engage in drill-down queries to further analyze the results of simple queries and reports. These users need access tools that combine the simplicity of predefined queries and reports with a certain degree of flexibility.

■ *Experts.* These users tend to create their own complex queries and perform a sophisticated analysis on the information they retrieve from the warehouse. These users know the data, the tools, and the database well enough to demand tools that allow for maximum flexibility and adaptability.

Therefore, when implementing the warehouse, an analysis of the end-user requirements has to be coupled with an evaluation of the user sophistication levels, and the selected end-user tools have to satisfy both the business needs and the capabilities and preferences of the end users. Other considerations can be found in App. D.

15.8.6 Integrated solutions

Most data warehouse vendor solutions consist of a relational database used for the data warehouse, data warehouse management software, and data access and reporting tools, along with the necessary database connectivity software. What follows is a brief look at some of the solutions available on the market today.

A number of vendors participate in data warehousing by providing a suite of services and products that go beyond one particular component of the data warehouse. These vendors tend to establish internal centers of data warehousing expertise and often engage in partnership relationships with specialized independent software vendors for the products and expertise.

Digital Equipment Corp.

Digital has combined the data modeling, extraction, and cleansing capabilities of Prism Warehouse Manager with the copy management and data replication capabilities of Digital's ACCESSWORKS family of database access servers in providing users with the ability to build and use information warehouses. ACCESSWORKS runs on the Digital OpenVMS platform and provides the necessary data access back-end gateways and front-end connections.

Hewlett-Packard

Hewlett-Packard's client/server-based HP OpenWarehouse comprises multiple components including a data management architecture, the HP-UX operating system, HP 9000 computers, warehouse management tools, an Allbase/SQL relational database, and the HP Information Access query tool. HP offers single-source support for the full HP OpenWarehouse solution. This allows customers to choose components that best suit their needs, without having to work with multiple vendors for support. HP also provides a suite of consulting services for designing and implementing a data warehouse. HP OpenWarehouse integrates a number of third-party products, including Red Brick Warehouse from Red Brick Systems, Prism Warehouse Manager from Prism Solutions, EXTRACT from Evolutionary Technologies, Enterprise Data Access/SQL from IBI, and Open Development Environment from Open Environment Corp.

IBM

The IBM Information Warehouse framework consists of an architecture; data management tools; OS/2, AIX, and MVS operating systems; hardware platforms including mainframes and servers; and a relational DBMS (DB2). Other components of the IBM Information Warehouse family include:

- DataGuide/2—provides a catalog of shared data and information objects which can be listed and described in everyday business terms, and searched with keywords. Once the information is identified, DataGuide/2 can start applications to retrieve and process it.

- DataPropagator—automates data replication across an enterprise, using a graphical user interface (see discussion on DataPropagator in Chap. 11).

- DataRefresher—provides copy management capability for moving large amounts of data from a broad range of data sources.

- DataHub—manages complex client/server relational database environments and provides the base for IBM's family of copy management and replication tools.

- Application System (AS)—provides a set of general data access, query, reporting, and charting facilities and specialized tools for planning or modeling, project management, linear programming, document processing, and application development.

- Personal Application System/2 (PAS/2)—decision support software designed for Windows and OS/2 PCs. The user can select from a list of decision support objects that can manage and analyze data, produce reports and charts of the data, and create procedures to automate regular work. Optionally includes business planning, project management, statistical analysis, and application development.

- Query Management Facility (QMF)—a host-based facility that provides query, reporting, and graphics functions from menu options.

- IBM FlowMark—workflow management product designed to help database administrators document their system management tasks and automatically execute these tasks.

Sequent

Sequent Computer Systems Inc.'s DecisionPoint Program is a decision support program for the delivery of data warehouses dedicated to on-line complex query processing (OLCP). The program combines Sequent symmetric multiprocessing (SMP) architecture with a variety of client/server products and services, including UNIX-based Sequent Symmetry 2000 Series, Red Brick Warehouse for Red Brick Systems, and ClearAccess Query Tool from ClearAccess Corp. DecisionPoint is targeted to information service organizations looking to meet the data access demands of knowledge workers and executives. ClearAccess Query Tool provides DecisionPoint users with a transparent window into the Red Brick Warehouse. Using a graphical interface, users query the data warehouse by pointing and clicking on the warehouse data items they want to analyze. Query results are placed on the program's clipboard for pasting onto a variety of desktop applications, or they can be saved to a disk.

Clearly, this is not a complete list. Database vendors are all positioning themselves as providers of integrated data warehouse services and products. Oracle, Sybase, and Informix all offer integrated data warehouse solutions that are based on recent acquisitions, development of in-house consulting expertise, and strategic partner alliances.

15.9 BENEFITS OF DATA WAREHOUSING

Data Warehouse usage includes:

- Locating the right information
- Presentation of information (reports, graphs)
- Testing of the hypothesis
- Discovery of information
- Sharing the analysis

Using better tools to access data can reduce outdated, historical data. Likewise, users can obtain the data when they need it most, often during business-decision processes, not on a schedule predetermined months earlier by the IS department and computer operations staff.

Data warehouse architecture can enhance overall availability of business intelligence data, as well as increase the effectiveness and timeliness of business decisions.

15.9.1   Tangible benefits

Successfully implemented data warehouse can realize some significant tangible benefits. For example, conservatively assuming an improvement in out-of-stock conditions in the retailing business that leads to a 1 percent increase in sales can mean a sizeable cost benefit (i.e., even for a small retail business with $200 million in annual sales, a conservative 1 percent improvement in sales can yield additional annual revenue of $2 million or more). In fact, several retail enterprises claim that data warehouse implementations have improved out-of-stock conditions to the extent that sales increases range from 5 to 20 percent. This benefit is in addition to retaining customers who might not have returned if, due to out-of-stock problems, they had to do business with other retailers. Other examples of tangible benefits of a data warehouse initiative include the following.

- There are improved product inventory turns.

- Costs of product introduction are decreased, with improved selection of target markets.

- More cost-effective decision making is enabled by separating (ad hoc) query processing from running against operational databases.

- Better business intelligence is enabled by increased quality and flexibility of market analysis available through multilevel data structures which may range from detailed to highly summarized. For example, determining the effectiveness of marketing programs allows the elimination of weaker programs and enhancement of stronger ones.

- Enhanced asset and liability management means a data warehouse can provide a "big" picture of enterprise-wide purchasing and inventory patterns and can indicate otherwise unseen credit exposure and opportunities for cost savings.

15.9.2   Intangible benefits

In addition to the tangible benefits just outlined, a data warehouse provides a number of intangible benefits. Although they are more difficult to quantify, intangible benefits should also be considered when planning for the data warehouse. Examples of intangible benefits include:

- Improved productivity, by keeping all required data in a single location and eliminating the rekeying of data.

- Reduced redundant processing, support, and software to support overlapping decision support applications.

- Enhanced customer relations through improved knowledge of individual requirements and trends, through customization, improved communications, and tailored product offerings.

- Enablement for business process reengineering—data warehouse can provide useful insights into the work processes themselves, resulting in developing breakthrough ideas for the reengineering of those processes.

Chapter

16

Technology and Advanced Applications of Data Warehousing

The previous chapter discussed general concepts of data warehousing, with the focus on the architecture, components, technical, design, and implementation issues. However, a number of key technology aspects of data warehousing have been discussed too briefly. These technologies are extremely important to understanding and successfully implementing a data warehouse. Therefore, although the breadth of these topics and the wealth of the material that should be rightfully included here are clearly beyond the scope of this book, this chapter attempts to provide a closer look at the relational and specialized database technology for data warehouse, on-line analytical processing (OLAP), and data mining tools. In addition, this discusses a number of vendor products, their features, and directions.

16.1 RELATIONAL DATABASE TECHNOLOGY FOR DATA WAREHOUSING

Although the basics of parallel database technology were already discussed in Chap. 12, this section attempts not to repeat that discussion, but rather to provide a data warehouse-centric viewpoint on the technology and its implications.

The organizations that embarked on data warehousing development deal with ever-increasing amounts of data. Generally speaking, the size of a data warehouse rapidly approaches the point where the search for better performance and scaleability becomes a real necessity. This search is pursuing two goals:

- *Speed-up*—the ability to execute the same request on the same amount of data in less time
- *Scale-up*—the ability to obtain the same performance on the same request as the database size increases

An additional and important goal is to achieve *linear* speed-up and scale-up—doubling the number of processors cuts the response time in half (linear speed-up) or provides the same performance on twice as much data (linear scale-up).

These goals of linear performance and scaleability can be satisfied by parallel hardware architectures (discussed in Chap. 4), parallel operating systems, and parallel database management systems.

Parallel hardware architectures are based on multiprocessor systems designed as a shared-memory model (symmetric multiprocessor or SMP), shared-disk model, or distributed-memory model (massively parallel processor or MPP, and *clusters* of uniprocessors and/or SMPs).

16.1.1 Types of parallelism

Database vendors started to take advantage of parallel hardware architectures by implementing multiserver and multithreaded systems designed to handle a large number of client requests efficiently. This approach naturally resulted in *interquery parallelism,* where different server threads (or processes) handle multiple requests at the same time. Interquery parallelism has been successfully implemented on SMP systems, where it increased the throughput and allowed the support of more concurrent users. However, without changing the way the DBMS processed queries, interquery parallelism was limited— even though multiple queries were processed concurrently, each query was still processed serially, by a single process or a thread. In other words, if a query consists of a table scan, join, and sort operations, then this would be the order in which these operations execute, and each operation would have to finish before the next one could begin.

To improve the situation, many DBMS vendors developed versions of their products that utilized *intraquery parallelism.* This form of parallelism decomposes the serial SQL query into lower-level operations such as scan, join, sort, and aggregation (see Fig. 16.1, Case 1). These lower-level operations then are executed concurrently, in parallel. By dedicating multiple resources to the processing, a single request can be processed faster. Operations other than queries—INSERTs, DELETEs, UPDATEs, index creation, database load, backup, and recovery—can also be parallelized and thus speeded up.

Parallel execution of the tasks within SQL statements (intraquery parallelism) can be done in two ways:

- *Horizontal parallelism* means that the database is partitioned across multiple disks, and parallel processing occurs within a specific task (i.e., table scan) that is performed concurrently on different processors against different sets of data (Fig. 16.1, Case 2).

- *Vertical parallelism* occurs among different tasks—all component query operations (i.e., scan, join, sort) are executed in parallel in a pipelined fashion. In other words, an output from one task (e.g., scan) becomes an input into another task (e.g., join) as soon as records become available (see Fig. 16.1, Case 3).

A truly parallel DBMS should support both horizontal and vertical types of parallelism concurrently (see Fig. 16.1, Case 4).

16.1.2 Data partitioning

Data partitioning is a key requirement for effective parallel execution of database operations. It spreads data from database tables across multiple disks so that I/O operations such as read and write can be performed in parallel. Partitioning can be done randomly or intelligently.

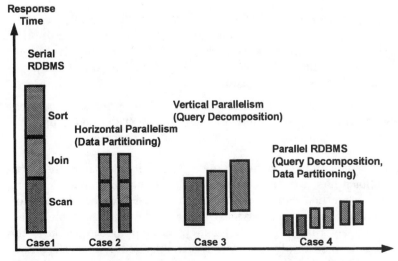

Figure 16.1 Types of DBMS parallelism.

Random partitioning includes random data striping across multiple disks on a single server. Another option for random partitioning is round-robin partitioning, where each new record is placed on the next disk assigned to the database. Although random partitioning can be effective in reducing I/O contention for multiple concurrent requests against the same table, its effectiveness can be significantly reduced depending on data distribution and query selectivity—since DBMS does not know where each record (row) resides, it is possible that all partitions may have to be fully scanned in order to satisfy a query.

Intelligent partitioning assumes that DBMS knows where a specific record is located and does not waste time searching for it across all disks. Intelligent partitioning allows a DBMS to fully exploit parallel architectures and also enables higher availability. For example, not only can the DBMS avoid reading certain disk segments where the selection criteria are not met, intelligent partitioning allows query processing even if a disk partition is unavailable, as long as the DBMS determined that the partition data is not required to satisfy the query. Intelligent partitioning techniques include:

- *Hash partitioning.*   A hash algorithm is used to calculate the partition number (hash value) based on the value of the partitioning key for each row.

- *Key range partitioning.*   Rows are placed and located in the partitions based on the value of the partitioning key (e.g., all rows with the key value from A to K are in Partition 1, L to T are in Partition 2, etc.).

- *Schema partitioning.*   This is an option not to partition a table across disks; instead, an entire table is placed on one disk, another table is placed on different disk, etc. This is useful for small reference tables that are more effectively used when replicated in each partition rather than spread across partitions.

- *User-defined partitioning.*   This is a partitioning method that allows a table to be partitioned based on a user-defined expression (i.e., use state codes to place rows in one of 50 partitions).

Since a table can be partitioned in only one way at a time, the partitioning choice has to satisfy database access requirements—a wrong partitioning method can create "hot spots" which defeat the advantages of parallel hardware and software. For example, if a table is partitioned by key ranges and accessed by a nonpartitioned key, the processing may be totally ineffective and may result in performance characteristics that are worse than that of a serial database.

16.2   DATABASE ARCHITECTURES FOR PARALLEL PROCESSING

Software parallelism is a natural follow-on to hardware parallel architectures. In addition to the parallel operating system, an adaptable parallel database software architecture is required to take advantage of parallelism in shared-memory and distributed-memory environments. In fact, the parallel database architecture is what determines the ultimate scaleability of the solution.

16.2.1   Shared-memory architectures

In shared-memory SMP systems, the DBMS assumes that the multiple database components executing SQL statements communicate with each other by exchanging messages and data via the shared memory. All processors have access to all data, which is partitioned across local disks (see Fig. 16.2).

This DBMS architecture is optimized for a single tightly coupled system—an SMP platform. It is relatively easy to develop, it uses a familiar programming paradigm, and it is not as sensitive to data-partitioning schema as a shared-nothing design. Unfortunately, the scaleability of shared-memory architectures is limited. SMP systems do not demonstrate linear growth in direct proportion to the number of processors. Depending on the processor and system bus speed, the

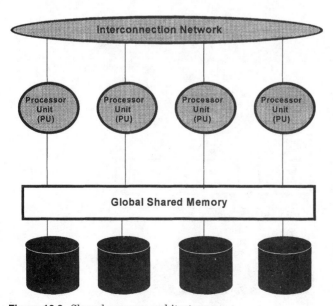

Figure 16.2 Shared-memory architecture.

SMP throughput does not increase (and can even decrease, due to a local cache coherency problem) when the number of processors exceeds some (machine-specific) number.

16.2.2   Shared-disk architecture

In a shared-disk system the DBMS assumes that all processors have access to all disks. They may or may not share memory. The shared-memory model (i.e., SMP) is shown in Fig. 16.2, and the distributed-memory model is illustrated in Fig. 16.3. In the latter case, the processors have to communicate with each other via messages and data transmitted over the interconnection network. In addition, an extra software layer—a distributed cache manager—is required to globally manage cache concurrency among processors. The shared-disk distributed-memory design eliminates the memory access bottleneck typical of large SMP systems and helps reduce DBMS dependency on data partitioning. However, because of the overhead of sharing database locks while maintaining cache concurrency, it also introduces a potential limitation on the overall system scaleability for distributed-memory systems.

16.2.3   Shared-nothing architecture

In a shared-nothing distributed-memory environment (Fig. 16.4) the data is partitioned across all disks, and the DBMS parallelizes the

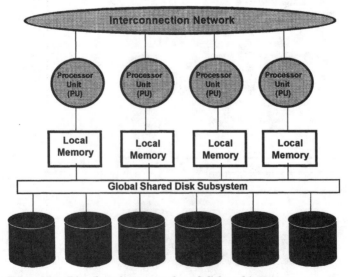

Figure 16.3 Distributed-memory shared-disk architecture.

execution of a SQL query across multiple processors. Each processor has its own memory and disk, and communicates with other processors by exchanging messages and data over the interconnection network. This architecture is optimized specifically for the MPP and cluster systems.

The shared-nothing architectures offer near-linear scaleability. Theoretically, the number of processor nodes is limited only by the hardware platform limitations (and budgetary constraints), and each node itself can be a powerful SMP system.

However, the shared-nothing distributed-memory architecture is the most difficult to implement. There are a number of reasons for that difficulty—it requires a new programming paradigm, new operating system or parallel extensions to an existing one, new compilers, new or enhanced programming languages, etc. (see Chap. 4 for more details). From a parallel DBMS viewpoint, however, there are a number of issues and requirements unique to the shared-nothing architecture. Among these requirements are:

- *Support for function shipping.*   Decomposed SQL statements have to be routed to and executed on the processor that has the needed data in order to drastically reduce the interprocessor communications.

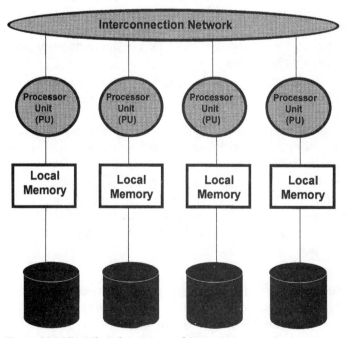

Figure 16.4 Distributed-memory architecture.

- *Parallel join strategies.* A join between two tables is called a *co-located* join when the rows to be joined reside on the same partition. However, if the rows of the two tables reside on different partitions (e.g., are controlled by different processors), a parallel DBMS has to be able to select an effective strategy to perform the join with minimum interprocessor communication traffic. Choices include *re-directed* joins, where the rows of one table are sent to the node where the corresponding rows of another table reside or the matching rows of both tables are sent to a third node to be joined; *repartitioned* joins, where the rows of both tables are repartitioned on the join column and then redirected to enable colocated joins; and *broadcast* joins, where the entire table is sent to all nodes. The data shipment from one processor node to another is an implied requirement for the distributed-memory parallel DBMS.

- *Support for data repartitioning.* When one of the processors or a local disk fails, the DBMS must be able to repartition the database across remaining processor nodes automatically.

- *Query compilation.* This is the process of selecting an access path throughout the database. The shorter the path, the quicker is the query. The DBMS optimizer uses statistical information about data partitioning, data values, cardinality, indexes, etc., stored in the database catalog to make optimal choices. In a distributed-memory environment, each processor node contains its own database partition and, thus, may have its own database catalog. The DBMS should be able to compile the query on any processor node using both the local and the global catalog.

- *Support for database transactions.* Since a parallel distributed-memory DBMS is, in fact, a distributed DBMS, it should comply with many of the rules for a distributed DBMS (see Chap. 10 for C. J. Date's 12 Rules of Distributed DBMS). For example, a global lock manager and global deadlock detection mechanism are required to support database transactions in a distributed-memory system.

- *Support for the single system image of the database environment.* A parallel DBMS has to be managed as a single logical entity and must present a consistent view to database administrators and developers regardless of how many processor nodes it is supporting.

16.2.4 Combined architecture

Interserver parallelism of distributed-memory architecture means that each query is parallelized across multiple servers (e.g., processor nodes of the MPP or clusters), while intraserver parallelism of the shared-memory architecture means that a query is parallelized within the server (i.e., across multiple processors of an SMP). Clearly, each approach has its own advantages and disadvantages.

A true, flexible, constraint-free architecture should take full advantage of its operating environment and, at the same time, reduce the disadvantages associated with a particular approach. In other words, a combined hardware architecture could be a cluster of SMP nodes (see Chap. 4 for details). Then, a combined parallel DBMS architecture should support interserver parallelism of distributed-memory MPPs and clusters and intraserver parallelism of SMP nodes.

16.3 PARALLEL RDBMS FEATURES

Data warehouse development requires a good understanding of all architectural components, including the data warehouse DBMS platform. Understanding the basic architecture of warehouse DBMS is the first step in evaluating and selecting a product. Understanding the specific features of the product and the way these features are implemented helps make an intelligent decision when choosing a particular DBMS. First, let's look at what state-of-the-art parallel features the developers and users of the warehouse should demand from the DBMS vendors:

Scope and techniques of parallel DBMS operations. This includes queries (SQL statements based on the SELECT verb), other Data Manipulation Language (DML) operations such as INSERT, DELETE, and UPDATE, and DBMS utilities. In queries, many atomic operations (i.e., scan, sort, join) can all be parallelized both horizontally and vertically. Existing DBMS products perform these parallel operations differently—some can parallelize a table scan but not an index scan; some support vertical parallelism but limit the pipeline to a small number of concurrent tasks. Clearly, the fewer the limitations on parallelism, the better the product can leverage the parallel hardware platform.

Similarly, parallel execution of INSERT, DELETE, and UPDATE operations is extremely valuable not only for OLTP, but also for query processing—indeed, when a DBMS creates a temporary table to sort or join large tables, an INSERT operation is involved to populate the table. These operations require locking strategies that are optimized for parallel execution. There, a DBMS that uses multiple log files, for example, is better positioned to reduce an update bottleneck. Finally, a DBMS that supports parallel database load, backup, reorganization, and recovery is much better positioned to handle very large databases (VLDB).

Optimizer implementation. A cost-based optimizer that is cognizant of the parallel environment and data partitioning will produce an execution plan that is the most efficient and results in the shortest execution path. The optimizer has to be able to recognize the parallel environment it operates in and automatically invoke strategies best suited for a given situation. For example, different approaches should be taken when a query is executed in a shared-nothing environment, where the main goal is to minimize interprocessor communications, compared with a shared-memory SMP system, where the interprocessor communications are done via a shared memory and are not nearly as expensive.

Application transparency. Basically, an application developer should not be aware that the database application is designed for a parallel DBMS environment. At a minimum, a parallel DBMS should not force a developer to modify an existing application to take advantage of the parallel system. That should be true not only for queries, but also for DBMS server features such as stored procedures, triggers, and rules.

DBMS needs to be aware of the parallel environment. This is a complementary requirement to the application transparency. Such an awareness allows the DBMS server to take full advantage of the existing facilities on a very low level.

DBMS management tools. These tools should help configure, tune, administer, and monitor a parallel DBMS as effectively as if it was a serial DBMS. Because, frequently, a given data-partitioning schema results in unbalanced "hot spot" data partitioning, a tool that allows a DBA to repartition the database dynamically could prove invaluable.

Price/performance. From a performance and scaleability viewpoint, a parallel DBMS should demonstrate near linear speed-up and scale-up. The key, however, is to obtain these characteristics at reasonable costs. Industry-standard benchmarks can be used to measure price and performance of a parallel DBMS. Transaction Processing Council's TPC-C measures price and performance of complex transactions, while TPC-D is designed to measure price and performance of decision support queries.

16.4 ALTERNATIVE TECHNOLOGIES

In addition to parallel database technology, a number of vendors are working on other solutions for improving performance in data warehousing environments. These include:

- Advanced database indexing products
- Specialized relational database management systems designed specifically for data warehousing
- Multidimensional databases

The multidimensional databases and specialized relational databases are covered in the sections of this chapter that discuss on-line analytical processing. This section will briefly describe new indexing techniques used to speed up relational queries.

16.4.1   Advanced indexing techniques

A new approach to increasing performance of a relational DBMS is to use innovative indexing techniques to provide rapid direct access to data. SYBASE IQ is an example of a product that uses innovative bit-wise index structure of the data stored in the SYBASE DBMS. In fact, the SYBASE IQ is not a database, but a complementary add-on product that accepts queries and attempts to resolve them through its proprietary bit-mapped index structures. Those queries that cannot be resolved through the index are sent directly to the SYBASE SQL Server for processing.

Products like this promise increased performance without deploying expensive parallel hardware systems. However, the close relationship between the database data and its index structure may be an obstacle to OLTP processing (indexes need to be rebuilt when the underlying data is changed). This nonupdateable nature of the index has a negative effect on scaleability. Also, while the bit-mapped indexes significantly accelerate data access, they are best suited for low cardinality data and tend to lose their effectiveness for high cardinality data. It is also unclear how such a technique can handle new data types such as image, voice, and multimedia.

16.5   PARALLEL DBMS VENDORS

This section provides an overview of several vendors' strategies and products for parallel database processing.

16.5.1   Oracle

Oracle supports parallel database processing with its add-on Parallel Server Option (PSO) and Parallel Query Option (PQO). The PSO was originally designed for loosely coupled clusters of shared-disk systems (i.e., VAXclusters), and it enables multiple instances of ORACLE running on multiple computers to share the same data using a distributed cache manager. The PQO is optimized to run on SMPs or MPPs in conjunction with the PSO, and is supported on all ORACLE platforms except NetWare, OS/2, and Windows NT—all these are targeted for the future.

With the acquisition of IRI Software, Oracle now is positioned to offer a comprehensive data warehousing solution that exceeds its parallel DBMS offering.

Architecture

The fundamental component of Oracle's design is the notion of the virtual shared-disk capability. Oracle considers this point a key that makes almost every hardware platform commercially viable. The Parallel Query Option uses a shared-disk architecture which assumes that each processor node has access to all disks. The Parallel Server Option is required on any distributed-memory platform (MPP or clusters), where the shared-disk software is provided by the operating system vendor. PQO supports parallel execution of queries that include at least one full table scan, user-defined functions, and subselects statements. PQO supports parallel operations such as index build, database load, backup, and recovery. The users have full access to all database functionality in parallel environments.

Data partitioning

Oracle has chosen the approach that allows its customers to move into a parallel environment without having to deal with the administrative overhead of partitioning data. ORACLE (version 7) supports random striping of data across multiple disks. Because of their random nature, partitions cannot be backed up and recover at the partition level, and ORACLE cannot skip partitions that don't contain relevant data. ORACLE supports dynamic data repartitioning, which is done in memory using key range, hash, or round-robin methods to facilitate joins where data spans nodes.

Parallel operations

ORACLE's approach to parallelization of query processing is external and manual. ORACLE executes all queries serially unless two conditions are met. First, the optimizer must include at least one full table scan. Second, the DBMS must be instructed to parallelize operations. The instructions can be specified as a start-up parameter for the ORACLE instance, as a parallelization factor assigned by a DBA at a table level, or as optimizer hints that are submitted with each individual query.

The ORACLE PQO query coordinator breaks the query into subqueries and passes these to the corresponding pool server processes. The server processes work in parallel and return their results to the coordinator for any postprocessing. The ORACLE PQO can parallelize most SQL operations, including joins, scans, sorts, aggregates, and groupings. In addition, ORACLE can parallelize the creation of indexes, database load, backup, and recovery.

When executing in parallel, PQO supports both horizontal and vertical parallelism. Vertical parallelism is currently limited to two levels—

in a query that contains scan, join, and sort, only two operations can be pipelined.

16.5.2 Informix

Informix Software has partnered with Sequent Computers in reengineering its DBMS engine to build in full parallelism from the ground up (Sequent had an exclusive six-month window before the product was ported to other platforms). INFORMIX runs on a variety of UNIX platforms, and its version 7 of the product is available on Windows NT. INFORMIX OnLine version 8 MPP platforms include IBM SP2, AT&T 3600, and ICL Goldrush, with Sequent, Siemens/Pyramid, and others to follow.

Architecture

Informix developed its Dynamic Scaleable Architecture (DSA) to support shared-memory, shared-disk, and shared-nothing models. Parallel query processing implementation was first available for the shared-memory SMP systems, with other parallel architecture support built into subsequent releases. INFORMIX OnLine version 7 is a shared-memory implementation that supports parallel query processing and intelligent data partitioning. The next release of the product (INFORMIX 8) allows a partitioned table to be distributed across nodes on the network and is designed to support MPP and clusters. The Extended Parallel Server (XPS) option of INFORMIX 8 supports distributed-memory architectures and can support shared-disk environments to handle node failures.

Data partitioning

INFORMIX OnLine 7 supports round-robin, schema, hash, key ranges, and user-defined partitioning methods. Both data and indexes can be partitioned. The number of partitions is user-defined. Repartition is done dynamically, on-line, and in parallel.

Parallel operations

All database functionality is preserved in parallel versions of the product. INFORMIX OnLine 7 executes queries, INSERTs, and many utilities in parallel. XPS adds parallel UPDATEs and DELETEs. INFORMIX supports multiple physical logs on each processing node. Full parallel point-in-time recovery is available. The cost-based optimizer is fully aware of the parallel environments and generates parallel query execution plans.

Partnerships

Informix has established several strategic relationships that provide added functionality to its product line:

- *Data modeling*—Through its relationship with Prism Solutions.
- *Management tools for data extract, transformation, and maintenance*—Prism and Carleton Corp.
- *Open systems*—Through relationships with all the hardware vendors that offer scaleable, high-end, open systems hardware solutions.
- *Front-end and gateway access*—Like Oracle and Sybase, Informix has relationships with several vendors, including Business Objects, Inc., Clear Access/Fairfield Software, Gupta Technologies, Information Advantage, Inc., IBI, PowerSoft Corp., Trinzic Corp., and Uniface Corp.

Note. To enchance its functionality, Informix acquired Stanford Technology Group with its MetaCube OLAP tool, and Illustra with its support for complex data types and data access through the Web.

16.5.3 IBM

IBM's parallel client/server database product, DB2 Parallel Edition (DB2 PE), is a database product that is based on DB2/6000 server architecture. To date, DB2 PE is targeted only for IBM SP2 and clusters of RS/6000, all running AIX, although the company may decide to port the product to other platforms in the future. The first release of the product has not yet been optimized to support SMP systems, triggers, and BLOBs. The next version aims to close the gap between DB2 PE and functionality-rich DB2/6000 version 2 (see Chap. 12 for more details).

Architecture

DB2 PE is a shared-nothing architecture where all data is partitioned across processor nodes. All database operations and utilities are fully parallelized where possible. IBM internal and some customer benchmarks show that the product demonstrates excellent scaleability. Although DB2 PE can run on a LAN-based cluster of RS/6000, its design is optimized for high-performance SP2 with its very high speed internal interconnect. True to the shared-nothing architectural model, DB2 PE does not implement a virtual shared disk or a distributed lock manager, although the product can take advantage of shared memory when communicating across virtual nodes on SMP systems. Each DB2 PE instance has its own log, its own memory, and its own storage devices. This allows for easy customization—nodes can be added and deleted relatively quickly. Each node is aware of other nodes and how the data is partitioned.

Data partitioning

DB2 PE supports hash partitioning and *node groups* that allow a table to span multiple nodes. The DBA can choose to partition a table on a table-by-table basis depending on the application workload. The DBA can rebalance (repartition) data across nodes when nodes are added or deleted or to improve application access to the database. Rebalancing is done on-line. The master system catalog for each database is stored on one node and cached on every other node. Data definition statements are automatically routed to the master catalog node, and changes are cascaded to other nodes.

Parallel operations

Parallelism is built into the basic architecture. All database operations—query processing, INSERTs, DELETEs, UPDATEs, load, backup, recovery, index creation, table reorganization, etc.—are fully parallelized. Many database utility operations (i.e., load, backup, restore) are done at the partition level. DB2 PE breaks SQL statements into fragments for each node, executing the same low-level processing in a parallel environment that is possible on a single node. DB2 PE's cost-based optimizer is aware of the parallel environment, data partitioning, and the cost of internodal messaging. DB2 PE supports function shipping (preferred) and a variety of join strategies, including colocated, redirected, broadcast, and repartitioned joins.

16.5.4 Sybase

Sybase has implemented its parallel DBMS functionality in a product originally called Navigation Server (it is now called SYBASE MPP). It was jointly developed by Sybase and AT&T GIS (formerly NCR), and its first release was targeted for the AT&T 3400, 3500 (both SMP), and 3600 (MPP) platforms. AT&T had an exclusive six-month window before the product was ported to other platforms that include IBM SP2, Sun, and HP. Sybase has developed another product aimed at improving DBMS performance—SYBASE IQ (see a brief discussion in Sec. 16.4.1)—and now faces the challenge of rationalizing positions of both the SYBASE MPP and SYBASE IQ for data warehousing and VLDB processing.

Architecture

Navigation Server is designed to make multiple distributed SQL Servers look like a single server to the user. It is a shared-nothing system that partitions data across multiple SQL Servers and supports both function shipping and data repartitioning. Navigation Server is an Open Server application that operates on top of existing SQL Servers. In other words, the database engine itself (SQL Server) is not aware of the parallel environment—all the knowledge about the environment, data partitions, and parallel query execution is maintained by the Navigation Server software. Therefore, some server-based features, such as triggers or any cross-server integrity constraints, are difficult to use in this release of the product. This architecture also means that SQL Servers have to send data to a coordinator for the query if, for example, a SQL statement includes a join involving data that is not local to a given SQL Server. Moreover, the query is not decomposed for the parallel environment—the entire SQL statement has to be sent to the SQL Server.

Navigation Server performs a unique two-level optimization—SQL statements are always optimized on a global level by the Navigation Server, and ad hoc queries are also optimized by the individual SQL Servers, which allows SQL Servers to effectively use local indexes. Internal benchmarks and early customer experiences show that Navigation Server demonstrates near linear scaleability on shared-nothing AT&T 3600.

Navigation Server consists of specialized servers:

- Data Server—smallest executable unit of parallelism that consists of SQL Server, Split Server (performs joins across nodes), and Control Server (coordination of execution and communications). Precompiled parallel plans are translated into appropriate SQL statements in the form of stored procedures for each Data Server.

- DBA Server—handles optimization, DDL statements, security, and global system catalog.

- Administrative Server—a graphical user interface for managing Navigation Server.

In addition to these servers, the Navigation Server comes with the Configurator, a tool for the initial planning and ongoing management of the Navigation Server configuration and data partitioning based on database design, planned transactions, and performance and capacity requirements. To date, Sybase is the only vendor that offers automated user assistance in designing parallel databases.

Data partitioning

Navigation Server supports hash, key range, and schema partitioning. Indexes are partitioned to match their table partitioning. Each SQL Server maintains its own local indexes and statistics.

Parallel operations

All SQL statements and utilities are executed in parallel across SQL Servers, but, in the first release of the product, all processing at the SQL Server level remains serial. Therefore, Navigation Server supports horizontal parallelism, but the vertical parallelism support is limited to the capabilities of the SQL Server engine (a more robust vertical parallelism available with SYBASE System 11 internal parallel capabilities).

16.5.5   Other RDBMS products

The vendor products discussed here represent a significant part of the parallel DBMS market. However, this market is not limited to these products. In fact, there are several established vendors and products that have been developing parallel database solutions for a number of years. Let's look at two vendors: Teradata and Tandem.

AT&T Teradata

Teradata, introduced in 1983, initially ran only on specialized platforms, although AT&T has recently moved it to UNIX and this version runs on AT&T 3500 (an SMP machine). Teradata employs hardware components as part of its architecture and has been seen traditionally as a proprietary architecture, although it demonstrates very good scaleability. Its architecture is a mature, fully parallel shared-nothing architecture that resembles SYBASE Navigation Server but is enhanced by leveraging hardware design. Its main drawback is its high cost and lack of DBMS functionality useful in OLTP environments. Teradata has been successfully used for very large decision support systems. For example, Teradata supports a 2.7-TB data warehouse for optimizing inventory for a major retailer.

Tandem NonStop SQL/MP

This is the latest version of Tandem's NonStop SQL RDBMS. Introduced in 1987, NonStop SQL was optimized for high-performance OLTP applications and high availability—fault tolerance was always Tandem's trademark. This focus on high availability led to development of parallel database utilities that were fast and dynamic—the database stays available at all times. NonStop SQL/MP is closely tied to and runs on Tandem's proprietary NonStop operating kernel and Himalaya distributed-memory servers. Similar to Teradata, despite its proprietary nature, NonStop SQL/MP is a mature parallel DBMS product. It uses a shared-nothing architecture, supports key range partitioning on the primary key, and parallelizes queries, other DML functions, and utilities. Log files are also partitioned, so that the concurrency is high and the recovery is fully parallel. The optimizer is aware of the environment and can generate both the serial and parallel plan—it is designed to choose the lowest-cost option. Data can be repartitioned dynamically in memory to optimize join or to parallelize a previously nonpartitioned table. NonStop SQL/MP is a highly scaleable parallel RDBMS that is well suited both for decision support processing against large databases and high throughput OLTP. In fact, Tandem has published audited TPC-C benchmark results that demonstrated almost 100 percent linear scaleability in supporting a large number of concurrent users on the database size reaching 1.3 TB. The major weaknesses of NonStop SQL/MP include its lack of standards compliance (at the time of this writing, NonStop SQL conformed to SQL89, not SQL92) and the fact that it currently runs only on Tandem's proprietary Himalaya platforms.

16.5.6 Specialized database products

The two products described as follows represent software (Red Brick) and hardware (White Cross) approaches to specialized data warehouse solutions.

Red Brick Systems

Red Brick Warehouse is an example of a specialized multirelational approach to the multidimensional requirements of modern data warehousing. Red Brick offers a relational data warehouse product specialized for decision support. The product is designed for query-intensive environments. Red Brick Warehouse consists of three components:

- *Table Management Utility,* a high-performance load subsystem that loads and indexes operational data

- *Database server* that stores and manages the warehoused information

- *RISQL Entry Tool,* an interactive query tool that provides decision-support extensions and direct user access to the Red Brick Warehouse database

Red Brick Warehouse is architected to work with very large databases (500+ GB), and can load and index data at up to 1 GB per hour. Incremental load capabilities update the Red Brick Warehouse with only the most current data.

Red Brick supports specialized indexes that include traditional B-Tree, STAR, and PATTERN index structures. STAR indexes are built automatically when tables are created and maintain relationships between primary and foreign keys using a *star* schema approach (see

Sec. 16.6.4). PATTERN indexes are fully inverted text indexes that greatly reduce search time for partial character string matching.

RISQL provides access to data stored in the Red Brick Warehouse and offers SQL extensions via functions such as rankings, running averages, and cumulative totals which are necessary for data analysis and decision support. RISQL Reporter is a report generator that provides enhanced report formatting, columnar formatting, and batch reporting capabilities.

Red Brick follows the ISO SQL 92 standard and has strategic relationships with Sequent, IBM, Sun, Sybase, and HP as well as many of the tool suppliers through a variety of relationship programs (Prism Solutions, Brio Technology, Trinzic, Microsoft, Clear Access, HP, Pilot Software, etc.).

White Cross Systems Inc.

White Cross Systems, a U.K.-based firm, offers the WX 9020 massively parallel processing data server as a specialized means of handling a data warehouse. It features over 300 processors, 6 GB of memory, 120 GB of mass storage, and the capability to add additional WX 9020 systems to scale up to solve performance or I/O constraints. The mass storage uses RAID technology. A separate communications processor lets the WX 9020 run as a separate server, interacting with user applications using standard SQL.

16.6 ON-LINE ANALYTICAL PROCESSING AND MULTIDIMENSIONAL DATABASES

On-line analytical processing (OLAP) describes a class of software comprising specialized database servers and front-end graphical analytical tools designed for live ad hoc data access and multidimensional analysis. While transaction processing usually relies on relational databases, OLAP has become synonymous with multidimensional database technology.

16.6.1 The need for OLAP

The original objectives in developing an abstract model known as the *relational model* were to address a number of shortcomings of nonrelational database management and application development. For example, the early database systems were complex to develop and difficult to understand, install, maintain, and use. The required skill set was expensive, difficult to attain, and in short supply.

Since the relational model is based on mathematical principles and predicate logic, existing relational database management systems

(RDBMSs) offer powerful solutions for a wide variety of commercial and scientific applications.

However, while the RDBMSs are good at retrieving a small number of records quickly, they are not good at solving modern business problems such as market analysis and financial forecasting that are array-oriented and *multidimensional* in nature. These problems are characterized by the need to retrieve large numbers of records from very large data sets (hundreds of gigabytes and even terabytes) and summarize them on the fly. The key driver for OLAP is the multidimensional nature of the problems it is designed to address. For example, marketing managers are no longer satisfied by asking simple one-dimensional questions such as "How much revenue did the new product generate?" Instead, they ask questions such as "How much revenue did the new product generate by month, in the northeastern division, broken down by user demographic, by sales office, relative to the previous version of the product, compared with the plan?"—a six-dimensional question.

The result set may look like a multidimensional spreadsheet (hence, the term *multidimensional*). Although all the necessary data can be represented in a relational database and accessed via SQL, the two-dimensional relational model of data and the Structured Query Language (SQL) have some serious limitations for such complex real-world problems. For example, this query may translate into a number of complex SQL statements, each of which may involve full table scan, multiple joins, aggregations and sorting, and large temporary tables for storing intermediate results. The resulting query may require significant computing resources that may not be available at all times and even then may take a long time to complete. Another drawback of SQL is its weakness in handling time-series data and complex mathematical functions. Time-series calculations such as a three-month moving average or net present value calculations typically require extensions to ANSI SQL rarely found in commercial products.

Response time and SQL functionality are not the only problems. OLAP is a continuous, iterative, and preferably interactive process. An analyst may drill down into this data to see, for example, how an individual salesperson's performance affects monthly revenue numbers. At the same time, the drill-down procedure may help discover certain patterns in sales of given products. This discovery can force another set of questions of similar or greater complexity. Technically, all these analytical questions can be answered by a large number of rather complex queries against a set of detail and presummarized data views. In reality, however, even if the analyst could quickly and accurately formulate SQL statements of this complexity, the response time and resource consumption problems still persist, and the analyst's productivity is seriously impacted.

Of course, as shown in previous sections of this chapter, one solution to this problem could be a parallel scaleable DBMS running on a high-performance multiprocessor system. In practice, however, not every business can justify this level of hardware investment. Therefore, OLAP has evolved as a client/server-based solution for multidimensional analysis applications.

16.6.2 Multidimensional data model

While the relational data model is represented by a two-dimensional table, the data model for multidimensionality is a cube (see Fig. 16.5). The table on the left contains detailed sales data by product, market, and time. The cube on the right associates sales numbers (units sold) with dimensions—product type, market, and time—with the UNIT variables organized as *cells* in an *array*. This cube can be expanded to include another array—price—which can be associated with all or only some dimensions (for example, the unit price of a product may or may not change with time, or from city to city). The cube supports matrix arithmetic that allows the cube to present the dollar sales array simply by performing a *single* matrix operation on all cells of the array {Dollar Sales = Units * Price}.

The response time of the multidimensional query still depends on how many cells have to be added on the fly. The caveat here is that, as the number of dimensions increases, the number of the cube's cells increases exponentially. On the other hand, the majority of multidimensional queries deal with summarized, high-level data. Therefore, the solution to building an efficient multidimensional database is to preaggregate (consolidate) all logical subtotals and totals along all dimensions. This preaggregation is especially valuable since typical

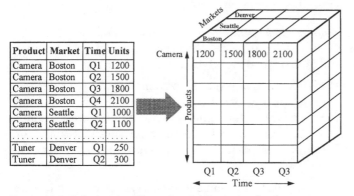

Figure 16.5 Relational tables and multidimensional cubes.

dimensions are *hierarchical* in nature. For example, the TIME dimension may contain hierarchies for years, quarters, months, weeks, days; GEOGRAPHY contains country, state, city, etc. Having the predefined hierarchy within dimensions allows for logical preaggregation and, conversely, allows for a logical drill-down—from the product group to an individual product, from annual sales to weekly sales, etc.

Another way to reduce the size of the cube is to properly handle *sparse* data. Often, not every cell has a meaning across all dimensions (many marketing databases may have more than 95 percent of all cells empty or containing 0). Another kind of sparse data is created when many cells contain duplicate data (i.e., if the cube contains a PRICE dimension, the same price may apply to all markets and all quarters for the year). The ability of a multidimensional database to skip empty or repetitive cells can greatly reduce the size of the cube and the amount of processing.

Dimensional hierarchy, sparse data management, and preaggregation are the keys, since they can significantly reduce the size of the database and the need to calculate values. Such a design obviates the need for multitable joins and provides quick and direct access to the arrays of answers, thus significantly speeding up execution of the multidimensional queries.

16.6.3 OLAP guidelines

Multidimensionality is at the core of a number of OLAP systems (databases and front-end tools) available today. However, the availability of these systems does not eliminate the need to define a methodology of how to select and use the products. Dr. E. F. Codd, the father of the relational model, has formulated a list of 12 guidelines and requirements as the basis for selecting OLAP systems. Users should prioritize this suggested list to reflect their business requirements and consider products that best match those needs:

1. *Multidimensional conceptual view*—A tool should provide users with a multidimensional model that corresponds to the business problems and is intuitively analytical and easy to use.

2. *Transparency*—The OLAP system's technology, the underlying database and computing architecture (client/server, mainframe gateways, etc.), and the heterogeneity of input data sources should be transparent to users to preserve their productivity and proficiency with familiar front-end environments and tools (e.g., MS Windows, MS Excel).

3. *Accessibility*—The OLAP system should access only the data actually required to perform the analysis. Additionally, the system

should be able to access data from all heterogeneous enterprise data sources required for the analysis.

4. *Consistent reporting performance*—As the number of dimensions and the size of the database increases, users should not perceive any significant degradation in performance.

5. *Client/server architecture*—The OLAP system has to conform to client/server architectural principles for maximum price and performance, flexibility, adaptivity, and interoperability.

6. *Generic dimensionality*—Every data dimension must be equivalent in both its structure and operational capabilities.

7. *Dynamic sparse matrix handling*—As previously mentioned, the OLAP system has to be able to adapt its physical schema to the specific analytical model that optimizes sparse matrix handling to achieve and maintain the required level of performance.

8. *Multiuser support*—The OLAP system must be able to support a workgroup of users working concurrently on a specific model.

9. *Unrestricted cross-dimensional operations*—The OLAP system must be able to recognize dimensional hierarchies and automatically perform associated roll-up calculations within and across dimensions.

10. *Intuitive data manipulation*—Consolidation path reorientation (pivoting), drill-down and roll-up, and other manipulations should be accomplished via direct point-and-click, drag-and-drop actions upon the cells of the cube.

11. *Flexible reporting*—The ability to arrange rows, columns, and cells in a fashion that facilitates analysis by intuitive visual presentation of analytical reports must exist.

12. *Unlimited dimensions and aggregation levels*—Depending on business requirements, an analytical model may have a dozen or more dimensions, each with multiple hierarchies. The OLAP system should not impose any artificial restrictions on the number of dimensions or aggregation levels.

In addition to these 12 guidelines, a robust production-quality OLAP system should also support:

■ Comprehensive database management tools that would allow an integrated centralized tool and database management for the distributed enterprise

■ The ability to drill down to detail (source record) level—that means that the tool should allow for a smooth transition from the multidimensional (preaggregated) database to the detail record level of the source relational databases

- Incremental database refresh—many OLAP databases support only full refresh, and it presents an operations and usability problem as the size of the database increases

- Structured query language (SQL) interface—an important requirement for the OLAP system to be seamlessly integrated into the existing enterprise environment

16.6.4 Multidimensional vs. Relational

Many companies driven by complex, multidimensional queries like the ones described in the previous section have often selected OLAP systems with true multidimensional database engines, like Pilot's Light-Ship or Information Resources' Express (IRI Software is a division of Oracle). However, the proprietary nature and limited scaleability of these multidimensional databases coupled with the requirements to drill down to the level of detail available only as rows of relational databases all lead to a growing need for on-line, multidimensional analysis of data that is stored in two-dimensional relational databases. To implement an efficient data warehouse using relational database technology, some vendors and consultants advocate a relational implementation of multidimensional design called a *star* schema (see Fig. 16.7). Among the benefits of this approach are reduced complexity in the data model that increases data "legibility," making it easier for users to pose business questions given the model. Data warehouse queries are answered up to 10 times faster because of improved performance.

These relational implementations of multidimensional database systems are sometimes referred to as *multirelational* database systems. To achieve the required speed, these products use the star or snowflake schemas—specially optimized and denormalized data models that involve data restructuring and aggregation. (The snowflake schema is an extension of the star schema that supports multiple fact tables and joins between them.)

Example—star schema

Consider a typical business analysis problem: Display the share of total sales represented by each product in different markets, categories, and periods, compared with the same period a year ago. To do so, you would calculate the percentage each number is of the total of its column, a simple and common concept. However, in a classical relational database these calculations and display would require definition of a separate view, requiring over 20 SQL commands. The star schema is designed to overcome this limitation of the two-dimensional relational model. (See Fig. 16.6.)

A star schema is a relational schema organized around a central table joined to a few smaller tables using foreign key references. The central table is called the Fact table, and it contains raw numeric items that represent relevant business facts (price, discount values, number of units sold, dollar value, etc.). The facts are typically additive and are accessed via dimensions. Since the fact tables are presummarized and aggregated along business dimensions, these tables tend to be very large.

Smaller tables are the dimensional tables that define business dimension in terms already familiar to the users. These dimensional tables contain a noncompound primary key (mktkey, timekey, etc.) and are heavily indexed. Dimensional tables typically represent the majority of the data elements. These tables appear in constraints and GROUP BY clauses, and are joined to the fact table using foreign key references. Typical dimensions are time periods, geographic and demographic regions, products, promotions and discounts, sales representatives, office numbers, account numbers, vendors, distributors, etc.

Once the star schema database is defined and loaded, the queries that answer questions similar to the one described here are relatively simple, and, what's more, the actual database work to derive to the answer is minimal compared to a standard relational model. A star schema can be created for every industry—consumer packaged goods, retail, telecommunications, transportation, insurance, health care, manufacturing, banking, etc. An example of star schema implementa-

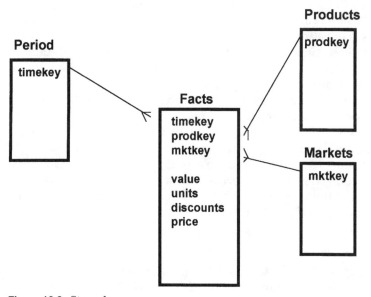

Figure 16.6 Star schema.

tion is Red Brick Warehouse VPT from Red Brick Systems, which was already discussed.

Interestingly, to further improve the speed, the concepts of parallel database processing can be applied to these multirelational solutions. In fact, Red Brick Systems has already implemented some parallel technology in its Red Brick Warehouse.

16.6.5   Alternative approach

Each of the OLAP approaches reviewed up to this point has its advantages and disadvantages, the most critical of which is the proprietary nature of the technology and/or the data model. These specialized data models aim at supporting specific applications, thus sacrificing technology independence. These techniques may increase the performance of one application, but they also may hamper the performance of a different application that may need some of the data. Therefore, many industry analysts predict that, except for the most complex analytical applications with extremely high performance requirements, specialized multidimensional databases will be eventually displaced by OLAP tools that leverage RDBMS technology.

Indeed, various data access tools (such as those from Business Objects) can hide the underlying data model's complexity by giving users an abstraction of the data structures they use to get data. This type of OLAP product gives users a simplified, multidimensional view of the physical data model, making complex data analysis much easier for the business analyst. Moreover, using summary tables instead of detail tables can boost performance for some applications, and using summary tables can cut the CPU resources required to perform the analysis by requesting only aggregated or summarized data. By using metadata information stored in tables within the relational database, the tool can reformat data to deliver a multidimensional view of the data from the enterprise data warehouse.

Using metadata to simulate a multidimensional view of the data will have some performance impact that needs to be evaluated on a case-by-case basis. However, the capabilities of supporting large databases and a large number of users without the need of subsetting the data into a separate proprietary database could represent an attractive alternative. Unifying the enterprise data warehouse using relational technology will improve the quality of business decisions made with data by reducing the inaccuracies.

16.6.6   OLAP tools

The OLAP segment of the tools market has grown because many data warehouse initiatives require on-line analysis. OLAP gained increased visibility after Dr. Edgar F. Codd introduced the term *OLAP* in a white paper. OLAP tools are emerging that provide access to relational database structures. Industry experts such as the Gartner Group recommend that users favor products that offer multidimensional-to-relational database reach-through and also promise direct access to relational databases.

OLAP examples include Essbase from Arbor Software, LightShip from Pilot Software, and NDR from New Dominion Resources.

The multirelational tools include Information Advantage's Decision Support Suite, MicroStrategy's DSS Agent, and Stanford Technology's MetaCube.

16.7 DATA MINING

As already mentioned, a critical success factor for any business today is its ability to use information effectively. This strategic use of data can provide the opportunity to discover hidden, previously undetected, and frequently extremely valuable facts about consumers, retailers, and suppliers, business trends and directions, and significant factors. Knowing this information, an organization can formulate effective business, marketing, and sales strategies, precisely target promotional activity, discover and penetrate new markets, and successfully compete in the marketplace from a position of informed strength. A relatively new and promising technology aimed at achieving this strategic advantage is known as *data mining*.

16.7.1 Data mining definition and drivers

Let's define data mining as the process of discovering meaningful new correlations, patterns, and trends by digging into (mining) large amounts of data stored in warehouses, using artificial intelligence and statistical and mathematical techniques. In that, data mining can reach beyond the capabilities of the OLAP, especially since the major attraction of data mining is its ability to build *predictive* rather than *retrospective* models (see Table).

Traditional DSS/EIS tools are retrospective:	Data mining tools are predictive:
"Print out last month's expenses by cost center."	"Predict and explain next month's demand."
"List the biggest spenders from the last mailing."	"Define concentrated micromarket to reduce future mailing costs and improve success rates."
"Using this model, tell me how well it describes last year's cancellations of our contracts."	"Explain why some customers defect to our competitors."
	"Find some new patterns of customer behavior we are not aware of yet."

Data mining is not specific to any industry—it requires intelligent technologies and the willingness to explore the possibility of hidden knowledge that resides in the data. Industries that are already taking advantage of data mining include retail, financial, medical, manufacturing, environmental, utilities, security, transportation, chemical, insurance, and aerospace industries, with the early success stories coming primarily from the retail, financial, and medical sectors. The organizations already using data mining techniques report gaining insights into their respective businesses by revealing implicit relationships, patterns, surprisingly significant facts, trends, exceptions, and anomalies previously unavailable through the human analysts. These experiences show that, although data mining is still an emerging discipline, it has a huge potential to gain significant benefits in the marketplace. Most organizations engage in data mining to:

- *Discover knowledge.*   The goal of knowledge discovery is to determine explicit hidden relationships, patterns, or correlations from data stored in an enterprise's database. Specifically, data mining can be used to perform:

    —Segmentation (e.g., group customer records for custom-tailored marketing)

    —Classification (assignment of input data to a predefined class, discovery and understanding of trends, text document classification)

    —Association (discovery of cross-sales opportunities)

    —Preferencing (determining preference of customer's majority)

- *Visualize data.*   Analysts must make sense out of a huge amount of information stored in corporate databases. Prior to any analysis, the goal is to "humanize" the mass of data they must deal with and find a clever way to display the data.

- *Correct data.*   While consolidating massive databases, many enterprises find that the data is not complete and invariably contains erroneous and contradictory information. Data mining techniques can help identify and correct problems in the most consistent way possible. The number of applications within this category is somewhat limited due to the difficult nature of the correction process. Replacing missing values or correcting what can be perceived as "wild" values requires judgment calls that are difficult to provide automatically.

The strategic value of data mining is time sensitive, especially in the retail/marketing and finance sectors of the industry. Indeed, organizations that exploit the data first will gain a strategic advantage in serving and attracting customers. Consequently, the benefits derived from the data mining process provide early adopters of the technology with a timely competitive advantage.

16.7.2 Data mining methodology

Data mining describes a collection of techniques which aim to find useful but undiscovered patterns in collected data. The goal of data mining is to create models for decision making which predict future behavior based on analysis of past activity. Data mining supports knowledge discovery, defined by William Frawley and Gregory Piatetsky-Shapiro (MIT Press, 1991), as "... *the nontrivial extraction of implicit, previously unknown, and potentially useful information from data* ..."

Some of the barriers to successful data mining include the highly sophisticated nature of its tools and techniques, and the limited number of qualified analysts and statisticians who can interpret the results of the analysis. Therefore, it is important to develop and follow an actionable data mining methodology. Let's consider the steps the organization may follow to successfully mine data:

1. *Database selection and preparation.*   This step includes the identification of databases and factors to be explored. Whenever possible, required records can be retrieved using a live data dictionary. Data preparation includes filling in missing values and removing errors. While the referential integrity controls of modern relational databases have done much to improve data quality, legacy databases may still be incomplete or error-filled. Interpreting missing data can be dangerous or misleading, particularly when dealing with small samples. However, it is important to understand why the values were missing in the first place, as this could influence a decision on how to deal with the missing values. After the data was selected and prepared, it is ready for the next step. However, the nature and the amount of the data can have a strong influence on which techniques will be the most effective or even possible. Consider the following factors:

   Data complexity.   Data complexity refers to the number of factors that must be considered and to the amount of interactions between the factors.

   Data variability.   Data variability has a direct effect on how much of the data must be analyzed. Relatively small samples of the homogeneous data allow building of general models. As variability increases, it becomes more important to analyze larger data samples and to cluster more carefully.

Data volume. The amount of data present is important from a number of perspectives. Too much data can overwhelm a technique and may require a compromise as to how many factors can be evaluated. Too little data can affect statistical validity. The number of factors considered also influences necessary sample size—more factors requires larger samples to be meaningful.

2. *Analysis.* This step consists of two substeps: first, the large database groups defined during the preparation phase are further divided using clustering techniques. Next, a more detailed (but still high-level) feature analysis is performed to find the factors that seem to be the most obvious contributors to the formation of these clusters, and to determine which factors are involved in the maximization of particular goals.

3. *Tool selection.* Many tools are available today, but most are not complete and often may need to be combined with existing techniques or systems already developed within the organization.

4. *Testing of hypothesis and knowledge discovery.* This is the step most often associated with the term "data mining." During this process, hypotheses are formed and tested (top-down process), new relationships are discovered (bottom-up process), and "what-if" analysis may be performed.

5. *Knowledge application.* In most cases, tested rules that were created from the discovery process can be directly added to either procedural code or (if the number of rules is large and the possibility for updates great) into a knowledge-based system. Prediction models can also often be directly integrated into application code.

16.7.3 Data mining techniques

A number of underlying techniques can be applied to the various functions of the data mining effort. Visualization, statistics, induction, and neural networks are the most popular. Most of these techniques have reached acceptable levels of maturity in building *predictive* models.

Data mining techniques fall into three major categories: supervised, unsupervised, and reinforcement learning. *Supervised* learning includes the most widely used techniques. It is equivalent to "programming by example." Supervised techniques involve a training phase during which historic training data whose characteristics map to known outcomes are fed to the data mining algorithm. This process trains the algorithm to recognize key variables and values which will later become the basis for making predictions when scanning new data. *Unsupervised* learning does not involve a training phase but instead depends on the use of algorithms which detect all patterns such as associations and sequences which occur above specified significance criteria in input data. This approach leads to the generation of many rules which characterize the discovered associations, clusters, and segments. These rules are then analyzed to determine those of significant interest. *Reinforcement* learning, though used less frequently than the other methods today, has applications in optimization over time and adaptive control. Reinforcement learning is the most like real life. It is very much like training on the job, where an employee is given a set of tasks requiring decisions and, at some point in time, is given a performance appraisal, which determines the employee performance and forces the employee to evaluate his or her decisions in light of the performance results. Because the reinforcement learning process does not provide immediate corrective actions, it can be used to solve some very difficult time-dependent problems.

Of course, successful data mining is based on more than the specific techniques employed. Modern data mining operations depend on sophisticated data capture, validation and correction, and management of very large volumes of information. Implementation of data mining techniques which take full advantage of massively parallel processing (MPP) hardware architectures is critical to full exploitation of today's huge and rapidly growing databases in such areas as consumer packaged goods marketing, credit management, effective advertising and promotion planning and tracking, and frequent shopper programs.

Techniques

Data mining is based on a variety of pattern recognition techniques including neural networks, case-based reasoning, genetic algorithms, fuzzy logic, and classification and regression trees. A number of these techniques are based on *induction*—the process of reasoning from specific facts to reach a hypothesis. The opposite of induction is *deduction,* which is reasoning from a hypothesis and trying to prove it by specific facts.

A brief overview of some important mathematical modeling and knowledge-based data mining techniques is given as follows.

Artificial neural networks (ANN). Neural networks are multilayered network architectures that "learn" how to solve a problem based on examples. Neural networks enable development of nonlinear predictive and classification models. Neural networks consist of inputs, each of which corresponds to an independent data field; one or more outputs which represent the dependent outcome fields; and one or more levels of intermediate hidden levels which are used in the calculation of the predictive response output. A particular neural network's topology (i.e., feedforward, limited recurrent, or fully recurrent) and the learning paradigm (i.e., supervised, unsupervised) define the neural network *model* (e.g., back propagation network). A neural network topology is designed to reflect the complexity of the model of the data to be analyzed. Each node in a neural network is connected to all nodes in the succeeding level. Each node of the network predicts the effect of the inputs which feed into that node. Each input connection to a node has an associated adjusting weight which is multiplied with the input value to increase or decrease the impact of that input on the node. The state of the neural network is adjusted by changing these weights during a training process. The value of any node is computed as a function of the weighted sum of the values of the nodes in the prior level.

Neural network techniques offer a number of benefits. A fundamental benefit is their ability to learn through training so that a model's effectiveness should improve with experience. Neural network topology naturally lends itself to parallel processing for improved system performance. Finally, neural networks are effective at recognizing patterns and trends among many factors.

On the negative side, neural networks require extensive data preprocessing. Only numeric input is possible, and the ranges of the variables must be carefully scaled. Neural networks require numerous parameter settings, some as basic as network structure and size, and these decisions can have a strong influence on the results. Another problem is that the resulting models are difficult to interpret, although some progress has been made in this area. Finally, neural networks are frequently criticized for their long training times.

Classification and regression trees (CART).   Classification and regression trees (CART) is a general classification method developed in the late 1970s. CART generates segmentation rules for clustering (classifying) data records based on a predicted outcome. Segmentation rules are represented by a tree, each node of which represents a rule (an assertion) which segregates incoming records into two result sets. For example, an assertion could be "Income greater than $5000," which is either true or false for each record.

The initial node in a tree is called its *root*. The root node partitions the full input records into two subsets. Each successive intermediate node further partitions the subset of records it tests. The end nodes, or *leaves,* of the tree partition the records into final subsets, each of which has associated an outcome which classifies that subset and a probability that the predicated outcome is correct. A path from the root node to a leaf node is called a *branch* of the tree.

Once a tree has been built against a set of initial training data, the efficiency of the tree as a predictor against future data is improved through what is called a *pruning* process. During this process, a succession of subtrees is created by removing one or more branches from the initial tree. Each subtree is evaluated against test data and its performance compared to the known outcomes. Finally, the subtree which provides the best relative error rate and appropriate performance characteristics is selected as the basis for the predictive model which can be used against new data.

Genetic algorithms (GAs).   Genetic algorithms simulate an evolutionary approach to optimizing parameters of classification or general functions. Genetic algorithms can be used in conjunction with classification tools such as neural networks to improve their modeling accuracy. For a function or model to be optimized, various combinations of parameter values, referred to as *genomes,* are specified and encoded as a string of values. Then, a *fitness function* is defined to evaluate each string to determine its fitness as a solution to the problem. Given an initial set of genomes, a general-purpose genetic algorithm simulates evolutionary activity to produce subsequent generations of modified genomes. Principles such as *selection, genetic mutation, gene crossover,* and *survival of the fittest* are simulated to direct the evolution of the genomes. At each stage, each genome is evaluated for its predictive quality and confidence, using the fitness function. Those which fall short of a specified fitness threshold are eliminated from contributing to the next generation. Ultimately, the parameters from the best-of-breed genome are fed back into the target model or function being optimized.

Case-based reasoning (CBR).   Case-based reasoning (CBR) systems represent a relatively new knowledge-based approach to data mining and pattern recognition. To date, CBR has largely been restricted to niche applications such as for equipment help-desk problem diagnosis. CBR tools categorize a new record, called a *case,* by analyzing descriptions of previous cases for the closest fit to the attributes of the new case. Unlike neural network models, CBR can handle complex data including both numeric and nonnumeric values which should offer CBR an increasingly important advantage in emerging object-oriented systems. With CBR, each attribute of a case is assigned a weight representing its importance in establishing a match. Determining the appropriate weights for each attribute often requires a significant knowledge engineering process involving domain experts.

Fuzzy logic.   The concept of fuzzy logic is based on fuzzy sets, first proposed by Dr. Lofti Zadeh in 1965. Fuzzy sets are based on a simple extension of standard binary sets, which allows for multivalued, partial membership. (Let's divide the entire population into two groups: short people who are less than 6 feet tall and tall people who are taller than 6 feet. Then all people who are exactly 6 feet tall do not belong to either set. Of course, we can define a third set of 6-foot-tall people, but the reality is that the decision whether a person is tall or short is subjective—somebody who is 6-feet, 1-inch may not be considered tall. The fuzzy set theory allows for partial membership, where this person can have a membership of 0.8 in the tall set and a membership of 0.2 in the short set.) This concept results in the formal logic theory that is not binary, but rather multivalued. One of the advantages of fuzzy logic is that it maps well to our intuitive understanding of the world. Because it allows for multivalued, partial membership and partial values, it allows for the development of systems that are much better adapted to real-life problems than binary logic would permit. For example, systems based on fuzzy logic can evaluate conditions in terms of "good," "OK," "so-so," "almost-ready," etc., and then take appropriate actions based on that evaluation. In data mining, fuzzy logic can be used in conjunction with neural networks to provide for preliminary classification of the input values and to determine the best values for the weights. This output is then refined in neural network processing, but the significant portion of the training phase can be avoided.

Statistics. Statistics are the most mainstream of the techniques applied to data mining problems. Statistics are used universally by traditional and advanced technology researchers to perform many functions, such as clustering, factor analysis, and prediction. Frequently used in combination with other technologies, statistics are often the technique of choice for initial analysis to identify predictive factors. New statistical techniques are constantly being developed, and this wide field continues to play a major role in data analysis. However, statistics often require up-front assumptions and are difficult for nonstatisticians to apply and interpret. They are also difficult to use with large numbers of variables.

Visualization. Visualization relies heavily on the human aspect of the analysis. Even the best set of rules or tables of data may reveal more information when visualized with color, relief, or texture in 2D, 3D, or 4D representations. Visualization techniques may be used throughout the data exploration process and are particularly useful during the initial stages for high-level grouping functions. Visualization can also be used in combination with other techniques, such as induction, where it might show the number of rules generated versus certain parameter settings.

One disadvantage of visualization is the difficulty of depicting relationships among more than four variables. Time is also difficult to envision, even with multiple graphs simultaneously displayed and animated time series data. More on the topic of data visualization can be found in Sec. 16.7.5.

16.7.4   Applications of data mining

Utilizing predictive models in decision making has several benefits. A model should explain why a particular decision was made. Adjusting a model based on feedback from future decisions will lead to experience accumulation and true organizational learning. Finally, a predictive model can be used to automate a decision step in a larger process. For example, using a model to instantly predict whether a consumer will default on his credit card payments will allow automatic adjustment of credit limits rather than depending on expensive staff making inconsistent decisions. Let's look at applications of data mining and predictive modeling.

Mass personalization

By categorizing customers according to subtle characteristics in their behavior patterns, companies can customize their interactions to provide personalized services to large numbers of customers (e.g., customized mailings, targeted direct marketing, personalized telephone service, direct sales assistance, improved customer retention).

Fraud detection

Using predictive models, an organization can detect existing fraudulent behavior and identify customers who are likely to commit fraud in the future.

Automated buying decisions

Data mining systems can uncover consumer buying patterns and make stocking decisions for inventory control.

Credit portfolio risk evaluation

A data mining system can help perform credit risk analysis by building predictive models of various portfolios, identifying factors, and formulating rules affecting bad risk decisions.

Financial planning and forecasting

Data mining provides a variety of promising techniques to build predictive models forecasting financial outcome on a macroeconomic scale.

Discovery sales

For companies that excel in data mining, an innovative source of revenue is the sale of some of their data mining discoveries. For example, credit bureaus can charge a premium for premined databases that yield more meaningful results to their clients.

Examples

Major retail and financial services organizations use data mining to finely target direct mail promotional campaigns. These firms have extended their established decision support systems with data mining technology to develop target customer profiles which improve response rates and so reduce marketing costs. When combined with advanced data management and compression techniques, data mining supports analysis of the more than 1 terabyte (TB) per day of supermarket scanner data. Using predictive data mining models, a leading bank discovered that it can increase credit card revenues by reducing minimum payments—a contradictory outcome that was not at all obvious from the conventional analysis.

Other examples of data mining usage include a service bureau's identification of likely payroll service customers, a major bank's detection of fraudulent credit card transactions, the IRS system predicting when individuals should be audited, and the U.S. Department of Energy's model to predict the likelihood of oil production for a site.

These examples prove that using data mining can be a powerful competitive advantage.

16.7.5 Data visualization

Data visualization is emerging as an advanced technology that may allow organizations to process vast amounts of information and present it in a usable format. It is an umbrella term for the use of interactive graphics and imaging to represent and manipulate volumes of data. Multiple dimensions can be presented by the position (e.g., coordinates x, y, or z), size, orientation (e.g., roll, pitch, or yaw), color, shape, and behavior (e.g., spin, vibration, or sound) of graphical objects. Since visualization is a natural form of human comprehension, visualization applications provide an opportunity to reach a broader audience of non-computer-literate users by allowing them to sift through volumes of data using an intuitive and natural interface.

Visualization first emerged in the scientific world, where over the past decade it gained popularity as a means to model and analyze such phenomena as air pollution, automobile crashes, and underground reservoirs. Since that time its scientific applications have expanded to include medical imaging, minimal invasive surgery techniques, three-dimensional underground reservoir simulation, weather modeling and forecasting, computational chemistry, and computational fluid dynamics.

But with the steady growth of corporate data, the demand for flexible tools helping the decision-making process has propelled data visualization into the commercial arena. In its higher form, visualization is seen as virtual reality, a three-dimensional representation of information, which requires that end users use specially equipped helmets, goggles, and gloves to immerse themselves in a virtual world where users can directly manipulate the "objects" they find.

The following are some examples of how data visualization is used today:

- A computer manufacturing company uses an internally developed data visualization tool to monitor sales activity in various geographic regions. Guided by a mouse, users can "fly" through sales territories and dynamically manipulate the level of detail shown (e.g., by product, salesperson, or region). Sales targets are represented by hovering disks that are broken when the target is exceeded.

- A large telecommunications company uses visualization techniques to represent its telecommunications networks in different countries. By plotting load factors in geographic regions, engineers can monitor systems before calls are "dropped" by overloaded networks.

- A financial services firm uses a data visualization tool from Maxus Systems (MetaphorMixer) to track stock and bond markets. The system uses real-time market data to drive changes in the color, shape, or action of company logos on a checkerboard to reflect changes in, for example, price/earnings ratios and volume.

- With a data visualization tool from Fiamass (Flo Analysis, which uses continuous flow lines representing cyclic movements measured at different time intervals), the banks and brokerage houses can track the likely direction and range of future movement in the market.

- Data visualization is successfully used in scientific applications—for example, Visual Numerics' PC-Wave Advantage is used to study solar wind and monitor sun spots, in part in an attempt to predict a major solar flare.

- Several manufacturing facilities have built visual models of their plants using data on stock levels, machine performance, inspection systems, and job distribution. The information is used to monitor and analyze the entire system's production levels.

Among the benefits of data visualization are:

- Users can dynamically interact with variables and explore how variables affect the phenomenon being represented.

- Users can view summarized data and quickly drill down to various levels of specificity.

- By using intuitive presentation devices, data navigation becomes self-explanatory and the interaction becomes easier and more natural.

- Increased data comprehension extends knowledge of existing information to facilitate the identification of hidden patterns and trends.

16.7.6 Criteria for data mining and visualization tools

Tools and platforms for data mining must be carefully selected and integrated, because data mining can easily overwhelm technology and products. The market itself is still emerging. As an illustration, there are many vendors that compete in the data mining and visualization market. Among them, a few are established large companies (e.g., IBM, Silicon Graphics, Lockheed, Software AG). They are competing with a number of new relatively small vendors. These include Epsilon, Logica, HNC, Cross/Z, 3Dlabs, Advanced Visual Systems, IDIS, BBN, and many others.

Since data mining and visualization tools are based on complex theory that goes beyond traditional data processing, organizations should consider the following when evaluating any technology or product for data mining:

- *Sample size limitation*—Many existing systems often cannot deal with more than 10,000 to 20,000 records at one time. This limitation is important when evaluating a large number of factors, since the number of examples the product can process may not be representative.

- *Preprocessing*—If a tool can handle only discrete value ranges, then the data will have to be preprocessed and normalized. Additionally, the preprocessing may have to deal with data transformation, since some products process only numeric input.

- *Testing of hypotheses*—Users should be able to substantiate hypotheses by testing them with specific facts or records (top-down analysis). In addition, the system should be able to build hypotheses from individual facts while allowing users to modify the facts to perform what-if investigations (bottom-up analysis).

- *System output* (rules, models, decision trees, etc.)—If an explanation of the results is the paramount goal, rules and induction techniques are appropriate. If finding the best combination of factors is the goal and a literal explanation is not required, neural networks and fractal techniques should be used.

- *Easy of use and adaptivity*—Discovery tools should be able to process all data, no matter how often the data changes or how fast it enters the system. Systems that require long training or processing times may not be appropriate with rapidly changing data. The same is true for the support staff—products range from highly automated tools that give the user little to adjust to manual systems that require considerable technical knowledge. The skill levels of users and developers should be taken into consideration when selecting a tool.

- *Scaleability and completeness*—Most tools address only portions of the problem, and many have difficulty dealing with huge data sets.

Client/Server Computing— Architecture for Today and Tomorrow

Those readers who arrived at this point by reading through the book have been introduced to the client/server computing model, which has been shown to include the specialized client and server platforms, connected with a specialized software layer—middleware. The analysis of the client/server architecture has extended a widely accepted view of client/server computing as the architecture for the distributed database environment. This extended view includes important issues such as distributed systems management, networks and data communications, distributed transaction processing, and data warehousing.

Most importantly, the client/server architecture has been discussed from the point of view of the standards and open systems. And, hopefully, the result of all these discussions has demonstrated the client/server paradigm as a special case of distributed cooperative processing. Client/server computing can bring to users some extremely important and tangible benefits, especially if the client/server architecture is built on and takes advantage of open systems.

17.1 CLIENT/SERVER APPLICATION DEVELOPMENT

The definition of an application has been changing for some time. As advanced organizations move beyond early client/server architectures, the increasing numbers of business solutions will be delivered by integrating a range of heterogeneous components from many sources. In general, as client/server computing becomes the architecture of the day, the industry is focusing its attention on the component-based application development environments that can help realize the enhanced productivity promise of the client/server architecture. This trend is evident in many client/server implementations and is actually emphasized by the characteristics of the development and production environments. For instance, the majority of desktop (client) systems today are running a version of Microsoft Windows. Although Windows NT-based server platforms are often used for small- to medium-scale client/server systems, many mission-critical client/server applications being built today still rely on the maturity, functionality, openness, and robustness of the UNIX-based server platforms.

Therefore, the need for effective, easy-to-learn tools that can be used to build and run client/server applications in heterogeneous environments has become clear. And many vendors have dedicated considerable resources to become major players in this market. Naturally, DBMS vendors were among the first. But, their tools did not find a warm reception from users. Often, the tool worked only for that vendor's DBMS. Also, the tool quality and usability were often rather poor—not every DBMS vendor could allocate sufficient time and resources to competitive tool development, since it was considered a "secondary" market opportunity. The resulting vacuum was rapidly filled by a number of independent software vendors who focused all their energies on competitive tool development.

In addition, the entire development paradigm is shifting from procedural to object-based. Universal acceptance of languages such as C++ and the proliferation and maturity of Microsoft's Object Linking and Embedding (OLE) are evidence of the growing popularity of object-oriented analysis, design, and programming. Further evidence can be found in the new way of building applications from reusable components—the gains in productivity and software quality can be quite dramatic.

As a result, the market for effective, portable, easy-to-learn, full-featured graphical development tools is very competitive. This market is not static. It continues to grow more competitive as Windows development and operating environments continue to mature and as de facto industry standards such as OLE, ODBC, and MAPI continue to proliferate. The market landscape is also changing as new alliances are formed and as vendors actively pursue partnerships, mergers, and acquisitions to place themselves into leadership positions. To discuss new application development methodologies and every popular tool is certainly beyond the scope of this book. Therefore, this chapter focuses on PowerSoft's PowerBuilder, Gupta's SQL Windows, and Forté—some of the best-known tools used for client/server application development. This choice should not be interpreted as an endorsement of these tools or as a recommendation to use them. It simply illustrates the state of the art in third-party software client/server application development tools.

17.1.1 PowerBuilder

Some of the key attractions of object-oriented application development include encapsulation of application objects, polymorphism, the ability to inherit forms and GUI objects, and the premise that, once an object has been created and tested, it can then be reused by other applications. These features have been emphasized in the latest generation of client/server development tools. One of the preferred tools for object-oriented client/server application development is PowerSoft's Power-Builder. The strength of PowerBuilder isn't just its object orientation, its ability to develop Windows applications, or its affinity toward client/server architecture. One of the greatest benefits attributed to PowerBuilder is its ability to dramatically increase the developer's productivity and shorten the development cycle when creating graphical client/server applications.

PowerBuilder offers a powerful fourth-generation language (4GL), object-oriented graphical development environment, and the ability to interface with a wide variety of database management systems. It can interface with such popular database engines as SYBASE SQL Server, IBM's DB2, Gupta's SQLBase, ORACLE Server, INFORMIX OnLine, XDB Server from XDB, and Allbase/SQL from Hewlett-Packard. In addition, it has its own database engine from Watcom International Corporation.

Object-orientation

PowerBuilder supports many object-oriented features. Among them is *inheritance,* which allows developers to change the attributes of child classes by modifying these attributes in the parent class of objects. *Data abstraction*—the encapsulation of properties and behavior within the object—is enabled through three classes of objects: window classes, menu classes, and user-defined classes. These classes contain objects that are defined and built by developers looking for enhanced reusability. Indeed, the encapsulation of the code and attributes generalized the functionality of the objects. Hence, if reusability is desired, objects should be created with clearly defined interfaces and encapsulated data and behavior. Polymorphism, another object term, allows one message to invoke an appropriate but different behavior when sent to different object types. Polymorphism support in PowerBuilder means that the same message can be sent to the object and its parent, and both would behave appropriately. A trivial example would be a message to add a title to a document. In the general case, the document class has subclasses of letters, resumes, and status reports, all of which inherit document properties. The message in question can add an appropriate title to each of the subclass documents according to their internal formats that were encapsulated into those documents.

To add to the list of object-oriented features of PowerBuilder, consider the SQL object that allows programmers to modify the application's data windows at run time. In addition, PowerBuilder supports execution of SQL commands at run time.

Windows facilities

A powerful Windows-based environment, PowerBuilder supports key Windows facilities. These include dynamic data exchange (DDE), dynamic link libraries (DLL), object linking and embedding (OLE), multiple document interface (MDI), and a familiar drag-and-drop metaphor.

PowerSoft also included collaborative workgroup enabling facilities such as code management feature in its flagship product. PowerBuilder code management supports the ability to check objects in and out of libraries, which facilitates joint workgroup development projects.

Features

PowerBuilder is known for its intuitive user interface, graphical development environment, and ease of use. With PowerBuilder, a developer can define the bulk of an application by creating windows and controls with various painter utilities. This work is done on a client platform running Microsoft Windows, and the entire development environment is designed to take advantage of the available Windows facilities. The PowerBuilder windows and controls can contain program scripts that execute based on different events that can be detected by Power-Builder. The scripting language—PowerScript—is a high-level, object-oriented, event-driven programming language similar to Visual Basic.

PowerBuilder controls include standard Windows objects such as radio buttons, push buttons, list boxes, check boxes, combo boxes, text fields, menus, edit fields, and pictures.

Among the events are standard Windows events such as *clicked* and *double-clicked* that represent pointing-device (mouse) handling. PowerBuilder allows developers to define application-specific events and create application messages that are used for communication between application objects.

Creation of a new window is a starting point for a new application. Ideally, this new window closely corresponds with a high-level user's view of the application, which clearly enhances the quality of the application (at least in the user's eyes). Let's examine how a client/server application can be constructed using PowerBuilder painters.

- *Application Painter.* This utility is used first to identify basic details and components of a new or existing application. Existing application maintenance is quite simple—double-clicking on the application icon displays a hierarchical view of the application structure. All levels can be expanded or contracted with a click of the right mouse button. Similarly easy, the Application Painter allows creation and naming of a new application, selection of an application icon, setting of the library search path, and defining of default text characteristics. As an event-driven system, the Application Painter has access to application-level events. Among them are Open (triggered when an application starts), Close (triggered when an application is terminated), Idle (triggered when an application remains inactive after a specified period of time), and a number of error events. These events control the main flow of the application. For example, an Open event, when triggered, executes the Open script for the application, which may direct control to initialization statements and open applications windows defined with the Window Painter. The Application Painter can be also used to run or debug the application.

- *Window Painter.* The Window Painter is used to create and maintain the majority of PowerBuilder window objects (with the exception of user-defined objects). Several types of windows are supported by the Window Painter: main, parent, child, pop-up, dialog, and MDI. For a new application, the process usually starts with the creation of a main application window (the one typically displayed first when the application starts). This window, like all others, has several attributes such as title, position, size, color, and font. These attributes, as well as objects within the window (various buttons, boxes, menus, etc.), are defined using the Window Painter. It is important to notice that all Window Painter operations are performed in an intuitive graphical fashion, by dragging and dropping and clicking mouse buttons. After the window and controls are created, the developer can select the Script Option to open the *PowerScript Painter,* which allows developers to select from a list of events and global and local variables, all of which can be pasted into the body of the code. From the PowerScript Painter the developer can invoke the Object Browser which displays attributes of any object, data type, and structure. The selected attributes can also be pasted into the code. Another useful action supported within the Window Painter is the Paste SQL window, which allows a developer to graphically select and paste SQL statements.

Windows created with the Window Painter possess such object properties as inheritance, where windows and controls can inherit properties from other windows.

■ *DataWindows Painter.*   DataWindows are at the heart of many PowerBuilder applications. These are powerful dynamic objects that provide access to databases and other data sources such as ASCII files. PowerBuilder applications use DataWindows to connect to multiple databases and files, as well as import and export data in a variety of formats such as dBase, Excel, Lotus, and tab-delimited text. Acting as primary data containers, DataWindows are used for such database operations as ad hoc queries, browsing and editing of tables, report writing, and data exchange with other applications. All basic DataWindows operations are supported transparently, without the need to code in SQL. Using DataWindows Painter, a developer can select a data source using DataWindows options such as Quick Select, SQL Select (DataWindows issues SQL Select statements), Query (a SQL statement created in another object), and External (data retrieval using PowerScript statements). In addition, DataWindows supports execution of stored procedures for those database engines that support this feature. That is one of the reasons why PowerBuilder is so popular with SYBASE developers.

DataWindows allows developers to select a number of presentation styles from the list of tabular, grid, label, and freeform. An option in DataWindows allows a user-specified number of rows to be displayed in a display line.

Associated with DataWindows Painter is the *Query Painter,* which allows the generation of SQL statements that can be stored in PowerBuilder libraries. These stored SQL statements can be used elsewhere in the current application as well as in other applications.

Thus, using basic Application Painter, Window Painter, and DataWindows Painter facilities, a simple client/server application can be constructed literally in minutes. When more complex applications are to be created, developers can code SQL statements into the scripts associated with other PowerBuilder objects. A rich set of SQL functions is supported, including CONNECT/DISCONNECT, DECLARE, OPEN and CLOSE cursor, FETCH, and COMMIT/ROLLBACK. Stored procedures are supported via DECLARE, EXE-

CUTE, UPDATE, and CLOSE procedure statements. PowerBuilder supports such SQL extensions as FETCH PRIOR and SELECT FOR UPDATE, if the DBMS supports these. Dynamic preparation and execution of SQL statements is also supported.

SQL scripts communicate with database engines via a special transaction object (SQLCA is the default), that manages communication parameters, identifies the target database, and monitors the status of database operations. This transaction object is created automatically by PowerBuilder when the application starts up. For database connectivity, PowerBuilder supports ODBC and DRDA. ODBC support comes with an ODBC administration utility, that allows the user to add new data sources; add, modify, and delete users; and install and (re)configure ODBC drivers. In addition, the Administration utility works with database views and stored procedures.

PowerBuilder supplies several other painters. Among them are:

- *Database Painter* allows developers to pick tables from the list box, and examine and edit join conditions and predicates, key fields, extended attributes, display formats, and other database attributes.

- *Structure Painter* allows the creation and modification of data structures and groups of related data elements.

- *Preference Painter* is a configuration tool that is used to examine and modify configuration parameters for the PowerBuilder development environment.

- *Menu Painter* creates menus for the individual windows and the entire application.

- *Function Painter* is a development tool that assists developers in creating function calls and parameters using combo boxes. In addition to facilitating the creation of new functions, Function Painter simplifies access to the function arguments and global variables of over 500 functions provided by PowerBuilder.

- *Library Painter* manages the library where the application components reside. It also supports check-in and check-out of library objects for developers.

- *User Object Painter* allows developers to create custom controls. Often, these custom controls are graphical objects that modify or combine existing objects. Once created, these custom controls can be treated just like standard PowerBuilder controls.

- *Help Painter* is a built-in help system, similar to the MS Windows Help facility.

Workgroup approach

PowerSoft recognizes that the appeal of the CASE approach is still strong. Therefore, PowerBuilder provides a new API for Open Repository CASE Architecture (ORCA) that is being given to third-party vendors. This allows CASE tools, source code control systems like PVCS from Intersolv, and other workgroup tools to interact with PowerBuilder. In addition, PowerBuilder's own Library Painter supports check-in and check-out of library objects for developers. These include application components, windows, and SQL statements.

Of course, PowerBuilder is not the end of all tools, nor is it by any means perfect. For example, its cost could be significant, especially if the number of required licenses is large. The need for the run-time environment could be annoying.

17.1.2 SQLWindows

As mentioned before, the competition in the area of application development tools is very stiff. PowerBuilder's main competitors include SQLWindows and ObjectView, both of which are excellent products vying for the same marketplace. Also, users should not discount Microsoft. Its Visual Basic and Visual C++ are viable alternatives for component-based client/server development. And, with the wider acceptance of object-oriented technology and the maturity of object-oriented tools, products such as SmallTalk deserve some close attention.

Gupta's SQLWindows is arguably one of the most object-oriented 4GLs on the market. SQLWindows runs on Intel-based PCs running MS Windows. The Corporate Edition of the products includes:

- Direct interfaces to SQLBase, SYBASE SQL Server, MS SQL Server, ORACLE, AS/400 DBM, INFORMIX, and CA/Ingres. Optional connectivity to DB2/MVS (requires CICS/ESA or VTAM), DB2/2 (for OS/2), Cincom's Supra.

- Support for ODBC (drivers for dBase and Paradox are included), OLE, MAPI, VIM, MHS.

- SQLWindows development environment.

- QuickObjects—a suite of reusable components.

- Quest—a database query tool.

- SQLConsole—a database tuning and administration tool.

- SQLWindows Compiler (requires Microsoft's Visual C++ compiler).

- Version control software—includes SQLTeam/Windows, PVCS, and development license for SQLBase (Gupta's RDBMS) that is used for the version control repository, that can support multiple concurrent projects. Optionally, the repository can be stored in SYBASE or ORACLE.

- SQLRouter—a database connectivity gateway to all supported databases. It is configured automatically at installation time once a user specifies databases that the system will be using.

- Visual Toolchest—a class library of objects and functions.

- CASE tool interface to LBMS Systems Engineer and Popkin's System Architect.

SQLWindows uses multiple document interface (MDI) windows for the development process and for the run-time application that it builds. As is typical for the MDI metaphor, the development environment has a main window, from which a user can invoke a child window containing the form painter. The same is true for a SQLWindows application—it contains a top-level window, with multiple child windows containing specific forms.

SQLWindows provides a flexible tool palette that is used to create windows and add objects to them. The palette allows the developer to choose objects from it and provides context-sensitive list boxes to help select additional parameters.

The tool palette provides access to the QuickObjects component, a suite of data access and data reporting objects. In addition to QuickObjects for accessing, adding, updating, and deleting records in relational databases, the product contains objects to access groupware solutions such as Lotus Notes databases, and e-mail systems such as Microsoft Mail (using MAPI) and Lotus cc:Mail (using VIM). A developer can extend the functionality of QuickObjects objects and can create new objects that will be added to the tool palette.

Typical application development with SQLWindows starts with selecting a data source. This can be accomplished by choosing *Query* QuickObject from the tool palette, which will initiate an interface to the Quest data access tool. Multiple Quest objects can be placed on a form, with one Quest object for each table, thus supporting a master-detail relationship. A SQLWindows default specifies that data is read into the form when the form is first invoked.

Similar to data access objects, a developer may choose user interface objects (e.g., a text box) by associating these objects with data fields from the tables accessed with Quest. For simple applications, SQLWindows provides Quick Commander objects that support user navigation through the forms and data tables. These navigational objects are pushbuttons encapsulating prewritten data access code and icons for various record-level operations (display first, last, next, or previous record, etc.).

Gupta's SQLWindows provides its own 4GL called SAL (SQL-Windows Application Language). SAL comes with on-line assistance that helps in building SAL code on-line. Unlike PowerBuilder, which structures an object's code into separate scripts associated with different events, SQLWindows places all code for an object into a single script. As a result, editing, viewing, and documenting an object's code is much easier. (One exception to this is that the inherited code is not visible through a standard editor—one must use a Class Editor to view the parent's code.) A helpful feature that facilitates SQLWindows application documentation is its Outline View, which provides a hierarchical view of the structure of the application, including global declarations, libraries, forms, objects, and SAL code.

As already mentioned, Gupta's SQLWindows supports single and multiple inheritance, with a child object capable of inheriting from multiple parents. SQLWindows will automatically keep the child object synchronized with its parents for the properties and methods it inherited.

Objects such as windows, forms, dialog boxes, functions, classes, global variables, and constants are stored in the object library, which facilitates their reuse within and among the applications.

Applications are deployed by either building a p-code executable file that is interpreted by the SQLWindows run-time engine or compiling parts of the application using the SQLWindows compiler that builds a C code. This C code is then compiled to a DLL using a C/C++ compiler (for example, the tool supports Microsoft's Visual C++). Although the run-time engine is still required (some p-code still remains), the second option could provide for better overall performance.

One drawback of SQLWindows is its inability to encapsulate a data field with its business rules. In other words, when a user creates an object for a particular data field, this object cannot be linked to the data until it is placed on a form. Conversely, when a data field is placed on a form, its business rules (e.g., a range of values, data type) are not automatically enforced until this data field is associated with a particular object.

17.1.3 Forté

As described throughout the book, in a three-tiered client/server computing architecture, an application's functionality is partitioned into three distinct pieces: presentation logic with its graphical user interface, application business logic, and data access functionality. Typically, in such a partitioned application, the presentation logic is placed on a client, while the application logic resides on an application server, and the data access logic and the database reside on a database server (see Fig. 17.1).

Clients   **Application Servers**   **Data Servers**

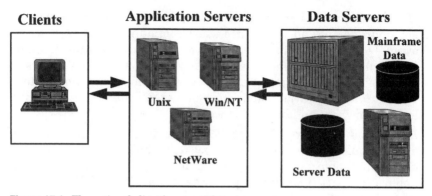

Figure 17.1   Three-tiered client/server architecture.

Forté (from Forté Software Inc.) is designed to provide application developers with facilities to develop and partition applications to be efficiently placed on the proper platforms of the three-tiered architecture. Forté provides an environment that encourages rapid development, testing, and deployment of distributed client/server applications across any enterprise. Forté's strength is in its ability to implement open, scaleable applications that are independent of database management systems, windows managers, communications software, and operating systems.

Forté offers comprehensive life-cycle support through three functional components:

- *Application Development Facility (ADF)* is based on the distributed object computing framework and is used to define user interfaces and application logic. It includes a GUI designer for building user screens, a proprietary 4GL called Transactional Object-Oriented Language (TOOL), a set of standard class libraries, an interactive debugger, and a development repository. Developers construct applications using *workshops* (a set of tools similar to PowerBuilder's painters). A GUI is not a necessary component—Forté supports building distributed client/server applications that do not have a user interface (e.g., a telephone switch support system). Screens and 4GL routines are stored and managed in a repository as objects to permit a modular approach and facilitate reuse.

- *System Generation Facility (SGF)* assists developers in partitioning the application, generating executables for distribution. Forté's most powerful feature is its ability to automate partitioning of the application into client and server components. SGF automatically puts processes on the appropriate device based on the application's logic and platform inventory—a developer supplies the information about eligible platforms. Forté maps this proposed architecture to the target environment and sets up necessary communications. SGF generates C++ source code for compilation into native executable code on target platforms. To enhance flexibility, Forté allows developers to override the proposed partitioning with a graphical partitioning tool. In addition, application partitions can be replicated for scaleability, load balancing, and fault resilience.

- *Distributed Execution Facility (DEF)* provides tools for managing applications at run time, including system administration support, a distributed object manager to handle communications between application partitions, and a performance monitor. DEF provides a unified collection of run-time services and control structures to deploy partitions, administer applications, distribute objects, perform load balancing, provide for fail-over scenarios, and dynamically tune performance.

Forté generates portable code across all supported platforms that include VMS, HP-UX, Dynix (Sequent), AIX, SunOS, Solaris, and DG-UX. Client support includes MS Windows, Apple Macintosh, and Motif.

Forté provides general-purpose object wrappers to interface with legacy applications. Legacy support is provided via RPCs (Netwise) and gateways (SYBASE/MDI and ORACLE), with integration via DDE and object request broker (Digital's Object Broker). Forté facilitates synchronization of processes by supporting transactions across heterogeneous platforms.

Application development is simplified since developers do not have to know the networking protocol, how the application is partitioned, and on which platforms each of the partitions would run. Forté enables multitasking within applications by providing simple commands to invoke asynchronous communications.

In short, Forté is representative of a class of tools that provides developers with the power and flexibility to quickly build three-tiered client/server applications.

17.1.4 Others

Of course, there are many other front-end and development tools on the market today. With the acceptance of ODBC as standard database access API, the database connectivity ceased to be an issue. Therefore, the tool selection process should be based on business application requirements, ease of use, openness, portability to different hardware and operating system platforms, robustness of the applications, integration with other applications and system environments, costs, etc.

Among the tools used today for client/server development are Microsoft Visual Basic and Visual C++, Uniface, SQR and Easy SQR,

Forest & Trees, Microsoft Excel, Lotus 1-2-3, Q+E, Huron, Dynasty, Delphi, and many others.

A detailed discussion on this subject is certainly beyond the scope of this book, but even this short list demonstrates that the choices are many, and each choice comes with its own advantages and disadvantages.

17.2   APPLICATION TESTING

As client/server computing matures to the point where it can be often deployed for mission-critical applications, the need for reliable and rigorous testing has become even more critical. Interestingly, some of the advantages of client/server development tools—their ease of use and the support for rapid iterative development methodologies (RAD)—can also cause developers to overlook the complexity of client/server application testing. To achieve production-grade quality, client/server applications—like their predecessors, legacy applications—must be both functionally and technically sound. Therefore, client/server applications must be tested, preferably according to the best practices and proven methodologies.

Logically speaking, application testing includes these three phases:

- *Phase 1*—Business users should ensure that the application provides the functionality required and that it meets ease-of-use and ease-of-learning requirements.

- *Phase 2*—This involves technical testing designed to ensure that all aspects of the application, from the user interface components to application logic and data access, contains no errors.

- *Phase 3*—The application should be stress-tested to ensure that it will support the user base.

Experience shows that organizations that have omitted these testing phases in the development process have paid the price in ongoing repair.

Historically, when PC-based application development and deployment was limited to the desktop, testing of applications was often informal at best. Errors ("bugs") were not proactively searched and removed. Instead, developers waited until the application software produced an unexpected response before taking action. However, this approach cannot support the ever-increasing demands on the availability of client/server applications and systems. Analysis of the development trends shows that, while programming tasks in building client/server applications are decreasing in complexity, the tasks associated with effective and thorough testing of a client/server application are increasingly challenging, as procedures and tools for ensuring the technical and functional quality of client/server applications are still immature.

Client/server application testing requires new extensions to the standard test planning process. These new extensions include client/server components—the client software, the connectivity software, and the server software—that first must be tested individually with individual test plans and then tested as a cohesive integrated (but still distributed!) system.

For the *server* components, many concepts of mainframe application testing may be preserved, including the creation of test data and data values, verification of output, verification of inputs, and stress testing.

For *connectivity,* the testing is twofold:

- First, the single communication between client and server needs to be tested.
- Second, the system must be tested with the maximum amount of possible users stress-testing the application at one time for both response times and accuracy of data passing between application components.

On the *client* side, testing should start with the usability of the user interface and the applications (even though this will have been done during the requirements and prototyping phases already). Then, the testing plan should include the response times and data accuracy. Plus, all window objects, such as push buttons and slide bars, and each application function available through the GUI windowing features (e.g., "save," "save as," "print") must also be individually tested. Finally, because client/server applications tend to be event/action driven, rather than procedural, the test plan must ensure that each user will exercise applications functions in a different order. The testing plan must consider each possible path through the application for testing.

Another important aspect of client/server application testing is the *technical quality* testing. In a traditional mainframe-centric environment, many tools from multiple vendors are available to assist with the technical testing. Tools for defect detection, performance monitoring, coverage analysis, capture and playback for data entry, test data generators, and comparators are successfully deployed and used for quality assurance testing. Unfortunately, the situation is different in the world of client/server where not only the mainframe code but the server and client components must be tested as well. For example, to test applications that use character-based terminal devices, there exist tools that allow a data stream from an on-line screen to be easily captured. In a windowed environment, such as MS Windows and

OSF/Motif, the picture is much more complex since every possible action from mouse click to keystroke must be simulated. A similar situation exists in regard to performance monitors, resource utilization analyzers, and the like. Although it is highly probable that existing vendors of testing technologies will extend their product offerings to provide similar functionality for client/server applications, in the meantime, many organizations are forced to extend testing tools, methodologies, and procedures to include the unique functions of client/server technologies. These extensions include procedures for creating test data to test all potential data values, performing manual performance benchmarks, and verifying the results of all client/server interactions. Often, additional procedures must be developed to monitor a client/server application's internals, such as memory allocations, network traffic, database, and gateway functionality, all of which can impact performance.

17.3 PUTTING IT ALL TOGETHER

This is a book about architecture. To review, the purpose of architecture is to guide the understanding, building, and maintenance of systems. In general, a system architecture (and that certainly includes client/server architecture) can be viewed as a topology map that defines the system as a set of related components and their interfaces. The components of such a topology may include applications, utilities, and databases. The data content of the interactions among the components is defined through the interfaces. One of the benefits of having such an architecture map is that it can be used to evaluate the impact of a change on system components which allows the implementation of the change with less interruption to existing systems.

Chapter 2 of this book looked at the first-generation, two-tiered client/server systems and noticed the limitation of that architecture in scaleability, performance, manageability, and reliability to be deployed as enterprise-wide solutions. A more robust three-tiered client/server architecture was described as an information model where the client components, application services, and data services are functionally and technically separated from one another and distributed across the network. But even that model was demonstrated to have limitations. Another model, a services-based model that includes clients, servers, and middleware, was offered as the most comprehensive and best-suited for enterprise-wide client/server computing.

The bulk of this book's material is dedicated to discussions on various aspects and components of this services-based model, their interfaces and the interaction between the components The reader has been introduced to the notions of client and server specialization, communications and middleware, distributed database processing and data replication, distributed systems management, and data warehousing, to name just a few.

Let's select *data access* as an example through which to illustrate the power of the services-based architecture. Data access is the key functional component of the client/server architecture, and, using the services-based approach, we can map all client/server components related to data access into one cohesive model (see Fig. 17.2).

17.3.1   Data access services architecture for DSS and OLTP applications

The services-based approach to data access in the client/server computing model implies that applications rely on two underlying sets of services to access various forms of data: *common services* and *specialized services*. From the data access viewpoint, these sets of services are designed to:

- Provide a well-defined and consistent way to access various data sources from any application

- Provide application-independent data management facilities

- Insulate applications from the intricacies of the underlying data storage, manipulation, and management technologies

- Provide reasonable (business-defined) levels of performance, throughput, and robustness for all access to structured and unstructured data under management by utilizing access methods optimized for specific data stores

While the first three requirements are the responsibility of the common data access services, the fourth requirement represents a data store-specific set of services and drivers highly tuned to maximize the underlying technology of a given data management system. In general, this services-based approach to data access can be applied equally well to two major application classes: Decision Support Systems (DSS) and on-line transaction processing (OLTP) systems. In this context, the services-based architecture should satisfy two opposing but complementary requirements:

- To provide *common* data access services software layer by supporting *common reusable* data access objects and data management facilities

- To support diverse and often specialized processing and data requirements typical of DSS and OLTP application classes by providing *distinct subsets* of the architecture that are specialized for DSS and OLTP environments, respectively

The latter requirement implies that the DSS-oriented subset of services should rely on an implementation of a data warehouse and a common metadata repository for the majority of its data access services, while the OLTP-oriented services work with the "operational" data and employ services of a robust transaction manager. It also means that while the DSS-oriented services may benefit from common data access APIs such as ODBC, the OLTP-based architecture may have to (directly or indirectly) employ "native" DBMS drivers and APIs.

17.3.2 Common services—data access middleware

This data access services architecture (see Fig. 17.2) is *services-based* and is organized into three distinct architectural layers. As such, this architecture can be easily mapped into the three-tiered client/server model without sacrificing any benefits of the latter.

Indeed, from the client's perspective, the architecture provides a number of data access objects that use well-defined APIs to interact with a set of common data access services—*data access middleware.* This layer helps insulate client applications from the intricacies of the underlying database technology as well as from the complexity of heterogeneous distributed data environments.

On the server side, however, the effectiveness, throughput, robustness, and performance requirements of data access mechanisms

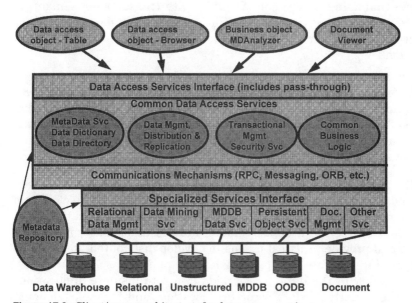

Figure 17.2 Client/server architecture for data access services.

demand a high degree of specialization. This is especially true given the heterogeneity of various data stores, supporting hardware, and software platforms. This need for specialization of data access services is reflected in the set of *specialized services interfaces* that support a number of data access technologies and corresponding data stores.

The architecture is designed to coexist with OMG's CORBA and with OLE-based data access objects residing on the first tier (client). An object request broker mechanism can be employed to deliver data access requests to the second tier that acts as the data access middleware.

The data access middleware tier contains *common data access services* that are accessed via a well-defined data access API. The common data access services component of the architecture consists of the several major service classes, which work cooperatively to deliver proper data access services support:

- *Common dictionary, data directory and metadata services.* Provide data definitions, data location, and other relevant information about all types of data under management. This group of services interacts directly with the metadata repository and the data warehouse.

- *Data management, distribution, and replication services.* Provide services necessary to support remote and distributed data access, timeliness and consistency of replicas, workload distribution, and overall management of the archiving and disaster recovery services.

- *Transactional management and support services.* Provide applications and data management facilities with transactional semantics, ensure data integrity and reliability, and provide general recovery services. These services are primarily targeted toward OLTP applications.

- *Common business logic (common application services).* A set of shareable multitasking components that interact with clients, peer services, and the data stores. These components provide a common set of reusable library functions that may include the enforcement of business rules and policies, application-specific security mechanisms, and utilities.

By definition, the scope of data access middleware services is well beyond a single technology. Rather, it is an integrated suite of system software services that provide universal (i.e., for any application, from any data source) data access, enable flexible multiplatform applications, and provide practical means to develop distributed applications that can interoperate with existing legacy applications and data.

The ability of the data access middleware to insulate applications from the underlying data structure, location, and technology should remove traditional obstacles to flexibility and portability. Thus, implementing data access middleware will provide for application scaleability and deployment portability, and will minimize the impact on the applications when hardware and software platforms change.

The clean architectural separation of the common data access services from the DBMS-specific specialized services can be implemented by placing common data access services on a separate platform(s) that can act as a new middleware server added to the client/server network. Using this approach should provide an opportunity to manage, recover, tune, and scale the data access middleware server platform in order to maximize the overall performance and robustness of the entire architecture.

This approach will also have a significant positive impact on the application development. Indeed, data access middleware should eliminate the need for the labor-intensive and often expensive training in specific DBMS APIs, and will allow application developers to focus on how data is being used to solve business functions.

Client view

To take full advantage of the capabilities offered by data access middleware, the data access services architecture utilizes an object-oriented approach to requesting data access services. Applications should be structured in such a way that all data access requests are encapsulated into a number of reusable data access objects. These data access objects will invoke object request brokers to communicate the requests to the data access services components (server objects).

Specialized services

The common data access services component validates, parses, and prepares the application request to be processed by the *specialized data services* component. It resides on the third tier of the architecture, where all data stores and corresponding specialized servers exist. Due to a wide variety of existing and new data structures, and the high complexity of the processing associated with each individual type of data, this tier contains a number of vendor solutions designed to be most efficient for a specific data store or type. Each of these solutions may provide its own proprietary or standards-based specialized services interface. It is the responsibility of the common data access services to parse incoming data requests and translate them into appropriate interface calls. For example, the specialized data access services layer contains:

- *Relational data management component* handles all accesses to relational data stores and supports ANSI SQL, X/Open RDA, ODBC, and vendor APIs such as SYBASE DB-Lib and CT-Lib, ORACLE OCI, and IBM's DRDA.

- *On-line analytical processing and data mining services* provide a set of software tools designed to support the advanced analytical requirements of business units. These services provide interactive access to multidimensional data for applications such as portfolio analysis and market segmentation, and may exploit the capabilities of unorthodox processing techniques such as neural networks, genetic algorithms, and case-based reasoning. To achieve desired performance and throughput, these services may employ a number of high-performance computing architectures.

- *Persistent objects services* provide storage and management capabilities for business and application objects.

- *Document management services* support storage, retrieval, search, and version control capabilities for documents.

- *Web services* provide access to HTML-encoded pages and Java applets on the World Wide Web.

- *Others* (image, animation, video-on-demand, etc.)—these services support access to unstructured data.

To summarize, the aforementioned data access services architecture is a good illustration of the power and flexibility of the services-based approach to architecting enterprise-wide client/server solutions. The services-based architecture spans the boundaries between application, data, technology, and support architectures to focus on services that have to be provided to consumers of these services—businesses. This services-based approach facilitates completeness of the solution and provides a unified framework of designing and deploying large-scale client/server environments.

17.4   CLIENT/SERVER COSTS

A number of industry consultants maintain that the driving force behind client/server computing is the ability to save money by running applications on inexpensive (compared to traditional mainframe) hardware platforms. However, experience shows that as client/server systems move from departmental levels to the larger enterprise, cost savings do not materialize, and frequently the expenses grow higher than was anticipated (and higher than the system was budgeted for). The main reason for this phenomenon is the fact that hardware represents only a small fraction of the total cost of client/server computing. Enterprise client/server computing is pushing beyond the boundaries of the first-generation, departmental client/server systems along the following trends:

- Extending the capabilities of local area networks into wide area networking

- Integrating client/server applications with the legacy data stores and systems, which often requires companies to run newer client/server systems and legacy systems in parallel

- Extending the availability attributes of client/server systems into a data center-like environment, attempting to achieve 24-x-7 continuous operation

- Extending the data center systems management disciplines into the new client/server environment

- Introducing new challenges related to the distributed and open nature of client/server computing, including, but not limited to, electronic software distribution, distributed security, the rapid pace of changes in technology, and the lack of immaturity of several key standards.

All these trends and requirements of new client/server systems affect the development, deployment, and operational costs. In fact, we can probably group all costs into the immediate, obvious costs and hidden, future costs.

The first group includes client and server hardware, operating system software, DBMS software, networking hardware and software, front-end software tools, network installation, application development and/or legacy application conversion, and training. Even though these costs could be quite significant, they do not take into account the reality of building a distributed client/server environment.

Therefore, consider the second group of cost factors, which may include pilot development, legacy system conversion, systemwide administration and management, potential network bandwidth upgrades, backup and recovery solutions, cost of planned and unplanned downtime, security implementation, upgrades of hardware and software, maintenance of the applications and systems, and training for the upgrades.

Let's look at some of these hidden costs more closely. A typical departmental LAN may have a set of systems management and security tools, but they are rarely robust enough and capable enough to be integrated with the enterprise tools installed in and operated from the corporate data center. Current LAN systems management is poorly automated and therefore is labor-intensive and expensive. Since the systems management, troubleshooting, backup and recovery, availability, and security requirements of enterprise client/server computing have to satisfy stringent data center standards, the costs involved in upgrading to these levels may be quite high. Indeed, while the downtime of a LAN system can reach several hours, often without any serious impact on the company's business, the situation is by definition quite different for the enterprise, and high availability is always expensive.

The diversity of platforms, operating systems, databases, and software components that is typical of an enterprise client/server system not only requires a multidiscipline, cross-trained system administration and database administration staff, but also makes the problem identification and resolution process very difficult.

Another source of difficulty (and additional cost) comes from the need to internetwork multiple (sometimes heterogeneous) local area networks. The LAN integration often becomes a project unto itself.

In addition, when the original LAN was designed, it probably did not take into account the need to accommodate high network traffic often associated with enterprise transaction processing. Coupled with the need for the two-phase commit traffic, this may force the requirement to increase the network bandwidth—a clear source of additional, often unanticipated costs.

Finally, let's consider client/server application development. It is often true that using intuitive, graphical client/server application development tools boosts the developer's productivity. However, at the same time, organizations do not realize that testing event-driven applications (i.e., GUI-based applications) often takes as much as three times as many testing professionals (and corresponding time) as testing old-style procedure-driven applications.

17.5 BENEFITS AND ADVANTAGES OF CLIENT/SERVER COMPUTING

Client/server computing has evolved from the first-generation, simple two-tiered client/server model to the current complex, three-tiered, enterprise-wide, mission-critical generation of client/server computing. Client/server computing continues to proliferate and advance, mainly because its current and prospective users—extensive networked enterprises and organizations looking to decentralize, downsize, and distribute their data processing operations—continue to demand enhancements in functionality and technology, shorter time to market for new products, higher productivity, and improvement in the cost effectiveness of solutions.

Among these demands is the need to move toward open distributed systems. As a rule, most users are facing the problems of portability and interoperability in heterogeneous networked environments. Indeed, portability and interoperability, and not a particular operating system, are what users are looking for in the open systems arena. Such openness can be achieved by:

- Building the entire computing environment and its various components in compliance with the international and industry-accepted standards

- Distributing various application components between clients and servers and interconnecting them via efficient, standards-based networks

- Integrating all distributed system, heterogeneous hardware and software platforms, various presentation and database management systems into a seamless, cohesive, reliable, and secure single system image

- Providing tools and mechanisms to effectively manage and control this new, open, distributed client/server environment

- Ensuring that the openness of the environment does not compromise the security and integrity of applications and data

The client/server architecture is not the end of all architectures, and it has some serious drawbacks. Complexity is one of them. However, users can find that there are real benefits in adopting the client/server architecture. Specifically, client/server architecture:

- Allows corporations to better leverage emerging microcomputer computing technology. Today's workstations deliver considerable computing power, previously available only from mainframes, at a fraction of mainframe cost.

- Delivers applications quickly to end users. Because of specialization of client/server platforms and distribution of application components, application functionality can be delivered and refined in relatively short intervals. Client/server architecture helps speed up the implementation of new systems by eliminating ambiguity and defining components and APIs.

- Helps achieve systems interoperability, data sharing, and the general improvement in the system quality and the increased flexibility to make modifications more easily in the future.

- Facilitates implementation of business process reengineering (BPR), which is aimed at helping companies to redesign jobs and workflows to achieve orders-of-magnitude operational improvements. Additionally, client/server architecture defines the architected process which is the communication of a common direction throughout the organization.

- Allows the processing to reside close to the source of data being processed, therefore reducing network traffic and the response time. As a result, the effective network throughput is increased, and the network bandwidth requirements and associated costs can be reduced.

- Facilitates the use of standards-based graphical user interfaces (GUIs). These new, intuitive, easily navigated, and consistent interfaces can be delivered to customers in a variety of visual presentation techniques. As a result, investment in training and education can be better leveraged, and new products exceeding customer expectations can be developed faster. End-user resistance in accepting new products can be minimized.

- Improves maintenance and control of the distributed client/server environment through a more consistent approach to system management.

- Enables organizations to achieve and maintain competitive advantage, especially by leveraging emerging technologies for the strategic use of data. Building data warehouses and employing powerful client/server analytical tools (OLAP, data mining, data visualization) can position an organization to expand its market share, improve customer support, and in general win competitively.

- Allows for and encourages the acceptance of open systems. Indeed, by its own nature, the client/server computing model calls for the specialization of the client and server platform. The need to interconnect heterogeneous systems, to port applications between client and server systems, and to be able to participate in cooperative processing allows end users to free themselves from proprietary architectures. Thus, users are able to take economical, marketing, and competitive advantage of the open systems market.

The client/server computing model holds many promises both to developers and to end users. Some of these promises are achievable today, while others will hopefully be solved tomorrow. And while client/server architecture will not turn nontechnical users into professional software developers, it can, if properly implemented, reduce software maintenance costs, increase software portability, boost performance of existing networks, and even eliminate application backlog by increasing developers' productivity and shortening the development life cycle.

17.6   WHAT IS NEXT?

It is difficult to predict the future. Some things, however, have a relatively high probability of becoming reality based on the analysis of current trends and dynamics of the marketplace. Among those trends, several are quite clear: object-orientation, data warehousing, distributed heterogeneous computing, interactive multimedia, mobile computing, commercialization of the Internet reinforced by the Information Superhighway, OLAP and data mining, maturing of data quality tools and techniques, and high-performance commercial computing. All these are well suited to the client/server computing model.

Indeed, the World Wide Web, the wide variety of Web browsers (e.g., Mosaic, Netscape), and the new distributed computing model represented by Sun Microsystem's Java are all examples of the multimedia graphical client/server environments designed to access information on the Internet in an intuitive graphical fashion. And it's not just multimedia—RDBMS vendors and companies such as Illustra offer attractive and easy ways to access data on the Web, as well as to support complex, unstructured, user-defined data types and functions.

Parallel commercial computing reflects the notion of server and client specialization. For a database server, it means a move toward a scaleable parallel database management system. Unfortunately, the world continues to undergo rapid and dramatic changes. For example, the computing power of microprocessors doubles every 18 months, and it is not difficult to imagine a hand-held computer capable of performing tasks that today require a three-tiered client/server system. It is also clear that the size of business data accumulated and managed by organizations is also doubling at about the same rate (indeed, supermarket scanners can collect about 1 TB of data a day!). And the need for ever-higher computing power; opportunities to discover extremely valuable and previously unknown information in the oceans of data; and the ability to process previously unmanageable data types such as multimedia, images, voice, and video, will continue to drive computing architectures and technology to new horizons.

Let's look at the requirements that the rapidly changing business world imposes on the current and emerging technology architecture:

- New systems must be cost effective, scaleable, reliable, and powerful enough to handle current and future processing requirements.

- New systems must be able to provide application, management, information, and communication services to the growing population of users and other interconnected systems.

- New systems must be able to interoperate with existing client/server and legacy systems.

- New computing environments must be open and flexible to accommodate future technological innovations with a minimal impact on existing systems.

- New systems management environments must be able to simplify and reduce the overhead of managing distributed heterogeneous systems and networks.

In short, what appears to be a possible future direction of client/server computing is an emergence of the enterprise server platform, which can be envisioned as a collection of services that satisfy the preceding requirements and are distributed across the network for the best price and performance, high availability, and manageability.

An example of the client/server computing evolution toward this enterprise server platform is the continued specialization of clients and servers, and the recognition of the value of scaleability, availability, and manageability that resulted in the second-generation three-tiered client/server architecture of today, and possibly a services-based multitiered architecture of tomorrow.

However, even the client/server architecture is not the end of the evolution of the computing environment. The next evolutionary step in client/server computing could be a client/network/server model, where remote servers and clients cooperate over the network (most probably, the Internet) to do work. In contrast to a well-defined and heavily tuned client/server arrangement, here any client can engage in any session *without* prearranged setup.

For example, any user could get on the Internet, go to a home page, click on a session, receive executable code automatically, and instantly engage in a rich multimedia connection. While traditional client/server computing limits applications to a small neighborhood of prearranged users, the new model lets millions of Internet-connected clients have access to a rapidly growing population of dynamic applications. An even higher degree of evolution could be towards a peer-to-peer computing model where all participant systems are equals and can request and provide services to and from each other. Very few products today even claim to support peer-to-peer processing.

This architecture appears to be the ultimate in distribution of application processing. The processing is performed wherever there are available computing resources, including shared devices, CPU, and memory. A single system in peer-to-peer processing can act as a client for other servers and a server for itself and other clients. In intelligent peer-to-peer processing, one server can not only distribute a workload among available servers, but can even optimize such a distribution based on network characteristics, available routes, and system resources. This computing model holds the promise of being able to satisfy many requirements in an evolutionary fashion.

If the client/server architecture presents system designers with a wealth of complex, not always easily solvable issues, the spectrum of outstanding technical issues relevant to the implementation of a peer-to-peer computing architecture is far greater. However, the client/server computing model, as an evolutionary step towards the goal of peer-to-peer computing, is a promising and powerful architecture. It provides business solutions that allow the development of open distributed systems *today*.

Appendix

Glossary

Access method A method used to move data between the main storage and peripheral devices (e.g., I/O devices such as tapes or disks). Access can be sequential (records are accessed one after another in the order in which they appear in the file), random (individual records can be referred to in any order), and dynamic (both sequential and random access is allowed).

Advanced Interactive eXecutive (AIX) IBM's version of the UNIX operating system.

Advanced Peer-to-Peer Networking (APPN) Data communication support that routes data in a network between two or more APPC systems that are not directly attached.

Advanced Program-to-Program Communications (APPC) Peer-level data communication support, based on SNA's Logical Unit Type 6.2 protocols.

Alert An error message sent to a central network control point (e.g., SSCP) at a host system.

American National Standard Code for Information Interchange (ASCII) The code, developed by ANSI, for information exchange between data processing systems, data communication systems, and associated equipment. The ASCII character set consists of 7-bit characters plus one bit for parity check.

American National Standards Institute (ANSI) An organization sponsored by the Computer and Business Equipment Manufacturers Association for establishing voluntary industry standards.

API See **Application programming interface.**

Application program   (1) A program written for or by a user that performs the user's work. (2) A program used to connect and communicate with stations on a network.

Application programming interface (API)   The formally defined programming language interface between a program (system control program, licensed program) and its user. In VTAM, API is the interface through which a program interacts with the access method.

Application requester (AR)   In DRDA, the source of a request sent to a remote relational database management system.

Application server (AS)   In DRDA, the target of a request from an AR.

APPC   See **Advanced Program-to-Program Communications**.

APPN   See **Advanced Peer-to-Peer Networking**.

Architecture-Neutral Distribution Format (ANDF)   A way to develop and distribute software independently from the hardware architecture platform on which the software is intended to run.

Artificial neural network (ANN)   See **Neural network**.

AS/400   Application System/400. A family of IBM's midrange computers.

Asynchronous processing   A series of operations that are done separately from the job or transaction in which they were requested.

Asynchronous transmission   In data communication, a method of transmission in which the sending and receiving of data is controlled by control characters rather than by a timing sequence.

Back-end program   In CICS, a program that is initiated by the front-end program in order to support an LU6.2 conversation.

Batch   In contrast with interactive, a group of jobs to be run on a computer sequentially, with little or no operator intervention.

Binary code   A binary data representation for discrete data. Each distinct category is assigned an integer value and coded as a standard binary string.

Binary large object (BLOB)   Very large (may be several gigabytes in size) binary representation of an image data type.

Binary synchronous communications (BSC)   A data communications line protocol that uses a standard set of transmission control characters and control character sequences to send binary-coded data over a communication line. Contrast with **synchronous data link control**.

BIND   A request to activate a session between two logical units.

Boundary function   In SNA, (1) the capability of a subarea node to provide protocol support for adjacent peripheral nodes, such as transforming network addresses to local addresses, performing session sequence numbering, or providing session-level pacing support. (2) A component that provides these capabilities.

Bridge   A means (device) of connecting two similar environments at relatively low protocol levels (such as two LANs at the logical link level).

Buffer   A portion of storage for temporarily holding input or output data.

Carrier Sense Multiple Access with Collision Detection or Collision Avoidance (CSMA/CD, CSMA/CA)   Popular LAN networking protocols.

CCITT   The International Telephone and Telegraph Consultative Committee.

Change-direction protocol   A data flow control function in which the sending logical unit stops sending requests, signals the receiver using the change-direction indicator, and prepares to receive requests.

Channel   A path along which signals can be sent—e.g. System/390 data channels.

Channel-attached   Attachment of a device directly to the computer channel.

Character Data Representation Architecture (CDRA)   In DRDA, the architecture that defines codes to represent characters and conversion to/from these codes.

CICS (Customer Information Control System)   A teleprocessing and transaction management system which runs as a VTAM application.

Classification (in data mining)   The process of learning to distinguish and discriminate between different input patterns using a supervised training algorithm. Classification is the process of determining that a record belongs to a group.

Classification and regression trees (CART)   A computer software technique that finds rules for making predictions by repeatedly breaking up historical examples of data into ever smaller subgroups.

Client   A system entity (combination of hardware and software components) which requests particular services to be done on its behalf from another entity—a server.

Cluster controller   A channel-attached or link-attached device that can control the input/output operations of more than one device connected to it (e.g., IBM 3174).

Clustering (in data mining)   The process of grouping similar input patterns together using an unsupervised training algorithm.

Commit   The process that causes the changes to the protected resources to become permanent. See also **Syncpoint.**

Common Gateway Interface (CGI)   In WWW, an interface designed to allow access from the client application directly to the remote relational database.

Communication controller   Communication hardware that operates under the control of the network control program (NCP) and manages communication lines, cluster controllers, workstations, and routing of data through the network.

Complex Instruction Set Computing (CISC)   The opposite of RISC (**Reduced Instruction Set Computing**), a computer system architecture that utilizes a relatively large set of complex instructions, where each instruction requires more than one CPU cycle to execute.

Configurator   In the SYBASE Navigation Server, a tool used for up-front planning and ongoing management of the Navigation Server configuration.

Congestion   An overload condition caused by traffic in excess of the network's capabilities.

Control server   A component of the SYBASE Navigation Server that acts as a front-end request processor.

Conversation   The logical connection between a pair of transaction programs for serially sharing a session between two type 6.2 logical units. Conversations are delimited by brackets to gain exclusive use of a session.

CORBA (Common Object Request Broker Architecture)   An architecture developed by the Object Management Group (OMG) to provide portability and interoperability of objects over a network of heterogeneous systems. CORBA defines an object-oriented switching mechanism, the object request broker, for the messages passed between objects.

Cryptography   The transformation of data to conceal its meaning.

CS-Library   A library of routines that are useful to both client and server applications. All Client-Library applications will include at least one call to CS-Library. Client-Library routines use a structure which is located in CS-Library. CS-Library is included with both the Open Client and Open Server products.

CT-Library   A call-level interface also used to write client applications. Client Library is new to System 10 and is designed to accommodate cursors and other advanced features in the SYBASE 10 product line. Advanced programming features such as asynchronous programming and callback events are supported. Connection processing and error and message handling have all been improved.

Data mining   The process of efficient discovery of nonobvious valuable information from a large collection of data.

Data channel   A device that connects a processor and main storage with I/O control units.

Data Definition Language (DDL)   A part of the Structured Query Language (SQL) that consists of the commands responsible for the creation/deletion of the database objects.

Data flow control (DFC) layer   The SNA layer within a half-session that controls whether the half-session can send, receive, or concurrently send and receive RUs; groups related RUs into RU chains; delimits transactions through the use of brackets; controls the interlocking of the requests and responses; generates sequence numbers; and associates requests with responses.

Data link control (DLC) layer   The SNA layer that consists of the link stations that schedule data transfer over a link between two nodes and perform error control for the link.

Data Manipulation Language (DML)   A part of the Structured Query Language (SQL) that consists of the operators responsible for the data manipulation (e.g., SELECT, DELETE, UPDATE, INSERT).

Data Server Interface (DSI)   An Open Client connection from a Replication Server to a data server that maps to a connection.

Data stream   A continuous stream of defined-format data elements being transmitted or intended to be transmitted.

Database cursor   A mechanism for accessing the results of a SQL select statement one row at a time. Using cursor applications can process each row individually rather than having to process the entire set of rows returned by the select.

Database device   In SYBASE, a logical device that is mapped to a raw disk partition or an operating system file.

Database management system (DBMS)   A software system that controls and manages the data to eliminate data redundancy and to ensure data integrity, consistency, and availability, among other features.

Database mirroring   The DBMS capability to maintain a duplicate of the database and the transaction log, each on separate devices.

DB-Library   A call-level interface used to write client applications. DB-Library includes a bulk copy library and a special two-phase commit library.

Decipher   To return enciphered data to its original form.

Definite response   A protocol that directs the receiver of the request to unconditionally return a positive or negative response to that request.

Digital Network Architecture (DNA)   A network architecture developed by Digital Equipment Corporation.

Directory services   Services for resolving user identifications of network components to network routing information.

Distributed Computing Environment (DCE)   The standards-based environment developed by the Open Software Foundation (OSF) that provides interoperability and portability across heterogeneous distributed systems.

Distributed data management (DDM)   An architecture that allows application programs or users on one system to access data stored on remote systems.

Distributed Management Environment (DME)   A standards-based computing environment proposed by the OSF that provides a distributed management solution for the DCE.

Distributed Relational Database Architecture (DRDA)   A connection architecture developed by IBM to provide access to relational databases distributed across various (IBM) platforms.

Distributed request   An extension of the **distributed unit of work (DUW)** method of accessing distributed relational data where a single SQL statement may reference data residing in different systems. Distributed request support includes unions and joins across distributed DBMSs.

Distributed transaction processing (DTP)   A type of transaction processing that is characterized by synchronous communication between partners, accomplished via LU6.2 protocols.

Distributed unit of work (DUW)   A method of accessing distributed relational data where each SQL statement may reference only one system location, but the unit of work may consist of several SQL statements that can read and write data from several distributed DBMSs.

Document Interchange Architecture (DIA)   Protocols within the transaction services layer, used by distributed office application processes for data interchange.

Duplex   Simultaneous two-way independent data transmission in both directions.

EBCDIC   Extended binary-coded decimal interchange code.

Emulator High-Level Language Application Programming Interface (EHLLAPI)   An API that provides a way for users to access the 3270 host presentation space.

Encipher   To scramble or convert data prior to transmission in order to hide the meaning of the data from an unauthorized user.

End user   The ultimate source and destination of data in an SNA network.

Ethernet   LAN architecture that uses CSMA/CD for media access control.

Event callback model   A presentation logic technique used in some graphical user interface (GUI) routines to handle events.

Event control block (ECB)   A control block used to represent the status of an event.

Event loop model   A presentation logic technique used in some graphical user interface (GUI) routines to handle events.

Exception response   A protocol that directs the receiver to return a response only if the request is unacceptable or cannot be processed.

Exit routine   Special-purpose, user-written routine.

Expert system   A data-processing system comprising a knowledge base (rules), an inference (rules) engine, and a working memory.

Fiber Distributed Data Interchange (FDDI)   High-performance networking standard based on the token-passing technique used in the optical fiber cable.

Finite-state machine   An architectural entity that can be placed in a limited number of defined states as the result of applying allowed input sequences.

Flow control   The process of managing the rate at which data traffic passes through a network.

Formatted Data Object Content Architecture (FD:OCA)   An architected collection of constructs used to interchange formatted data.

Front-end program   In CICS, a program that is responsible for starting an LU6.2 conversation with the back-end program.

Full duplex   See **Duplex.**

Function shipping A CICS facility that allows certain CICS functions, requested in one CICS system, to access resources on another, remote CICS system.

Fuzzy logic A system of logic based on the fuzzy set theory.

Fuzzy set A set of items whose degree of membership in the set may range from 0 to 1.

Fuzzy system A set of rules using fuzzy linguistic variables described by fuzzy sets and processed using fuzzy logic operations.

General data stream (GDS) Data and commands that are defined by length and identification bytes.

Genetic algorithm A method of solving optimization problems using parallel search, based on Darwin's biological model of natural selection and survival of the fittest.

Genetic operator An operation on the population member strings in a genetic algorithm which are used to produce new strings.

Graphical user interface (GUI) An interface used by display workstations to interface with end users, that provides a consistent API and a standard look and feel. Microsoft's Windows, OSF/Motif, Sun's Open Look, and OS/2 Presentation Manager are some of the most popular GUIs.

Half-duplex In data communications, alternate, one-way-at-a-time, independent transmissions.

Host processor In SNA, a processor where a telecommunication access method resides.

HTML (Hypertext Markup Language) A document formatting language used to build WWW pages.

HTTP (Hypertext Transport Protocol) Communications protocol used on the World Wide Web to transmit HTML-encoded pages.

Intelligent agent A software application which assists a system or a user by automating a task. Intelligent agents must recognize events and use domain knowledge to take appropriate actions based on those events.

Interclient Communications Conventions Manual (ICCM) A set of specifications published by the X Consortium that allow client applications to communicate and work together.

Interface Definition Language (IDL) A language used to define interfaces to interconnect clients and servers. Examples include RPC IDL in the OSF's DCE and ORB IDL in CORBA.

Internet Protocol (IP) A part of the TCP/IP protocol suite that performs data packet segmentation and routing.

Intersystem communications (ISC) In CICS, a way of providing communications between two CICS systems residing in different processors by using the ACF/VTAM access method. This contrasts with CICS Multiregion Operations (MRO).

ISQL (Interactive Structured Query Language)   The SYBASE interface to the SQL Server.

Layer   An architectural grouping of related functions that are logically separated from the functions of the other layers.

Link   The combination of the link connection and link stations that join adjacent nodes in the network.

Link connection   The physical equipment that provides two-way communication between link stations.

Link station   The combination of hardware and software that allows a node to attach to, and provide control for, a link.

Local area network (LAN)   The physical connection that allows information exchanges among devices (typically, personal computers) located on the same premises.

Log transfer manager (LTM)   A component of SYBASE Replication Server that facilitates replication of changes throughout the replicated sites.

Logical unit (LU)   A port through which an end user accesses an SNA network in order to communicate with another end user.

Logical unit of work (LUW)   Work that is performed between the start of a transaction and COMMIT or ROLLBACK of the same transaction.

Loose consistency   In SYBASE Replication Server, the data consistency protocol implemented via replication (contrast with *tight consistency* that is based on the two-phase commit protocol).

LU6.2   Logical unit type 6.2—a special type of logical unit, that supports Advanced Program-to-Program Communications (APPC) between programs in a distributed processing environment. APPC/LU6.2 is characterized by peer-to-peer communication support, comprehensive end-to-end error processing, optimized data transmission flow, and a generic application programming interface.

Management services   In SNA, one of the types of network services in the network control point and physical units (PU) that provide functions for problem management, performance, accounting, configuration, and change management.

Mapped conversation   In APPC, a type of conversation in which the data can be sent and received in a user-defined format, while the data transformation is performed by APPC/LU6.2.

Massively parallel processors (MPP)   A computing architecture based on a distributed-memory, shared-nothing approach.

Memory-based reasoning (in data mining)   A technique for classifying records in a database by comparing them with similar records that are already classified.

Message unit   A generic term for the unit of data processed by a communication system.

Metropolitan area network (MAN) A network using a city infrastructure to connect nodes within the geographical limits of a city.

Middleware A generic term that defines a set of run-time software services designed to insulate clients and servers from the knowledge of environment-specific communications and data access mechanisms.

MIME (Multimedia Internet Mail Enhancements) A freely available standard-ized method of sending and receiving attachments.

Modem A device that modulates and demodulates signals transmitted over data communication facilities in order to convert digital signals into and from an analog form.

Motif A popular window manager selected by the Open Software Foundation for presentation management in its version of the open system environment.

Negative response A response indicating that a request did not arrive suc-cessfully or was not processed successfully by the receiver.

Network address An address that identifies a link, a link station, or a net-work addressable unit.

Network File System (NFS) Popular method of accessing remote files in a UNIX system environment (developed by Sun Microsystems).

Network operating system (NOS) A generic term for the operating system level software used to manage and control networks.

NetView An IBM product used to monitor, manage, and diagnose a network.

Neural network A computing model based on the architecture of the brain. A neural network consists of multiple simple processing units connected by adaptive weights.

Node An endpoint of a link, or a junction common to two or more links.

Object A named unit that consists of a set of characteristics that are encap-sulated within the object and describe the object and data. Certain character-istics of an object are inherited from its *parents* and can be inherited to its *children*. Operations valid for the object are stored together with the object as its methods. In computer architecture, an object can be anything that exists in and occupies space in storage (e.g., programs, files, libraries) and on which operations can be performed.

Object request broker (ORB) A key component of CORBA—an object-oriented message-switching mechanism designed to provide portability and interoperability of objects over a network of heterogeneous systems.

On-line analytical processing (OLAP) Computer-based techniques used to analyze trends and perform business analysis using multidimensional views of business data.

Open Look A popular window manager that is used primarily by the mem-bers of UNIX International (UI).

Open Network Computing (ONC) UNIX International's architecture for an open distributed computing environment.

Open Software Foundation (OSF) Not-for-profit technology organization that intends to develop an open computing environment by selecting technology solutions from its members.

OS/2 (Operating System/2) A multiprogramming, multitasking operating system, developed for the PS/2 family of personal computers.

OSI (Open Systems Interconnection) A layered architecture that is designed to allow for interconnection between heterogeneous systems.

Pacing A technique by which a receiver controls the rate of transmission by the sender.

Packet A data transmission information unit, consisting of a group of data and control characters.

Packet switching The process of routing and transferring data by means of addressed packets.

Parallel sessions Two or more concurrently active sessions between two logical units using different pairs of network addresses.

Positive response A response indicating that a request has been successfully processed.

Presentation Manager (OS/2 PM) An OS/2 component that provides graphical API.

Protocol boundary A synonym for the architecturally defined application program interface.

Queued attach In OS/2 APPC, an incoming allocate request that is queued by the Attach Manager until the transaction program issues an appropriate APPC verb.

Queuing A store-and-forward communication mechanism often employed by messaging middleware.

RAS programs *Reliability, availability,* and *serviceability* programs that facilitate problem determination.

Recommendation X.21 The Consultative Committee on International Telephone and Telegraph (CCITT) recommendations for a general-purpose interface between data terminal equipment and data circuit equipment for synchronous operations on public data networks.

Recommendation X.25 The Consultative Committee on International Telephone and Telegraph (CCITT) recommendations for an interface between data terminal equipment and packet-switched networks.

Reduced Instruction Set Computing (RISC) The opposite of CISC (Complex Instruction Set Computing), a computer system architecture that utilizes a relatively small set of computer instructions where each instruction is "simple" enough to require one CPU cycle to execute.

Reinforcement learning (in data mining) A training model where an intelligence engine (e.g., neural network) is presented with a sequence of input data followed by a reinforcement signal.

Relational database (RDB) A database built to conform to the relational data model; it includes the catalog and all the data described therein.

Remote Data Access (RDA) A proposed ANSI standard to access remote relational databases.

Remote procedure call (RPC) A connectionless method of communication between two programming systems where a requester (client) issues an RPC to execute a procedure on a remote system (server).

Remote request The form of SQL distributed processing where the application runs on a system different from the one housing the RDB. Contains a single SQL statement referencing data located at a single site.

Remote unit of work (RUW) The extension of the remote request form of SQL distributed processing where multiple SQL statements may reference data located at a single remote site.

Replication Server Interface (RSI) An asynchronous interface from one Replication Server to another.

Replication Server Manager (RSM) A GUI-based administration tool for managing the Replication Server system.

Replication Server System Database (RSSD) The SYBASE System Catalog for the Replication Server.

Rhapsody Workflow management software developed by AT&T.

Rollback The process of restoring protected resources to the state at the last commit point.

SA Companion The SYBASE front-end tool for SQL Server administration tasks.

Schema Server A component of the SYBASE Navigation Server used to control the Global Directory.

Server A system entity (combination of hardware and software components) which performs particular services on behalf of another entity—a client.

Server-Requestor Programming Interface (SRPI) An API used by requestor and server programs to communicate with a PC or hosts.

Session A logical connection between two network addressable units that allows them to communicate.

Session-level pacing In SNA, a flow control technique that permits the receiver to control the data transfer rate.

Shared-nothing architecture A computing architecture for parallelizing work in a computer system where multiple processors, each with its own private memory and disk, are interconnected and communicate via messages.

Split Server A component of SYBASE Navigation Server used primarily to process join requests in parallel systems.

SQL Debug The SYBASE source-level debugger for Transact-SQL code.

Stored procedure   An advanced design technique employed by SYBASE to allow a collection of SQL statements and flow-control directives (e.g., IF, THEN, ELSE) to be parsed, verified, compiled, bound, and stored at the DBMS server. Stored procedures are invoked by client applications in a fashion similar to RPC and provide a significant performance improvement over a traditional embedded SQL.

Structured Query Language (SQL)   A standard for the nonnavigational data access and definition language used in relational databases.

Subscription   In SYBASE Replication Server, a technique that allows all or parts of data tables to be replicated to the subscribers of that data. It uses a **Subscription Resolution Engine** (SRE) to match primary data with the subscription for that data.

Supervised learning (in data mining)   A training model where the intelligence engine (e.g., neural network) is presented with an input pattern and a desired output pattern.

SYBASE Backup Server   A component of SYBASE System 10 designed specifically to perform backup operations.

SYBASE Navigation Server   A component of SYBASE System 10 that is designed to provide database scaleability and performance by taking advantage of SMP and MPP computing architectures.

SYBASE OmniSQL Server   The SYBASE gateway product (an Open Server application) designed to provide a transparent access to distributed heterogeneous databases.

SYBASE Open Client   A programmable client component (a set of library routines and the corresponding APIs, such as DB-Lib and CT-Lib) of Sybase's suite of client/server products.

SYBASE Open Server   A programmable server component of Sybase's suite of client/server products.

SYBASE Replication Server   A SYBASE System 10 component that implements and manages database replication.

SYBASE SQL Monitor   A SYBASE System 10 tool used to monitor SYBASE SQL Server performance.

Symmetric multiprocessing (SMP)   A computer architecture where several tightly coupled CPUs share a common memory and common workload.

Synchronization level   In APPC, the specification indicating that the conversation allows no synchronization (SYNCLEVEL=NONE) and supports confirmation exchanges (SYNCLEVEL=CONFIRM) or full synchronization (SYNCLEVEL=SYNCPT).

Synchronous Data Link Control (SDLC)   A communication protocol for managing synchronous code-transparent, serial-by-bit information transfer over a link connection.

Synchronous transmission   In data communication, a method of transmission where the sending and receiving of characters is controlled by timing signals.

Syncpoint   (1) A point in time when all protected resources accessed by an application are consistent. (2) An LU6.2 verb that causes all changes to protected resources to become permanent, and, therefore, the resources are consistent. See also **Commit.**

Systems Network Architecture (SNA)   The description of the logical structure, formats, protocols, and operational sequences for transmitting information through and controlling configuration and operation of networks.

Systems Network Architecture Distributed Services (SNADS)   An IBM architecture that defines a set of rules to receive, route, and send electronic mail across networks.

System Services Control Point (SSCP)   In SNA, a central location point within an SNA network for managing the configuration, coordinating network operator and problem determination requests, and providing directory support and other session services for end users.

Targeted marketing   The marketing of products to select groups of consumers that are more likely than average to be interested in the offer.

Terminal   In data communication, a device capable of sending and receiving information.

Threads   A unit of context management under the control of a single process that can be implemented within the server process or via operating system services.

Time-series forecasting   The process of using a data mining tool (e.g., neural networks) to learn to predict temporal sequences of patterns, so that, given a set of patterns, it can predict a future value.

Time-sharing option (TSO)   A feature of an operating system (i.e., MVS) that provides conversational time sharing of system resources from remote stations.

Top End   A transaction monitor developed by the NCR Corporation to provide transaction management in the open systems (UNIX-based) distributed environment.

Transaction   In communications, a unit of processing and information exchange between a local and a remote program that accomplishes a particular action or result.

Transaction Monitor/Transaction Manager (TPM)   Software system that provides control and management functions to support transaction execution, synchronization, integrity, consistency, atomicity, and durability.

Transaction program (TP)   In APPC, a program that uses the APPC API to communicate with a partner transaction program on a remote system.

Transaction routing   In CICS, a facility that allows CICS transactions, initiated on a local CICS system, to be executed on a remote CICS system.

Transact-SQL   Sybase's proprietary programming and control language.

Transmission Control Protocol/Internet Protocol (TCP/IP)   Communication protocol popular because of its openness and easy interoperability features.

Threshold Manager A feature of SYBASE System 10 that monitors the amount of free space available on a particular database segment and executes a predefined stored procedure when a threshold is reached.

Triggers In a DBMS, triggers can be viewed as a special type of stored procedure that have the ability to initiate (trigger) certain user-defined actions based on a particular data-related event. Triggers are often used to implement referential integrity constraints.

Tuxedo A transaction monitor developed by AT&T to provide transaction management in the UNIX system distributed environment.

Two-phase commit (2PC) A protocol that ensures the integrity and consistency of all protected resources affected by a distributed transaction.

Unit of work The amount of processing that is executed from the time the transaction is started to the time the transaction is ended.

Universal resource locator (URL) A format used to specify addresses on the Web.

Unsupervised learning A training model where an intelligence engine (e.g., a neural network) is presented with input data, and it self-organizes the data into clusters or segments by learning to recognize statistically significant similarities between the input patterns.

Verb In APPC, an LU6.2 command, defined in the APPC API.

Virtual Machine/System Product (VM/SP) An IBM licensed program, which is an operating system that manages the resources of a real processor to provide virtual machines to end users.

Virtual Telecommunications Access Method (VTAM) An IBM licensed program that controls communication and data flow in an SNA network.

Visualization Graphical display of data which helps the user in understanding the structure and meaning of the information contained in the data.

VTAM application program A program that (1) has identified itself to VTAM by opening an ACB and (2) can issue VTAM macro instructions.

WAIS (Wide Area Information Servers) A program that allows relatively easy searching and retrieval from indexed text databases on remote computers.

Web Browser A client/server program that lets users navigate and view documents on the World Wide Web. Examples include Mosaic (invented at the National Center for Supercomputing Applications at the University of Illinois) and Netscape.

Wide area network (WAN) A network connecting nodes located across large geographical areas.

World Wide Web (WWW) A network of computers that presents information graphically through a hypertext-based system that lets users search for related "pages" globally by pointing and clicking with a mouse.

Workstation A terminal or personal computer at which a user can run applications.

X Windows System   A distributed presentation management system developed by MIT for UNIX-based environments.

XA Interfaces   X/Open's proposed standards for the portable application programming interfaces between transaction managers and resource managers (DBMS).

X/Open   Nonprofit organization founded to develop standards for interoperability between unlike systems. Its specifications for system interoperability and portability are listed in the X/Open Portability Guide (currently, in its fourth issue—XPG4).

X.21   See **Recommendation X.21.**

X.25   See **Recommendation X.25.**

C. J. Date's 12 Distributed DBMS Rules

The following rules have been compiled from the Summer 1987 article on distributed database systems published by Chris J. Date in *InfoDB* magazine.

RULE 1—LOCAL AUTONOMY

Definition: The sites in a distributed system should be autonomous or independent of each other.

Comments: A DBMS at each site in a distributed system should provide its own security, locking, logging, integrity, and recovery. Local operations use and affect only local resources and do not depend on other sites.

RULE 2—NO RELIANCE ON CENTRAL SITE

Definition: A distributed database system should not rely on a central site, because a single central site may become a single point of failure, affecting the entire system. Also, a central site may become a bottleneck affecting the distributed system's performance and throughput.

Comments: Each site of a distributed database system provides its own security, locking, logging, integrity, and recovery, and handles its own data dictionary. No central site must be involved in every distributed transaction.

RULE 3—CONTINUOUS OPERATION

Definition: A distributed database system should never require downtime.

Comments: A distributed database system should provide on-line backup and recovery, and a full and incremental archiving facility. The backup and recovery should be fast enough to be performed on-line without noticeable detrimental affect on the entire system performance.

RULE 4—LOCATION TRANSPARENCY
AND LOCATION INDEPENDENCE

Definition: Users and/or applications should not know, or even be aware of, where the data is physically stored; instead, users and/or applications should behave as if all data was stored locally.

Comments: Location transparency can be supported by extended synonyms and extensive use of the data dictionary. Location independence allows applications to be ported easily from one site in a distributed database system to another without modifications.

RULE 5—FRAGMENTATION INDEPENDENCE

Definition: Relational tables in a distributed database system can be divided into fragments and stored at different sites transparent to the users and applications.

Comments: Similar to the location transparency rule, users and applications should not be aware of the fact that some data may be stored in a fragment of a table at a site different from the site where the table itself is stored.

RULE 6—REPLICATION INDEPENDENCE

Definition: Data can be transparently replicated on multiple computer systems across a network.

Comments: Similar to the data location and fragmentation independence rules, replication independence is designed to free users of the concerns of where the data is stored. In the case of replication, users and applications should not be aware that replicas of the data are maintained and synchronized automatically by the distributed database management system.

RULE 7—DISTRIBUTED QUERY PROCESSING

Definition: The performance of a given query should be independent of the site at which the query is submitted.

Comments: Since a relational database management system provides nonnavigational access to data (via SQL), such a system should support an optimizer that can select not only the best access path within a given node, but also can optimize a distributed query performance in regard to the data location, CPU and I/O utilization, and network traffic throughput.

RULE 8—DISTRIBUTED TRANSACTION MANAGEMENT

Definition: A distributed system should be able to support atomic transactions.

Comments: Transaction properties of atomicity, consistency, durability, isolation, and serialization should be supported not only for local transactions, but also for distributed transactions that can span multiple systems. An example of a distributed transaction management issue is transaction coordination in the distributed two-phase commit processing.

RULE 9—HARDWARE INDEPENDENCE

Definition: A distributed database system should be able to operate and access data spread across a wide variety of hardware platforms.

Comments: Any truly distributed DBMS system should not rely on a particular hardware feature, nor should it be limited to a certain hardware architecture or vendor.

RULE 10—OPERATING SYSTEM INDEPENDENCE

Definition: A distributed database system should be able to run on different operating systems.

Comments: Similar to Rule 9, a truly distributed database system should support distribution of functions and data across different operating systems, including any combination of such operating systems as DOS, UNIX, Windows NT, MVS/VM, VSE, and VAX.

RULE 11—NETWORK INDEPENDENCE

Definition: A distributed database system should be designed to run regardless of the communication protocols and network topology used to interconnect various system nodes.

Comments: Similar to Rules 9 and 10, a truly distributed database system should support distribution of functions and data across different operating systems irrespective of the particular communication method used to interconnect all participating systems, including local and wide area networks. In fact, networks and communication protocols can be mixed to satisfy certain business, economic, geographical, and other requirements.

RULE 12—DBMS INDEPENDENCE

Definition: An ideal distributed database management system must be able to support interoperability between DBMS systems running on different nodes, even if these DBMS systems are unlike (heterogeneous).

Comments: All participants in distributed database management systems should use common standard interfaces (APIs) in order to interoperate with each other and to participate in distributed database processing.

E. F. Codd's
12 Guidelines for OLAP

Dr. E. F. Codd, the father of the relational model, has formulated a list of 12 guidelines and requirements as the basis for selecting OLAP systems. Users should prioritize this suggested list to reflect their business requirements and consider products that best match those needs.

1. *Multidimensional conceptual view*—A tool should provide users with a multidimensional model that corresponds to the business problems and is intuitively analytical and easy to use.

2. *Transparency*—The OLAP system's technology, the underlying database and computing architecture (client/server, mainframe gateways, etc.), and heterogeneity of input data sources should be transparent to users to preserve their productivity and proficiency with familiar front-end environments and tools (e.g., MS Windows, MS Excel).

3. *Accessibility*—The OLAP system should access only the data actually required to perform the analysis. Additionally, the system should be able to access data from all heterogeneous enterprise data sources required for the analysis.

4. *Consistent reporting performance*—As the number of dimensions and the size of the database increases, users should not perceive any significant degradation in performance.

5. *Client/server architecture*—The OLAP system has to conform to client/server architectural principles for maximum price/performance, flexibility, adaptivity, and interoperability.

6. *Generic dimensionality*—Every data dimension must be equivalent in both its structure and operational capabilities.

7. *Dynamic sparse matrix handling*—The OLAP system has to be able to adopt its physical schema to the specific analytical model that optimizes sparse matrix handling to achieve and maintain the required level of performance.

8. *Multiuser support*—The OLAP system must be able to support a workgroup of users working concurrently on a specific model.

9. *Unrestricted cross-dimensional operation*—The OLAP system must be able to recognize dimensional hierarchies and automatically perform associated roll-up calculations within and across dimensions.

10. *Intuitive data manipulation*—Consolidation path reorientation (pivoting), drill-down and roll-up, and other manipulations should be accomplished via direct point-and-click, drag-and-drop actions upon the cells of the cube.

11. *Flexible reporting*—The ability to arrange rows, columns, and cells must exist in a fashion that facilitates analysis by intuitive visual presentation of analytical reports.

12. *Unlimited dimensions and aggregation levels*—Depending on business requirements, an analytical model may have a dozen or more dimensions, each of which has multiple hierarchies. The OLAP system should not impose any artificial restrictions on the number of dimensions or aggregation levels.

D

10 Mistakes for Data Warehousing Managers to Avoid*

MISTAKE 1: STARTING WITH THE WRONG SPONSORSHIP CHAIN

A data warehousing project without the right sponsorship chain is like an automobile with insufficient gasoline and oil and a linkage problem between the steering wheel and the wheels.

The right sponsorship chain includes two key individuals above the data warehousing manager (the person who leads the data warehousing project). At the top is an executive sponsor with a great deal of money to invest in effective use of information. Corporate presidents, vice presidents of marketing, and vice presidents of research and development often fit the bill. A good sponsor, however, is not the only person required in the reporting chain above the warehousing manager. When a data warehousing project fails, the cause can sometimes be traced to the lack of a key individual between the sponsor and the data warehousing manager. That person is often called the project *driver* because he or she keeps the project moving in the right direction

---

* This has been adapted from "Ten Mistakes to Avoid for Data Warehousing Managers," by Dr. Ramon Barquin, Allan Paller, and Herb Edelstein, The Data Warehousing Institute, Washington, D.C., 1995.

and ensures that the schedule is kept. A good driver is a business person with three essential characteristics: (1) One who has already earned the respect of the other executives, (2) has a healthy skepticism about technology, and (3) is decisive but flexible.

Table D.1 shows the price paid when these sponsorship elements are missing.

TABLE D.1

Problem with sponsorship chain	Price paid by project
Sponsor is an IT executive rather than a business executive outside IT.	Project is seen as a technology experiment rather than a strategic investment in the business.
Sponsor has a limited budget.	Every unexpected technical challenge is a crisis, as budget dollars are hard to get. Project gains reputation as problem-prone and a budget buster.
There is no driver; DW Manager reports directly to sponsor.	No one on the project has authority to broker peace among competing data definitions. Sponsor soon tires of data definition wars and withdraws support.
Driver has not earned the respect of peers at the executive level.	Content of data warehouse is not trusted, in part, because no one can vouch for the validity of the definitions used.
Driver is excited rather than skeptical about technology.	Project is viewed as a technical experiment (or toy); most business people avoid it.
Driver is indecisive or unwilling to act quickly.	Project slows, executive support dissolves, interest fades, users find alternative solutions.

MISTAKE 2: SETTING EXPECTATIONS THAT CANNOT BE MET

Data warehousing projects have at least two phases. Phase one is the selling phase in which you attempt to persuade people that, by investing in your project, they can expect to get wonderful access to the right data through simple, graphical delivery tools. Phase two is the struggle to meet the expectations you have raised in phase one. Sadly, it is not uncommon for overeager project managers to make claims that their data warehouse will give people throughout the enterprise easy access to all the information they need, when they need it, in the right format. Along with that promise (explicit or implied) comes a bill for one to seven million dollars. Business executives who hear those promises and see those budgets cannot help but have high expectations.

But users do not get all the information they need. All data warehousing is, by necessity, domain specific, which means it focuses on a particular set of business information. Worse still, many warehouses are loaded with summary information—not detail. If a question asked by an executive requires more detail or requires information from outside the domain, the answer is often, "we haven't loaded that information, but we can; it will just cost (a bunch) and take (many) weeks."

MISTAKE 3: ENGAGING IN POLITICALLY NAIVE BEHAVIOR

A common error made by many data warehousing managers is promoting the value of their data warehouse with arguments to the effect of, "This will help managers make better decisions." When a self-respecting manager hears those words, the natural reaction is "This person thinks we have not been making good decisions and that his/her system is going to 'fix' us." From that point on, that manager is very, very hard to please.

Those IT professionals who have been in the industry for at least 10 years know that the objective of data warehousing is similar to the one that fueled the fourth-generation language boon of the late 1970s and the DSS/EIS activities of the 1980s—giving users better access to important information. While 4GL products have had a long and useful life, the DSS/EIS activities had a quick rise and even quicker fall, probably because DSS/EIS initiatives were often promoted as change agents that would improve business and enable better management decisions. Most people will support the concept of a data warehouse when it is presented without the fanfare as the place people can go to get useful information.

MISTAKE 4: LOADING THE WAREHOUSE WITH DATA JUST BECAUSE IT IS AVAILABLE

Some inexperienced data warehousing managers send a list of tables and data elements to end users along with a request asking which of those data elements should be included in the warehouse. Sometimes, the users are asked to categorize the elements as "essential," "important," or "nice to have." Typically, the results are very long lists of marginally useful information that radically expands the data warehouse storage requirements and slows the responsiveness.

Loading extraneous data leads to very large databases, which are difficult to manage and support, and which take too long to load. Additional hardware required to support this load can be justified only when all data is useful for the decision-making process; otherwise, it becomes a very expensive and inefficient white elephant.

MISTAKE 5: BELIEVING THAT DATA WAREHOUSE DATABASE DESIGN IS THE SAME AS TRANSACTIONAL DATABASE DESIGN

Since the goals of transaction processing systems differ from the goals of data warehouses, the database designs must be different as well. In transaction processing, the goal is speed to access and update a single record or a few records. Data warehousing is fundamentally different. The goal here is to access aggregates—sums, averages, trends, and more. Another difference is the user. In transaction systems, a query will be used tens of thousands of times. In data warehousing, an end user may formulate a query that may be used only once. Data warehousing databases are often denormalized to enable easy navigation for infrequent users. Transaction processing databases are often normalized to ensure speed and data integrity.

An even more fundamental difference is in content. Where transactional systems usually contain only the basic data, data warehousing users increasingly expect to find aggregates and time-series information already calculated for them and ready for immediate display (this has been an impetus behind the multidimensional database market).

MISTAKE 6: CHOOSING A DATA WAREHOUSE MANAGER WHO IS TECHNOLOGY-ORIENTED RATHER THAN USER-ORIENTED

One data warehousing user complained that the biggest mistake made on a large data warehousing project was to put a "propeller-head" as a data warehousing manager. This user-hostile project manager made so many people angry that the entire project was in jeopardy of being canceled. Although many technologists make excellent project managers, remember that data warehousing is a service business and making clients angry is a near-perfect method of destroying a service business.

MISTAKE 7: FOCUSING ON TRADITIONAL, INTERNAL RECORD-ORIENTED DATA AND IGNORING THE POTENTIAL VALUE OF EXTERNAL DATA AND OF TEXT, IMAGES, AND—POTENTIALLY—SOUND AND VIDEO

A study conducted by the White House in the early '80s showed that senior-level management in over 50 large companies rely on outside data (news, telephone calls from associates, etc.) for more than 95 percent of all the information they use, and the higher people are in the organization, the less value they place on internal data. Because of this preferential treatment of external data, senior executives sometimes see data warehousing as irrelevant. It is not that they are uninterested in key operating indicators; they just don't have time to bury themselves in the sort of detailed data a warehouse provides. Thus, a data warehouse that makes every piece of internal data available to senior management will likely be seen as only marginally useful. Therefore, it is imperative to extend the project focus to include external data.

In addition, consider expanding the forms of information available through the warehouse. Today, data warehousing solutions employ data visualization techniques and multimedia, and they often present the information in the form of images, full-motion video, and sound.

MISTAKE 8: DELIVERING DATA WITH OVERLAPPING AND CONFUSING DEFINITIONS

The Achilles heel of data warehousing is the requirement to gain consensus on data definitions. Conflicting definitions each have champions, and they are not easily reconciled, especially if the definitions reflect the way some organizational units operate (e.g., "sales" can be defined differently by the Finance and Marketing departments). Solving this problem is one of the most important tasks of the data warehousing project. If it is not solved, users will not have confidence in the information they are getting. Worse, they may embarrass themselves by using the wrong data, in which case they will inevitably blame the data warehouse.

MISTAKE 9: BELIEVING THE PERFORMANCE, CAPACITY, AND SCALEABILITY PROMISES

Recently, CIOs from three companies—a manufacturer, a retailer, and a service company—reported an identical problem: within four months of getting started, each had to purchase at least one additional processor of a size equal to or larger than the largest computer they had originally purchased for the data warehouse. They simply ran out of power.

Bigger problems may lie in wait on the software side. Often, counting on a promise of a powerful (and expensive) parallel database system may be a mistake since the software may not always perform as advertised. Problems with performance and scaleability can also come from front-end applications that can use nonscaleable tools (or non-scaleable design) to fail in delivering an acceptable performance. An even more common capacity problem arises in networking, with abundant examples of network saturation. Network overloads are a very common surprise in client/server systems in general and in data warehousing systems in particular.

MISTAKE 10: BELIEVING THAT ONCE THE DATA WAREHOUSE IS UP AND RUNNING, YOUR PROBLEMS ARE FINISHED

Each happy data warehouse user asks for new data and tells others about the great new tool. And they, too, ask for new data to be added, and want it immediately. At the same time, each performance or delivery problem results in a high-pressure search for additional technology or a new process. Thus, the data warehousing team needs to maintain high energy levels over long periods of time. A common error is to place data warehousing in the hands of project-oriented people who believe that they will be able to set it up once and have it run itself.

Data warehouses need to be intensely nurtured for at least a year after their initial launch. Even after that, without a dynamic leader, they can easily lose their momentum and their sponsorship. Data warehousing is a journey, not a destination.

MISTAKE 11: FOCUSING ON AD HOC, DATA MINING, AND PERIODIC REPORTING

As you can see, this is mistake number 11. It is true that believing that there are only 10 mistakes is also a mistake (R. Barquin et al.).

This is a subtle error, but an important one. Fixing it may transform a data warehousing manager from a data librarian into a hero.

The natural progression of information in a data warehouse is (1) extract the data from legacy systems, clean it, and feed it to the warehouse; (2) support ad hoc reporting until you learn what people want; and then (3) convert the ad hoc reports into regularly scheduled reports.

This is the natural progression, but it isn't the best one. It ignores the fact that managers are busy and that reports are liabilities rather than assets unless the recipients have time to read the reports. (Reports are like inventory; if they are not used they just generate costs.)

Alert systems can be a better approach and they can make a data warehouse mission-critical. Alert systems monitor the data flowing into the warehouse and inform all key people with a need to know, as soon as a critical event takes place.

One key to an effective alert system is infrequency—if alerts are sent too often, they become a burden rather than an asset. To determine the contents and the thresholds of that critical information, one must fully understand what's going on in the mind of a business person who will receive the alert. Data warehousing drivers and managers with solid ties to senior managers are in the best position to do that job well.

Suggested Publications

Berson, Alex, *Client/Server Architecture,* McGraw-Hill, New York, 1992.

Berson, Alex, and George Anderson, *SYBASE and Client/Server Computing,* McGraw-Hill, New York, 1995.

Blakeley, B., H. Harris, and R. Lewis, *Messaging and Queuing Using the MQI,* McGraw-Hill, New York, 1995.

Chen, H., "Machine Learning for Information Retrieval: Neural Networks, Symbolic Learning, and Genetic Algorithms," *Journal of the American Society for Information Science,* 1995.

Gray and Reuter, *Transaction Processing Concepts and Techniques,* Morgan Kaufman Publishers, San Francisco, 1993.

Inmon, W. H., *Building the Data Warehouse,* QED Publishing Group, Wellesley, Mass., 1992.

McGovern, D., with C. J. Date, *A Guide to SYBASE and SQL Server,* Addison-Wesley, Reading, Mass., 1993.

Paller, Alan, *The IS Book: Information Systems for Top Management,* Doc Jones Irwin, 1990.

Piatetsky-Shapiro, G., and W. Frawley, *Knowledge Discovery in Databases,* MIT Press, 1991.

Stonebraker, M. (ed.), *Readings in Database Design,* Morgan Kaufman Publishers, San Francisco, 1994.

Widrow, Rumelhart, and Leht, "Neural Networks: Applications in Industry, Business, and Science," *Communications ACM,* vol. 37, no. 3 (March 1994).

Winter, R. A., and S. A. Brobst, "An Introduction to Parallel Database Technology," *Enterprise Systems Journal,* August 1994.

IBM PUBLICATIONS:

An Architecture for a Business and Information System (Information Warehouse) (G321-5311).

CICS/VS Application Programmer's Reference Manual (Command Level) (SC33-0241).
CICS/VS Intercommunication Facilities Guide (SC33-0230).
DDM Reference Guide (GC21-9526).
DRDA: DDM General Information (GC21-9527).
DRDA Distributed Data Management Level 3 Architecture (GC21-9526).
DRDA Reference (SC26-4651).
Introduction to Distributed Relational Data (GC24-3200).
SNA Format and Protocol Reference Manual: Architecture Logic for LU Type 6.2 (SC30-3269).
SNA Technical Overview (GC30-3073).
VTAM Programming for LU6.2 (SC30-3400).

STANDARDS DOCUMENTS:

ANSI: Database Language SQL, X.3.135-1986.
ANSI: Database Language SQL With Integrity Enhancement, X.3.135-1989.
ANSI Database Language: Language Embedding, X.3.168-1989.
ISO: Database Language SQL, ISO-9075-1987.
ISO: Database Language SQL With Integrity Enhancement, ISO-9075-1989(E).
OMG: Object Management Architecture Guide, 1991.
OMG: Common Object Request Broker: Architecture and Specifications, 1991.

Acronyms

ACB	Application Control Block; Access Method Control Block
AFS	Andrew File System
AIX	Advanced Interactive eXecutive
ANDF	Architecture-Neutral Distribution Format
ANN	Artificial Neural Network
ANSI	American National Institute of Standards
API	Application Programming Interface
AEI	Application Enabling Interface
APPC	Advanced Program-to-Program Communications
APPN	Advanced Peer-to-Peer Networking
AR	Application Requester (in DRDA)
AS	Application Server (in DRDA)
AS/400	Application System/400
ATM	Asynchronous Transfer Mode
BCP	Bulk Copy Program
BIU	Basic Information Unit
BLOB	Binary Large Object
BSC	Binary Synchronous Communications
CART	Classification and Regression Trees

CDDI	Copper Distributed Data Link
CDRA	Character Data Representation Architecture
CDS	Cell Directory Services
CCITT	International Telephone and Telegraph Consultative Committee
CGI	Common Gateway Interface
CICS	Customer Control Information System
CISC	Complex Instruction Set Computing
CLI	Call-Level Interface
CMIP	Common Management Interface Protocol
CNM	Communication Network Management
COM	Component Object Model (Microsoft); Common Object Model (Digital)
CP	Control Point
CORBA	Common Object Request Broker Architecture
COS	Class of Service
CSDA/CA	Carrier Sense Multiple Access/Collision Avoidance
CSDA/CD	Carrier Sense Multiple Access/Collision Detection
DB2	Database 2 (IBM)
DBCC	Database Consistency Checker
DBMS	Database Management System
DCE	Distributed Computing Environment
DDF	Distributed Data Facility
DDL	Data Definition Language
DDM	Distributed Data Management
DFC	Data Flow Control Layer
DFS	Distributed File System
DIA	Document Interchange Architecture
DLC	Data Link Control Layer
DLL	Dynamic Link Libraries
DLR	Dynamic Link Routine
DME	Distributed Management Environment
DML	Data Manipulation Language
DNA	Digital Network Architecture
DNS	Domain Name Server
DSI	Data Server Interface
DSOM	Distributed System Object Model
DTP	Distributed Transaction Processing

DRDA	Distributed Relational Database Architecture
DS	Database Server
DUW	Distributed Unit of Work
EBCDIC	Extended Binary-Coded Decimal Interchange Code
ECB	Event Control Block
EHLLAPI	Emulator High-Level Language Application Programming Interface
FCS	Fiber Channel Standard
FDDI	Fiber Distributed Data Interface
FD:OCA	Formatted Data Object Content Architecture
FR	Frame Relay
FSM	Finite-State Machine
FMH	Function Management Header
FTP	File Transfer Protocol
GA	Genetic Algorithm
GDS	General Data Stream
GUI	Graphical User Interface
HTML	Hypertext Markup Language
HTTP	Hypertext Transport Protocol
ICCM	Interclient Communications Conventions Manual
ICF	Intercommunication Function
ISC	Intersystem Communications
ISDN	Integrated Services Digital Network
ISQL	Interactive Structured Query Language (SYBASE)
ISV	Independent Software Vendor
LS	Link Station
LAN	Local Area Network
LR	Logical Record
LTM	Log Transfer Manager
LU	Logical Unit
LUW	Logical Unit of Work
LU6.2	Logical Unit type 6.2
MAN	Metropolitan Area Network
MAPI	Mail API
MAP/TOP	Manufacturing Automation Protocol/Technical and Office Protocol
MCA	Micro-Channel Adapter
MDA	Multidimensional Analysis

MDI	Multiple Document Interface
MFLOPS	Millions of Floating-Point Instructions per Second
MFC	Microsoft Foundation Classes
MIME	Multimedia Internet Mail Enhancements
MIPS	Millions of Instructions per Second
MPP	Massively Parallel Processors
MQI	Messaging and Queuing Interface
MRO	Multiregion Operations
NAU	Network Addressable Unit
NCP	Network Control Program
NFS	Network File System
NLM	NetWare Loadable Module
NOS	Network Operating System
ODBC	Open Database Connectivity
OLAP	On-Line Analytical Processing
OLE	Object Linking and Embedding
OLCP	On-Line Complex Processing
OLTP	On-Line Transaction Processing
ONC	Open Network Computing
ORB	Object Request Broker
OS/2	IBM Operating System/2
OSF	Open Software Foundation
OSI	Open Systems Interconnection
QBIC	Query By Image Content
PM	OS/2 Presentation Manager
POSIX	Portable Operating System Interface
PROFS	Professional Office System
PU	Physical Unit
PWS	Programmable Workstation
RAS programs	Reliability, Availability, and Serviceability programs
RDA	Remote Data Access
RDBMS	Relational Database Management System
RISC	Reduced Instruction Set Computing
RPC	Remote Procedure Call
RPL	Remote Program Link
RSI	Replication Server Interface
RSM	Replication Server Manager
RSSD	Replication Server System Database

RUW	Remote Unit of Work
SAA	Systems Application Architecture
SCSI	Small Computer System Interface
SDLC	Synchronous Data Link Control
SLU	Secondary Logical Unit
SMP	Symmetric Multiprocessing
SMTP	Simple Mail Transfer Protocol
SNMP	Simple Network Management Protocol
SOM	System Object Model
SRPI	Server-Requestor Programming Interface
SNA	Systems Network Architecture
SNADS	Systems Network Architecture Distributed Services
SQL	Structured Query Language
SVID	UNIX System V Interface Definitions
SVR4	UNIX System V Release 4
TCOS	Technical Committee on Open Systems
TCP/IP	Transmission Control Protocol/Internet Protocol
TP	Transaction Program
TPM	Transaction Processing Manager
TPS	Transactions per Second
TSO	Time Sharing Option
UI	UNIX International
UOW	Unit of Work
URL	Uniform Resource Locator
VAN	Value Added Network
VIM	Vendor Independent Messaging
VLDB	Very Large Database
VM/SP	Virtual Machine/System Product
VR	Virtual Route
VTAM	Virtual Telecommunications Access Method
WAIS	Wide Area Information Servers
WAN	Wide Area Network
WOSA	Windows Open Services Architecture
WWW	World Wide Web
XPG4	X/Open Portability Guide Issue 4
XRF	Extended Recovery Facility

Index

ABOUT THE AUTHOR

Alex Berson has more than 20 years of experience in information technology as a systems architect and consultant, lecturer, and writer. He specializes in client/server and commercial high-performance computing, distributed transaction processing, data warehousing, and more. He is the coauthor of *SYBASE and Client-Server Computing* and the author of *APPC: Introduction to LU6.2.*